Qian Qianyi's
Reflections on
Yellow Mountain

The Chiang Ching-kuo Foundation
for International Scholarly Exchange
蔣經國國際學術交流基金會
sponsored the publication of this book

Qian Qianyi's Reflections on Yellow Mountain

Traces of a Late-Ming Hatchet and Chisel

Stephen McDowall

香港大學出版社
HONG KONG UNIVERSITY PRESS

Hong Kong University Press
14/F Hing Wai Centre
7 Tin Wan Praya Road
Aberdeen
Hong Kong

© Hong Kong University Press 2009

ISBN 978-962-209-084-2

Secure On-line Ordering
http://www.hkupress.org

British Library Cataloguing-in-Publication Data
A catalogue copy for this book is available from the British Library.

Printed and bound by Liang Yu Printing Factory Co. Ltd. in Hong Kong, China

Contents

Acknowledgements

An annotated translation of a portion of Qian Qianyi's essay "You Huangshan ji" 游黃山記 appeared in my article "Qian Qianyi's (1582–1664) Reflections on Yellow Mountain," *New Zealand Journal of Asian Studies* 7 (2) (2005): 134–52, and a revised version of that section is reproduced here with permission from the *NZJAS*.

I am extremely grateful for the financial support I received during the early stages of this project from the J. L. Stewart Foundation, the Asia New Zealand Foundation and the New Zealand Asian Studies Society. I have been the fortunate recipient of several grants from the Faculty of Humanities and Social Sciences at Victoria University of Wellington, and more recently, a Postdoctoral Fellowship within the School of Languages and Cultures at the same institution and a Colmar Brunton NZ Research Excellence Award have afforded me the opportunity to bring the project to its completion. The production of colour illustrations was made possible through a generous grant from the Chiang Ching-kuo Foundation for International Scholarly Exchange.

Of the many people whose advice, assistance or support I have enjoyed since this study began in 2004, I would like to acknowledge in particular Bai Limin, James Beattie, Jonathan Chaves, Hamish Clayton, Stephen Epstein, Anne Gerritsen, Pauline Keating, Joy McDowall, Stefanie Michel, Shirley Pack, Tony Quinn, Monica Rogers and Lynette Shum. Staff at the Staatsbibliothek zu Berlin and at the Shanghai Library were extremely helpful during two research trips, and Naomi Eisenthal, formerly of Victoria University Library, devoted many hours to tracking down and sourcing a number of important texts in a language she did not understand. The judicious comments of Professors Geremie Barmé, John Minford and Brian Moloughney helped to refine earlier versions of the manuscript, and Michael Duckworth, Clara Ho and their colleagues at Hong Kong University Press worked with enthusiasm and professionalism to ensure that the project never stalled.

I am, above all, grateful for the years of encouragement and guidance I have received from my friend, colleague and mentor Duncan Campbell, without which this book would have proved impossible.

SM.

List of Illustrations

Explanatory Notes

Translations of official titles follow those given in Charles O. Hucker, *A Dictionary of Official Titles in Imperial China* (Stanford: Stanford University Press, 1985). Unless otherwise stated, people mentioned in this book are referred to by their official names (*ming* 名), while sobriquets (*zi* 字 and *hao* 號) and lifespan dates are given in parentheses at first mention where possible. In the body of this volume, I have included Chinese characters at the first appearance of proper nouns, and occasionally at subsequent appearances to avoid ambiguity, while for the convenience of the reader, characters have been provided again for most personal names and book titles that appear in the translation notes of Chapter Five. English translations of titles of books are provided in parentheses at first appearance only. For consistency, I have used only traditional Chinese characters in this study, and Chinese names and terms are romanized according to the *Hanyu pinyin* system, except on a few occasions where an alternative spelling has been accepted into English (such as Confucius). All translations not otherwise attributed are my own.

Abbreviations Used

DMB   L. Carrington Goodrich ed. *Dictionary of Ming Biography 1368–1644*. Two volumes. New York: Columbia University Press, 1976.

ECCP   Arthur W. Hummel ed. *Eminent Chinese of the Ch'ing Period*. Two volumes. Washington DC: Government Printing Office, 1943–44.

ICTCL   William H. Nienhauser, Jr. ed. *The Indiana Companion to Traditional Chinese Literature*. Two volumes. Bloomington: Indiana University Press, 1986 (vol. 1) and 1998 (vol. 2).

MRSM   Yang Tingfu 楊廷福 and Yang Tongfu 楊同甫 ed. *Ming ren shiming biecheng zihao suoyin* 明人室名別稱字號索引. Two volumes. Shanghai: Guji chubanshe, 2002.

QMZQJ   Qian Zhonglian 錢仲聯 ed. *Qian Muzhai quanji* 錢牧齋全集. Eight volumes. Shanghai: Guji chubanshe, 2003.

QRSM   Yang Tingfu 楊廷福 and Yang Tongfu 楊同甫 ed. *Qing ren shiming biecheng zihao suoyin* 清人室名別稱字號索引 [*zengbuben* 增補本]. Two volumes. Shanghai: Guji chubanshe, 2001.

SBCK   *Sibu congkan* 四部叢刊 collection. Shanghai: Shangwu yinshuguan, 1919–1936 [初編: 1919–1922; 續編: 1934; 三編: 1936].

attrib.	attributed		*fl.*	*floruit* [flourished]
b.	born		*jr.*	*juren* 舉人
BCE	Before the Common Era			[provincial graduate]
	[Before Christ]		*js.*	*jinshi* 進士
CE	Common Era			[metropolitan graduate]
	[*Anno Domini*]		r.	reigned
comp.	compiled		rpt.	reprinted
d.	died		trans.	translated
ed.	edited			

Approximate Values of Ming Measurements

1 *chi* 尺 (foot) = 32 cm
1 *gong* 弓 [= *bu* 步] = 5–6 *chi* 尺
1 *ren* 仞 = 8 *chi* 尺
1 *zhang* 丈 = 10 *chi* 尺
1 *li* 里 = 360 *bu* 步 = 536 m
1 *mu* 畝 = 567 m²
1 *jin* 金 [= *liang* 兩] = 36.9 g of silver
1 *juan* 卷 = (fascicle/chapter) = a traditional unit of book-division

Dynastic Reign Periods 1500–1750

Ming 明

Xiaozong 孝宗 (Hongzhi 弘治)	[1488]–1505
Wuzong 武宗 (Zhengde 正德)	1506–21
Shizong 世宗 (Jiajing 嘉靖)	1522–66
Muzong 穆宗 (Longqing 隆慶)	1567–72
Shenzong 神宗 (Wanli 萬曆)	1573–1620
Guangzong 光宗 (Taichang 泰昌)	1620
Xizong 熹宗 (Tianqi 天啟)	1621–27
Sizong 思宗 (Chongzhen 崇禎)	1628–44

Qing 清

Shizu 世祖 (Shunzhi 順治)	1644–61
Shengzu 聖祖 (Kangxi 康熙)	1662–1722
Shizong 世宗 (Yongzheng 雍正)	1723–35
Gaozong 高宗 (Qianlong 乾隆)	1736–[96]

Introduction

If an artist desires to paint an object's appearance, he should select its appearance. If he desires to paint an object's substance he should select its substance. But he should not mistake appearance for substance 物之華取其華物之實取其實不可執華為實.

Jing Hao 荊浩 (*fl.* 907–23) attrib.,
"Bifa ji" 筆法記 [Account of Brush Methods][1]

Some decades ago in his classic study, the eminent Viennese art historian E. H. Gombrich (1909–2001) marvelled "how long and arduous is the way between perception and representation" in sixteenth-century painted landscapes. To the landscape painter, he continued, "nothing can become a motif except what he can assimilate into the vocabulary he has already learned."[2] It was an articulation of a concept that had been at the core of the visual arts for centuries; Jing Hao's concern to select 取 either appearance or substance reveals already an important distinction between meaning and form. Centuries later, Leonardo da Vinci (1452–1519) could assert that painting was a *cosa mentale* — a thing of the mind — dismissing those painters who draw by the judgement of the eye and without the use of reason as no better than mirrors,[3] while more recently, René Magritte (1898–1967) explained his *La condition humaine* (1933) with the comment that the world "is only a mental representation of [that which] we experience inside ourselves."[4]

This book focuses primarily on landscape presented in written rather than visual form, specifically the ways in which a particular mountain was depicted in the *youji* 遊記 (travel accounts) produced during roughly the final century of Ming rule (1550–1644). This might seem far removed from the concerns of Gombrich, but the study has emerged out of a sense that we have been far too slow in literary criticism to recognize the vital role of the viewer in the process of representing the natural world. There remains in secondary scholarship a tendency to read the landscape descriptions found in *youji* as accurate historical and physical records of given sites, while ignoring the specific cultural contexts in which these descriptions were formed. James Hargett's 20-year-old definition of the genre remains typical of the way in which travel essays are understood:

> To begin with, they contain a first-hand account of a brief excursion or an extended journey. The language used therein to describe the details of the trip is predominantly narrative. Second, they provide facts about the physical environment such as climate, relief, vegetation and land-use in a given region ... *The descriptions in these types of reports are "objective" or "impersonal" in that the author himself plays no direct role, but simply observes and reports on what he sees* [my emphasis]. Third, *youji* works invariably reveal the author's attitudes or opinions ... This "subjective" or "personal" quality is the one characteristic that most clearly distinguishes the travel record from the geographical tracts found in most local histories (*fangzhi*).[5]

Drawing from the same framework, a more recent treatment of one late-Ming traveller discusses his work in terms of an "ability to transcend different categories, drawing on both subjective and objective strands of travel writing."[6]

It is not my intention here to pick holes in Professor Hargett's outstanding study of the travel literature of the Song (960–1279), but it does seem to me that the notion of "facts about the physical environment," in which "the author himself plays no direct role" implies of the observer a disinterest that can no longer be accepted so uncritically. All "objective" non-fictional writings are created not only by the descriptive tools at an author's disposal, but by entire systems of cultural, political, social and aesthetic schemata that, at various levels of the observer's consciousness, impose themselves on the world. By making a case here for a more nuanced and subtle treatment of *youji* in secondary literature, I hope to go some way towards removing the genre from its elemental *you* 遊 and *ji* 記, which, in Chinese as well as its usual English equivalent of "record" is freighted with connotations of verisimilitude not carried by other literary forms. Abandoning the oversimplified subjective-objective framework, my analysis begins with the assumption that all representations of landscape are culturally creative acts.

The specific case study around which this book revolves is the "Account of My Travels at Yellow Mountain" (You Huangshan ji 游黃山記), a ten-part essay written by the poet, scholar, official and literary historian Qian Qianyi 錢謙益 (1582–1664) in early 1642. Written to complement a set of poems, the essay recounts a journey Qian made during the previous year to Yellow Mountain (Huangshan 黃山), the range of peaks that makes up the major orographic feature of southern Anhui 安徽, within the region immediately south of the Yangzi River known as Jiangnan 江南. While today, images of its iconic, mist-shrouded peaks decorate the halls of railway stations throughout the country, the relatively inaccessible Yellow Mountain was far slower than many other significant Jiangnan landscapes to attract the attention of travellers and poets. The Wanli 萬曆 reign (1573–1620) of the Ming dynasty, during which Qian Qianyi was born, marks the beginning of the site's representational history in any meaningful sense, and part of what this study sets out to do is to introduce at least some of the ways in which this landscape began to be presented in writing during this crucial period. Rather than attempt any kind of objective description or history of the site (hopefully it will become clear that I regard such a possibility as problematic), my aim here is to recreate the landscape of Yellow Mountain as it existed for a select group of highly educated élite males, most of whom lived within a relatively confined area, and who chose to present their world in *youji* form during the decades leading up to the end of the Ming period (1644). By drawing into this discussion a wider representational tradition that necessarily includes depiction in visual as well as textual form, I present a reading of late-Ming Yellow Mountain as the product of a discourse rather than as an empirically verifiable space. I argue that what this mountain meant, how it functioned, even what it looked like to Qian Qianyi and his seventeenth-century contemporaries are far more usefully viewed as products of the complex world in which these men lived, than as evidence about the landscape itself.

While this approach runs somewhat against the grain of traditional readings of travel literature, I have sought throughout to remain alert to branches of recent scholarship that have developed across a number of diverse disciplines. Over a decade on from the publication of Craig Clunas' seminal work *Fruitful Sites: Garden Culture in Ming Dynasty China* (1996), it seems to me that the implications of his study for our understanding of late-Ming prose in general have yet to be fully explored.[7] Clunas seeks to challenge conventional histories of "the Chinese garden," preferring to read such a category as the product of "discursive practice" rather than as a pre-existing object of representation. He draws the discussion of Ming gardens back into a context in which landownership and luxury consumption had become key components of élite self-representation and identity construction, showing that what gardens in southern China meant in 1600 had shifted dramatically from what they had meant just a century earlier. His project is particularly significant here, as it bridges the divide between art and landscape, and between the visual and verbal, a theme I take up below. In an earlier essay, W. J. T. Mitchell had remarked that "the intensive, almost compulsive collaboration between practitioners of the word and practitioners of the image" represents one of the most salient features of modern culture, noting the sense in which nature has been "pictorialized" by the audio and written commentary that often now accompanies the outdoor experience.[8] The idea of the pictorialization of landscape is one I wish to explore here, although I hope that what follows is at the very least the beginnings of an argument against such processes being the preserve of something called *modern* culture.

In another context, British historian Simon Schama recently claimed that "landscapes are culture before they are nature; constructs of the imagination projected onto wood and water and rock." He argues that "once a certain idea of landscape, a myth, a vision, establishes itself in an actual place, it has a peculiar way of muddling categories, of making metaphors more real than their referents; of becoming, in fact, part of the scenery."[9] This kind of category-muddling is a particular feature of the religious pilgrimage, of course, and the present study is also in part a response to the important work of Coleman and Elsner, in which "physical and myth-historical landscapes provide the backdrop to movement, so that in progressing through the physical geography a pilgrim travels and lives through a terrain of culturally constructed symbols."[10] The foundations of such studies in twentieth-century Western scholarship may well have been laid by geographers such as Donald Meinig, who has long argued that "any landscape is composed not only of what lies before our eyes but what lies within our heads,"[11] but the concept was already understood by Jia Zheng 賈政, who knew that for the observer, the meaning of Grand Prospect Garden 大觀園 would be created by reading "that touch of poetry which only the written word can lend a scene" in Cao Xueqin's 曹雪芹 (*zi* Qinpu 芹圃, *hao* Mengruan 夢阮; 1715?–63) classic novel *Hongloumeng* 紅樓夢 [Dream of the Red Chamber].[12]

The example of the pine (*song* 松) might usefully preface my underlying thoughts here. The pine is one of the famed Four Perfections of Yellow Mountain 黃山四絕, a phrase now so much a part of modern consciousness that it featured as a question in a recent competition for international students of Chinese language and culture.[13] It is impossible now to imagine that pines were not always one of the most important features of the landscape, and certainly no visitor to Yellow Mountain today would ever leave without viewing the famous Welcoming Guests Pine 迎客松, one of the more recognizable cultural icons of the Jiangnan region. But the fact that the earliest-surviving topographical source for the site, the Song-dynasty *Huangshan tujing* 黃山圖經 [Topographical Classic of Yellow Mountain], mentions pines only in passing, provides a very real challenge to what we think we know about this mountain and this tree.[14] What happened between the Song dynasty and the end of the Ming to transform the pine from an incidental footnote of a landscape into one of the most important of its visual features? Or, to put it another way, did the character *song* 松, which I am perhaps too casually rendering into "pine," mean the same thing in the Song dynasty as it did in the Ming? We are told in Jing Hao's tenth-century treatise that a pine tree grows "with the virtuous air of a gentleman" 如君子之德風也. Some paintings depict them as coiling dragons in flight, their branches and leaves growing wildly, but this "does not capture the true spirit of pines" 非松之氣韻也.[15] How is it then, that pines of the early seventeenth century are *almost invariably* of serpentine form, if such a portrayal does not capture their true spirit? In Jing's world, a pine was, like a man of integrity, upright and unwavering in the face of political oppression or poverty. By the late Ming, the twisted, coiling pine embodied the ideal of the eccentric and exceptional man 奇士. Such a dramatic shift in meaning provides a sober warning against accepting on face value any description of landscape, without attempting to understand the cultural context from which it came.

Qian Qianyi was one of the great literary figures of the seventeenth century, a man who, in the words of Huang Zongxi 黃宗羲 (*zi* Taichong 太冲, *hao* Nanlei 南雷; 1610–95), "presided over the literary world for fifty years" 主文章之壇坫者五十年.[16] But if Qian were the *sommo poeta* of his generation, he was also, politically, one of the more problematic figures of the Ming-Qing transition period, having served both ruling houses during his official career. In 1769, over a century after Qian's death, the Qianlong 乾隆 Emperor (Gaozong 高宗; r. 1736–96), by far the most vociferous of Qian's detractors, issued the following decree:

> Qian Qianyi was a man of great natural ability, but of no character. In the time of the Ming, he held official posts; likewise after our house had seized control he was one of the first to follow our house in service as a director of one of the minor courts. He was lacking in loyalty and truly does not deserve to be remembered by mankind . . . If Qian Qianyi had courted death for the sake of the last dynasty and refused to turn coat, and with brush and ink ranted against [us], this would have been appropriate and reasonable. But having accepted office under our rule how could he continue to use this wild, howling language of former days in his writings? In my opinion, it was due to his wish to cover up the shame of having been disloyal to the Ming, which only makes his disgrace worse.[17]

While subsequent proscriptions did not succeed in preventing the eventual transmission of his works, the stigma of disloyalty did prevent any meaningful scholarly research into Qian Qianyi and his works before the end of the Qing era, and our knowledge of the man and his writings has been adversely shaped by this scholarly lacuna. Critical examination of Qian's literary works, particularly his prose texts, has barely begun, and the vast majority of his essays remain unannotated and unstudied. At present there exists no adequate critical biography of this remarkable literary figure.

The present project is explicitly not an attempt to fill this biographical void, and I would certainly not claim to have mastered in any sense the wealth of material that exists and continues to be generated on Qian Qianyi and his writings.[18] Nor do I seek here to emulate the work of Brian Dott, whose important recent treatment of Taishan 泰山 [Mount Supreme] in the late imperial period examines multiple readings of that sacred space by gentry, clergy, pilgrims and emperors.[19] The far more modest objective of this book is to attempt to read closely a single individual's account of one particular landscape in light of what we know of its late-Ming context. For this essay at least, the formula of objective description coupled with personal opinion does not begin to approach the level of sophistication required to attain any meaningful understanding of the text. The "objective descriptions" that make up Qian Qianyi's Yellow Mountain lie at the intersection of an existing textual tradition, late-Ming aesthetic, cultural and religious values, and traditional cosmology, all of which is filtered through the memory of one of the greatest literary historians of his generation, and presented in an essay composed for a specific rhetorical purpose. The "Account of My Travels at Yellow Mountain" was one of just a handful of travel essays in Qian's voluminous corpus, but despite its inclusion in several anthologies, it has never received adequate attention in secondary scholarship. This project not only includes the first complete English-language translation of the essay, but also represents the first critical study of the account, and of the various existing versions of the text, to appear in any language.[20]

The late-Ming world in which Qian Qianyi sat down to compose his essay was a complex place. While corruption and factionalism at court threatened to plunge the empire into political crisis, banditry, famine and plagues provided a daily more evident challenge to social and economic order. In Chapter One of this study I examine some of the social changes taking place within this world, arguing that self-representation through text had by the turn of the seventeenth century become an essential part of élite life. Drawing on recent studies that have highlighted the link between conspicuous consumption and identity construction in the late Ming, I argue that representations of engagements with landscape are usefully viewed alongside writings about collecting and connoisseurship that characterize the period. We are not justified in reading travel accounts as innocent sources of information that stand apart from a late-Ming society in which, in representational terms at least, status markers had assumed such an important role in élite discourse. This chapter also seeks to place Qian Qianyi himself into this world, briefly sketching his early career, before focussing in particular on the years surrounding the composition of the Yellow Mountain essay in 1642. If part of what we read in the landscape is a reflection of Qian, then the fact that he made the journey at such a critical juncture in his public and personal life necessarily informs our reading of his essay.

Chapter Two examines the Yellow Mountain we find in writing up to the end of the Ming period. By presenting in chronological order the represented experiences of travellers since the Tang era (618–907), this chapter traces the gradual accretion of layers of cultural, historical and religious meaning that become part of the way the mountain is experienced, and how this experience is related in essay form. My analysis shows that by the time the important Wanli reign had come to an end in 1620, the significant sites and sights of Yellow Mountain had been defined, and an appropriate traveller's itinerary prescribed. We find, on close reading, a remarkable similarity of recorded experience on the part of late-Ming travellers, not only with regard to the language used to describe individual features of the mountain, but also in the recurring themes that pervade the various texts. This unravelling of the meaning of the mountain is continued in Chapter Three, which focuses on the representational tradition of the site in visual form, a dimension that I argue is usefully viewed alongside the textual tradition as part of the general understanding of the landscape being formed by the mid-seventeenth century. Mirroring the way in which representations of Yellow Mountain developed in text, visual depictions of the site become, by the early Qing period, conceptual works that tend to emphasize distinct views, often at the expense of spatial consistency. Textual and visual accounts of the mountain produced during the seventeenth century not only give the impression of being a progression from one individual scene to the next, but also seem increasingly to rely on the consensual presentation of shared historical and descriptive information.

Against this background, Chapter Four introduces the "Account of My Travels at Yellow Mountain" by Qian Qianyi, highlighting some of the main themes that pervade the text. The essay is one rich in the language of religious pilgrimage, and it seems that for Qian, the landscape can be read appropriately in accordance with Confucian, Buddhist and Daoist tradition. I argue here that representational conventions by now established for Yellow Mountain direct Qian's writing process, and that the necessity of engaging with certain important sites may actually have led to the deliberate distortion of parts of his itinerary. The complete picture of his trip of 1641 cannot be grasped by reading the essay alone, and the fact that details included elsewhere in Qian's collected works, the *Muzhai chuxueji* 牧齋初學集 [Collected Early Scholarship from Shepherd's Studio], are omitted from the *youji* is revealing. Qian's account of the landscape is very much a product of late-Ming cultural and aesthetic values, but it also fixes the canonical literary sources as the means by which the natural world is to be interpreted and represented.

Discussion of such issues is intended to prepare the reader to make sense of my full translation of Qian's essay, which appears as Chapter Five. While I have endeavoured to produce an English rendition of the essay that flows as freely as is possible (and should be accessible to specialist and non-specialist alike), the annotations that supplement the text are necessarily dense, and highlight some of the complexities of the essay and its composition that have been discussed in previous chapters. A close analysis of the narrative reveals considerable reliance on the works of others, providing a significant challenge to the idea of author as objective observer that a reader might gain at first glance. Indeed, reading the text in annotated form shows the Yellow Mountain of Qian's essay to be the product of a highly complex creative process, and one that in the end reveals far more about the author and élite writing in the late Ming than about the mountain itself.

Finally, a note on the title of this book, which borrows a phrase — "traces of hatchet and chisel" 斧鑿痕 — that appears in Part IV of Qian's essay, as we come upon a monk cutting into the rock at the foot of a peak. The expression is used literally in this instance, but it had also come to refer metaphorically to traces of artistry in a written composition; those passages in a text at which the interventions of the poet's brush onto the natural scene were most evident. Rather than highlighting these traces in a pejorative sense (the sense, indeed, in which such a phrase would normally have been understood in Qian's world), the present study seeks to enrich our reading of the text by revealing the intricacies behind the fascinating cultural practice of *youji* composition. We have long since accepted that the very process of capturing landscape in visual art invalidates any attempt to present a site as standing apart from other historically contingent contexts in which meaning is created (even the once innocent photograph, for example, is no longer read in such a naïve way).[21] And almost a century after Wang Guowei 王國維 (*zi* Jing'an 靜安, *hao* Guantang 觀堂; 1877–1927) reminded us that "all scenic description [in poetry] involves the expression of emotions,"[22] it seems appropriate to apply the same level of sophistication to the analysis of prose. For the truth is that the way the late-Ming élite chose to write about their landscapes and why, is an infinitely more interesting story than we have hitherto acknowledged. Those traces of hatchet and chisel visible in Qian Qianyi's Yellow Mountain represent the great achievement of seventeenth-century literary culture, and the essays of Qian and his contemporaries can be understood only as we begin to recognize, in Gombrich's terms, just how "long and arduous" these literary journeys really were.

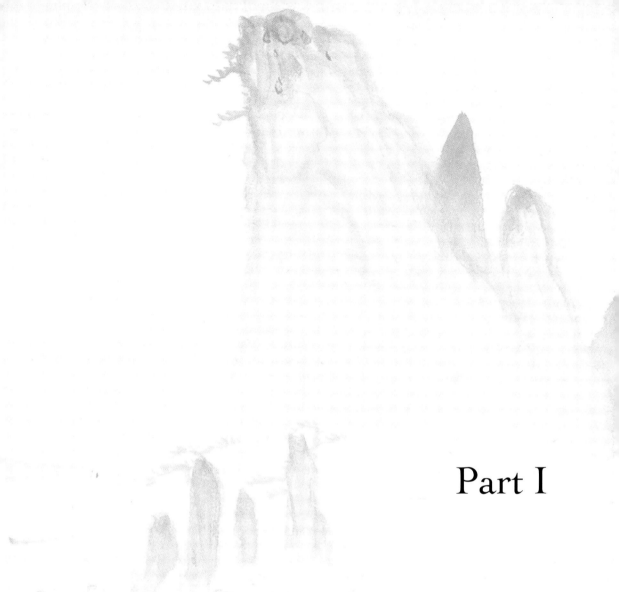

Part I

1

Of Trivial Things

Writing the Self in Late-Ming Literary Culture

The world in which the Jiangnan man-of-letters found himself during the course of the final century of Ming rule was a fast-paced and in many ways a rather troubling place. While the population had more than doubled, and the number of degree holders had increased fivefold since the beginning of the dynasty nearly three centuries earlier, the size of the public service, the traditional destination for an educated male, had remained relatively static.[1] Success in the imperial examinations could no longer guarantee a candidate a government position, while the expanding salt and textile industries in particular produced a new generation of wealthy mercantile families, further challenging the boundaries of élite society. Factionalism, corruption and an expansion of eunuch power characterized a court unable to quell the increasing incidence of banditry and violence reported throughout the empire, as state infrastructure continued to decline, with the Chongzhen 崇禎 Emperor (Sizong 思宗; r. 1628–44) giving approval for the closure of up to one-third of the stations in the already weakened imperial courier system beginning in 1629.[2] Now famine and plague not only threatened further destabilization of the social and economic order, but in symbolic terms, also represented the final stages in the erosion of the Ming ruling house's moral claims to imperial authority.

The immense social impact of such changes on the late-Ming world has proven to be a fruitful source of some particularly fascinating scholarship in recent years.[3] The virtually hereditary claim to leadership and élite status that the literati had enjoyed for centuries was being challenged, perhaps for the first time in history, as educated scholars increasingly found themselves marginalized by the political system. At the same time, the perception that surplus capital was shifting the balance of economic power out of élite hands and into those of the merchant class was for many deeply unsettling. As Craig Clunas has shown, the quest of the educated literatus to find new avenues of self-definition saw the enjoyment of fashionable items such as antiques shift "from being a personal predilection, one of a number of potential types of privileged activity, to being an essential form of consumption which was central to the maintenance of élite status."[4] For those living through the early decades of the seventeenth century this shift had happened at an almost frightening pace. The historian Shen Defu 沈德符 (*zi* Huchen 虎臣, *hao* Jingbo 景伯; 1578–1642) found remarkable the changes that had taken place in the Hangzhou antique markets over his lifetime:

> When I was a child I did not think of [cups] as valuable treasures. A pair of Chenghua 成化 [1465–87] wine cups now fetches 100 ounces, and a Xuande 宣德 [1426–35] incense burner almost as much. It is all due to the leaders of fashion from Suzhou making these things the subject of their 'elegant discussions', which the imperial relatives and big merchants blindly and frivolously imitate, that the flood of rising prices has reached this point.[5]

As status competition increasingly played itself out around the complicated arenas of fashion and taste, ever more commodities became subject to the whims of the unpredictable marketplace, while consumptive practices that had previously been the preserve of the élite were coming within the reach of a wider range of the population than in any previous period in the empire's history. A decade after government sumptuary restrictions began to be relaxed around the 1560s, Chen Yao 陳堯 (*zi* Jingfu 敬甫, *hao* Wugang 梧岡; *js.* 1536?) lamented, "Take simple clothes to a country fair, and not even country people will buy them."[6] The claim made in the gazetteer of Tongcheng 桐城 county, Anhui, that "by the Chongzhen period, extravagance became excessive and distinctions were confused,"[7] echoed Zhang Tao's 張濤 (*zi* Zhenhai 振海, *hao* Shanshi 山是; b. 1560?) now famous lament of 1609, that "[t]he lord of silver rules heaven and the god of copper cash reigns over the earth."[8]

    Such, at least, is how society is portrayed in the myriad complaints about the excesses of rampant commercial expansion we find in the works of late-Ming literati. Did these complaints reflect a genuine unease about the reality of the evolving world? Jonathan Hay is one critic who, addressing Clunas' study, cautions against taking "too much at face value" the rhetoric of the literati, and underestimating "the degree to which the educated gentry élite was itself in a process of dissolution and mutation."[9] Certainly it would be a mistake to accept uncritically élite mistrust of commercialism without taking into account the increasing degree to which gentry income depended on the commercial economy,[10] or indeed the fact that merchant patronage of the arts was becoming ever more essential to the maintenance of the élite way of life. Clunas himself notes that the late-Ming unease about extravagance was "to a certain extent conventional."[11] But to whatever degree gentry writings reflect a genuine anxiety about the changing world, there is no doubt that a significant number felt the need not only to complain about the excesses before them, but also to record their complaints in writing.

This chapter examines the key role of text in the ways in which the educated élite sought to portray itself during the late Ming. It argues that, whatever the realities of merchant-gentry relationships during the period, in representational terms, the establishment and maintenance of clear markers of social status had become, by the final decades of the sixteenth century, so fundamental to élite life that such concerns could not but permeate even the most apparently trivial pieces of writing. Complaints such as that of He Liangjun 何良俊 (*zi* Dengzhi 登之, *hao* Zhehu 柘湖; 1506–73) of Huating 華亭, who labelled one of Jiangnan's wealthiest families "the acme of common vulgarity incapable of being outdone,"[12] are so prevalent in élite discourse that they simply cannot be ignored. Hay's warning against taking literati complaints at face value is unquestionably sound, and as we learn more about the structure of late-Ming society we may well find that many of them complain a little too loudly. But it is precisely the face value of such claims that is so pertinent to the present study. As we examine some of the ways in which members of the late-Ming élite wrote about their world, I argue that as a marker of social status, the appropriate engagement with landscape functioned for these men in much the same way as the connoisseurship of material objects, on which so much ink was spent during the period. This chapter also introduces Qian Qianyi, briefly sketching his early life, and examining his place in this complex élite world in the lead up to his Yellow Mountain trip of 1641.

Connoisseurship

Much of the anxiety of self-representation that plagued literati of the period was concerned with the changing patterns of consumption that threatened to redefine the merchant class. While mercantile families had always spent money, the new levels of conspicuous purchasing we find emerging in the last century of Ming rule represented a new challenge to the élite. Sandi Chin and Ginger Hsü note in their study that merchant spending often included the sponsorship of large construction projects; shrines, bridges and roads were all built using merchant money in the late Ming.[13] One can imagine that in terms of its visibility this kind of large-scale public spending would have heightened the feeling of disempowerment that comes through in the works of the élite during the period. But, after all, a road was still just a road. More troublesome seems to have been the massive appropriation of cultural capital that occurred in the form of art sales to merchants or those of merchant backgrounds. Shen Defu notes with a degree of amazement the insatiable appetite of wealthy Anhui merchants for antique paintings: "They spend hundreds and thousands of cash to compete in the purchase [of antiquities]."[14] The Jiangnan educated élite, traditional custodians of the culturally significant artefacts of the empire, were now being outbid.

Wai-yee Li separates the late-Ming discourse on objects into two distinct categories: the first including books on the art of living and taste manuals such as the *Zhangwu zhi* 長物志 [Treatise on Superfluous Things] by Wen Zhenheng 文震亨 (*zi* Qimei 啟美, *hao* Yujuzhai 玉局齋; 1585–1645), and the second including the more personal and anecdotal accounts usually taking the form of *biji* 筆記 [notes] or *xiaopin* 小品 [vignettes].[15] Running parallel with developments in an expanding commercialized publishing industry,[16] the explosion of works in both of Li's categories during the period reveals much about the complex role of tradable commodities in late-Ming society.[17] In a world in which the consumption of luxury goods had become available to a growing number of wealthy buyers, appropriate consumption seems early to have become even more important than consumption itself. By the turn of the seventeenth century it was no longer enough to own a collection of rocks, scrolls or vases; one had to own such things with discrimination. At the same time, and in keeping with the introspective turn that could more generally be said to characterize artistic practice of the period,[18] self-representation had become critical to the maintenance of élite status, a means by which the true connoisseur might draw a line between himself and the ignorant, but increasingly wealthy, merchant-collectors.

The important autobiographical function of the late-Ming essay has in my view yet to be fully understood. We have been far too willing to listen to Ming assurances about the inconsequence of anecdotal prose, accepting at face value the name *xiaopin* 小品 (meaning a "short piece," but also something written "of trivial things"), while ignoring the vital role these vignettes played in the way élite society was defined and maintained. This approach is typified in the introduction to a recent anthology of translations of Ming *xiaopin* by Yang Ye, who claims that the genre "primarily served to amuse and entertain its reader."[19] Ye cites a preface by Chen Jiru 陳繼儒 (*zi* Zhongchun 仲醇, *hao* Meigong 眉公; 1558–1639) in which Chen, Dong Qichang 董其昌 (*zi* Xuanzai

玄宰, *hao* Sibai 思白; 1555–1636) and Zheng Yuanxun 鄭元勳 (*zi* Chaozong 超宗, *hao* Huidong 惠東; 1603–44) shut themselves away, decline all visitors and produce essays purely for their own amusement,[20] a romanticized self-depiction that must be understood more in terms of literary convention than as a reflection of the realities of late-Ming life. Such allegedly meaningless sketches were all carefully preserved and published not only in the collected works of various men-of-letters, but also, as Ye himself notes, as separate collections during the period.[21] The fact that the same essay dates the rise of *xiaopin* to the Longqing 隆慶 (1567–72) and Wanli reign periods,[22] precisely the period during which issues of taste and fashion had become so important, is a clue to the significance of this style of writing. Rather than reading the *xiaopin* as a trivial form of entertainment, "intended for close associates," as one scholar recently put it,[23] we need to read the genre as a further attempt at the self-definition that had become such an important aspect of late-Ming life. Its *raison d'être* was not private reflection but the very public portrayal of the author's appropriate engagement with the trappings of élite society.

Lu Shusheng's 陸樹聲 (*zi* Yuji 與吉, *hao* Pingquan 平泉; 1509–1605) "Yanshi ji" 硯室記 [Account of Inkstone Studio], a piece included in Ye's anthology, is typical of this kind of autobiographical essay that raises the self to a level of importance seldom seen in other genres.[24] Lu is a connoisseur of inkstones, who concedes that not one of his collection is of any great quality, "and yet my obsession [for them] cannot be reasoned away" 余之癖未解也. Presenting himself as continuing a discourse on inkstones that began with such notables as Ouyang Xiu 歐陽修 (*zi* Yongshu 永叔; 1007–72) and Su Shi 蘇軾 (*zi* Zizhan 子瞻, *hao* Dongpo 東坡; 1037–1101), Lu gives himself the sobriquet "Master of Ten Inkstones" 十硯主人, thus drawing an explicit link between the author/collector and his collected objects. Here Lu's distinction is that he spurns the too-obvious approach of collecting only valuable or tradable pieces. The process of acquisition, he wants us to believe, was not planned or considered, but simply arose from the very nature of his self. Given the conclusions of scholars such as Clunas and Li, that by the late Ming, collecting and conspicuous consumption had become essential to the maintenance of élite status, it seems somewhat naïve to regard Lu's essay as no more than trifling entertainment.[25] Such accounts were in many cases the only difference between conspicuous consumption and the socially useless consumption in solitude.

True connoisseurship was also implied by certain key linguistic markers. When Gu Qiyuan 顧起元 (*zi* Taichu 太初; 1565–1628) commented on the relaxation of sumptuary laws at the start of the Wanli era, he suggested that the change had allowed people to "present their exceptionality" 獻奇,[26] invoking an important concept that will recur throughout this study. Ideas about the exceptional, the strange, the eccentric, and the bizarre had begun to fill the essays of men-of-letters by the late sixteenth century, although reading these works tends to bear out Qianshen Bai's observation that late-Ming scholars "seemed unconcerned to define [the concept] and used it rather loosely."[27] In any case one can read something of the complexity of the term and its use in Gu's rather exasperated follow-up to his observation above, that "[i]t never ends; there is always more and more exceptionality,"[28] an inherent contradiction that was apparently acceptable (or at least comprehendible) to his late sixteenth-century audience. Ideas about the exceptional were linked implicitly to another important concept of the age, obsession 癖, an affliction (the ideogram 癖 suggests illness) that by the turn of the seventeenth century had itself become something of a fashionable commodity.[29] Lu Shusheng cites an obsession to justify his collection of inkstones, while Qi Biaojia 祁彪佳 (zi Youwen 幼文, hao Shipei 世培; 1602–45) refers to the construction of his garden as a "crazy obsession" 癡癖 in an essay dated 1636.[30] Connoisseurship was distinguished from mere collecting by the very irrationality of these men's activities. This strange world was one in which Zhang Dai 張岱 (zi Zongzi 宗子, hao Taoan 陶庵; 1597–1689?) could claim that "one cannot befriend a man without obsessions, for he lacks deep emotion" 人無癖不可與交以其無深情也.[31]

Connoisseurship of Landscape

Gu Qiyuan's linking the presentation of the exceptional to the relaxation of sumptuary laws is revealing, suggesting that already by the beginning of the Wanli era (1573) the establishment of one's uniqueness was becoming inextricably linked to issues of consumption and ownership. Indeed, late-Ming writings about tradable commodities tend to support Gell's general observation that consumption "involves the incorporation of the consumed item into the personal and social identity of the consumer"[32]— Lu Shusheng's adoption of the sobriquet "Master of Ten Inkstones" reveals an instinctual awareness of this relationship between object and owner. But when one examines the kinds of pseudonyms used by the late-Ming literati, it is far more frequently landscape that one finds associated with the self in this way. The sobriquet of the scholar Huang Ruheng 黃汝亨 (zi Zhenfu 貞父, hao Nanping 南屏; 1558–1626), a man we will meet below on Yellow Mountain, carries with it far more than simply the fact of his growing up in Hangzhou (Nanping 南屏 [Southern Screen] is a hill overlooking West Lake 西湖). We read here an explicit association of man and landscape, and an implication that the exceptional qualities of West Lake are reflected in the exceptional qualities of Huang himself.[33]

It is a small but essential part of the argument of the present study that, at least during the period under examination here, engagements with important landscapes, spaces of cultural significance, are usefully viewed as part of the same process of identity construction and self-representation that surrounds issues of consumption and ownership of tradable commodities. In the present context, the link is perhaps best revealed in a colophon composed by Qian Qianyi in 1642, following his acquisition of a painting at Yellow Mountain the previous year, an episode he declines to include in the *youji* that is the focus of this study. As a prelude to an examination of engagement with physical landscapes, it seems useful to spend a moment here examining his account of this engagement with an object that represented at once both a purchasable cultural relic and a landscape scene. That object was the *Jiangshan xueji* 江山雪霽 [Rivers and Mountains after Snow], a painted handscroll attributed to the great Tang artist and poet Wang Wei 王維 (*zi* Mojie 摩詰 *hao* Youcheng 右丞; 701–61).[34] A work of this importance would have been considered one of the most valuable cultural treasures circulating at the time, yet, perhaps surprisingly, it changed hands a number of times around the turn of the seventeenth century, twice being viewed by the pre-eminent painter, calligrapher and art historian of the age, Dong Qichang. A letter dated 1595 and sent to Feng Mengzhen 馮夢禎 (*zi* Kaizhi 開之, *hao* Beiyuan 北園; 1546–1605), a Jiaxing 嘉興 native and at that time the owner of the handscroll, documents Dong's request to view it: "I am extremely anxious to see your scroll. I have specialized in painting, but if your ancient masterpiece could enlighten me [as to the style of Wang Wei's brushstrokes], you would be doing me a great favour."[35] A note made by Dong later that year reveals something of the value of the work in the minds of the two men:

> In autumn, I heard that a handscroll by Wang Wei, *Rivers and Mountains after Snow*, had been acquired by Feng Kaizhi [Mengzhen]. I immediately sent a friend to Wulin 武林 [Hangzhou] to borrow the scroll. Kaizhi considered the scroll to be as precious as his own head and eyes, his brain and bone marrow, but because of my special passion for Wang's painting, he reluctantly agreed to my request. I fasted for three days before unrolling the scroll.[36]

The work eventually survived both this, and another journey in 1604, before Feng Mengzhen's death at Yellow Mountain the following year, and after several changes of ownership the scroll ended up in the possession of a Cheng Jibai 程季白 of Xin'an 新安, sometime after 1618.[37]

In 1642 Feng's grandson Feng Wenchang 馮文昌 (*zi* Yanxiang 研祥, *hao* Kuaixuetang 快雪堂) had three letters sent to his late grandfather by Dong

Qichang regarding the viewing of the handscroll (dated 1595, 1596 and 1604) mounted into an album, to which, in the tenth month of the same year, Qian Qianyi appended the following colophon:

> Chancellor Feng Kaizhi [Mengzhen] obtained the *Rivers and Mountains after Snow* by Wang Youcheng [Wei], and stored it in his Pleasure in Snow Hall 快雪堂, becoming the crowning glory of his lifetime of connoisseurship. Dong Xuanzai [Qichang], who was at that time working at the Historiography Institute 史館, sent Feng a letter asking to borrow the work for viewing. The Chancellor bound and sent the painting over three thousand *li*, and, after a year, it was returned to him. Now, the Chancellor's grandson Yanxiang [Wenchang] has had Dong's handwritten letters concerning the borrowing of the painting mounted into an album, which he has entrusted to me in order that I might record this colophon. The Wanli reign was a time of peace within the seas, when scholars fluttered around the halls and academies, and derived mutual pleasure from the movement of brush and ink . . . [but] after the death of the Chancellor, when this scroll was purchased by a wealthy man from Xin'an, an immortal example of brush and ink became buried under a mountain of copper cash, there languishing for over thirty years. Only when I travelled to Yellow Mountain was I able to recover it, bringing it out from its prison like the divine objects of Fengcheng 豐城.[38] If Dong and Feng have spirits, they will certainly have applauded this.[39]

Qian's story of the handscroll provides a good illustration of the attitude of educated scholars towards the wealthy men (rather predictably, this one is from the great centre of commercial activity Xin'an) who, scandalously, were becoming the great collectors of the age by virtue of fiscal means alone. Such trends extended to areas other than just art collecting — Harriet Zurndorfer has shown in her study that Huizhou 徽州 merchants were particularly zealous in their imitation of élite cultural activities such as drinking wine and playing the zither.[40] Even so, Chin and Hsü's analysis that by the seventeenth century "the social positions of 'merchant' and 'literatus' were all but interchangeable,"[41] seems far too simplistic. The attempts of wealthy merchants to appropriate literati culture are seldom met in élite discourse with anything other than contempt. Whatever the reality of the relationships between men such as Qian Qianyi and those who had become wealthy through commerce, the fact is that in representational terms it was still essential for Qian to separate the "us" from the "them." Merchants and literati might now have been purchasing the same types of painting, but clearly their respective social positions remained anything but interchangeable.

Self-Representation in Travel Literature

Of course the association of self and landscape was not just a one-way process. The inscription of a painting with a colophon, or indeed the literal inscription of characters into the face of a cliff inevitably altered the character of the landscape. But more symbolically there is a sense in Qian's account of the Wang Wei handscroll that the very meaning of the work changes with each new buyer. The exaggerated distinction Qian draws between such an object in his own hands and one in those of a Xin'an merchant (un-named) almost brings to life the landscape in question; there is a definite implication that the scroll wanted to be freed from its prison by the right sort of owner.

This sense of the intertwining of identities of owner and object is similarly evident in late-Ming *youji*, or travel accounts. Indeed, if self-representation had become a vital component of élite identity construction with regard to collecting and connoisseurship, it was even more essential in the case of élite travel practices. Lu Shusheng's inkstones at least provided a tangible reminder of his discriminating connoisseurship, even if his collection required textual justification. One's travels, though, would disappear forever without the immortality that only text could provide. Ignoring for a moment the fact that travel is not an "object" in the strictest sense of the word, what should become clear as this study continues is that inasmuch as it required a degree of "specialized knowledge as a prerequisite for its 'appropriate' consumption" and there existed a "high degree of linkage of its consumption to body, person, and personality," late-Ming travel meets two important criteria of Appadurai's definition of a luxury object, "whose principal use is rhetorical and social."[42] The important rhetorical function of *youji* makes sense of the fact that travel essays almost inevitably fill a significant part of late-Ming *xiaopin* collections, placed alongside works dealing with art, rocks, antiques and various other accoutrements of élite society. Certainly many, although not all, examples of *youji* share the same surface impression of lightness and informality we see in other *xiaopin*. But the heightened sense of the self, and the eagerness of the author to define himself in opposition to other, vulgar tourists are of greater significance here in terms of the characterization of the genre.

It is important also to note that the popularity of travel began to reach its peak during the period in which the commodities markets were, if our sources are to be believed, spiralling out of control. Facilities available through the official courier system were easily replaced by commercial services after the former had begun to decline by the turn of the seventeenth century. Boats, sedan chairs, porters and guides are seldom remarked upon in late-Ming writings in terms of their scarcity or difficulty to purchase.[43] The publication in 1570 of Huang Bian's 黃汴 (*zi* Liangfu 梁甫, *hao* Dongjiao 東郊) *Yitong lucheng tuji* 一統路程圖記 [Comprehensive Illustrated Record of Routes][44] reflected a growing interest in travel that saw in the following decades the production of ever more topographical gazetteers, mirroring what Clunas classes as "an explosion of publishing interest in the fields of what might loosely be called luxury consumption" during the same period.[45] Undoubtedly the market for travel guides was part of an expanding book culture that both fed off and contributed to an increase in literacy during the late-Ming period, but there is also no doubt that these guides were being used. The world was one in which Huang Liuhong 黃六鴻 (*zi* Sihu 思湖) could claim that reading ten thousand books and travelling ten thousand *li* were the requirements of an accomplished gentleman,[46] while by 1637, Song Yingxing 宋應星 (*zi* Zhanggeng 長庚; 1587?–1666?) had already noticed that "carriages from Yunnan may be seen traversing the plains of Liaoyang [modern Liaoning Province], and the officials and merchants from the southern coast travel freely in Hebei."[47]

One further reason for reading late-Ming travel essays in the same way as essays on the other fashionable things of the age is the obvious similarity in the choice of language employed across these types of writings. When Yuan Hongdao 袁宏道 (*zi* Zhonglang 中郎, *hao* Shigong 石公; 1568–1610) claimed that travel was an "obsession" among the men of Suzhou 蘇人好遊自其一癖,[48] he might easily have been referring instead to rocks, calligraphy or inkstones. Yuan uses the same term in a self-description dated 1597:

> By nature I am carefree, and I cannot bear any kind of restraint. Unfortunately I share an obsession 癖 with Dongpo [Su Shi] and Banshan 半山 [Wang Anshi 王安石 (1021–1086)]. Whenever I stay inside for a day, I fidget about as if sitting on a hot stove. So even on frosty days, dark nights, or when I have a pile of trivial matters to attend to, my mind never ceases to tour the hills and rivers.[49]

Yuan's self-deprecatory admission must be read in the context of the period; the same "restless itch to rove" that had prevented Dante's (1265–1321) Ulysses from returning home had by now become almost *de rigueur* of élite late-Ming society.[50] Zou Kuangming 鄒匡明, whom we will meet below at Yellow Mountain, cites an "obsession for springs and rocks" 泉石之癖 as the reason for his roaming.[51] This idea of a force beyond the control of the traveller still resonates today; as the editor of one recent anthology of travel literature claims, "what makes [the writers in this anthology] different from the commissioned traveloguers, is that they set out because of an inner compulsion to do so, or are driven by some sort of necessity . . ."[52] It is precisely the fact that men such as Yuan Hongdao were (usually by their own accounts) *compelled* to set out, that raises them above the wrong sorts of traveller.[53]

For the seventeenth-century writer though, producing an appropriate textual response to landscape was a complicated business. James Hargett dates the rise of the *youji* in China to the Song period, during which improved and more extensive land and water arteries afforded an expanded civil bureaucracy greater access to the more remote and inaccessible of the empire's sites.[54] Strassberg notes that by the end of the Song "a number of influential texts had emerged to form a canon,"[55] and indeed, the period produced probably China's first collection of travel accounts, Chen Renyu's 陳仁玉 (*zi* Degong 德公, *hao* Biqi 碧棲; *js.* 1259) *Youzhi* 遊志 [Chronicles of Travels].[56] So for the late-Ming man-of-letters, the culturally important landscapes were cluttered with the histories and inscriptions (both metaphoric and literal) of men dating back centuries. The scholar faced not only T. S. Eliot's concern that every poet "fulfils once for all some possibility of the language, and so leaves one possibility less for his successors,"[57] but also the question of how meaningfully to incorporate the works of his famous predecessors into those of his own. Responding to landscape now inevitably involved the recollection of a famous line of poetry, or the comparison of a view with one famously described long before. No account of a visit to Orchid Pavilion 蘭亭 would be complete without some mention of Wang Xizhi 王羲之 (*zi* Yishao 逸少; 303?–61?), whose preface had established the site as central to China's literary heritage. If travelling had always been about writing, as Michel Butor observes,[58] by the late Ming the writing process also necessarily involved reading.

In some ways the expansion of the travel guide industry had made the process of responding appropriately to landscape an easier one. A visitor to the important landscapes of the empire at the turn of the seventeenth century could easily discover the historical significance of a site, or find a quote or two for his *youji* in one of the many gazetteers now filling the local book markets. But this accessibility of information came with its own set of problems. It was one thing for Yuan Hongdao to refresh his literary memory at West Lake by consulting Tian Rucheng's 田汝成 (*zi* Shuyao 叔禾, *hao* Yuyang 豫陽; *js.* 1526) *Xihu youlanzhi* 西湖遊覽志 [Touring Gazetteer of West Lake],[59] first published in 1547 and, significantly, reprinted twice during the Wanli period; it was quite another for an ignorant merchant to be provided with a neat summary of the Lake's literary history without having to lift a finger. As the educated literatus increasingly found the once solitary landscapes of the empire filling with tourists, his textual engagement with the site became ever more important as a means of fortifying social distinctions. Feng Mengzhen was already unimpressed with the flood of tourists in 1590s Nanjing who wanted simply to see the famous sites, but who, in his view, had no understanding of what they signified.[60] The pleasure of the exquisite reflections and shadows of West Lake were, Yuan Hongdao recorded in 1597, "to be enjoyed by monks and travellers alone" 此樂留與山僧遊客受用, while later he found that a "rabble of bondservants" made Stone House 石屋 Cave "seem like a noisy market" 為傭奴所據嘈雜若市.[61] Such complaints come across as startlingly "modern" to us now, and indeed are remarkably reminiscent of those that came out of the nineteenth-century onset of mass tourism in the West, when one critic could describe tourists as "noxious animals," while slightly later Osbert Sitwell (1892–1969) observed as "a swarm of very noisy transatlantic locusts" the tourists crowding Amalfi in the 1920s.[62] What we are reading here are expressions of distaste for travellers written by other travellers; responses perhaps, to what Alan Brien described some decades ago as "a gnawing suspicion that after all you've said you are still a tourist like any other tourist."[63] The degree to which the distaste expressed was genuine is difficult to answer, but what is clear is that the expression of distaste had become a virtual necessity.

Looking back some years after 1644, Gu Yanwu 顧炎武 (original *ming* Jiang 絳, *zi* Ningren 寧人, *hao* Tinglin 亭林; 1613–82) would regard the decline, and then the scaling down of the official courier system beginning in 1629, as the principal reason for the collapse of the Ming ruling house.[64] While Timothy Brook is probably correct in his view that the fate of the courier system cannot on its own account for such a dramatic failure,[65] Gu's claim at least gives a good indication of the scale of the transformation taking place. While private, commercial travel services quickly filled the void, the change here is unmistakable; travel had shifted from being almost exclusively the domain of the élite, who used the courier system even when not on active government service (although this was officially prohibited), to being a purchasable commodity, freely available to anyone with the means to pay for a sedan chair or a boat. The massive expansion of the publishing industry during the period had likewise made knowledge a purchasable commodity; the fact that after 1580 the explosion in the numbers of topographical gazetteers, in one sense taste manuals for the consumption of landscape, paralleled the appearance of taste manuals for the consumption of things, such as Wen Zhenheng's *Zhangwu zhi*, is hardly a coincidence. Élite representations of the glut of travellers on the important landscapes of late-Ming Jiangnan parallel those of the glut of buyers in the commodities markets, and in text the consequences were remarkably similar, shifting the emphasis from the act of travel/ownership to the manner in which such behaviour was carried out. Those composing *youji* during the final half century of Ming rule appear almost overly anxious to go beyond "other 'mere' tourists" to what Dean MacCannell calls "a more profound appreciation of society and culture."[66] While such impulses undoubtedly existed prior to the sixteenth century, it does seem that by around 1600 the important business of standing out from the crowds of tourists populating the great sites had become more important, and indeed more complex, than in any previous period in history.

Qian Qianyi and the Literary World

Adshead dates the beginning of late-Ming China's "smouldering" political crisis to 1582, the year that saw the death of Grand Secretary Zhang Juzheng 張居正 (*zi* Shuda 叔大, *hao* Taiyue 太岳; 1525–82).[67] But in the small and bustling city of Changshu 常熟, some 360 *li* to the east of Nanjing, something else had occurred during this, the *renwu* 壬午 (and tenth) year of the Wanli reign — the birth of the future poet, official and literary historian Qian Qianyi 錢謙益 (*zi* Shouzhi 受之, *hao* Muzhai 牧齋, Muweng 牧翁, Banyetang 半野堂, Jiangyunlou 絳雲樓, Dongjian 東澗, Yushan laomin 虞山老民, Tianzi mensheng 天子門生; 1582–1664).[68] The Qian clan was an educated one, headed by Qianyi's grandfather Qian Shunshi 錢順時 (*zi* Daolong 道隆; b. 1532), who had placed highly in his *jinshi* examination of 1559.[69] Qianyi spent his early years reading the classics, and, under the influence of his father Qian Shiyang 錢世揚 (*zi* Shixing 士興, *hao* Jingxing 景行; d. 1610), establishing an extensive social network that would serve him well in later life.[70] In the 28th year of the Wanli reign (1600), Qianyi married a woman surnamed Chen 陳 (d. 1658), whose father was an associate of Qian Shiyang, and who would later bear him his son Qian Sun'ai 錢孫愛 (*zi* Ruyi 孺貽; *jr.* 1646).[71] Qianyi passed his *juren* examination in 1606, and four years later, in the spring of 1610, he graduated as *jinshi* with high honours, being appointed Junior Compiler 編修 at the Hanlin Academy 翰林院 in his twenty-ninth year.

Three and a half centuries after the fall of the Ming ruling house, the name Qian Qianyi remains inextricably linked to issues of dynastic loyalty, and to this day his service of both the Ming and the Qing courts stands out as the most notable aspect of his biography. In the twelfth month of the 41st year of his reign (1777), eight years after his initial edict (see above), the Qianlong Emperor established a new biographical category of "twice-serving officials" 貳臣 in order to accommodate those men who, disgracefully, had served both houses over the Ming-Qing transition period. Later published as *(Qinding guoshi) Erchen zhuan* (欽定國史)貳臣傳 [Imperially Ordered Biographies of

Figure 1: Yang Pengqiu 楊鵬秋. *Qian Qianyi* 錢謙益. Drawing from Ye Gongchuo 葉恭綽 (1880–1968) comp., *Qingdai xuezhe xiangzhuan dierji* 清代學者象傳第二集 (1953). [Rpt.; *Qingdai xuezhe xiangzhuan heji* 清代學者象傳合集. Shanghai: Guji chubanshe, 1989].

Twice-Serving Officials],[72] the biographies of these 120 officials were divided into superior 甲 and inferior 乙 classes (Qian was placed in the latter), with the emperor explaining the distinction in a further proclamation of 1778:

> Qian Qianyi's character was unworthy. When the Ming house was losing power he was one of the first to turn to us for orders, yet in his poetry and prose he dared secretly to vilify us. He had no principles to guide him in taking office or in retiring, and was something less than a man. If his record is placed in the *Erchen zhuan* on a par with that of Hong Chengchou 洪承疇 [1593–1665] and others the different degrees of shameful conduct are not brought out. How then would the distinction between good and evil people be made manifest?[73]

By the time the *Erchen zhuan* biographies had become *juan* 78 and 79 of the *Qingshi liezhuan* 清史列傳 [Biographies of the Qing History] in 1928, Qian's works had already been consigned to the margins of literary history for a century and a half, having been omitted from the monumental *Siku quanshu* 四庫全書 [Complete Library of the Four Treasuries of Literature] collection initiated in 1772.[74] While Qianlong's proscriptions essentially failed in terms of preventing the transmission of Qian's works,[75] they did ensure that the name Qian Qianyi remained shrouded in infamy until the end of the Qing era, occupying a dubious position from which it has never fully recovered.[76]

The complex range of choices faced by the educated élite at various stages between the years 1644 and 1684, when the Qing finally achieved control of the empire in its entirety,[77] has only recently begun to receive adequate treatment in secondary literature.[78] It is becoming ever more apparent that analyses of political developments during the early Qing cannot usefully be based around such rudimentary frameworks as the simple loyalist-collaborator opposition. Tobie Meyer-Fong's acknowledgement that our reading of issues of loyalism has been "over-influenced by the values of the Qianlong era . . . and by the anti-Manchu rhetoric of the late nineteenth and early twentieth centuries" represents a crucial step towards a deeper understanding of the complexities of relationships formed in élite society after 1644.[79] While this is not to deny that men such as Qian Qianyi earned the scorn of some of their contemporaries,[80] the precise nature of their position in early Qing society needs to be approached carefully. Qianshen Bai's trenchant examination of the life of the calligrapher Fu Shan 傅山 (*zi* Qingzhu 青主, *hao* Selu 嗇廬; 1607–84?) is one study that brings new perspective to the developing interactions of all those who lived through the transition period, whether or not they decided to serve the new regime, and further advances in our understanding of the early Qing world will, one feels, require more such careful approaches.[81]

In the present context, however, neither Qian Qianyi's surrender to Manchu forces in 1645, nor his service of both the Ming and the Qing ruling houses, will be addressed.[82] My concern here is to place Qian back into the context of 1641–42, when, however serious the political and economic crises seemed to scholars of the time, the total collapse of the Ming house could still barely be imagined. Indeed, if Qian's political career became complicated during the transition to Qing rule, it had been no less so under the Ming. The death of his father meant that Qian spent only a few months at the Hanlin Academy after graduating in 1610, returning home to spend the following years in mourning. In 1615 he printed his late father's *Gushi tanyuan* 古史談苑 [Discussions of Ancient History], which had been completed the year before Shiyang's death.[83] Resuming his official career in 1620, Qianyi was in the following year appointed to the highly regarded position of Zhejiang provincial examiner. At the end of 1622 he again asked for leave, this time for reasons of ill health, and his recall in 1624 lasted less than a year before he was dismissed for his affiliations with the Donglin Party 東林黨.[84] When the Chongzhen reign commenced in 1628, Qian was appointed vice-minister 右侍郎 (rank 3a) at the Ministry of Rites 禮部, only to be dismissed again the same year after being accused by Wen Tiren 溫體仁 (*zi* Zhangqing 長卿, *hao* Wensizhai 文似齋; d. 1638) of corruption during the Zhejiang provincial examination of 1621. In 1637 Qian and his disciple Qu Shisi 瞿式耜 (*zi* Qitian 起田, *hao* Jiaxuan 稼軒; 1590–1650) were incarcerated following a further dispute involving Wen Tiren, but were released shortly afterwards when the latter was forced from office. Returning to Changshu, Qian remained in retirement until his brief period of service at the Nanjing Southern Ming court in 1645.

Qian's challenging career as an official under the Ming was not atypical for a man of his time. Government service still provided the necessary point of entry into the sophisticated literati society of Jiangnan, but for many, the vicissitudes of late-Ming official life, captured by Nelson Wu in his treatment of the life and career of Dong Qichang,[85] proved too difficult to endure. After the death of his father in 1610, Qian continued for years to style himself "former historiographer" 舊史官, despite having served less than three months in the role. By the time he retired to Changshu in 1638, Qian had spent almost his entire official career out of office, yet he was already regarded by his contemporaries not only as the greatest poet of his generation, but also as the pre-eminent literary critic of the age, finding himself in the constant demand of young writers seeking corrections to their drafts.[86] Clearly the world of the Jiangnan scholarly community was one in which a reputation could be forged outside of government service, with the enjoyment of literature, music, wine, tea, antiques and the various other trappings of élite culture providing ample avenues for social networking.

In terms of literary theory, Qian was to some extent the inheritor of the movement of self-expression championed by Yuan Hongdao and the Gongan 公安 School, centred around Jiading 嘉定, the home of Qian's close friend Cheng Jiasui 程嘉燧 (*zi* Mengyang 孟陽; *hao* Songyuan 松圓; 1565–1644).[87] For Yuan and his followers, poetry was achieved only when a poet allowed his "natural sensibility" 性靈 to flow onto the page, rather than striving to achieve perfection of metre or diction.[88] The resulting natural and spontaneous composition would, according to Gongan theory, better reflect the personality of the poet; Yuan could claim admiringly in 1608 that "those who do not know [the poet] Yuanding 元定 [Liu Kanzhi 劉戡之] can examine his poems, while those who have never seen Yuanding's poems, [need only] examine the man."[89] Many of Qian's statements about literature echo those of Yuan. He believed that "the writer of [real] poetry is compelled only by his natural aspiration" 所謂有詩者惟其志意偪塞 and does not "go against his inclinations" 矯厲氣矜,[90] and that aspects such as stanza length, metre and form were mere physical characteristics 體態, incidental to the spirit 氣 of a poem.[91] But Qian was also a step removed from the literature of his age; as the corrector of drafts, the writer of prefaces, and later, as the compiler of the monumental *Liechao shiji* 列朝詩集 [Collected Poetry Ordered by Reign].[92] When in the spring of 1640 Zheng Yuanxun held on his estate a poetry contest among the literary luminaries of the age, it was Qian Qianyi to whom the poems were eventually sent to be judged.[93]

Qian's literary theory also placed more emphasis than those of the Gongan poets on sound literary scholarship. "Poetry and prose sprout from the inner spirit . . ." he claimed, "are nourished by the age and raised up by scholarship" 詩文之道萌折于靈心蟄啟于世運而苗長于學問.[94] Indeed, by the late 1630s Qian's self-confessed "obsession for books" 好書之癖[95] had seen his own collection of volumes become one of the great personal libraries of the age, one that would later be housed in the Tower of Crimson Clouds (Jiangyunlou 絳雲樓), partially destroyed by fire in 1650.[96] Huang Zongxi would later observe, "[o]f the books I desired to view there was not one volume not housed in the Tower of Crimson Clouds" 絳雲樓藏書余所欲見者無不有,[97] while some years after the loss of the collection, Niu Xiu 鈕琇 (*zi* Shucheng 書城, *hao* Linyetang 臨野堂; d. 1704) claimed that "not one of the book collectors south of the Yangzi has amassed a collection as rich as that of Qian."[98] In terms of conspicuous consumption, Qian's library was the connoisseur's collection *par excellence*. Cao Rong's 曹溶 (*zi* Jiegong 潔躬, *hao* Qiuyue 秋嶽; 1613–85) claim that Qian "collected only Song- and Yuan-dynasty [1279–1368] editions and would not touch either imprints or manuscript copies of anything written by men of recent ages,"[99] was based on the *Jiangyunlou shumu* 絳雲樓書目 [Catalogue of the Tower of Crimson Clouds Library], a rather problematic source that should probably be read more as a connoisseur's self-portrait than as a listing of the actual holdings of his library.[100] The practice of affixing a collector's seal 藏書印 to the books held in a particular library reveals their significance as collected objects, as the Qing collector Huang Peilie 黃丕烈 (*zi* Shaowu 紹武, *hao* Fuweng 復翁; 1763–1825) noted some years later.[101] Of a Song-dynasty edition of the *Zuozhuan* 左傳 [Zuo Commentary on the *Spring & Autumn Annals* 春秋] Qian noted in 1631 "books of this class have a sense of ancient fragrance 古香 all about them, and are surely under the protection of spirits."[102] And, predictably, the term used by Qian to account for his collection is obsession 癖; after the fire of 1650 it is an "obsessive book-miserliness" 惜書癖 for which he playfully chastises himself.[103]

But Qian's personal library was also the collection of a true scholar. "Whenever we discussed a book . . ." Cao Rong recalled,

> [Qian] was able to speak in detail about both the old and new editions of the work, and the various differences between them; when we looked out the books themselves to test the veracity of what he had said, we would invariably find that he had been correct to the smallest detail. There was not a book that he seemed not to have read; how very different he was to those who claim to love books but who leave them sitting on the highest shelves![104]

Now, at the end of the 1630s, Qian seems to have felt himself adding new depth to his understanding of the canonical texts. In the spring of 1638, while still in prison, he had re-read the *Shiji* 史記 [Historical Records] and the two *Hanshu* 漢書 [Histories of the Former and Latter Han Dynasties], finally "understanding thoroughly the similarities and differences of the texts . . . where previously such aspects had been blurred" 茫如.[105] Elsewhere he regretted that, although he had read both the *Shiji* and the *Hanshu* as a child, it was "as if I had never engaged with them at all" 猶無與也.[106] Retiring to Changshu, he continued his commentary on the works of Du Fu 杜甫 (*zi* Zimei 子美, *hao* Shaoling 少陵; 712–70), a study that would eventually represent one of the most fascinating (and still understudied) works of commentary produced in late imperial China.[107] Wang Qi 王琦 (1696–1774), the Qing editor of the collected works of the great Li Bai 李白 (*zi* Taibai 太白, *hao* Qinglian jushi 青蓮居士; 701–62), would later admit that Qian's work had been a profound influence on his own editing practice, although this fact would eventually prove problematic as we will see below.[108] What distinguishes Qian as a commentator is his textual grounding in the classics; the catalogue to his personal collection lists, for example, 165 volumes of commentaries or editions of the *Yijing* 易經 [Book of Changes] alone.[109] In a self-conscious age in which "much creative energy was channelled into achieving insights that would enable one to propose a new interpretation of an old poem or an apter choice of words in somebody else's line,"[110] Qian was the pre-eminent literary scholar of the age. Thus when the great bibliophile Mao Jin 毛晉 (*zi* Zijin 子晉, *hao* Qianzai 潛在; 1599–1659) produced a new commentary on the *Thirteen Classics* 十三經 in 1639 (a year before Zheng Yuanxun's poetry contest), it was only natural that for the composition of a preface he should turn to Qian.[111]

This period also marks the beginning of a further chapter in the life of Qian Qianyi, for it was now that he met for the first time another remarkable figure of the Ming-Qing transition, Liu Shi 柳是 (original surname Yang 楊; *zi* Rushi 如是, *hao* Hedongjun 河東君; 1618–64), the courtesan and brilliant literary talent with whom Qian would spend the remaining years of his life.[112] After a brief meeting at some point during the previous month, the two were apparently reunited during the eleventh month of 1640 when Liu, unaccompanied and disguised as a man, came to call on Qian in Changshu. Liu had arrived on a skiff, evidently her preferred mode of transport around the prosperous Jiangnan cities. "I will marry no man whose talent does not match that of Scholar Qian of Yushan" 吾非才學如錢學士虞山者不嫁, she is recorded in the murky annals of literary mythology to have stated, while Qian's reply was "I will take as a wife no woman whose poetry does not match that of Liu Shi" 吾非能詩如柳如是者不娶.[113] By the following month, Liu had taken up residence in the Thus Did I Hear Studio 我聞室 on Qian's estate.[114]

Timothy Brook ascribes the rise of courtesanship in the late Ming to a society in which factionalism at court and the loss of official recognition had brought about a sense of impotence in élite men.[115] Certainly the ideal of the talented beauty seems to have flourished briefly during this period, a trend that may indeed have paralleled an actual increase in literary and social freedom experienced by women at the upper end of society.[116] Much of what we know about the figure of Liu Shi is suggestive of a blurring of traditional gender distinctions — dressing as a man, matching the literary talents of her partner, travelling independently, and adopting the sobriquet *Rúshì* 如是, which could be read as a pun on the traditional designation *rúshì* 儒士 (Confucian scholar). But Liu's literary talent, like that of so many seventeenth- and eighteenth-century women of fact and fiction (the boundaries between which are not always clear), is always described as an accompaniment to her beauty, and one suspects that it would be a mistake to ascribe too much independence to this figure who, after all, had lost her identity in early life with her change of name (a common practice among courtesans).[117] Sadly, Qian Qianyi's death in 1664 ignited a bitter dispute over family property, a dispute that eventually left Liu destitute, and, in the final confirmation of her vulnerability, ultimately induced her suicide.

As Qian Qianyi and Liu Shi welcomed in the first day of the *xinsi* 辛 巳 year (1641) together at Changshu,[118] those difficulties that the post-Ming world would bring were still some way off. Like those of so many of his contemporaries, Qian's official career under the Ming had been characterized by frustration and disappointment, but in his sixtieth year, he could reflect on the fact that he was widely recognized as the most brilliant poet and literary scholar of his generation, not to mention the owner of one of the finest collections of books south of the Yangzi. Now, he had entered into an affair with a beautiful courtesan who was not yet twenty-four. Just six months later, in the face of vociferous opposition from the family of Qian's first wife, Qian and Liu would be married. In the intervening period, Qian Qianyi set off for Yellow Mountain.

2

Landscape of Brush and Ink

Literary Tradition at Yellow Mountain

The mountain 山 in traditional China stood at the centre of a wide range of often competing practices relating to art, politics and most significantly, to religion, where it occupied a position both as a site of ritualistic pilgrimage activity and as a numinous object of worship. As the solid components of the landscape compound (which comprised hills and waterways 山水), mountains came to represent stability and permanence, and had early become inextricably linked to the ruling house both as delineators and as protectors of the imperial realm. Most important in this regard were the mountains that made up the system of Marchmounts 嶽, which at various times consisted of Mounts Tai 泰, Huo 霍, Heng 衡, Hua 華, Heng 恒 and Song 嵩, representing as a group the four (later five) limits of the habitable world, and the sites of the ritual tour of the emperor.[1] The *Shujing* 書經 [Classic of History] records the mythical Emperor Shun 舜 as having been the first to perform ritual worship at each of the Marchmounts in his domain.[2] Increasingly, the success of an emperor or dynasty was thought to be linked in particular to Taishan in the east (see Figure 2), at which the performance of the important *feng* 封 and *shan* 禪 rituals documented in the *Shiji* became during the first millennium CE a method by which a worthy emperor might emulate his legendary predecessor.[3] More visibly perhaps, the prevalence of imperial tumuli, both natural and artificial, as "monuments to China's imperial institution" provided an implicit link between mountains, heaven and the imperial house.[4] Even after the performance of the *feng* and *shan* sacrifices had fallen out of favour with later emperors, mountains continued to function as important symbols of imperial power, symbols that were continuously exploited by rulers such as

Figure 2: *The Imperial Tour of Inspection at Taishan* 巡守岱宗圖. Woodblock print from Sun Jianai 孫家鼐 ed., *Qinding Shujing tushuo* 欽定書經圖説. Beijing: [Jingshi] daxuetang, 1905.

Kangxi 康熙 (Shengzu 聖祖; r. 1662–1722), Qianlong and more recently Mao Zedong 毛澤東 (1893–1976).[5]

The sacred geography of China was continually reinterpreted and redefined by the development of systems that existed concurrently with, but stood in opposition to, that of orthodox Confucian ritual. From the late sixth century on, Daoists attempted to appropriate the Marchmount system by incorporating that set of peaks into their own cosmology.[6] While Chan Buddhism developed its own set of Five Mountains and Ten Monasteries 五山十剎,[7] of far greater significance was the prescription of an alternative system of mountains linked to the four major bodhisattvas in the Mahāyāna pantheon. These Four Famous Mountains 四大名山 of the Buddhist tradition, Mounts Putuo 普陀 (associated with Avalokiteśvara 觀音), Jiuhua 九華 (for Kṣitigarbha 地藏), Emei 峨嵋 (for Samantabhadra 普賢) and Wutai 五台 (for Mañjuśrī 文殊) were, in the words of one prominent Ming Buddhist, the sites at which "the old Buddhas have incarnated and manifested themselves to aid in the propagation of Buddhism and bring all living beings to salvation."[8] The Four Famous Mountains continued to function as a pilgrimage network well into the late imperial era; Zhang Dai's account of the spring fair in Hangzhou captures evocatively the atmosphere created by the masses of pilgrims on their way to Putuoshan during the late Ming.[9] Occupying a space within competing religious and intellectual traditions, mountains were at times the sites of violent conflict, as competing religious groups attempted to impose their own schemata onto landscapes at the expense of those of others. More often a mountain could exist simultaneously within different worlds, embodying different sets of meanings at various stages of its life.[10]

And, of course, the history of painting in China during the last millennium is largely the history of the representation of the mountain. But if Yellow Mountain lay outside the traditional systems of Marchmounts ascribed importance in religious terms, it for centuries also lay outside this less formal system of culturally significant landscapes, to which meaning had been attached by virtue of their contribution to the world of the scholar. Hubei's Red Cliff 赤壁, for example, had been immortalized in the poetry of Su Shi, while the Wang River 輞川 was for scholars inextricably linked to the name of Wang Wei. By contrast, it is revealing that when the great Northern Song landscape artist Guo Xi 郭熙 (*zi* Chunfu 淳夫; 1020?–1100?) listed seventeen "famous mountains and magnificent massifs of the empire," in his important *Linquan gaozhi ji* 林泉高致集 [Collection of Lofty Ambitions in Forests and Springs], Yellow Mountain did not rate a mention.[11] Indeed, as late as 1500, the number of visitors to the mountain who would later be felt worthy of inclusion in the 1679 gazetteer *Huangshan zhi dingben* 黃山志定本 [Gazetteer of Yellow Mountain: Definitive Edition] numbered only a few dozen.[12] Undoubtedly the inaccessibility of Yellow Mountain played a significant part in its relatively late development as a site of cultural significance, but as at other landscapes, the various identities of the mountain competed with each other over time, as the site was appropriated by Daoist, then Buddhist scholars, and finally by the Confucian literati. Ultimately it was this final group that was responsible for the mountain's rise to fame during the seventeenth century, but for those writing of or painting the mountain at that time, its peaks remained the dwelling places of Daoist immortals, while access to the mountain was itself a product of the imperially sponsored Buddhist presence.

This chapter is an attempt to read Yellow Mountain as a product of a discursive tradition; as a landscape, the shifting meanings and fortunes of which depended first and foremost on its representation in text. Increased access both to the mountain itself and to writings about the landscape during the early decades of the seventeenth century brought about two major developments in the history of the site. Most obviously, interest in travel to Yellow Mountain increased sharply, although few travellers explicitly acknowledge the presence of existing text as an inducement to travel (the Hangzhou writer Yao Wenwei 姚文蔚 (*zi* Yuansu 元素, *hao* Yanggu 養谷; *js.* 1592), who after an illness was finally able to make the trip in the tenth month of 1609, is one of few who does, citing the essay of Huang Ruheng as the impetus for his trip).[13] But more significantly for present purposes, it is clear that travellers to the site from around the turn of the seventeenth century onwards had access to and contributed to a developing representational tradition that informed, directed and mediated their experiences of the landscape. The gradual accretion of knowledge and prescription of culturally significant sites that can be traced below, not only transformed Yellow Mountain into one of the major cultural landmarks of the empire, but also set in place accepted patterns of textual description, many of which survive to this day.

Topographical Sources of Yellow Mountain History

The earliest dedicated, and by far the most influential, extant written source of information on Yellow Mountain is the *Huangshan tujing*, an anonymous Song dynasty text that fixes the site firmly within the Daoist mythological tradition, a tradition that in some form probably dated centuries earlier.[14] In this work, the mountain is said to be the site at which the Yellow Emperor 黃帝, aided by his assistants Rongcheng 容成 and Fuqiu 浮坵, succeeded in developing an *elixir vitae*, with the emperor's eventual ascension to the heavens transforming the site into a realm of immortals. A separate, similar tradition had certainly existed around Taishan; the Yellow Emperor's ascension to immortality at that site had been celebrated in a poem by Cao Zhi 曹植 (*zi* Zijian 子建; 192–232) in the third century CE.[15] The Han Emperor Wudi's 漢武帝 (Liu Che 劉徹 r. 140–87 BCE) ritualistic ascent of Taishan in 110 BCE was in part probably an emulation of that of the Yellow Emperor, whose hat and robes were said to have been buried at the site and marked with a tomb.[16] Nevertheless, the Daoist appropriation of Yellow Mountain is revealed by toponyms that reflect its supposedly central place in Daoist lore; peaks and other landmarks being labelled with such names as Immortals 仙人, Ascension 升昇 and Alchemists' 煉丹. The famous "Thirty-six Peaks" 三十六峰 of the mountain itself mirrored the number of cave heavens 洞天 in the Daoist cosmology.[17]

The original accompanying pictures for the *Huangshan tujing* have been lost, and for the existing edition have been replaced by copies of works attributed to notable seventeenth-century artists, among them Zheng Zhong 鄭重 (*zi* Qianli 千里, *hao* Tiandu lanren 天都懶人; *fl.* 1590–1630), Hongren 弘仁 (original name Jiang Tao 江韜, *zi* Wuzhi 無智, *hao* Jianjiang 漸江; 1610–64), Hongren's nephew Jiang Zhu 江注 (b. 1623?), and Mei Qing 梅清 (*zi* Yuangong 淵公, *hao* Qushan 瞿山; 1623–97). The extent to which these replacements resemble their Song antecedents is unknown, but as none of the Ming travellers who carried the work with them mention any accompanying pictures, it seems likely that it began circulating as unaccompanied text at some point prior to the sixteenth century. Editions of the *Huangshan tujing* must have been reasonably easy to come by in the Anhui book markets; many of the Ming scholars whose essays we will examine below make use of the text, without feeling the need to remark on its scarcity.[18] This work remained the standard reference for travellers until the Qing period.

Much of the significance of the *Huangshan tujing* lies in its treatment of names. It provides the earliest extant listing of Yellow Mountain's famous Thirty-six Peaks, and reveals, in startlingly precise terms, the origins of the site's official change of name, from its pre-Tang *Yishan* 黟山 (sometimes 黝山 or 北黝山), which I translate here as "Blackmount":

> Yellow Mountain, formerly called Blackmount . . . is the place where the Yellow Emperor Xuanyuan 軒轅 became immortal [i.e. cultivated his realized self 棲真]. [So] on the seventeenth day of the sixth month of the sixth year of the Tianbao 天寶 reign [747 CE] of the Tang dynasty, [the Emperor Xuanzong 玄宗 issued] an imperial edict changing the name to Yellow Mountain.[19]

This explanation would become the standard account of the origins of the name Yellow Mountain, a remarkable fact given the absence of any external evidence for the change of name (no such imperial decree was recorded in the official Tang histories).[20] Some in the Yuan and Ming periods would later come to the conclusion that the Daoist significance of the name had been overplayed by Tang scholars, who had invented the apparently ancient sources then cited by the Song gazetteer.[21] Zhao Fang 趙汸 (*zi* Zichang 子常; 1319–69) was one who rejected the *Huangshan tujing*'s explanation, preferring to read the colour yellow in traditional geomantic terms,[22] while Wu Du 吳度 noted the troublesome occurrence of the name "Yellow Mountain" in the text of the *Lie xian zhuan* 列仙傳 [Biographic Accounts of Transcendent Ones], a work completed several centuries before the name is supposed to have been changed.[23]

The issue of individual site names on the mountain was no less complicated. The most important named features of Yellow Mountain are, of course, the Thirty-six Peaks, each identified and given a brief description (as we have seen, often in terms of a peak's particular role in the Daoist lore of the mountain) in the *Huangshan tujing*. The extent to which the anonymous editor of the work relied on existing peak names in his listing cannot, sadly, be known without reference to textual evidence that simply does not exist, but it is quite possible that the gazetteer's role in naming was as much prescriptive as it was descriptive. Certainly the White Goose Peak 白鵝峰 of Li Bai's poem "On Seeing Wen the Recluse Back to His Former Residence at Yellow Mountain's White Goose Peak" 送溫處士歸黃山白鵝峰舊居 is conspicuous by its absence, a fact we will see noted in Qian Qianyi's essay. But that the mountain was composed of Thirty-six Peaks (which may not necessarily have been named) must have been known before the Song period. While Li Bai, notably, mentions just thirty-two peaks, another poet of the Tang period, the monk Daoyun 島雲 reveals knowledge of the Thirty-six: "Of steeps we are handed down [just] thirty-six, / But how can the number of these hills not exceed a thousand?" 峭拔雖傳三十六參差何啻一千餘.[24] If the names of the Thirty-six Peaks had also been "handed down" 傳 to the poets of the Tang era, then the listing in the Song gazetteer would have been based on this existing textual or oral tradition.

In any case the influence of the *Huangshan tujing* on the writings, and indeed on the experiences, of Ming and Qing travellers to Yellow Mountain would prove to be a substantial one. The named Thirty-six Peaks as catalogued in that text became the standard list, reproduced precisely in later topographical and historical sources. Even more important was the relative prominence ascribed the various peaks, numbered from one to thirty-six in a sequence that would also be reproduced in later works. Even the most cursory glance through the poetic and prose accounts of Ming and Qing travellers reveals the comparative frequency of references to peaks numbered from one to ten in the Song sequence. In the present case, Qian Qianyi's lengthy essay is limited, with just three exceptions (Verdant 翠微 [19], Stone Gate 石門 [24] and Cloud Gate 雲門 [27]), to descriptions of the first twelve.[25]

One explanation for this tendency to focus only on a certain selection of peaks is the difficult issue of identification. For Qian and his contemporaries, the Thirty-six Peaks that existed on paper were in practice not easily identifiable as visitable sites. The major peaks, such as Heavenly Capital 天都 and Lotus Blossom 蓮花 were well known, and these could be recognized and named by porters, monks, or residents of the region. But, as we will learn from Qian in the final section of his essay, these known peaks numbered "no more than ten or so." Since the publication of the Song text, he laments, "scholars and officials [have been] unable to settle on [all] of their names, while monks and shepherds are unable to point out [all] of their locations," a problem particularly troublesome in the case of the mysterious White Goose, a peak immortalized in a poem by the great Li Bai, and yet one that by 1641 proved unidentifiable.[26] While late-Ming scholars regarded the *Huangshan tujing* as the authoritative source on Yellow Mountain, there remained a degree of uncertainty as to the precise relationship between text and landscape, an uncertainty that in representational terms presented a daunting challenge. Even the very essence of the mountain, where its foothills began and ended, was, during the Ming era, hard to define in the absence of the authority of textual sources.[27]

The early seventeenth century marks the beginnings of an interest in Yellow Mountain on the part of compilers of illustrated compendia, interest probably both produced by and contributing to an increasing awareness of the region among the general population that had begun some decades earlier. Commodities such as wood, tea and ink sticks from the wider Yellow Mountain region, particularly Huizhou, had been known in other parts of China since at least the Southern Song period [1127–1279], but by the turn of the seventeenth century, Xin'an merchants had become famous throughout the empire, largely on the back of the expanding salt markets.[28] Even allowing for the fact that Huang Bian was a Huizhou native, his 1570 route book *Yitong lucheng tuji* is revealing in terms of the significance of southern Anhui in the merchant network; the road from Hangzhou to Qiyunshan 齊雲山 [Cloud-Level Mountain, also referred to as White Mount 白嶽], which Qian Qianyi would follow in 1641, was already important enough to be plotted by distance.[29] Somewhat ironically given the attitudes of literati travellers portrayed in the writings of the period, there is no doubt that at the turn of the seventeenth century, as Yellow Mountain gradually began to acquire cultural significance in élite society, it did so on the back of thriving mercantile transportation networks that linked southern Anhui with larger metropolitan regions.[30]

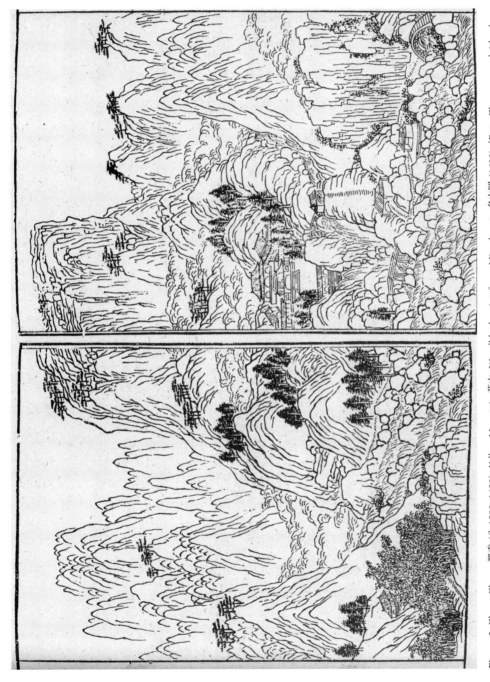

Figure 3: Zheng Zhong 鄭重 (*fl.* 1590–1630). *Yellow Mountain* 黃山. Woodblock print from *Mingshan tu* 名山圖 (1633). [Rpt.; *Zhongguo gudai banhua congkan erbian* 中國古代版畫叢刊二編. Shanghai: Guji chubanshe, 1994.]

The most comprehensive treatment of Yellow Mountain dating from this period is the section in Yang Erzeng's 楊爾曾 *Hainei qiguan* 海內奇觀 [Extraordinary Sights within the Seas] of 1609, an entry that includes drawings of the major peaks and some of the buildings (see Figure 5).[31] Yang's listing of the Thirty-six Peaks is essentially a reshuffle of information provided in the *Huangshan tujing*, while his introductory paragraphs seem to rely heavily on the essay of the Yuan scholar Wang Zemin 汪澤民 (*zi* Shuzhi 叔志; 1273–1355), whose account will be examined below. On Wang's essay also is based the entry in another work from around the same year, *Sancai tuhui* 三才圖會 [Collected Pictures of the Three Realms] compiled by Wang Qi 王圻 (*zi* Yuanhan 元翰, *hao* Hongzhou 洪洲; *fl.* 1565–1614) and supplemented by his son Wang Siyi 思義.[32] Zheng Zhong's ink drawing of Yellow Mountain (the original of the work that now illustrates the *Huangshan tujing*) is included in the *Mingshan tu* 名山圖 [Pictures of Famous Mountains] collection of 1633, a good indication of the mountain's growing importance during this period (Figure 3).

It was not until the Kangxi era that the next dedicated Yellow Mountain geographical source appeared in the form of the ten-fascicle *Huangshan zhi* 黃山志 [Gazetteer of Yellow Mountain] compiled by the monk Hongmei 弘眉 in 1667. This work is a far more extensive treatment of Yellow Mountain than had hitherto appeared in print, drawing on the *Huangshan tujing* (the earlier work's sequence of the Thirty-six Peaks is retained), but now including grottos, waterways and buildings among its listed named sites. This work was soon followed by the *Huangshan zhi dingben* 黃山志定本 [Gazetteer of Yellow Mountain: Definitive Edition] compiled by Min Linsi 閔麟嗣 (*zi* Binlian 賓連, *hao* Tanlin 檀林; 1628–1704) in 1679.[33] The work of that year is reputed to have been replete with errors, corrected for the second edition of 1686, upon which the present existing editions are based.[34] Min's gazetteer is based on Hongmei's 1667 edition, but was later criticized for its rather hubristic title, at least partly in reaction to which was compiled the *Huangshan zhi xuji* 黃山志續集 [Gazetteer of Yellow Mountain: Continued Collection] by Wang Shihong 汪士鋐 (*zi* Fuchen 扶晨, *hao* Liting 栗亭; 1658–1723) of She County, probably in 1691.[35] Two further works would appear by the turn of the century: the *Huangshan Cuiweisi zhi* 黃山翠微寺志 [Gazetteer of Yellow Mountain's Verdure Temple], compiled by the monk Anlan Chaogang 安懶超綱 and postfaced 1691,[36] and a second, shorter work by Min Linsi, the *Huangshan song shi pu* 黃山松石譜 [Register of Pines and Stones at Yellow Mountain], which appeared in 1697.[37] The shift of Yellow Mountain to the forefront of élite consciousness is clear; by the late seventeenth century the site could no longer be omitted from any list of the empire's great peaks.

Early Travellers

The travel essays included in the *Huangshan zhi xuji* date from the Qing period; many, indeed, are by Wang Shihong himself, whereas the previous two collections include the personal travel writings (in prose and poetry) of travellers from the Tang onwards. Probably a good number of these essays were in circulation, at least in manuscript form, during the first half of the seventeenth century — Qian Qianyi and many of the other writers of the period show an awareness of the textual tradition of the mountain, and at least some familiarity with the essays that would later be included in the early Qing collections. Reading through the essays of travellers to the mountain in chronological order is revealing, and one can trace the gradual accretion of knowledge pertaining to Yellow Mountain in the successive texts, as the appropriate responses to the landscape begin to be prescribed.[38] The nature of the Yellow Mountain experience changes remarkably as the landscape gradually becomes populated with travellers, and by way of a contrast to the works of the seventeenth-century writers below, it seems useful here to mention briefly what I believe to be the earliest extant prose account of a trip to the mountain, the essay by Wu Longhan 吳龍翰 (*zi* Shixian 式賢, *hao* Gumei 古梅) of She County, dated 1268.[39] Wu and his two companions spend just three days on the mountain, drinking a toast to Heavenly Capital Peak before their descent. What is remarkable about the journey is that the men apparently met nobody else over the entire three days. Even allowing for the probability that Wu would have omitted from the essay any monks he and his friends had encountered along the way (or who had acted as guides — Wu shows some knowledge of site names and routes, suggesting that the men were probably assisted), such an unpeopled landscape contrasts starkly with that encountered by later travellers.

Wang Zemin's longer essay of 1340 is probably the most influential Yellow Mountain *youji* written prior to the seventeenth century.[40] Wang was a native of nearby Wu 婺 (modern Jiangxi), and made the trip with the help of the Song-dynasty *Huangshan tujing*, the earliest extant documented instance of this text being used as a travel guide. Qian Qianyi would later cite Wang's description of the singing of the birds, and probably also draws from here the fact that the medicinal herb gatherers take three days to reach Heavenly Capital's summit. Of greater significance though, is the overall tone of Wang's text, in particular the Daoist reading of the mountain he presents. Drawing on the *Huangshan tujing*, Wang establishes Yellow Mountain as the home of the immortal Yellow Emperor and his assistants Rongcheng and Fuqiu, an image that returns throughout the mountain's history in text. Judging by the frequency of references to Wang's essay (attributed or otherwise) in the essays of subsequent travellers, we can assume that it was in circulation, in some form at least, well before its publication in the Kanxi-era gazetteers.

The brief essay by Pan Dan 潘旦 (*zi* Xizhou 希周, *hao* Shiquan 石泉), also a Jiangxi native, dated the winter of 1519, is worth mentioning here, as it marks an important stage in Yellow Mountain's textual development in its otherworldly description of the landscape.[41] Pan made the trip with a few relatives and friends, climbing to a point where they could view the Thirty-six Peaks, "like pillars of jade supporting the heavens" 如玉柱撐天. The group eventually loses its way and is forced to return to Auspicious Emblem Temple 祥符寺 (in the foothills of the mountain), but what is interesting here is the language used: "[We no longer] knew where the world of men was to be found" 不知人世復在何處, a trope that appears again and again in subsequent accounts (including Qian's). Pan does not appear to have had the *Huangshan tujing* to guide him on his journey, unlike another sixteenth-century traveller, Wang Xuanxi 汪玄錫, who as a consequence is able to give names to his sites.[42] Wang draws on the gazetteer's image of the mountain range's outward projection into neighbouring counties, and is also one of the first to highlight the life-giving properties of the hot springs. But Wang is aware too of the literary heritage of the site, mentioning in particular the Tang poets Li Bai and Jia Dao 賈島 (*zi* Langxian 浪仙; 779–843) as early visitors.[43]

A very different sort of essay to Wang's is that of the She-County physician Jiang Guan 江瓘 (*zi* Minying 民瑩; 1503?–65?).[44] Jiang made the trip in 1548, highlighting what one assumes was a particular point of interest for him — the various medicinal herbs found on the mountain. He clearly draws from the important essay of Wang Zemin examined above, borrowing the latter's description of the birds' song just as Qian Qianyi would do a century later. Jiang records the existence of some of the steps that were being cut into the rock at the time, but his journey still reads as a fairly difficult climb. What separates Jiang's text from those of earlier travellers is the amount of route information he provides; as James Cahill has noted, Jiang moves from one named site to another in the manner of an itinerary.[45] One of the results of this change can be seen in the language Jiang uses, with many more verbs of action (*xing* 行 [walked], *shang* 上 [climbed], *ru* 入 [entered], and so forth) than we find in previous accounts. Significant also is the fact that accommodation (旅舍) was available to travellers at Yanggan 楊干 near Tangkou (Fang Dazhi 方大治 [*zi* Zaiyan 在宥, *hao* Jiuchi 九池] also lodges here in his trip of 1569),[46] a sign perhaps of the beginnings of a tourist culture in the region.

An early prose account we have from the important Wanli era is one by Xie Zhaozhe 謝肇淛 (*zi* Zaihang 在杭; 1567–1624) of Changle 長樂, Fujian, one of few extant Yellow Mountain essays of the period written by travellers whose family roots stem from outside of the immediate Anhui-Jiangxi-Zhejiang area.[47] Xie is a significant figure in Ming literary terms, known as an important poet, scholar and collector of art, and for his compilation of the important *Wuzazu* 五雜俎 [Five Assorted Offerings]. Xie also compiled a number of topographical and institutional gazetteers during the early seventeenth century, and seems to have been something of a traveller in later life.[48] In this case his brief essay is beautifully crafted, but notable more for what it omits than for what it includes; there is very little of the route information or even the named sites we find in Jiang Guan's essay. Xie is only a little more specific about his route towards the mountain, approaching from the south and lodging in Fragrance Hamlet 芳村, where he keeps indoors during the night to avoid tigers.

Xie's essay contrasts markedly with those of another traveller from outside the region, Xu Hongzu 徐弘祖 (*zi* Zhenzhi 振之, *hao* Xiake 霞客; 1586–1641), who made two trips to the mountain, in 1616 and 1618.[49] Xu's accounts take the form of diary entries, meticulously recording paths taken and sites passed. In modern terms Xu, judging by the number of editions of the *Xu Xiake youji* 徐霞客遊記 [Travel Diaries of Xu Hongzu] that now line the shelves of Chinese bookshops, would probably rank as the most famous Yellow Mountain traveller of his age. It is doubtful though, that his contemporaries would have considered him as such, and in any case we should be careful not to overestimate the significance of his two essays on the textual history of Yellow Mountain during this period. The fact that neither of Xu's essays appeared in Min Linsi's *Huangshan zhi dingben* is revealing — in his brief biography of Xu in the same gazetteer Min regrets that Xu's diaries are no longer extant (literally, "have not been transmitted to the world" 惜未傳世).[50] Xu's considerable achievement of climbing Heavenly Capital Peak also goes unmentioned in the essays of subsequent Ming travellers, suggesting that his essays were at that time unavailable even in manuscript form.[51]

For the moment then, we shall continue to examine the essays of those scholars whose compositions were adding further layers to the understanding of the site being built up by the literati of the region. The brief and undated essay by Tang Shu 唐樞 (*zi* Weizhong 惟中, *hao* Yian 一庵; 1497–1574) is labelled the Wanli period by Min Linsi, which, if true, would place it at the very end of Tang's life.[52] Certainly it belongs to the Wanli era in its description of the Thirty-six Peaks: "myriad exceptional [sights] competing to present themselves 萬奇爭獻," a description that echoes Gu Qiyuan's account of the Jiangnan élite we noted in the previous chapter. The fact that for Tang, myriad (literally "ten thousand") instances of the exceptional 奇 could exist simultaneously, adds further weight to the feeling that the term was becoming bound up in aesthetic issues and moving away from the idea of the strange or unusual. The search for the exceptional would now become an indispensable adjunct to travel for the writer of the Yellow Mountain *youji*, almost in itself a justification of the effort required for the climb. But the effort required was also diminishing; there were now more lodgings and cut steps on the mountain than ever before, while writers begin to reveal a greater knowledge (probably through their guides) of the names of important peaks. One of the first of this new breed of Yellow Mountain travellers was Feng Mengzhen, the owner of the Wang Wei handscroll examined in Chapter One.[53] Feng made the trip in 1605, recording details such as the fact that Cloud Gate Peak is commonly called Scissors 剪刀 Peak, one of the causes of Qian Qianyi's frustration decades later. Feng also confidently follows convention by ranking Heavenly Capital as the tallest of the peaks, the one that "travellers do not dare to climb" 遊客無敢登者. Among the many exceptional 奇 sights he records, Feng is one of the first to use this term to describe the Yellow Mountain pines.

Buddhist Yellow Mountain

Feng Mengzhen was assisted in his travels by Pan Zhiheng 潘之恒 (*zi* Jingsheng 景升; 1556?–1621), a native of She County who retired to the mountain and helped to establish the Buddhist presence there during the Wanli reign.[54] Pan features in many of the essays of the period; he was evidently more than willing to act as a guide.[55] Pan would be joined the following year (1606) by the monk Pumen 普門 (original surname Xi 奚, *ming* Huaian 淮安 [or Weian 惟安]; 1546–1625), whose arrival at the mountain marks the beginning of the period of greatest religious activity at the site.[56] Pumen was able, in 1610, to secure the vital patronage of the Wanli Emperor and the Empress Dowager Cisheng 慈聖 (original surname Li 李; 1546–1614),[57] who, somewhat controversially, had opened the imperial treasury to sponsor the monastic projects of the monk Fudeng 福登 (original surname Xu 續, *hao* Miaofeng 妙峰; 1540–1613) some years earlier.[58] In addition to the enormous sums of money donated by the imperial palace, Pumen and his monks received robes, staffs and a complete bound set of Buddhist sūtras to be housed on the mountain. Such bestowals cemented during this period a link between the mountain and the state that probably existed already in the minds of late-Ming visitors. The Wanli period was an era in which the construction of temples, in the words of Chün-fang Yü, "approached its most lavish scale," with copies of Buddhist scriptures being printed and distributed to monastic buildings all over the empire.[59] In this case, the colour yellow, traditionally reserved for use by the imperial family, probably carried with it an implicit suggestion of the imperial house (*huáng* 黃 [yellow] being an exact homophone of *huáng* 皇, used to designate the throne). More visibly, there already existed by 1599 a formal financial relationship between the palace and one of the temples on Yellow Mountain, the official function of which was to protect 保 the dynasty.[60]

The significance of Pumen's Yellow Mountain project for the development of secular tourism at the site in the first decades of the seventeenth century cannot be overstated. New paths and steps suddenly afforded scholars access to peaks that had hitherto been out of the reach of most. The temples and monasteries that were springing up year by year provided welcome lodgings for weary travellers, and gone were the days of having to haul one's own supplies up ill-defined tracks. Moreover, the ever-increasing numbers of monks on the mountain meant that there would always be educated guides available to the traveller. Yellow Mountain had become a much more appealing destination, and the era of Pumen had truly ushered in a new chapter in the history of the landscape.[61] But a part of that appeal was also based around aesthetic ideals, for if Yellow Mountain was linked to the Ming state politically, it was also linked to late-Ming society in cultural terms. Most of the characteristics for which the landscape was quickly becoming known reflect late-Ming sensibilities and an artistic movement that, in the words of Qianshen Bai, had begun to prize the concepts of "deformation, fragmentation and awkwardness."[62] The bizarre rocks, the dense "sea" of cloud and the grotesque pines for which the mountain remains famous today were particular favourites of late-Ming viewers.[63] It should not be surprising to find that the linguistic terms employed in the early seventeenth century to articulate the aesthetic qualities and formal features of Yellow Mountain were precisely those terms used in reference to collecting and connoisseurship we saw in the previous chapter. In the case of the Yellow Mountain pines, it was the ubiquitous yet ill-defined concept of the exceptional 奇 that was beginning to generate their demand as luxury items; greedily consumed by a society in which the concepts of taste and fashion effected frequent changes to the way the wealthy participated in their sophisticated world. In a passage of his 1610 essay that we will find echoed by Qian Qianyi below, Zou Kuangming notes that collectors are "always carrying [the pines] off to be the ornaments for their window boxes" 往往取去為軒窗之玩. The practice, he observes, is a particular obsession 癖 among the men of She County.[64]

The two essays by Wang Zhijie 王之杰 dated 1606 and 1608 are typical of the *youji* written around this period.[65] Wang shows a good awareness of the activities of Pumen on the mountain, and pays the monk a visit at the Dharma Sea Hermitage 法海庵 in 1608. Other monks too assist Wang on his trip; he admits to being "supported under the arms" during the climb 僧扶掖以登, a common mode of ascent for seventeenth-century travellers. Wang notes on his first trip the presence of bizarre pines 怪松 and exceptional rocks 奇石,

and then inverts the terms in 1608, in what appears to be the earliest extant articulation of the "exceptional pines and bizarre rocks" 奇松怪石 formula that survives on the mountain to this day. The classification of the mountain (and especially its pines) as exceptional 奇 had now well and truly taken hold among travellers, no doubt fuelled by the direct and indirect contacts these men had with each other, and in some cases probably through the fact that they shared monk guides. In the 1605 essay of Feng Mengzhen examined above, the author records his guide as using the term to describe the Nine Dragons Pool 九龍潭.

The Hangzhou scholar Huang Ruheng's essay is further suggestive of the significant role played by the ever-increasing number of Yellow Mountain monks in the travels of the educated élite.[66] Huang spent ten days on the mountain, of which, he tells us, seven were spent walking, while three were spent inside avoiding the rain. He shows no sign of having with him any textual aids such as the *Huangshan tujing*, and as such he is completely reliant on his guides for the identification and naming of sites. The monks provide the names of peaks, but also more detailed knowledge; through them Huang learns the names of the flowers — the Rock Lotus 石蓮, the Violet Orchid 紫蘭 and so on. His description of the pines again betrays the increasingly complex range of meanings embodied by the term *qi* 奇 discussed above; they are *shen qi* 甚奇, literally "extremely exceptional." Huang's account more than any by previous scholars has a schematic character, gradually mapping out the approach from the south, then touring the important sites. He particularly enjoys the Spreading Sea 鋪海 of clouds, which "is called Yellow Mountain's most splendid site" 稱黃山最勝處矣, a subtle indication of the representational tradition developing around the mountain.

Missing from Huang's essay is the kind of Daoist imagery one finds in the accounts of those previous travellers who had used the *Huangshan tujing* to direct their gaze. From this point on, most of the essays emphasize the activities of Pumen and the other monks on the mountain; that is, they tend to evince far more of a Buddhist flavour than the more Daoist-oriented earlier works. To this group of essays belongs one of the most important for the present study, that of the Fujianese scholar Xie Zhaoshen 謝兆申 (*zi* Baoyuan 保元, *hao* Erbo 耳伯), who visited Yellow Mountain in 1614–15.[67] Xie recounts his own conversation with Pumen in which the latter explains the construction of his famous four-faced Buddha figure; Xie's superior access to the monks on this occasion was probably a result of his association with Pan Zhiheng ("my friend Jingsheng" 吾友景升氏), who, we noted above, had joined the grand Buddhist project on the mountain some years earlier. Xie's approach from the south is of particular interest here; he carefully maps and names each site in turn — Qiankou 潏口, Poplar Trunk Temple 楊干寺, Rong

Brook 容溪, Long Pond 長潭, Stone Anvil Ridge 石碪嶺, Scentgrass Stone 蓀石, Fragrance Hamlet 芳村 — in a series that had now become standard, and that would reappear in the accounts of others such as Dai Ao 戴澳 (*zi* Youfei 有斐, *hao* Feijun 斐君), who made the climb in 1617.[68] Reading through Xie's essay one gets a strong sense that the correct route had already been prescribed, that travellers were tending more and more towards following a pre-set pattern rather than roaming freely. The same is suggested in an account by Tang Binyin 湯賓尹 (*zi* Jiabin 嘉賓, *hao* Shuian 睡庵; *js.* 1595), who in 1612 could declare confidently that "Yellow Mountain travels begin at the Springs [i.e. Auspicious Emblem] Temple" 黃山之遊發自湯寺.[69]

Yellow Mountain in the Post-Wanli Era

So by 1620, with the long Wanli era at an end, Yellow Mountain had been transformed from an extremely difficult and unmapped climb, into a far more accessible destination, in both physical and intellectual terms. Wang Zemin had opened his essay of 1340 by locating the mountain in relation to the various prefectures of Anhui,[70] an explanatory note that had by the first few decades of the seventeenth century become somewhat redundant. But the grand era of financial and ideological imperial support for the site's Buddhist presence had now come to an end, and so too, five years later, would the era of its greatest champion; Pumen died in 1625.

It would be far too great a simplification to suggest that the Buddhist presence on Yellow Mountain came to an end with the death of Pumen. Many of the monastic buildings, such as Lotus Summit Hermitage 蓮頂庵 and Tushita Hermitage 兜率庵, were rebuilt or repaired during the Chongzhen reign,[71] and indeed, notable monks, including Xueqiao 雪嶠 (original surname Zhu 朱, *ming* Yuanxin 圓信) and Yunwai 雲外 (original surname Wang 汪, *ming* Xingze 行澤), continued to arrive throughout this period.[72] The important Mañjuśrī Cloister 文殊院 was quickly rebuilt after it had been partially destroyed by fire in 1637, and travellers who arrived at the mountain at this time had no trouble finding lodgings or guides. But even so, reading through the extant *youji* written during the period leading up to the fall of the Ming, one does sense that the Wanli reign was something of a golden age in the Buddhist history of the mountain, one that was never replicated. Although the paths and steps remained, the level of religious activity (as opposed to secular tourism) on the mountain would never again attain the heights of the pre-1620 period.[73]

This, at least, is how travellers to Yellow Mountain after 1625 tend to react to the site. If anything Pumen becomes even more a feature of the landscape following his death, in part through the presence of his stūpa, but also, symbolically, through the Temple of Compassionate Radiance 慈光寺, a permanent reminder of the monk's fund-raising abilities. Fang Gongqian 方拱乾 (*zi* Suzhi 肅之, *hao* Tan'an 坦庵) of Tongcheng, who travelled to the mountain in 1632, was perceptive in his observation that "on all the famous mountains under the heavens the monks are many, but before the time of Pumen it was as if there were no Yellow Mountain" 但未有普門時若未有黃山.[74] Fang and his travelling companion Yang Bu 楊補 (*zi* Wubu 無補, *hao* Gunong 古農; 1598–1657) tour the standard sites, focussing in particular on the Mañjuśrī Cloister.[75] The two men travel with a monk guide, whose function seems to be the identification of named sites, drawing responses where appropriate from the two scholars. At a tree identified as "Convenient Pine" 方便松, for example, Fang notes rather grumpily the unsuitability of the name, ignoring as it does the fact that "a pine also has [intrinsic] value" 松品亦貴.[76]

Two essays from Wu Tingjian 吳廷簡, the second dated 1635 (the first is undated) follow roughly the same pattern.[77] Wu approaches the mountain from the south, passing through Fragrance Hamlet along the way. He lodges and bathes at Auspicious Emblem Temple, and visits the four-faced Buddha at Compassionate Radiance. His experience is enhanced by his "long whistling" 長嘯, an old technique designed to produce the atmospheric conditions considered apposite to the occasion.[78] This whistling is also noted in previous essays — those of Pan Dan, Luo Qinceng 駱駸曾 (*zi* Xiangxian 象先, *hao* Hangxie 沆瀣),[79] Yang Bu, and Xu Chu 許楚 (*zi* Fangcheng 方城, *hao* Xiaojiangtan 小江潭) (see below), and is performed by Qian Qianyi when he reaches Mañjuśrī Cloister (although he does not mention this in his essay),[80] an indication perhaps, that physical behaviours and responses to sites were beginning to be prescribed as well as intellectual responses. The textual response had by now already been standardized to a certain extent; the sights and emotions of the trip make Wu, somewhat predictably, forget about the world of man 不復知有人間世矣. Whistling aside, Xu Chu's 1635 essay is similar in tone and route.[81] Xu, a native of She County, approaches from the south, and bathes at the foot of the mountain, where the spring waters are "hot enough to brew tea" 熱可點茗. He meets his friend She Shusheng 佘書升 (*zi* Lunzhong 掄仲), the man who had restored the Peach Blossom Source Hermitage 桃源庵, and who was starting to feature as an important presence on the mountain (Wu Tingjian's party had asked that She accompany them, but was rebuffed). Xu admires the pines and the four-faced Buddha, and stares awestruck at the imposing Heavenly Capital Peak: "there are no ropes for one's hands, no holds for one's feet" 無繘受手無凹受足. Only Pumen, we are told, had managed to scale successfully the peak; a decade on from the monk's death, his imprint on the mountain seemed to be in no danger of fading.

3

Hills and Waterways

Yellow Mountain in Seventeenth-Century Visual Culture

The intimate connection between fine art and travel had been established for centuries by the time Guo Xi failed to mention Yellow Mountain among the empire's great peaks. The "recumbent travelling" 臥遊 associated with Zong Bing 宗炳 (*zi* Shaowen 少文; 375–443) had early become an important part of the world of the literati, a means by which the hapless scholar might break from the drudgery of yamen life without leaving his desk, or by which an ailing man might still roam the great landscapes long after his youth had left him. The idea still resonated with literati of the Ming; the desire expressed by a man such as He Liangjun to "travel to the Five Marchmounts from my couch," would have been understood as an explicit reference to Zong.[1] Painted images seem also to have become accepted as an adjunct to the travel experience, and in 1541 we find Lu Shusheng viewing landscapes "in wind and rain, by dusk or dawn, under lamplight or by fireside," while on his way to the capital for his *jinshi* examination.[2]

Did Qian Qianyi complement his journey of 1641 with a viewing of painted images of Yellow Mountain? That he probably did is suggested strongly by what we can read both inside and outside of his essay. His friend, the noted painter Cheng Jiasui is unable to make the trip, but remains a strong metaphorical presence, accompanying Qian in the form of a painted fan (presumably a view of the mountain) that appears in Part V. To find a replacement travelling companion Qian stops first in Xiuning, where he enlists the company of Wu Shi 吳栻 (*zi* Quchen 去塵), whose family owned one of the largest and most important art collections of the region. Wu family patronage seems to have been directly or indirectly responsible for a significant portion of Yellow Mountain paintings produced during the Ming; in this case they could be regarded almost as portraits of the family estate, as much of Huizhou including large sections of the mountain itself was actually owned by the Wu clan.[3] Presumably a viewing of the Wu collection would have prefaced the two men's travels, and the acquisition of the Wang Wei handscroll seems likely to have been mediated by a member of the clan (Qian is frustratingly vague about how the purchase occurred). Such treasures, we saw above, acquired real meaning only in the hands of a worthy owner. In the hands of a merchant it was "buried under a mountain of copper cash."

This at least is how Qian Qianyi relates the story of the painting. In reality, of course, the role of the market in late-Ming art production and consumption was extremely complex, and one that has only in recent years begun to receive adequate scholarly attention.[4] It is becoming clear that the demand created by an expanding population of art buyers in the early seventeenth century was at the very least crucial to the maintenance of élite status for those men who preferred to see themselves as fitting within the traditional scholar-artist ideal. Patronage of visual arts by wealthy merchants took a range of forms, from short-term commissions to long-term friendships between patron and artist.[5] The number of painting inscriptions referring, sometimes rather obliquely, to favours and obligations, attests to the important role such objects could play in the complex web of interactions that made up élite society. However much Qian Qianyi professed to be appalled by the reduction of a cultural treasure to a mountain of copper cash, he was himself a willing participant in the market for cultural relics; it was his sale in 1643 of a rare Song-dynasty volume (that had once belonged to the eminent Ming scholar Wang Shizhen 王世貞 [*zi* Yuanmei 元美, *hao* Fengzhou 鳳洲; 1526–90]) to his student Xie Sanbin 謝三賓 (*zi* Xiangsan 象三, *hao* Saiweng 塞翁) that would allow him to pay for the construction of his ill-fated Tower of Crimson Clouds.[6] Qian must also have understood that a part of the monetary value of the Wang Wei handscroll was being created by his self-inscription, not to mention that of Dong Qichang, into the provenance of the work, with the composition of the colophon suggesting at least implicit recognition of this process.

The considerable task of undertaking a thorough analysis of the effects of patronage and the rapidly changing marketplace on the way visual depictions of Yellow Mountain were produced during the late Ming would clearly fall well beyond the scope of the present study, and is in any case hampered somewhat by the paucity of extant works that date from prior to 1644.[7] As a preface to the discussion that follows, however, it seems necessary at least to speculate on some of the areas that may have informed the Yellow Mountain images produced during the period. Most of the depictions of the mountain

produced during the seventeenth century follow a certain stylistic pattern: narrow overlapping peaks reduced to rather abstract, bare compositions, almost always at the expense of spatial consistency. In terms of antecedents, one cannot help but be reminded of works by the Yuan master Ni Zan 倪瓚 (original *ming* Ting 珽, *zi* Yuanzhen 元鎮, *hao* Yunlin 雲林; 1301?–74), and the limited range of brush textures and pale ink effects of such works tend to support this impression.[8] Contemporary theorists tended to categorize the works of seventeenth-century Anhui painters the same way. Wang Shizhen tells us that "Xin'an [i.e. Anhui] painters followed Ni Zan and Huang Gongwang 黃公望 (*zi* Zijiu 子久, *hao* Yifeng 一峰; 1269–1354), taking the monk Hongren as their trailblazer."[9] Given the high monetary value afforded Yuan paintings during the seventeenth century — a phenomenon that Wang attributed to Anhui collectors[10] — it does not seem unreasonable to assume that identifiable stylistic attributes of late-Ming Yellow Mountain works probably reflected, at least in part, contemporary marketplace demand, and perhaps even the specific articulated demands of the major art patrons of the period.

Such conjectures are complicated not only by the lack of extant works dating from prior to the fall of the Ming, but also by the lack of frank accounts of commercial art transactions written by those involved. As we assess the stylistic choices made by individual artists it is important to be aware of the range of possible meanings embodied in certain identifiable styles during different periods. Joseph McDermott has shown in his analysis of the development of the Yellow Mountain image after the fall of the Ming that the works of Hongren in particular tend to reveal certain Ming-loyalist themes.[11] Certainly as a *subject* of depiction, Yellow Mountain tends to be associated during the first decades of Qing rule with the activities of the loyalist scholars, and Ni Zan's own status as one of the Yuan *yimin* 遺民 (leftover subjects) warns against reading any imitation of his detached, unpeopled works in purely aesthetic terms.

It is worth remembering, too, that when we examine the works of Dong Qichang, Ni Zan, Wang Wei et al. we are dealing with objects that fall very much within the category of "art" at its most rarefied and exclusionary. It is much more difficult to get any accurate sense of the kind of landscape imagery that existed outside of such élite constructions of value, but that nonetheless must have played a part in giving meaning to a site. A woodblock illustration in a gazetteer might not have been considered significant in the same sense as a Wang Wei handscroll, but it must still have formed part of a broad range of visual material that contributed to the accepted appearance of a generic or specific landscape. Almost certainly the images of Yellow Mountain printed in books, painted on ceramics and carved in lacquer at the turn of the seventeenth century would have significantly outnumbered those paintings that qualified as high art, even if their marginality meant that they are seldom mentioned in the writings of the period, and that, in the case of the latter two, few examples are extant. The eccentric, gnarled Yellow Mountain pines that were prized by collectors for use in their bonsai arrangements (these will be discussed below) must have added to the body of visual material representing the mountain throughout the Jiangnan region. And the ways such images were received must also have varied greatly across media, for while Su Shi could criticize as naïve anyone who judged a painting on the basis of formal likeness,[12] a landscape image painted on a souvenir ceramic bowl would presumably have been expected to achieve at least some degree of representational accuracy.[13]

Despite the difficulties presented by the lack of available visual material, it seems reasonable at least to speculate on the ways in which visual representations of Yellow Mountain may have complicated and informed the discussion of the previous chapter. In a culture in which painted landscapes were almost always inscribed with text, and in which, at the beginning of the dynasty, the statesman Song Lian 宋濂 (*zi* Jinglian 景濂; 1310–81) had claimed that writing and painting "reach the same point by different routes,"[14] it should hardly be surprising that there seems to exist a close relationship between textual and visual representations of landscape in élite consciousness. The complexity of an essay such as that of Qian Qianyi is suggested by the term at the heart of this project, *shanshui* 山水, or landscape, a compound of which the individual components denoting hills 山 and waterways 水 combine to form an idea that encompasses a far greater range of meanings. If much of what lies behind my reading of prose responses to landscape comes by way of art history, then this is in part because this term itself (in English as in Chinese) was early appropriated into the world of the visual arts. Certainly the *youji* of Qian Qianyi and other late-Ming travellers are notable for their use of terminology related to the visual arts in the evaluation of the natural world. But it seems also that the early written tradition of Yellow Mountain informed to a significant degree the development of a visual system of representation of the site during the mid-seventeenth century. That the mountain in *youji* and in various visual forms eventually reduces to a set of distinct independent scenes is a strong indication that these representational traditions were complementary in their formation of layers of meaning around the site.

Printed and Painted Landscapes

Of the limited number of visual depictions we have of Yellow Mountain produced before the fall of the Ming, the majority are in woodblock print form. At least seven sets of prints of the site were published in Huizhou prior to 1644, the earliest extant work being the illustration to the 1462 edition of the *Huangshan tujing*.[15] These works present the stratified rock formations towards the back of the compositions, and the wildly inaccurate spatial organization of key features that are fairly typical in woodblock prints of the period, but they also tend to show the sparse, thinner qualities one associates with the Yuan masters. This is evident in a print such as that in the *Hainei qiguan* of 1609 (Figure 5), an example of a landscape depicted in upright linear forms (named), where the spatial organization has been reoriented to such a degree that the cloud has literally become a sea. No doubt this was partly a thematic choice of the artist, to capture something of the Daoist Isles of the Immortals idea in the higher peaks, but the resulting empty foreground with its few pines is so reminiscent of any number of Ni Zan's iconic images (Figure 6) that one cannot discount the possibility that this was a deliberate imitation of a Yuan-style landscape.

The significance of woodblock images for the present study is highlighted by the fact that Huizhou's rise in printing, which coincided with the height of Yellow Mountain's popularity, occurred during the period in which the empire's appetite for route books and gazetteers was likewise reaching its zenith. Indeed, the portability of illustrated books may well have rendered the woodblock prints contained therein more influential than paintings in at least the early development of the Yellow Mountain image. The publisher's colophon to a 1498 illustrated edition of the play *Xixiang ji* 西廂記 [Account of the Western Chamber] makes it clear that such a format was intended for a travelling audience, offering "a combination of narrative and pictures, so that one may amuse his mind when he is staying in a hotel, travelling in a boat, wandering around, or sitting idle."[16] The map-like quality of many of the woodblock prints of the age is a reminder that the illustration of text was, indeed, the principal purpose of woodblock technology during the late Ming. In this sense, text and image often existed concurrently, but even where this was not the case, textual and visual depictions of Yellow Mountain seem very much to feed off and inform each other, and it is not surprising to find that the seventeenth century marks a peak in the production of Yellow Mountain visual art. One imagines that the relationship between painted and printed depictions of Yellow Mountain was a close one at least until the fall of the Ming, and that factors such as, for example, the suitability of certain styles to be adapted to the woodblock form, must have informed the development of the painted tradition to some degree at least.

In terms of subject, the close relationship between textual and visual representations of the mountain is fairly clearly shown in two album leaves depicting Lotus Blossom Peak, one by Mei Qing (Figure 7) and the other by his almost exact contemporary Dai Benxiao 戴本孝 (*zi* Wuzhan 務旃, *hao* Qianxiu 前休; 1621–93) (Figure 8). In this case the text is the name of the peak, passed down in writings since at least the Song period, and every element of the two images is subordinate to this lotus blossom idea. Both works present a wildly inaccurate scale (discernable by the lone traveller just below the pine in Mei's work, and by the building, presumably the Mañjuśrī Cloister, in that of Dai), compressing what was a long and difficult climb into just a few paces. The images omit or minimize the background peaks, allowing the form of the subject peak to stand out against the sky. And in both cases that form fulfils the expectations established by the text; a lotus blossom unfurls before the viewer's eyes, exaggerated to the point of absurdity. What is clear here is that while both works are named, we are expected to be able to identify Lotus Blossom Peak by its form alone, and this indeed may provide one further explanation for the apparent disappearance of some of the Yellow Mountain's Thirty-six Peaks discussed in the previous chapter. We will see the same lotus image appear in Part IV of Qian's essay, in which "Lotus Blossom flaunts its calyx," the name imposing its meaning on the viewer's description, perhaps even his experience of the famous peak.

Another image that seems to complement textual depiction is Ding Yunpeng's 丁雲鵬 (*zi* Nanyu 南羽, *hao* Shenghua jushi 聖華居士; 1547–1621?) *Tiandu xiaori* 天都曉日 [Morning Sun over Heavenly Capital] of 1614, probably the earliest extant painting that takes Yellow Mountain as its principal subject (Figure 9).[17] The most significant feature of the work is not, in fact, the morning sun, but rather the waters washing over Heavenly Capital and the other background peaks, eventually flowing into the foreground. Ding is far more (although not completely) successful than the artist of the *Hainei qiguan* print (Figure 5) in accommodating the differences of scale inherent in the work, separating foreground and background with a fence of cloud that momentarily hides the flow of the waters. An inscription at the top right corner reveals the specific purpose of the work (the commemoration of the fiftieth birthday of a family friend), but it is also one of the better illustrations of the cleansing process described in the *Huangshan tujing* centuries earlier. This outflow of evil forces from the capital is an image that reappears in Qian Qianyi's essay; it may, indeed, have appeared in a woodblock print that originally accompanied the *Huangshan tujing* text. The combination of cloud and haze from the morning sun transforms Heavenly Capital and the other peaks into the Isles of the Immortals, a Daoist image probably considered an appropriate suggestion of longevity for the recipient of the work.

Such parallels suggest strongly that the tradition of Yellow Mountain visual art should be considered as complementary to the textual tradition in terms of the development of the landscape prior to the end of the seventeenth century. But a far more crucial parallel seems to exist in the way such depictions developed formally over the same period. I touched earlier on the idea that woodblock depictions in particular tend to present more of a collection of identified features than a "realistic" scene. Spatial relationships seem in most cases to be subordinate to the forms and names (often given) of the individual sites. Painted depictions of the mountain tend to share certain spatial qualities with the topographical woodblock prints, particularly those in the handscroll format, a medium designed to be gradually unrolled, distinct scene by distinct scene. One of the few extant panoramic depictions of the mountain from the Kangxi period is a handscroll by the monk-painter Yuanji 原濟 (original name Zhu Ruoji 朱若極, hereafter referred to by his better-known sobriquet Shitao 石濤; 1641–1718?) dated 1699 (Figure 10), the unrolling of which allows a peak-by-peak discovery of the mountain very much in keeping with the textual tradition as far back as the *Huangshan tujing*. Despite its "panoramic" impression, in other words, what we see in the Shitao scroll is not Yellow Mountain in its entirety but rather a collection of quite distinct, recognizable scenes. As modern viewers of art we often find ourselves examining such objects from behind glass, the scene (or the curator's choice of section) having already been revealed. In the case of pre-twentieth-century works we are seldom now afforded the opportunity to participate actively in the process of revealing scenes, but it is worth remembering here that this is the way in which such a work would normally have been experienced by a seventeenth-century viewer.

A good example of the subordination of space to form within a non-panoramic scene is the woodblock print depicting the Mañjuśrī Cloister by Wu Yi 吳逸 (*zi* Shulin 疎林), from the 1690 edition of the *Shexian zhi* 歙縣志 [Gazetteer of She County] (Figure 4). The work, which the artist describes as drawn after the manner of Yunlin 雲林 (i.e. Ni Zan), is particularly interesting for its organization of peaks. The Cloister is flanked by Lotus Blossom Peak to the left and Heavenly Capital to the right, a fairly common image in textual as well as visual depictions. Notwithstanding a token attempt to separate them in scale by concealing the bases of the two flanking peaks, an attempt negated somewhat by the similarity in size of the pines and paths, all three landforms stand more or less level. The scene, in other words, is an impossible one (in reality Heavenly Capital and Lotus Blossom stand at over a hundred metres above the Cloister). I am not suggesting here that the deliberate manipulation of scale was the primary motivation of the artist; no doubt the formal requirements of the composition — to have the central Jade Screen Peak 玉屏

峰 (on which the Mañjuśrī Cloister sits) rise most of the way to the top of the print — was the greatest concern. But the fact that Wu was happy to produce such a spatially distorted print is revealing. With few exceptions one cannot but feel that the individual features of Yellow Mountain compositions are to be viewed as distinct components, not as part of an overall picture.

This impression is supported by the fact that as we move through the works produced over the seventeenth century we find that Yellow Mountain tends to be portrayed less as a single all-encompassing image, and increasingly in the form of sets or albums of views. Cahill's "partial list" of Yellow Mountain paintings is dominated by albums and sets of panels, including multiple examples by the three major Yellow Mountain artists of the period, Hongren, Mei Qing and Shitao.[18] A full list would certainly include more; Cahill omits at least two of which I am aware, Dai Benxiao's 1675 album of twelve scenes in the Guangdong Provincial Museum (from which Figure 8 is taken) and his four-panel screen, *Huangshan sijingtu* 黃山四景圖 [Four Scenes of Yellow Mountain], now in the Shanghai Museum.[19] The development of the album of scenes as the preferred medium for depicting Yellow Mountain suggests to me a further stage in the subordination of space to form; where previously space had been unimportant and distorted, increasingly now it was being excised completely from the viewing experience. Not only do these sets help to define the iconic scenes of Yellow Mountain, they can also prescribe the appropriate physical responses to each site, clearly evident in leaf #8 from Shitao's twenty-one scene album *Huangshan tu* 黃山圖 [Pictures of Yellow Mountain] depicting the "Spreading Sea" of clouds (Figure 11). Two travellers are visible on top of the principal peak, one with arms raised in exultation at the sight of the peaks emerging like islands from the sea. The image alludes once again to the Isles of the Immortals idea, and reinforces the ecstatic viewing from above as one of the appropriate scenes of the Yellow Mountain itinerary, one that recurs in the *youji* of Qian and his contemporaries as well as in subsequent painted works.

Scenic Yellow Mountain

This concept of the distinct scene (*jing* 景) is essential to our understanding of the way landscape was viewed in the late Ming, and is of course inextricably linked to the representation of gardens and garden design. Hui Zou has shown that while the "scene" had been a concept associated with the garden for centuries, scenes from within the garden did not begin to be represented visually until the Ming period.[20] This accords with what we know about the idea of the garden in late imperial China — Craig Clunas notes that the

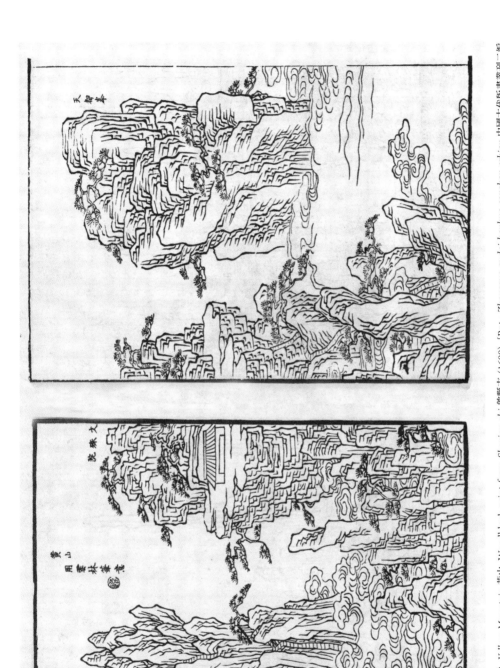

Figure 4: Wu Yi 吳逸. *Yellow Mountain* 黃山. Woodblock print from *Shexian zhi* 歙縣志 (1690). [Rpt.; *Zhongguo gudai banhua congkan erbian* 中國古代版畫叢刊二編. Shanghai: Guji chubanshe, 1994].

terminology of garden making came by the late Ming to be dominated by the theory of painting, linking this trend to the shift of the garden itself towards being represented exclusively as an aesthetic (as opposed to a productive) space.[21] Features of the garden, such as rocks and lengths of bamboo, are routinely categorized in Ming garden literature by the extent to which they approximate the styles of certain famous landscape painters of old. Thus Wang Xinyi 王心一 (*zi* Chunfu 純甫, *hao* Yizhi 一止; 1572–1645?) describes two groups of rocks in his Returning to the Fields Garden 歸田園: those that are intricate, as in the style of Zhao Mengfu 趙孟頫 (*zi* Ziang 子昂, *hao* Songxue daoren 松雪道人; 1254–1322), and those that are clumsy, after that of Huang Gongwang.[22]

Landscape could also be manipulated, of course, through economic necessity (the control of the floods by the legendary Yu the Great 大禹 [traditionally r. 1989–1981 BCE] is an early example), or to accord with aesthetic expectations, most clearly evident in the case of bonsai arrangements (*panjing* 盤景, literally "dish scenes"), a practice that became widespread only in the sixteenth century. When Tian Rucheng described the bonsai at West Lake in 1547, he noted that they "mostly imitate a pictorial idea 畫意."[23] In his important treatise on garden design written around the year 1631, Ji Cheng 計成 (b. 1582) advises that in the placement of rocks the designer should "imitate the brush-ideas of the old masters" 仿古人筆意.[24] A century later the Qing poet Yuan Mei 袁枚 (*zi* Zicai 子才, *hao* Jianzhai 簡齋; 1716–98) would go to great lengths to transform a section of his Garden of Accommodation 隨園 in Nanjing into a miniature version of West Lake, an arrangement that eventually included the Six Bridges 六橋, Flower Harbour 花港 and other features of the Hangzhou original.[25] There is a certain irony in Yuan's claim that his garden was a model of that which had been "created by Heaven" 天造; West Lake being itself a grand-scale example of a landscape manipulated to accord with an aesthetic ideal.[26]

What is interesting in the present context is not so much the manipulation of landscape, but rather the underlying impetus for that manipulation; that the same aesthetic criteria used to evaluate landscape paintings were being used to judge natural landscapes. The kinds of comparisons with painterly styles we find in the garden literature of the late Ming are extremely common in the *youji* of the period. The diarist Li Rihua 李日華 (*zi* Junshi 君實, *hao* Jiuyi 九疑; 1565–1635) is one of many travellers who explicitly compares types of landscapes with certain identifiable styles of old masters.[27] Particularly prevalent was the formula "Even such-and-such could not have painted this scene [because it is so remarkable]." At Hangzhou's Flew Here Peak 飛來峰, Yuan Hongdao is so impressed that "the calligraphy of Madman Zhang 張 [Xu 旭; *fl.* 742–55] or the crazy brushstrokes of Wu Daozi 吳道子 [alternative *ming* Daoxuan 道玄;

fl. 710–60] could not match its ever-changing twists and turns."[28] At Yellow Mountain Wu Tingjian also uses Wu Daozi as a comparison: "Wu Daozi or Gu Hutou 顧虎頭 [Gu Kaizhi 愷之; 345?–407?] could never have depicted even a ten-thousandth of this 不能寫其萬一."[29] Whether or not an artist such as Wu Daozi had the ability to describe a ten-thousandth of a scene could no doubt be debated at length by those making the observations, but the fact that art provided the aesthetic criteria for the evaluation of actual landscapes was taken for granted.

This process of framing landscape as art, and the tendency to reduce a site to individual scenes (a term loaded with a sense of the make-believe as Yi-fu Tuan reminds us)[30] is highly significant for the way we understand both textual and visual depictions of Yellow Mountain. The painted scenes of the landscape that emerge during the seventeenth century become a standardized set; the same set of sites/sights that we find repeated in *youji* appear over and over again in painted form. Where we find the same terms being used in the written descriptions of sites/sights, the same brush techniques recur at the same locations in the works of the visual artists. On the basis of an examination of written and visual portrayals of Yellow Mountain up to the end of the seventeenth century one could easily prescribe a set of ten or twelve "must see" scenes, although in contrast to many other important sites of the empire, a set of scenes was never officially delineated.[31] The list would include the peaks Heavenly Capital and Lotus Blossom, the "Spreading Sea" of clouds, Mañjuśrī Cloister, and the other names that recur throughout the works examined above. By the seventeenth century it was becoming possible for a traveller to recognize the various sites of the mountain before he had even left his studio.

The Scholarly Community

That such sites could be *known* before they were ever actually *seen* is a major part of the argument of the present study, challenging the truth of the eyewitness travel account implicit in the over-simplified subject/object dichotomy through which we usually read non-fictional essays. Wai-kam Ho discusses the importance of common acceptance in the power of literary icons to invoke pictorial images and to create metaphorical meaning.[32] Similarly, certain images that existed in élite consciousness would not only have been instantly recognizable, but also paintable by an artist who had never seen the subject in the original. Such a process was of course fairly commonplace in the case of human or divine subjects (many painters knew what the Luo River Nymph 洛神 looked like, although few claimed to have seen her), but perhaps less obvious in the case of landscape. It does seem though, that its consensual establishment in visual culture allowed Yellow Mountain to be depicted by seventeenth-century artists drawing on the collective memory of their peers and predecessors, rather than on first-hand observation, on more than one occasion. A preface to a collection by the eighteenth-century monk Xuezhuang 雪莊 refers to earlier works by Xiao Chen 蕭晨 (*zi* Lingxi 靈曦, *hao* Zhongsu 中素; *fl.* 1677–99) and Zheng Zhong as having been achieved by imagination rather than first-hand experience.[33] Cahill attributes the large album of Yellow Mountain panels now in the Beijing Palace Museum to Xiao Yuncong 蕭雲從 (*zi* Chimu 尺木, *hao* Shiren 石人; 1596–1673), who had himself never visited the mountain.[34] At least two of the scenes in one of Mei Qing's later albums are inscribed by the artist as being based on works by Shitao, representing places to which Mei had never been,[35] while Shitao himself records that one of his own Yellow Mountain images was based not on his own observation, but on a section of a poem by the Song prime-minister Cheng Yuanfeng 程元鳳 (*zi* Shenfu 申甫, *hao* Nezhai 訥齋; 1200–69?).[36] Moreover, just as it was common for an artist's oeuvre (in China and the West) to include studies of the works of old masters, it is not difficult to find examples of Yellow Mountain labelled as being depicted in a style other than the artist's own. Mei Qing, for example, inscribed several of his Yellow Mountain scenes as being imitations of the style of others such as Wu Zhen 吳鎮 (*zi* Zhonggui 仲圭, *hao* Meihua Daoren 梅花道人; 1280–1354),[37] while the imitation of Ni Zan remained popular throughout the seventeenth century.

What is particularly significant here is the lack of any sense of dishonesty surrounding these copied or imagined works; it seems to have been understood and accepted that the mountain's representational tradition was as much the object of depiction here as the landscape itself. This communal interpretation of landscape supports Craig Clunas' proposition that "many acts of élite looking were indeed precisely acts of communal looking, occasions on which élite values were exchanged, tested, reasserted and spread to members of the younger generation."[38] Instances of late-Ming art-viewing are for the most part represented as social occasions at which multiple viewers are present, although the extent to which such portrayals genuinely reflect élite practice is unclear. What we are building up here is a picture of a community of scholars, interpreting, reinterpreting and feeding off each other's ideas as the correct way of constructing the Yellow Mountain image developed over time. If we turn our attention back to the written accounts of the mountain discussed in the previous chapter, it is clear that this body of writing exhibits precisely the same communal development of a representational tradition as exists in the visual arts.

James Cahill has posited already that the structure of the typical Yellow

Mountain travel experience as reported in *youji* seems to have become more conventionalized as time went on. Referring in particular to the eighteenth-century essays of Yuan Mei and Liu Dakui 劉大櫆 (*zi* Caifu 才甫, *hao* Haifeng 海峯; 1697?–1779), he notes that in later works, sites tend to be named rather than described, as the travellers move in "a set passage from one designated place to the next."[39] Cahill's observation is a perceptive one, but as the present study is necessarily more comprehensive in terms of Yellow Mountain prose, we can refine his view and be a little more precise about the emergence of this set passage. It is fairly clear from the analysis of the previous chapter that the structure of the typical Yellow Mountain *youji* began to take shape during the Wanli era, and that by the end of that period the key elements that make up the conventionalized travel experience, at least the travel experience that was reported, were already in place. The titles of the Kangxi-era essays and poems included in the *Huangshan zhi xuji* almost without exception refer only to those sights and landmarks prescribed in the essays above — Pumen's four-faced Buddha, the "Spreading Sea" of clouds and so on. As we have seen though, responses to such locations had also become conventionalized to a degree. By 1620 it was virtually inevitable that a traveller would use the term *qi* 奇 to describe Yellow Mountain's pines, or *guai* 怪 to describe its rocks.[40]

Further supporting this sense of the communal development of a representational tradition are the origins of those whose written works have been discussed above. With few exceptions these men are natives of Xiuning, Jiaxing, Huizhou, Shexian and so on — areas within the greater Yellow Mountain region. Indeed, by 1635, the date of the last of the essays examined above, it seems that the mountain had barely been noticed by travellers from the far reaches of the empire. Xu Hongzu was known to have visited the site, but as yet his essays had not been widely read (his travels and his *youji* in any case tended to be exceptional in the context of the period), and the next dedicated gazetteer of Yellow Mountain to follow the Song-dynasty *Huangshan tujing* was still to be published. If, in other words, a set itinerary and a conventionalized written response to Yellow Mountain were developing during the Wanli period, then one assumes that a certain amount of manuscript sharing must have gone on among the region's travel-minded élite during the first decades of the seventeenth century. Pumen had indeed made the landscape more accessible, but access to the all-important written word that accompanied it must for the traveller have required some degree of contact with the local literati.

In this respect, it is difficult to imagine many men in late-Ming Jiangnan having more extensive networks of friends, family, colleagues and disciples than Qian Qianyi. A noted literary historian and the owner of one of the great book collections of the age, Qian may well have had in his possession a number of manuscript copies of the works he needed for his trip, and in any case appropriate reference materials and guides would certainly have been made available to a man of his status on his arrival in Huizhou. But reading through Qian's collected works one also finds associations with the community of Yellow Mountain scholars, the essays of whom had been so crucial in the literary development of the site. Qian had known Feng Mengzhen, and still associated with his sons and his grandson Wenchang, who requested of Qian an epitaph for his grandfather some thirty-eight years after the latter's death in 1605,[41] as well as the colophon to the letters we examined in the previous chapter. Huang Ruheng appears in a piece accompanying an epitaph written by Qian after 1637,[42] and the late Xie Zhaoshen is described as a "lost friend" 亡友 in an essay composed by Qian on his way to the mountain in 1641.[43] Yang Bu was a long-standing acquaintance of Qian,[44] while Tang Binyin had served as Associate Examining Official 同考官 at Qian's *jinshi* examination in 1610.[45] Wu Tingjian must have been known, at least indirectly, through other members of the Wu clan; Wenli 聞禮 (*zi* Qufei 去非, *hao* Yunxin 筠心) and Dazhen 大震 (*zi* Zhangyu 長宇, *hao* Zhangru 長儒), Tingjian's nephew, appear in the preface to Qian's Yellow Mountain essay, as well as in other writings.[46] We should remember also Qian's friendship with Cheng Jiasui, whose Yellow Mountain poetry and paintings seem to have provided at least some of the original impetus for the trip.[47]

    That Qian Qianyi had access to the appropriate textual knowledge pertaining to the landscape is significant for our examination of his essay below, for as we shall see his travels are informed by the entire Yellow Mountain literary tradition, from the poetry of Li Bai through to the *youji* of the post-Wanli period. His familiarity with this tradition manifests itself in different ways, from casual allusions to the borrowing of entire passages. What these chapters have attempted to bring out is the degree to which the experiences of late-Ming travellers and the representation of such experiences were not so much influential as, to borrow a phrase used in another context by Stanislaus Fung, "mutually generating."[48] It will become clear below that Qian Qianyi's essay is as much an engagement with an entire tradition of landscape representation as it is with the mountain itself.

Figure 5: Yang Erzeng 楊爾曾. From *Yellow Mountain* 黃山圖. Set of woodblock prints from *Hainei qiguan* 海內奇觀 (1609). [Rpt.; *Zhongguo gudai banhua congkan erbian* 中國古代版畫叢刊二編. Shanghai: Guji chubanshe, 1994].

Figure 6: Ni Zan
倪瓚 (1301?–74). *Woods
and Valleys of Yushan*
虞山林壑. Hanging
scroll dated 1372. The
Metropolitan Museum
of Art, Ex coll.: C. C.
Wang Family, Gift of
The Dillon Fund, 1973
(1973.120.8). Image
© The Metropolitan
Museum of Art.

Figure 7: Mei Qing 梅清 (1623–97). *Lotus Blossom Peak* 蓮花峰. Album leaf from *Huangshan tuce* 黃山圖冊 (1691–93). Image © The Palace Museum, Beijing.

Figure 8: Dai Benxiao 戴本孝 (1621–93). *Lotus Blossom Peak* 蓮花峰. Album leaf from *Huangshan tuce* 黃山圖冊 (1675). Image © Guangdong Provincial Museum, Guangzhou.

Figure 9: Ding Yunpeng 丁雲鵬 (1547–1621?). *Morning Sun over Heavenly Capital* 天都曉日. Hanging scroll dated 1614. The Cleveland Museum of Art, Andrew R. and Martha Holden Jennings Fund 1965.28. Image © The Cleveland Museum of Art.

Figure 10: Yuanji 原濟 [Shitao 石濤] (1641–1718?). Two sections of *Yellow Mountain* 黃山圖. Handscroll dated 1699. Image © Sen-oku Hakuko Kan, Sumitomo Collection, Kyoto.

Figure 11: Yuanji 原濟 [Shitao 石濤] (1641–1718?). Album leaf from *Huangshan tuce* 黃山圖冊 (before 1667). Image © The Palace Museum, Beijing.

Figure 12: View of Thread of Heaven 一綫天 route, Yellow Mountain, 2005. Photograph by the author.

4

Traces of Hatchet and Chisel

Qian Qianyi's Reflections on Yellow Mountain

Qian Qianyi's "Account of My Travels at Yellow Mountain" is an essay in nine parts, to which is attached a tenth part in the form of a preface 序. In total it consists of over 5,300 characters, most sections being of approximately equal size, with the exception of Part V, which at 927 characters approaches double the length of any other section. Written as an accompaniment to a set of poems composed on the mountain, the prose essay is based around a trip Qian made during the *xinsi* 辛巳 year (1641), but was not itself written until the first month of the following year, 1642.

Almost two decades ago in his treatment of Qian's Yellow Mountain poems, Jonathan Chaves noted the existence of two distinct groups: #1– 18 providing a "detailed, sequential account of the actual trip," and #19–24 offering "a reprise of the trip by highlighting certain major spots that [Qian] visited" (with a final poem written upon Qian's descent giving a total of twenty-five).[1] Chaves noted also that the two groups — the "narrative" and the "lyric" — are further distinguished by their metre: seven-character lines in the former and five-character lines in the latter, arguing that the presence of the narrative style of poem allows one to read the set as a type of *youji*.[2] In the present context, Chaves' analysis is particularly interesting, as my own reading of the nine sections of the prose essay similarly reveals two distinct groups that might be said to correspond to Chaves' narrative and lyric voices. Although perhaps not immediately evident on first reading, only Parts I–VI provide a sequential narrative, while Parts VII–IX are more reflective, corresponding to the reprise we find at the end of the poem set.[3] This division serves as a reminder that Qian's own poems would have been his most immediate source of information for the prose essay, which was written not on the mountain itself but in his studio some months later.[4]

Several features of the essay prove problematic when examined in relation to external textual evidence. The first of these concerns the proposed participation in the trip of Qian's friend Cheng Jiasui. The wording of the Preface (辛巳春余與程孟陽訂黃山之游) is somewhat ambiguous on the issue of when this plan was forged, suggesting on first reading that the agreement was made only in the spring of the *xinsi* 辛巳 year (1641). Cheng Jiasui's own account is that the plan was made during the twelfth month of the *gengchen* 庚辰 year (1640),[5] a date that makes more sense given the subsequent movements of the two men. In the end, Cheng did not take part in the trip, although textual explanations for this tend to be somewhat contradictory. Qian's Preface has it simply that "[w]hen a month had passed with [Jiasui] still not having arrived . . .", while in his biography of Cheng in the *Liechao shiji* Qian removes all mention of his friend's planned participation.[6] Cheng admits that Qian was forced to start without him after he arrived late, not setting out for Hangzhou until the first day of the third month.[7]

Chen Yinke speculates that Cheng's apparent reluctance to reach the meeting point on time was the result of uncertainty over whether the young Liu Shi, to whom Cheng had not warmed, would make the ascent with Qian. We know that Liu and Qian were together during the early part of that year, as the two left several poems composed during this period (see below). According to Chen, by the time it became clear that Liu would not climb the mountain, it was already too late for Cheng to meet Qian as originally planned (Chen invokes the "pitiful" image of a septuagenarian "playing hide-and-seek like a child").[8] That he wished to omit this episode from his Yellow Mountain story is one possible explanation for Qian's spurious dating of the trip we find in Part I of the essay ("I started out from Shang Hill on the fifth day of the second month") and in his essay "Shao Youqing shicao xu" 邵幼青詩草序 [Preface to the Poetic Drafts of Shao Youqing], which similarly dates the trip to the second lunar month of that year. However, a reconstruction of the itinerary based on Cheng Jiasui's comment (above) and the dates we find elsewhere makes it clear that the journey did not start until early in the *third* month of 1641. The opening poem of Qian's Yellow Mountain collection is dated the seventh day of the third month; Qian and Liu Shi respond to each other in verse in and around Hangzhou during the second month before the two part (*Muzhai chuxueji* 18; *Liu Rushi ji* [東山詶和集 1–2]),[9] and a set of four poems written at Qiyunshan confirms Qian's presence at that site on at least the final day of the second month 二月晦日 and the first day of the third 三月朔日 (*Muzhai chuxueji* 18).[10]

So based on the evidence from all available sources, it is possible to reconstruct in skeletal form the following itinerary (although being more precise about Qian's movements is problematic, as we will see below):

Twelfth Month of the *Gengchen* 庚辰 Year (1640): Qian and Cheng Jiasui make a plan to travel to Yellow Mountain the following year, arranging "to meet at Western Creek in Hangzhou when the flowering plum blossoms [had come] out" (Preface).

Twelfth Month of the *Gengchen* 庚辰 Year (1640) — Third Month of the *Xinsi* 辛巳 Year (1641): Qian travels in Zhejiang and Anhui, accompanied for a part of this period by Liu Shi (see Jin Hechong's *nianpu* [*QMZQJ*, Volume 8, pp. 930–52]). "When a month had passed with [Jiasui] still not having arrived, I found that I had matters to attend to at White Mount" (Preface).

Third Month of the *Xinsi* 辛巳 Year (1641):
Fifth Day (corresponding to 14 April 1641):[11] Qian sets out from Shang Hill (Part I) with his replacement companion Wu Shi (see discussion below).

Seventh Day: Qian sets out from Qiankou and reaches the Springs Cloister at the foot of Yellow Mountain, bathes, then lodges at Peach Blossom Source Hermitage (Parts I–II, Poems #1–5). Towards evening he receives a visit from Shao Liangqing and Shao Youqing (Part II; "Shao Youqing shicao xu" 邵幼青詩草序 and "Shao Liangqing shicao xu" 邵梁卿詩草序, *Muzhai chuxueji* 32). Rain falls heavily during the night (Part II; Poems #6–7).

Eighth Day: Qian sits watching the Heavenly Capital Peak waterfall (Part II; Poems #8–10). "The rains abated, but the spring waters seemed only to increase their rage, pounding against my chest like a pestle pounding a mortar. As the sun sank into the hills, for a short while we discussed our travels" (Part II).

Ninth Day: Qian starts his ascent from the Springs Cloister, and watches the spreading clouds from Old Man Peak 老人峰 (Part III; Poem #11). Further on, he views Heavenly Capital Peak, and arrives at Mañjuśrī Cloister where he finds cramped lodgings (Part IV; Poem #12). In the evening he rises to view the Thirty-six Peaks against the moon (Part IV; Poem #13).

Tenth Day: Qian leaves Mañjuśrī Cloister with two monks, who then plot out the itinerary for the remainder of the day, leading finally to the Heavenly Sea Hermitage 天海菴, at which Qian lodges for the evening (Part V; Poems #14–16).

Eleventh Day: Qian rises early and makes his way down to the Temple of Compassionate Radiance, whence he comes down off the mountain proper, bathes in the springs and lodges once again at the Peach Blossom Source Hermitage (Part VI; Poem #17).

Twelfth Day: Qian sets out from the Peach Blossom Source Hermitage and arrives at Qiankou (Part VI; Poem #18).

Thirteenth — Twenty-fourth Days: Qian makes his way home, calling first on Cheng Jiasui at Zhanghan Hill 長翰山 (Poems #25–28). This may be the period during which Qian purchases the Wang Wei handscroll ("Ba Dong Xuanzai yu Feng Kaizhi zhi chidu" 跋董玄宰與馮開之尺牘, *Muzhai chuxueji* 85), although I can find no evidence to date this more precisely.

First Month of the *Renwu* 壬午 Year (1642): Qian supplements his set of Yellow Mountain poems by composing "Account of My Travels at Yellow Mountain" 游黃山記 in nine parts, to which he adds a preface.[12]

Despite his eventual non-participation, the figure of Cheng Jiasui pervades the essay; he is without doubt the most important (mortal) presence in the essay other than Qian himself. Yellow Mountain would have presented a daunting challenge indeed to a man of 77 *sui*, and one is tempted to read his planned involvement more in terms of metaphor than of physical participation. But his presence in the text stands in stark contrast to the invisibility of Wu Shi, Qian's eventual travelling companion. Again, there is ambiguity in the wording of the Preface:

> It was a letter from Xu Weihan 徐維翰 [Xu Zhiyuan 之垣] that came to rouse me again — having read it my arms wanted to stretch out and take flight, so I grabbed Wu Quchen 吳去塵 [Wu Shi] and set out. Wu Zhangru 吳長儒 [Wu Dazhen] made ready a carriage and prepared us some grains and dried meats, and the cousins Zihan 子含 and Qufei 去非 [Wu Wenli] goaded each other to come, but in the end neither of them could make the trip 而皆不能從也.

The uncertainty created by the use of the character *jie* 皆 is obscured here in translation as "neither" — in fact, the term could be rendered as "none," referring to the entire Wu clan. Was Wu Shi forced to pull out of the trip at the last minute? This, indeed, would be a reasonable conclusion given that he is entirely absent from Qian's essay following this first mention, and fails to appear in even one of the 32 poems that make up the Yellow Mountain collection. But a reconstruction of the complete story of Qian's Yellow Mountain travels cannot be based upon a reading of these texts in isolation, and Wu does appear on the mountain in *juan* 32 of the *Muzhai chuxueji* in the preface "Shao Youqing shicao xu" 邵幼青詩草序.

Wu's absence from the essay is an important factor in the metaphoric underpinnings of the text, adding to the impression of solitary wandering that characterizes Qian's Yellow Mountain story. By way of introduction to that story, this chapter attempts to read between the lines of the account; to go beyond the cliffs and streams of Qian's Yellow Mountain and explore the motifs of immortality, religious pilgrimage and eremiticism that give flavour to the text. By presenting a discussion of such issues here, it is hoped that the essay itself, which appears in the following chapter, will be more easily understood as the product of the cultural tradition whence it came. As interesting as what appears in the essay is what is omitted, and we find that establishing a precise itinerary from Qian's narrative is fraught with difficulties. Above all, the journey Qian represents is one of spiritual awakening, in which the natural world can be correctly interpreted only with reference to the appropriate literary sources.

The Mortal

In his extensive examination of autobiographical writings in Chinese literature, Pei-yi Wu notes the obvious similarities between autobiography and travel literature, observing that the traveller and the autobiographer are both concerned with movement, and must adopt "at least an implied temporal scheme."[13] But travel to a significant cultural site inevitably carried with it another temporal dimension for the man-of-letters; contemplation of the literary, political or mythological history of the landscape. As Michelle Yeh argues in her discussion of twentieth-century poetry, "the sweeping view engages [the poet] in a reflection on time that encompasses an equally expansive scope of the past, present and future."[14] Probably this process was sharpened for the traveller by upwards movement, for to ascend, as Hans Frankel shows in his discussion of Tang poetry, is both to climb and see what is below, and to rise above the present and contemplate the past.[15] As a metaphor, Ming society understood height as an important marker of social status — the ideal of the *gao shi* 高士 [lofty scholar] referred to the heightened moral and political awareness that raised the élite above the rest of society, implying too a privileged position to observe and interpret the past. To the literatus therefore, the ascent of a mountain would always involve a degree of reflection on the journeys of his predecessors.

Inscriptions, too, gave landscape a temporal dimension, although by the seventeenth century these were not always welcomed by those who viewed them. During the time of Pumen, Qian observes in Part IX, when the tourists began to flock to Yellow Mountain, the rocks and peaks "suffered the grief of having their skin stripped and faces branded." He draws here from an essay by Yuan Hongdao, whose 1597 account of Qiyunshan had stated: "The Buddha speaks of every evil deed receiving retribution . . . What crimes have the green hills and the white rocks committed, that their faces are branded and their skin slashed 鯨其面裂其膚? The practice is truly inhumane."[16] Similar comments are recorded by Qian's contemporaries: at Taishan, Zhang Dai refers grumpily to travellers' "disgusting practice of inscribing on rocks,"[17] while at one point on his Yunnan travels, Xu Hongzu is moved to ask of an inscription "what have the mountain spirits done to deserve this?"[18]

Whether these men liked it or not, for the Ming traveller, inscriptions carved into the faces of cliffs had become unavoidable; an inextricable adjunct to the travel experience. Already at the beginning of the dynasty inscriptions were turning up in remote locations; the servant of the physician Wang Lü 王履 (*zi* Andao 安道, *hao* Qiweng 奇翁; b. 1332) had found four columns of characters inside a secluded cliff fissure during a trip to Huashan 華山 in 1381.[19] By 1743 the Nanjing scholar and official Fang Bao 方苞 (*zi* Fengjiu 鳳九, *hao* Wangxi 望溪; 1668–1749) was able to claim that of all the mountains he had visited, only Yandang 雁蕩 [Geese Pond Mountain] had preserved its "ancient appearance" 太古之容色 by escaping inscription.[20] At Yellow Mountain, Wu Tingjian had already noted some of the literary offerings that had been carved into the cliff faces prior to 1635,[21] and the list of inscriptions, some of which are no longer visible, in the 1988 edition of the *Huangshan zhi* numbers almost two hundred.[22]

One possible explanation for the antipathy towards inscriptions shown by men such as Yuan, Zhang and Xu is that as markers for how a landscape should be read they were too easily accessible, allowing a traveller to interpret a site/sight whether he possessed appropriate knowledge of aesthetic values or not. Artificial cues such as inscriptions may well have been seen as a further challenge to élite status in the way that the taste manual *Zhangwu zhi* allowed access to previously restricted knowledge. Landscape inscriptions in England during the Picturesque Movement in the late eighteenth century seem increasingly to have come to be viewed with distaste partly for this reason.[23] Certainly an inscription could provide more than indirect inspiration — one of the more interesting of such cases I have found at Yellow Mountain is Xie Zhaoshen's 1614 observation at Scentgrass Stone that "the rocks are dense while the forest is sparse" 石依林薄,[24] which on closer examination seems to have been taken directly from Wang Daokun's 汪道昆 (*zi* Boyu 伯玉, *hao* Nanming 南溟; 1525–93) inscription at the site.[25]

In any case, the presence of an inscription, whether literally carved upon the cliffs or written into the collected works of a previous traveller, inevitably carried with it a sense of history, and also perhaps a sense of the transitory nature of life itself. These considerations are important when we find that the passage of time and human mortality are motifs that pervade Qian Qianyi's essay. In one sense at least, this should not be a surprise. Yellow Mountain, as we have seen, was inextricably linked in the late-Ming mind to the Yellow Emperor, immortals, elixirs and medicinal herbs. For centuries, the ascent of the mountain had been made, as one Ming poet put it, to "pick medicinal [plants] and seek immortality" 采藥尋真.[26] Even without the aid of a topographical source such as the *Huangshan tujing*, the mountain's peaks, waterways and various other landmarks that bear the names of the Yellow Emperor and his assistants would have served as constant reminders to any Ming traveller of this aspect of the site's historical significance. But in 1641 Qian would have found on the mountain further visible signs of life's transience. The most obvious was probably the stūpa of the late Pumen, who had died some sixteen years previously, but a more subtle and more worrying reminder of the passage of time was the slow but unmistakable decline of Buddhist projects and religious activity on the mountain since the end of the Wanli reign. "The tolling of the great fish bells [that announce meal times to the monks] has all but ceased," Qian notes in Part VI. "Counting up the monasteries that once stood in Luoyang, one cannot but sigh for one's own ruined and disordered age."

It does not seem unreasonable then, to surmise that Qian Qianyi would have been conscious of his own passing years as he struggled his way up the mountain. We know that a century and a half later, the Qing poet Yuan Mei, then some 68 *sui*, could manage the climb only with the help of a porter (or "seahorse" 海馬): "At first I forced myself to walk on my own, but when I became terribly fatigued I had myself tied to a lad's back, and [in] this way I alternated equally between walking and being carried."[27] As much of Qian's narrative is couched in rather abstract terms, one wonders whether he was in fact carried for perhaps more of the journey than he would care to admit.

This may, indeed, have been on his mind when the following year he signed his Preface the "Old Man of Yu's Hill" 虞山老民, perhaps reflecting as he did on the arrival of the 60-year cyclical anniversary of his birth (i.e. the second instance of the *renwu* 壬午 year during his lifetime).[28] Any such anxiety, one imagines, must have been heightened by Qian's fledgling relationship with Liu Shi, the woman who would become his wife a few months after the Yellow Mountain trip, and who in 1641 was just 23 years of age. In some ways, one could read the entire trip as an attempt at invigoration in the context of this new relationship with a considerably younger woman. While this may be an over-determined reading, there is no doubt that she is on his mind when he bathes in the springs in Part II of his essay. Splashing around in the famous life-giving waters calls to Qian's mind the beautiful Yang Guifei 楊貴妃 (original *ming* Yuhuan 玉環; 719–56), consort of the Tang Emperor Xuanzong 玄宗 (born Li Longji 李隆基; r. 713–56), and, significantly, 34 years the emperor's junior. The set of four quatrains Qian composed at the springs were evidently written for and sent to Liu (they appear in her collected works suffixed with "sent off to Liu Shi" 遙寄河東君), who later mirrored them with a corresponding set of her own.[29]

Qian's anxiety over mortality is also evident in the attention he pays to names. We noted above that a large number of the famous Thirty-six Peaks could no longer be identified with any certainty, and that the important White Goose Peak of Li Bai's poem had apparently already disappeared by the Song dynasty. What must have troubled a man like Qian Qianyi was the apparent inability of text to define the landscape, and now, as he sat in his studio in 1642, he found further evidence of this deficiency. Foolish men were actually building at Alchemists' Peak, somehow unaware that "this is the place that was chosen by the Yellow Emperor as his private dwelling, and as such it is guarded by spirits" (Part V). Stone Gate Peak had been identified as early as the ninth century, identified and written into poetry (he cites the lines of the Tang poet Yu Dehui 于德晦 [*fl.* 840?–855?]), and yet now "even the mountain monks do not know this peak's exact location" (Part VII). The entries in the canonical *Shanhaijing* 山海經 [Classic of Mountains and Seas] and *Shuijing* 水經 [Classic of Waterways] continued to cause confusion among scholars, but even worse, travellers were now using the term "sea" 海 to refer to sections of the mountain, clearly a practice without any basis in the classics (Part IX).

How was it possible that the appropriate canonical sources pertaining to Yellow Mountain had been so flagrantly disregarded? As one entered the final phase of life, was not one's own immortality supposed to be ensured by one's textual legacy? How would future generations of scholars read one's own work when even a poem by the great Li Bai had been insufficient to prevent a peak from being lost to the world? The extent to which such questions may have lurked at the back of Qian's mind in 1642 can only be imagined, but there does seem to be an awareness in the text of an anonymous future generation of readers. He uses the words of Wu Shixian 吳時憲 to conclude his essay, because, he tells us, Wu is unknown to the people of Xin'an (literally, they "cannot raise his name" 無能舉其姓名 [Part IX]), and after commenting on the bizarre twists and turns of a fallen pine he concludes that "a thousand years from now, there is bound to be someone who will verify these words of mine and laugh about it" (Part VIII). This self-awareness pervades the essay; Qian seems conscious throughout of the need to imprint himself onto the landscape for travellers to come.

The Pilgrim

One element of the trip about which Qian leaves the reader in no doubt is its difficulty. Much of the Preface concerns the obstacles that had to be overcome before the trip could proceed: Cheng Jiasui fails to arrive in Hangzhou at the expected time; Qian's "matters to attend to" 有事 at White Mount (Qiyunshan) leads to a decline in enthusiasm, while even Xu Zhiyuan's letter concedes that the trip will be tiresome and long. In Part V the arduous nature of the journey itself is highlighted by Qian's being physically assisted by his monk companions, while in Part IV his lodgings are so mean that he can barely stretch out his legs on his bed. Such obstacles and privations play a crucial role in the overall narrative of the journey, and underscore the assumption that a true understanding of the mountain will be gained only through physical and intellectual exertion. It is Yellow Mountain's very inaccessibility that makes it worthwhile, in stark contrast with White Mount, even the most remote rocks of which have already been scribbled on by the vulgar.[30]

According to Pei-yi Wu, the use of the metaphor of life as a journey had become commonplace in Chinese literature by the sixteenth century. Wu cites Deng Yizan 鄧以讚 (*zi* Rude 汝德, *hao* Dingyu 定宇; 1542–99) on self-cultivation (*xue* 學): "Even though one may make a thousand false starts and ten thousand wrong moves, as long as one keeps on walking one will eventually find the right road at the end of the river and the foot of the mountain."[31] Here Qian Qianyi presents climbing as a self-cultivating process; there is a definite sense of a deeper understanding of the landscape developing as we read from paragraph to paragraph, section to section. In Part IV Qian relates his realization of the relative insignificance of a scene he had described

in Part III, one "which had earlier left me feeling so pleased with myself."
He represents his attainment of a kind of spiritual enlightenment in Part V,
and by Part VI, the Thirty-six Peaks are animate, old friends to whom he
is loathe to bid farewell. In Part VII, the subtle change to the site's former
name (Blackmount) evinces Qian's now complete understanding of both the
landscape and its representational tradition.

This sense that the traveller who interacts with the mountain in
an appropriate manner will achieve a kind of spiritual enlightenment is
suggestive of religious pilgrimage, and indeed, the Buddhist/Daoist flavour to
Qian's essay is undeniable. His companions are monks and his lodgings are
monasteries and temples. Buddhist terminology fills the pages of the essay:
the buildings around Alchemists' Terrace should be burnt in the flames of
the *kalpa* fires (Part V), while the Mañjuśrī Cloister, speckled with rocks,
resembles "a monk's patchwork kaṣāya" (Part IV). Landmarks such as the
Temple of Compassionate Radiance and the stūpa of the deceased monk
Pumen fill the visible landscape. In literary terms Qian borrows extensively
from the Daoist canon, the *Zhuangzi* 莊子 [Book of Master Zhuang] and the
Liezi 列子 [Book of Master Lie] in particular, while his Yellow Mountain is
a site of Daoist alchemical experiments, and the peaks the resting places of
immortal beings. But conspicuously absent from the essay is any detailed
description of religious activity. There is no sense that a particular temple
or monk is the goal of the journey, no ritualistic presentations of incense 香,
references to which in various compounds typically pervade the language of
religious pilgrimage.[32] Qian does not describe the interiors of, or the activities
performed inside any of the monastic buildings in which he lodges, nor does
he record any conversations with monks other than those concerned with the
immediate route and sightseeing details of the climb.

A further reason for caution in assessing the degree of religious meaning
in Qian's journey is the fact that the essay itself begins by placing Yellow
Mountain firmly within a context of orthodox Confucian philosophy. The
mountain is the geomantic embodiment of the true imperial capital, with
its principal peak, Heavenly Capital, screened by the surrounding hills, and
malevolent forces drawn away by its elaborate system of waterways. Although
the passage is heavily influenced by the *Huangshan tujing*, Qian draws here
from the *Guoyu* 國語 [Conversations of the States] and the *Shujing*, and quotes
directly from the *Zuozhuan* about the need to "wash away evil airs" 以流其
惡 (Part I). This early section of the essay is an important one, establishing
Yellow Mountain as a landscape that accords with the correct principles
of the Confucian classics, before moving on in his journey to a more
Buddhist/Daoist-oriented reading. That the mountain can be read properly in

accordance with all three traditions seems to be a major theme of the first half of the essay as a whole. In this sense, one needs to be careful not to place too great an emphasis on the Buddhist/Daoist aspects of Qian's Yellow Mountain, a dimension probably better understood in cultural rather than religious terms. The renewal of interest in Buddhist thought that took place in the late Ming had by 1641 profoundly altered the makeup of élite society. The literatus now conversed easily with educated abbots, sipped tea with monks and viewed monastic art collections at his leisure. The relationship was a symbiotic one; late-Ming monasteries increasingly relied on lay visitors for financial and political patronage, with the compilation of an institutional gazetteer one way by which an educated man could provide tangible support.[33]

Timothy Brook ascribes the revival of Buddhism in part to the emergence of the new gentry society in the late Ming, a group increasingly separated from political life, and seeking to redefine élite status in cultural terms.[34] State sponsorship of monastic projects, particularly by the Empress Dowager Cisheng (see Chapter Two), and the impact of several high profile monks of the era, with most of whom Qian Qianyi enjoyed associations,[35] combined to create a world in which Yuan Hongdao could praise a friend for possessing "a Chan heart under his scholar's robes."[36] In Daoist philosophy too, there had been a revival of interest. Daoist eremitic associations are implied of course by the number of men withdrawing from public life at the time, but alchemical Daoism seems also to have enjoyed a renewed period of popularity during the late Ming, reflected in the publication of such works as Li Shizhen's 李時珍 (*zi* Dongbi 東璧; *hao* Binhu 瀕湖; 1518–93) important *Bencao gangmu* 本草綱目 [Compendium of Materia Medica] in 1596. The Jiajing 嘉靖 Emperor (Shizong 世宗; r. 1522–66), having reached middle age, was reputed to have become obsessed with Daoist formulas for the manufacture of elixirs.[37] Some years later, Gu Yanwu would complain that the number of Daoist allusions used by examination candidates was indicative of the general confusion of the literati.[38] The era was one, indeed, in which Li Rihua could claim of the (imaginary) ideal private library of a scholar, "the east building houses the Daoist and the Buddhist sūtras, and the west building the Confucian classics."[39]

Another explanation for the presence of Buddhist/Daoist imagery in Qian's narrative is the ubiquity of names on the mountain with particular Buddhist/Daoist associations, a fact that must have imposed a degree of religious meaning onto the experiences of travellers even before they had set out. The mostly Daoist-influenced Thirty-six Peaks were complemented by the other named landmarks on the mountain, most of which, Qian tells us, had taken their names "in accordance with the wishes of the Mañjuśrī Cloister monks" (Part IX). Climbing the mountain by the typical western steps route probably carried with it a sense of pilgrimage under the guidance of Avalokiteśvara and Mañjuśrī, an implicit reference to the search for enlightenment in the *Avatamsaka sūtra* 華嚴經. But without any textual evidence, the extent to which Qian Qianyi might have engaged on the mountain in what he would have considered to be religious activity (the burning of incense, or the offering of prayer, for example) is difficult to gauge. It seems unlikely that a man educated and knowledgeable in Buddhist lore would have lodged with monks without participating in any of the ritual activities in which his hosts engaged, even if he were not himself a devout believer in Buddhist doctrine, as Qian Zhongshu 錢鍾書 (1910–98) has claimed.[40] Moreover, the large number of monks and active monastic institutions operating at Yellow Mountain towards the end of the Ming era suggests strongly that at least some amount of organized pilgrimage, of the kind we know was taking place at Taishan, occurred at the site.[41] Indeed, the resounding silence from Qian and other scholars on the issue tends to support Pei-yi Wu's suggestions that the narrative conventions of *youji* composition would have prevented a detailed description of the pilgrimage experience, and that a cultural gap may at least partly account for the absence of pilgrims in the essays of the travelling literati, who sought to distance themselves from the vulgar masses.[42] Certainly Qian associates with monks — the educated residents of the mountain would have been natural companions — but any serious discussions of the *Tripitaka* that may have taken place are left to the reader's imagination.[43]

However, there does exist in the narratives of Qian Qianyi and other travellers a very definite spiritual element that seems to lie beyond any organized religious activity that may or may not have been taking place. Notwithstanding McDermott's observation that the influence of Buddhist and Daoist establishments on Yellow Mountain began to decline by no later than the thirteenth century,[44] in late-Ming accounts, the landscape remains numinous 靈, possessed of a divine force that seems to observe, guide and limit human activity within its realm. Probably this divine presence was vaguely associated with Buddhist/Daoist conceptions of the world — at one point in his travels Xu Hongzu intones a Buddhist mantra to appease a mountain spirit 山靈 he fears he may have offended[45] — but there seems also to exist, certainly on Qian Qianyi's mountain, a sense of the awesome power of Nature that is in some ways analogous to the Western Romantic idea of the Sublime.[46] Part V in particular seems to resonate with what Shelley (1792–1822) would later describe as "a sentiment of ecstatic wonder, not unallied to madness."[47] In this sense the entire ascent may be read as leading towards a hoped-for communion with the divine forces of Nature, which for Qian will manifest itself in a form of enlightenment or "understanding" 知 (Qian uses the term several times) of himself and his world.

And of course, a mountain had to be climbed in a certain way, as Ge Hong 葛洪 (*zi* Zhichuan 稚川; 283–344?) had warned in the third century CE: "Mountains, whether large or small, are in all cases possessed of divine numina . . . Entering a mountain without being in possession of the [proper] technique 術, one is certain to find calamity and harm."[48] The Ming *Lingying Taishan niangniang baojuan* 靈應泰山娘娘寶卷 [Precious Volume by the Efficaciously Responsive Lady of Taishan] promises at Taishan an easy trip for the single-minded pilgrim and a difficult one for the insincere.[49] In the Western tradition, the importance of the correct mental and physical state for the spiritual journey is found in works such as Dante's *La Divina Commedia*, and is echoed later by Constable (1776–1837): "the landscape painter must walk in the fields with a humble mind. No arrogant man was ever permitted to see nature in all her beauty."[50] Preparing to climb Yellow Mountain, Qian is confident of his approach:

> I asked a fellow traveller: "Do you understand 知 Yellow Mountain? It is the great capital of the skies and the dwelling-place of the immortal Yellow Emperor. For two hundred *li* around there are the palaces and paths, where the many immortals come and go, and where the crowds of spirits rest, and among them there is a gate-keeping spirit, who can brush away the land, removing it from the sight of man. During my travels at Taishan, before I had climbed to Heaven's Gate 天門, and made it up to Sun-Gazing 日觀 Peak, I had no understanding of the respect that is due to that great mountain. Now, at the start of this journey, I am already respectful and pure of mind 清, silent and deferent; it is truly as if I had already made it to the summit of Heavenly Capital or Stone Gate Peak.

In his brief but thoughtful discussion of pilgrims' journeys of enlightenment in Western literature (drawing in particular on Dante and Bunyan [1628–88]), Jonathan Rée highlights the narrative technique of the journey-story as being "inescapably visual and perspectival," relying on the reader's ability "to see the journey both from the point of view of the traveller, and from the point of view of the gods or the birds, who can see the path beyond the traveller's horizon."[51] In the present case, crucial to the narrative structure of the essay is the fact that Qian foreshadows his journey; we see the ultimate goal (Heavenly Capital and Stone Gate Peaks) before his climb has begun, and we will mark his success by his eventually reaching those points. But there is also, I believe, a subtle allusion here to Li Bai's six-part poetic ascent of Taishan, in which that poet must first purify 清 body and mind before his climb can begin in earnest (Heaven's Gate and Sun-Gazing are the two peaks deemed appropriate for Li to begin his path to transcendence).[52] For Qian, a man so steeped in literary tradition, no action as important as the ascent of a mountain could take place without reference to the appropriate literary forefathers.

The divine forces to which Qian refers throughout his account are typical of those in the mountain essays of other late-Ming scholars: sometimes the "mountain spirit" 山靈, or sometimes, rather more vaguely, simply "Heaven" 天.[53] The précis of his journey Qian provides in Part VII highlights the crucial and providential role played by a higher power:

> In the past, every traveller who climbed Yellow Mountain in spring or summer had the vapours and mists press in all around him, and he could never make out more than a *zhang* from his face. The mountain monks all sighed with wonder at the clear skies that greeted us, something they had never seen before. No sooner had I left the mountain, than the heavy rains returned to saturate everything through, and seeing this, my companions and I congratulated each other even more.

On some level this passage was probably a response to the essay of one of Qian's recent predecessors, Wu Tingjian, who had recorded on his first visit made prior to 1635: "These travels have lasted a full five days, and whereas many previous visitors have suffered with the rains, for us . . . the sky has been light and the air clear, the ridges and peaks, the plants and trees all distinctly visible." 天朗氣清峰巒草木歷歷可數. On leaving the mountain, Wu notes, "On this day it began to rain, as if the heavens had waited for us to depart before opening up." 天若有待而然者.[54] At Qian's Yellow Mountain, the sense that the proper ascent of the mountain is possible by the grace of Heaven is ever-present, with the passage above mirrored in Poem #18,[55] and in Part V, in which "it seemed that Heaven itself was aiding me 天所相 on this trip." Both Qian and Wu were right about the fate of previous travellers; in his 1616 account Xu Hongzu watches while his sightseeing plans are "thwarted by Heaven" 竟為天奪 as he is enveloped by the mists.[56]

All three men would have been well aware of the historical precedence for this kind of meteorological observation. Sima Qian's classic account of Qin Shihuang's 秦始皇 (Ying Zheng 嬴政; r. 221–210 BCE) weather-beaten performance of the *feng* sacrifice at Taishan in the third century BCE is fairly clear in its implication that the unworthy emperor received his just deserts for an act of hubris.[57] Those who recorded the circumstances of the ascent of the same mountain by the Song Emperor Zhenzong 真宗 (r. 998–1022) in 1008 could compare the "royally perfect weather which their good emperor enjoyed and the storm of wind and rain which met the tyrant of Qin."[58] Some four decades after Qian's Yellow Mountain trip, an official account explicitly linked the Kangxi Emperor's ascent of Taishan to that of Han Wudi purely by virtue of favourable weather patterns:

> According to accounts in the *Hanshu*, when Wudi ascended Taishan, there were no wind and rain storms. Historical writings mark this as an auspicious event. Now, our emperor is examining all regions and inspecting the famous mountains. When he climbed up and down Taishan, the sky was clear and the weather was calm along all four frontiers. The myriad deities were numinous and favourable.[59]

It was the man of worth, entering the mountain gate respectfully and ascending in an appropriate manner, who was allowed to see nature in all its splendour, who could attain spiritual enlightenment, or indeed, to whom was conferred the Mandate of Heaven. But for mere mortals, these possibilities extended only so far. Li Bai's ascent of Taishan eventually ends in disappointment; a careless moment in the final lines of poem six having cost the great man his chance at immortality.[60] For Qian too, the ritual cleansing he performs daily in the sacred springs at the mountain's foot ultimately proves insufficient. There are parts of Yellow Mountain that he simply cannot reach, and by Part VII he has conceded that only by devoting himself to an ascetic life might he be permitted by the mountain spirit 山靈 to "put on [his] travelling shoes once again." Li and Qian are given a rare glimpse into the transcendent realm, but ultimately they both must return to the decaying world of man.

The Tourist

What becomes clear as one attempts this sort of analysis is that the terms "pilgrim" and "tourist," far from being diametrically opposed categories of traveller, are almost impossible to define in any mutually exclusive sense. The flag-waving leaders of the pilgrimage associations 香會 described by Dott at late-imperial Taishan bear more than a passing similarity to the package-tour leaders working their way around China's domestic tourist trail today.[61]

Alan Morinis' broad definition of pilgrimage as "movement away from the accustomed place toward a place or state that is held to embody ideals of importance to the pilgrim" is fairly easily applied to the travels of those men whose essays we have examined here.[62] Focussing on the motivations behind Qian Qianyi's journey suggests to me that his is an example of what Morinis calls "initiatory pilgrimage," a category that includes all travels that "have as their purpose the transformation of the status or the state of participants."[63] The sense in which Qian's ascent of the mountain is very much a spiritual journey pervades his essay, despite the fact that it appears to sit well outside the confines of what might be considered organized religious pilgrimage or ritual. And yet there *is* an element of ritual about the ascent, ritual that pertains not to shrines but to named sites. The literary lore of Yellow Mountain had been building up gradually for centuries, and, as we have seen in previous chapters, by 1641 the collective efforts of successive travellers had prescribed for the visitor something of a set itinerary. What shows through in the prose accounts of Yellow Mountain (and other important sites) written around this time is the sense that travellers already know before their arrival which sites they are supposed to see, because of what MacCannell describes as "a twofold process of sight sacralization that is met with a corresponding ritual attitude on the part of tourists."[64]

Rereading Qian Qianyi's narrative from this perspective is particularly interesting, and, with few exceptions and despite his attempts to distance his essay from those of others, the sites/sights he describes are the prescribed "true sights" (in MacCannell's terms) of Yellow Mountain. In one sense, the journey takes the form of a package tour; Qian moves from one named site to the next, and while his essay is rich in allusions and at times quite complex, the route essentially takes us past the standard landmarks of the mountain. Sections of the essay suggest the fulfilment of an obligation, particularly where Qian lists in Part I (drawing heavily on Xie Zhaoshen's essay) the names of sites with which he does not engage at all. We see this again in Part V, where the monks prescribe the suitable route for Qian to follow. Qian lists the sites in sequence before describing his own engagement with them (in some cases he does not even do this as we will see below), a passage that breaks the narrative flow of the essay, and that might have been omitted if literary quality had been the primary concern. In Part VIII, Qian names the two pines he had discussed in Part V, almost as if checking off a list of "must see" landmarks, proving that the mountain had indeed been visited correctly. In this sense the essay becomes a catalogue of sites visited, with the observation process seemingly reduced at times to one of recognition, where what is seen is not the sight itself, but its associated artistic tradition.[65]

The most revealing example of this sense of obligation with regard to visited sites is that of Illumination Crest 光明頂, one of the highest points on the mountain, and where today, on the former site of the Great Pity Cloister 大悲院, stands the climatology station. Occupying a position roughly at the intersection between the northern and southern sections of the mountain, the crest boasts arguably the most spectacular view of the whole landscape. In the Yuan era Wang Zemin had remarked that the Thirty-six Peaks "can be exhausted in one view 盡在一覽" from the site.[66] Fang Gongqian is among several seventeenth-century travellers whose essays describe a view from the crest that takes in Jiuhuashan, Lushan 盧山 and the Yangzi River, by my reckoning at least 60 kilometres to the northwest.[67] These descriptions tend to highlight the insignificance of the surrounding topographical features, an implicit emulation of Confucius' ascent of Taishan, at which the Master is said to have discovered the minuteness of the empire.[68] In 1617 Dai Ao remarked of the superiority of Illumination Crest: "every [sight] I had been unable to attain at Lotus [Blossom] Peak, I attained here 所不得於蓮峰者已得之此矣."[69]

Set against those of his predecessors, Qian Qianyi's essay is strikingly devoid of such descriptions. He notes the view of the exceptional 奇 Stalagmite Promontory 石筍矼 and the surrounding prefectures visible from Start to Believe Peak 始信峰, but despite the apparently "clear skies" that blessed the trip, Qian fails even to mention the view from what would have been (given that he did not scale Lotus Blossom or Heavenly Capital) the highest point he attained on the mountain. In this regard the omission that particularly stands out (apart from surrounding mountains) is Flew Here Rock 飛來石, an especially notable sight, visible from every point from Illumination Crest to Rosy Cloud Peak 丹霞峰 on the other side of the valley. This omission, and a close reading of both the prescribed itinerary of Part V and the subsequent narrative, leaves me quite convinced that neither Illumination Crest nor the adjunct Great Pity Crest 大悲頂 were ever reached. The two are subtly omitted from the appropriate sections of Part V of the essay, and one is inclined to think that they were bypassed in order to make an arduous walk more manageable. This conclusion is supported by a reading of the relevant poems (#14–16), from which the two sites are also absent.

That a site such as Illumination Crest could be seen as so integral to the Yellow Mountain experience that Qian Qianyi would fudge over its omission in his itinerary offers a revealing insight into the process of *youji* composition. What made the Crest so critical was its name, or more accurately, its having been identified and named by each of Qian's predecessors in turn. MacCannell's process of "sight sacralization" relies on names; for Qian and his contemporaries, the un-named locations on Yellow Mountain are meaningless precisely because they possess no rhetorical value. In the same sense the culturally significant sites at the mountain today are those that appear in the guidebooks, on the tourist maps (White Goose Peak is one already noted) and those that are marked with identifying features. For the traveller, the difference between the Thread of Heaven 一綫天 route and any number of other similar-looking pathways on Yellow Mountain is the small plaque attached to its wall (Figure 12), an act of naming that not only ascribes meaning to the site, but also establishes there the critical link between the traveller and his predecessors.

The Recluse

Qian Qianyi's essay then, is very much an account of his engagement with individual named sites on the mountain, rather than a journey between them. This is not to deny the movement in the narrative; there is, as we have seen, a dynamic aspect to the essay, and in any case an engagement with several of the named sites of late-Ming Yellow Mountain required movement (the Hundred-Step Cloudladder 百步雲梯, for example). Instead, it is a recognition that spatial relationships are subordinate to descriptions of the specific features of the landscape. Attempting to use the essay as a guidebook is, despite an appearance of topographical precision, virtually impossible, a consequence not only of deliberate ambiguity (as in the case of Illumination Crest) but also of a general lack of continuity in the narrative. In this sense the essay is strikingly similar to the Yellow Mountain albums of artists such as Mei Qing and Shitao discussed above, where unnecessary spatial details have been excised from the viewing process. As if drawing a visitor into a garden, Qian's narrative account takes the reader on a carefully directed and screened account of the landscape.

One obvious example of this screening process in Qian's essay is the invisibility of his travelling companion Wu Shi, and indeed, a cursory reading might easily produce the impression that Qian made much of the journey alone. Certainly he alone is the focus of each scene; it is *his* eyes that are filled with waves of cloud, spring waters pound against *his* chest, *he* becomes another Old Man Peak, and so on, even if, as we have seen, the essay at times lacks the active verbs that would suggest his moving through the space. Monks are mentioned only in passing, and other social interactions are few. But this again must be understood in terms of literary convention. Part of what this study has attempted to show is that the ascent of a mountain was to be portrayed in a certain way. Such trips would almost always be made with friends or other travelling companions, but in the travel literature of the late-Ming élite we seldom read much of the social side of these journeys. On a mountain, a scholar was more likely to assume the traditional role of the recluse, to use the time quietly to reflect on the unsatisfactory political circumstances of the day, and perhaps even to look forward to a time when the return of a sage ruler will result in recognition of his superior talents.[70] At Yellow Mountain, Qian could sigh over his own "ruined and disordered age" (Part VI), and for a man whose political career to that time had been marked by difficulties and controversy (more was to follow of course), the robes of a hermit detached from worldly affairs probably seemed a fairly attractive disguise to don.[71]

For the traveller, it seems likely that any existing associations between mountains and the eremitic tradition would have been reinforced at Yellow Mountain by names such as Peach [Blossom] Source Hermitage 桃源庵, at which Qian lodged during his stay. Although explained by Min Linsi in 1679 as a reference to the blossoms floating in its nearby waters,[72] the Hermitage would almost certainly have been linked (perhaps implicitly) in the minds of educated Ming travellers to Tao Qian 陶潛 (original *ming* Yuanming 淵明, *zi* Yuanliang 元亮; 365–427), the archetypal recluse figure of the Chinese tradition, whose fisherman had discovered at Peach Blossom Source 桃花源 a community detached from, and blissfully ignorant of, the outside world.[73] Written centuries later, Qian Qianyi's Yellow Mountain essay is particularly rich in such escapist language. He feels in Part II "as though I had risen above the dust of the world" after bathing at the hot springs, while nearby, alluding to a Wang Wei poem, he notes "it was truly as if there were no tracks here of man." In Part III, above Avalokiteśvara Crag 觀音崖, Qian "seems far removed from the world of man," while just a few lines later "it seemed as if I had crossed over into another world," while watching the Thirty-six Peaks piercing through dense cloud. The crossing 度 seems significant here, for the same term is used at the very beginning of this section (we *crossed* a stone bridge and proceeded north . . .). Indeed, Part III as a whole is suggestive of Tao Qian's short essay; Qian's edging his way between the cliffs until he reaches the point where, he tells us, the real journey begins, is reminiscent of Tao's fisherman crawling through the narrow passage towards his lost world.

The reality of Qian's Yellow Mountain journey would of course have been somewhat different. The simple number of buildings at the mountain during the period is enough on its own to suggest that the landscape must have been considerably more crowded than the essay suggests. Ever since the time of Pumen, Qian laments, an "endless procession" of carriages had been bringing tourists to the site (Part IX), and yet not one of these tourists makes his way onto the Yellow Mountain of the essay. There is something here of

Rousseau's (1712–78) *Les rêveries du promeneur solitaire*, where the landscape becomes in one sense a reflection of the intellectual solitude of the traveller. Porters and sedan-chair bearers are (less surprisingly) not mentioned in the text, but would almost certainly have played a role in Qian's ascent, with Ming travellers being accustomed to what Henry James (1843–1916) in another context would call the "servanted and avant-courier'd arts of travel."[74] But also absent is any real commentary on contemporary issues. Qian makes only a brief and rather oblique reference to famine in Part VI, but the fact is that while he toured Yellow Mountain, Jiangnan was in turmoil. The price of a peck of rice, which had been slowly increasing throughout the 1630s, spiked sharply between 1639 and 1642, leaving many unable to feed themselves; the 1641 entry in the *Shexian zhi* documents cannibalism as the direct result of the food prices for that year.[75] By the following winter, as Qian sat down to compose his essay, the great Jiangnan epidemic had begun to decimate an already-weakened population. Zhang Dai later estimated that half of the population of nearby Hangzhou (through which Qian passed on his way to the mountain) had died in the famine of 1640–41.[76]

What such omissions show is that rather than being a simple record of everything that occurred on the trip, the "You Huangshan ji" is a carefully fashioned composition by a man steeped in the literary culture of his forefathers. In this sense it anticipates the essays of the Japanese writer Matsuo Bashō 松尾芭蕉 (1644–94), whose *Oku no hosomichi* 奥の細道 [The Narrow Road to the Deep North], written retrospectively of a journey made in 1689, has been shown recently to have been a "highly 'constructed' representation of his professional practice as a *haikai* poet," rather than a factual log of events in chronological sequence.[77] The screening of scenes and the presentation of an account that gives the impression of reclusion rather than active social engagement is probably best understood as a product of the same social milieu that produced the body of late-Ming eremitic garden literature, with recent studies having highlighted the fact that in practice, withdrawal from society was seldom the objective of garden owners. Joanna Handlin-Smith's observation of Qi Biaojia's garden, that "its purpose was not scholarly solitude, but social solidarity with a local élite that shared an aesthetic appreciation for property with prize scenery"[78] serves here as a useful approach to thinking about the function of natural landscapes during the late Ming. By the late imperial period both types of space seem to have been freighted with the suggestion of a perfected realm.[79]

Of further significance in the present case is the fact that much of our knowledge of Qian's journey comes from a wider reading of the *Muzhai chuxueji*, rather than from the travel essay alone. Two prefaces written at the end of 1641 confirm the presence of Wu Shi on the trip, and expand on the role of the Shaos, referred to only briefly in the essay. From a colophon we learn that Qian actually purchased a rare and valuable painting at Yellow Mountain, and from poems we can establish the presence of Liu Shi on the first part of the journey (in Hangzhou). Standard publishing formats of Ming literary collections probably produced readers who were relatively comfortable understanding a body of information across several *juan*, but the point here is that what we read in the *youji* does not begin to tell the full story of Qian's journey, a fact that offers a significant further challenge to the documentary interpretation of the *youji* genre.[80] It suggests strongly that for Qian Qianyi at least, the composition of the travel essay was a chance to present an engagement with landscape in autobiographical terms, and that he understood his appropriately recorded response to the natural world in terms that raise the essay far beyond simple objective description.

The Reader

The existence of complementary accounts of Qian's Yellow Mountain trip in poetry and prose sets the journey apart from other works in his collections, and is worth considering briefly here. One imagines that one of the principal reasons for undertaking such a journey would have been the requirement for movement in the production of text. The sense of this goal and its achievement is suggested by the wording of Qian's Preface: "on my trip to Yellow Mountain I completed [得 i.e. attained] over twenty poems." This attitude appears to have been fairly common among scholars of the late Ming — Yuan Zhongdao 袁中道 (*zi* Xiaoxiu 小修, *hao* Kexuezhai 珂雪齋; 1570–1624), for example, had been quite explicit about the need for travel in his *Youju feilu* 遊居柿錄 [Notes Made Travelling and at Rest]: "If when studying at home I can understand not a word of what I happen to be reading, on board a junk I become intoxicated with the copiousness of my reading notes."[81] Qian Qianyi's literary collections are typical of those of scholars of the age in that his poems tend to have been written as accompaniments to movement, with "Seeing [Someone] Off" 送 and "Paying [Someone] a Visit" 訪 the most frequent actions that occasioned compositions. The adage that "when the superior man ascends the heights he must compose a poem" 君子登高必賦 had been attributed to no less an authority than Confucius some centuries earlier.[82] But that Qian, perhaps the greatest poet of his generation, felt the need to produce a *prose* accompaniment to his Yellow Mountain poems, in a culture that had for centuries anticipated Romantic assumptions about the supremacy of poetry as a literary genre, is intriguing. Searching the text itself for an explanation, one finds no more than his "I supplemented 補作 [the poems] with a prose account in nine parts," a term that offers up more questions than it answers. Were the poems thought to be too abstruse or allusive on their own to be grasped without a prose text to guide the reader? Chaves notes that at times the poetic and prose texts "help illuminate each other,"[83] but this explanation on its own is probably not adequate, particularly given the fact that his own poems would almost certainly have been Qian's most immediate source of reference when he composed his essay some ten months after leaving the mountain, and his view that the history of an age was embodied in its poetry, a theory later developed and captured by the term *shishi* 詩史.[84]

What then, caused Qian to add to his poetic account of Yellow Mountain with a prose account; to shift, in Joseph Brodsky's (1940–96) terms, "from full gallop to a trot"?[85] Reconstructing the circumstances behind the essay's composition in the first month of 1642, one imagines that the initial impetus for Qian's revisiting his Yellow Mountain trip, in addition to his preparation for the publication of the *Muzhai chuxueji*, would have come in the twelfth month of 1641, when he composed the two prefaces for Shao Youqing and his uncle Liangqing, who appear in Part II of the essay.[86] The first of these, as we have noted earlier, is the only textual evidence we have to confirm the physical presence of Qian's travelling companion Wu Shi on the mountain. The second, the "Preface to the Poetic Drafts of Shao Liangqing," is of critical importance to our understanding of Qian's Yellow Mountain:

> During my travels at Yellow Mountain, Shao Liangqing and his nephew Youqing caught up with me in the area between Fragrance Hamlet and Elixir Valley, and at that time I lamented the lateness of our meeting. Liangqing loves to write poetry, and whenever his poems form a collection, he brings them to me to seek my approval. But how was it that I truly came to understand Liangqing's poetry? It was by way of my travels at Yellow Mountain.
>
> The tallest of Yellow Mountain's Thirty-six Peaks reach as high as nine hundred *ren*, while the myriad peaks that stand at only two or three hundred *ren* are not listed in the *Huangshan tujing*'s brief account. The stone bridge on the tips of the downy peaks,[87] the places from which float Master Ruan's immortal notes,[88] the peaks where once perched the Green Ox 青牛,[89] and where once rested the Wild Man,[90] are all beyond the reach of anyone who cannot ride on the wind and the clouds, or be

carried along on the six essences 六氣 [i.e. beyond the reach of mortals]. Simply scaling the foothills of Blackmount [i.e. Yellow Mountain], without even reaching the verdant growth [halfway to the summit], one finds one's feet anchored in terror as if confronted by a moat. In the 120 *li* from the prefectural seat [of Huizhou 徽州] to the gate of the mountain the ravine rocks shimmer like gems, while the meandering creeks gleam like mirrors, with beautiful bamboo lining the walls and mystical herbs covering the cliffs. The impure dust from the putrid world of man can never enter a place such as this.

I consider Yellow Mountain's Heavenly Capital Peak to be the capital of the Sons of Heaven. Leading Mountain 率山, Hermitage Mountain 匡盧 and Great Screen Mountain 大鄣 are its screens, and everything within that 120 *li* can be likened to its imperial domain. One of my poems has a line "This mountain rules over a domain of spirits / All within these thousand *li* wait upon Her."[91] Otherwise, the topography of Yellow Mountain would not be worthy of reverence, its arteries would not be so long, and its splendid sights would be mediocre and easily exhausted. To engage in proper travel at Yellow Mountain, one must start down [in the foothills] between Fragrance Hamlet and Elixir Valley, moving back and forth and observing the ever-changing shapes of the peaks. Only then will the [true] face of Yellow Mountain fix itself in one's soul 心目中.

The [great] poetry of the Tang ranges from the brilliance of Li [Bai] and Du [Fu] and the vigour of Han [Yu 韓愈 (768–824)] and Meng [Jiao 孟郊 (751–814)], to the freedom of Yuan [Zhen 元稹 (779–831)] and Bai [Juyi 白居易 (772–846)], and the eccentricity of Li [He 李賀 (791–817)] and Li [Shangyin 李商隱 (813?–58)]. These men are like the Thirty-six Peaks of Yellow Mountain; at nine hundred *ren* high, they tower above all others. To engage in proper scholarship 學 [i.e. self-cultivation] is like climbing the mountain, starting in the foothills, reaching the verdant growth, selecting its splendid lines, and absorbing what stands apart from the rest. When, after a long while one attains [understanding], the faces of Li, Du, Han and Meng will also fix themselves in one's heart. When I met Liangqing it was down in the foothills, and having read and admired his poems, I realized that there is no better analogy to his poetry than this.

The tone of Liangqing's verses is profound and sure, his metre is harmonious and elegant. Beyond the reach of the impure dust from the putrid world of man, Liangqing stands in contrast to those of the present age who strive for the extraordinary and struggle towards the ancient, clambering towards greatness but with nothing on which to fall back for support, and losing what they long to attain in the confused enormity of it all. Only when one has ascended above Fragrance Hamlet and Elixir Valley, to where the clouds and mists are unbounded, and where the thunder showers occur below one's feet, can one say that one has really climbed Yellow Mountain. But as I said to someone: "Even if I could ride the clouds and were carried along by the wind, I would not stray from my lodgings at Fragrance Hamlet; to do so would be to give in to arrogance and delusion." So by travelling at Yellow Mountain and meeting Liangqing, I came to understand the way of both mountains and poetics, and it all happened before I had even left the foothills.

The association of the Thirty-six Peaks with the great poets of the Tang offers a revealing insight into Qian's conception of both landscape and literature, picking up on a line composed on the mountain itself (Poem #1), where "[Only] on reaching this place did I understand old Du [Fu's] poetry" 到 此方知杜老詩.[92] Paying homage to his literary forefathers, Qian not only reveals his system of understanding the natural world, but also enunciates the standards by which he knows his own work will be evaluated. It challenges the self-deprecatory note of his Preface, in which Qian wonders "whether there had been any real need to take up [his] brush," a conventional literary response that is in any case undercut by the essay's subsequent publication. Qian's collections contain relatively few travel essays in comparison with those of some of his contemporaries, a fact that suggests a far greater degree of significance for his "Account of My Travels at Yellow Mountain" than has previously been acknowledged.

The literary canon as a framework for understanding Yellow Mountain is shown clearly in the way Qian's travel essay is put together. Moving from scene to scene, his descriptions of sites are informed by the literary lore provided in the *Huangshan tujing*, while his reflections draw heavily on his knowledge of the Confucian and Daoist classics. A close analysis of the text reveals the extent to which it is built on the foundations of previous Yellow Mountain travellers, forming Kristeva's "*mosaïque de citations*," in which older texts are absorbed and transformed.[93] Even more fascinating is the fact that many of Qian's descriptions are taken directly from the works of such figures as Han Yu, Liu Zongyuan 柳宗元 (*zi* Zihou 子厚, *hao* Hedong 河東; 773–819) and Wang Wei, not one of whom had ever visited (or as far as I am aware, even mentioned) Yellow Mountain. By a careful examination of the annotated text we can understand Qian Qianyi's account of Yellow Mountain as the author's complex engagement with a wider literary tradition, his text as a sophisticated interweaving of his self and his world.

Part II

5

Account of My Travels at Yellow Mountain
by Qian Qianyi (1582–1664)

Translator's Note

My translation of "You Huangshan ji" below takes the version of the text found in the *SBCK* edition of the *Muzhai chuxueji* as its principal authority, and refers to alternative versions using the following abbreviations (for a full analysis of the text and its various versions, see appendices):

SBCK: *Muzhai chuxueji* 牧齋初學集, *SBCK* 四部叢刊 edition (Shanghai: Shangwu yinshuguan).

SHZ: *Muzhai chuxueji* 牧齋初學集, Suihanzhai 邃漢齋 edition (Shanghai: Wenming shuju, 1910).

QZL: Qian Zhonglian 錢仲聯 ed., *Qian Muzhai quanji* 錢牧齋全集 (Shanghai: Guji chubanshe, 2003).

HM: *Huangshan zhi* 黃山志 (1667), Hongmei 弘眉 comp. (rpt.; Beijing: Xianzhuang shuju, 2004).

MLS: *Huangshan zhi dingben* 黃山志定本 (1686), Min Linsi 閔麟嗣 comp. (rpt.; Shanghai: Anhui congshu bianyinchu, 1935).

LYM: Li Yimang 李一氓 ed., *Ming Qing ren you Huangshan jichao* 明清人遊黃山記鈔 (Hefei: Anhui renmin chubanshe, 1983).

WKQ: Wang Keqian 王克謙 ed., *Lidai Huangshan youji xuan* 歷代黃山遊記選 (Hefei: Huangshan shushe, 1988).

BYC: Bei Yunchen 貝運辰 ed., *Lidai youji xuan* 歷代遊記選 (Changsha: Hunan renmin chubanshe, 1980).

NQX: Ni Qixin 倪其心 ed., *Zhongguo gudai youji xuan* 中國古代遊記選 (Beijing: Zhongguo youji chubanshe, 1985).

LQS: *Huangshan zhi* 黃山志 (1988), Lü Qiushan 呂秋山 et al. comp. (Hefei: Huangshan shushe).

For the convenience of the reader, those who appear in the essay identified by literary names or other sobriquets have been rendered where possible into their original names (*ming* 名). Topographical and historical information on Yellow Mountain landmarks and sights that is not directly relevant to the essay is referenced to one or more of the most useful and accessible sources as follows:

《定本》 Min Linsi 閔麟嗣 ed., *Huangshan zhi dingben* 黃山志定本, 1686 ed. (rpt.; Hefei: Huangshan shushe, 1990).

《新志》 Lü Qiushan 呂秋山 et al. ed., *Huangshan zhi* 黃山志 (Hefei: Huangshan shushe, 1988).

《導遊》 Huang Songlin 黃松林, *Huangshan daoyou daquan* 黃山導遊大全 (Hefei: Huangshan shushe, 1993).

《文化》 Li Jiahong 李家宏 ed., *Huangshan lüyou wenhua da cidian* 黃山旅遊文化大辭典 (Hefei: Zhongguo kexue jishu daxue chubanshe, 1994).

The process of translation is inevitably one of compromise. Breaking through the endless *codes culturels* on which the classical Chinese essay is based, while retaining the style of the original text, is a goal that frequently appears far out of reach. For the purposes of the present study it is essential that Chinese characters, along with detailed textual and background information, accompany the text, and my annotations are therefore necessarily dense. However, lest reading Qian Qianyi should become "like viewing Flemish tapestries from the wrong side," it has also been my objective to produce a translation that provides for the English reader a sense of the elegance of the original essay.[1] To this end, while detailed comments intended for the specialist and germane to the study as a whole are provided as notes, it should also be possible for the non-specialist to read through the essay unhindered by scholarly appendages. In keeping with the intertextual nature of the original essay I have tried where appropriate to incorporate into my text existing translations of the classics by scholars such as James Legge (1815–97), although this has not always been possible. Although my rendering still founders far from John Minford's Atlantis, "where Chinese aristocrats converse in the Queen's English, Latin and French, while their servants swear in Cockney," I hope that the voice of Qian Qianyi, however muffled, might still make itself heard.[2]

Account of My Travels at Yellow Mountain
游黃山記

by

Qian Qianyi 錢謙益
(1582–1664)

Preface

In the spring of the *xinsi* year [1641], Cheng Jiasui and I planned to make a trip to Yellow Mountain,[1] arranging to meet at Western Creek in Hangzhou when the flowering plum blossoms came out.[2] When a month had passed with Jiasui still not having arrived, I found that I had matters to attend to at White Mount,[3] and my passion for the Yellow Mountain trip abated somewhat. It was a letter from Xu Zhiyuan that came to rouse me again[4] — having read it my arms wanted to stretch out and take flight,

---

1 余與程孟陽訂黃山之游 For biographical treatments of Cheng Jiasui 程嘉燧 see: *ECCP*, pp. 113–4; *Huangshan zhi dingben*, pp. 94–5, and *Liechao shiji xiaozhuan*, Volume 2, pp. 576–9. The works of Cheng and Li Liufang 李流芳 (*zi* Zhangheng 長蘅, *hao* Xianghai 香海; 1575–1629) are the subjects of a brief discussion and comparison (including plates) in Cahill ed., *Shadows of Mt. Huang*, pp. 62–6. For a discussion of Cheng's proposed participation in the trip, see Chapter Four.
2 約以梅花時相尋于武林之西溪 On the important flowering plum 梅 (*Prunus mume*), see Maggie Bickford's *Ink Plum: The Making of a Chinese Scholar-Painting Genre* (Cambridge: Cambridge University Press, 1996) and *Bones of Jade, Soul of Ice: The Flowering Plum in Chinese Art* (New Haven: Yale University Art Gallery, 1985). On the flowering plums at Hangzhou's Western Creek, see my note in Part VIII, below.
3 有事于白嶽 The name "White Mount" 白嶽 is a reference to Cloud-Level Mountain 齊雲山, which stands in the northwest of Xiuning, roughly 50 kilometres to the south of Yellow Mountain.
4 徐維翰書來勘駕 Xu Zhiyuan 徐之垣 (*zi* Weihan 維翰, *hao* Zaijianlou 在澗樓), a native of Yin 鄞 County, Zhejiang (*MRSM*, Volume 2, p. 314).

so I grabbed Wu Shi and set out.[5] Wu Dazhen made ready a carriage and prepared us some grains and dried meats,[6] and the cousins Zihan and Wenli goaded each other to come,[7] but in the end neither of them could make the trip.

Zhiyuan's letter to me read:

> The White Mount is remarkably steep, but it stands like one of those miniature scenes of landscape painters, and even its sheerest and most remote rocks have been scribbled over by vulgar Daoists. The remarkable peaks of Yellow Mountain, though, drive up from the ground, with the taller ones rising a few thousand *zhang*, and even the smallest rising several hundred. There is no way to approach the summit, as there is simply nothing on which to rest one's feet. The rocks have a sleek green quality, delicately exquisite with their intricate bends, and wherever a fissure appears there is always a pine cutting through it. With their short needles and ancient trunks, and truly myriad in their various forms, these pines all take the rocks for their earth.[8]

I have travelled as far as the Eastern and Southern Marchmounts,[9] roamed further north than Baha,[10] reached

---

5   遂挾吳去塵以行 Wu Shi 吳栻 (or 拭, *zi* Quchen 去塵) was a native of Xiuning, and a man who, according to Qian, "loved to roam the famous mountains and waterways" 好遊名山水 (*Liechao shiji xiaozhuan*, Volume 2, p. 636). See also Zhu Yizun's 朱彝尊 (*zi* Xichang 錫鬯, *hao* Zhucha 竹垞; 1629–1709) brief account of Wu in his *Jingzhiju shihua* 靜志居詩話 (rpt.; Beijing: Renmin wenxue chubanshe, 1998), pp. 604–5. On issues surrounding Wu's participation in the trip, see Chapter Four.

6   吳長孺為戒車馬庀糗脯 Wu Dazhen 吳大震 (*zi* Zhangyu 長宇, *hao* Zhangru 長儒), also of Xiuning (*MRSM*, Volume 2, p. 160), was the nephew of Wu Tingjian 吳廷簡, and features as a fellow traveller in the latter's "Record of My First Trip to Yellow Mountain" 黃山前遊記 [*Huangshan zhi* (1667), pp. 512–6; *Huangshan zhi dingben*, pp. 286–90; a slightly altered version appears in Li, *Ming Qing ren you Huangshan jichao*, pp. 18–24 under the title "Brief Account of Yellow Mountain" 黃山紀略]. I am unsure as to the precise relationship between Wu Shi and Wu Dazhen.

7   子含去非群從相向慫恿 Wu Wenli 吳聞禮 (*zi* Qufei 去非, *hao* Yunxin 筼心) was a native of Hangzhou (*MRSM*, Volume 2, p. 175). The formal name of Zihan 子含 is unknown to me.

8   奇峰拔地高者幾千丈庳者數百丈上無所附足無所逌石色蒼潤玲瓏夭曲每有一罅輒有一松逸之短鬚老骨千百其狀俱以石為土 Pei Shijun cites this passage in his brief discussion of Qian's Yellow Mountain essay, but erroneously attributes it to Qian himself rather than to Xu Zhiyuan (*Guwen shoutan*, p. 100).

9   歷東南二嶽 The reference here is to Taishan 泰山 (the Eastern Marchmount) and Hengshan 衡山 (the Southern Marchmount). On the various competing and complementary systems of Marchmounts in Chinese traditions, see Chapter Two.

10 北至叭哈以外 The name Baha 叭哈 is unknown to me. WKQ identifies it as a *Bahaga tuoershan* 巴哈噶托爾山, apparently now part of Mongolia.

Potaraka, Hermitage and Nine Blossoms Mountains in the south,[11] and nothing I have seen can compare to Yellow Mountain. Mere description cannot begin to exhaust its wonders, nor can the imagination approach them. Although it will waste a good many days, and the climb itself is an arduous labour, in the end it is a labour that one simply cannot forego.

On my trip to Yellow Mountain I completed over twenty poems, and afterwards, finding myself idle before my cold window, I supplemented this collection with a prose account in nine parts. When this essay was finished I immediately regretted writing it, and wondered, with Zhiyuan's description having already done full justice to Yellow Mountain, whether there had been any real need to take up my brush. Later though, a guest heard of my account, and soon those demanding to see it became too many; I could not refuse them. So now, I have arranged in order the nine parts to form a fascicle,[12] and am sending them to Cheng Jiasui at Zhanghan Hill,[13] including, as a starting point, this brief reference to Zhiyuan's letter.

This preface written in the first month of the *renwu* year [1642] by Qian Qianyi, the Old Man of Yu's Hill.[14]

Part I

Yellow Mountain rises elegantly to an extreme height, forming a range that is the principal massif of the region. Of all of the mountains south of the Yangzi, Heaven's Terrace and Heaven's Eyes are the best, but in terms of landforms the foothills of Yellow Mountain are level with the summits

---

11 南至落迦匡廬九華 The great Buddhist peaks. Potaraka 普陀山 (or 普陀洛伽山) lies off the coast of Zhejiang and represents one of the great sites of Buddhist pilgrimage during the late Ming. Hermitage 廬 Mountain (sometimes referred to as the Kuangs' Hermitage 匡廬) in Jiangxi was associated in Chinese minds with the monk Huiyuan 慧遠 (334–416) who had lived there for the latter part of his life. Nine Blossoms 九華 Mountain stands to the north of Yellow Mountain in Anhui and was in the late Ming an important repository of Buddhist scriptures.

12 遂撰次為一卷 Qian's prose account of his trip to Yellow Mountain, including this preface, makes up *juan* 46 of the *Muzhai chuxueji*.

13 詒孟陽于長翰山中 Zhanghan Hill 長翰山 was the site of Cheng Jiasui's estate in Xiuning, Anhui.

14 虞山老民 Yu's Hill 虞山 (or Bird's Eye Hill 烏目山) stands 261 metres above sea level in northwest Changshu, Qian Qianyi's hometown. According to tradition, the hill acquired its name by being the burial place of Yu Zhong 虞仲 of the Zhou (on whom see *juan* 31 of the *Shiji* [Volume 5, pp. 1445–76]). Yu's Hill is now the burial place of Qian, Liu Shi, and Qu Shisi.

of these other two.[15] Throughout East and West Zhe, the prefectures of Xuan, She, Chi, Rao, Jiang and Xin all boast hills that are the branches of the Yellow Mountain chain.[16] The waters of Yellow Mountain flow southeast into She, north into Xuan, south into Hang, Mu, and Qu, and from Qu west into Rao, and northwest into Guichi. Its highest peak is called Heavenly Capital,[17] being the capital of the heavens, and it is also called Three Heavenly Sons Capital.[18] To the north, south, east and west there is a screen. For several thousand *li* there are mountains that are vast, those that are bunched, those that extend, those that are towering, those that are connected, and those that stand alone.[19] Each of these is yet

---

15 江南諸山天台天目為最以地形準之黃山之趾與二山齊 Qian draws here from the *Huangshan tujing*, which reads: "The two mountains Heaven's Eyes and Heaven's Terrace are the largest of the various mountains south of the Yangzi . . . [but] the flatlands of Xuan and She [the two prefectures in which Yellow Mountain is situated] are already level with [the summits of] those two mountains" 江南諸山之大者有天目天台二山 . . . 宣歙之平地已與二山齊焉 (*Huangshan tujing*, 1a). This observation is repeated in the works of other travellers, see for example Fang Dazhi's 方大治 1569 essay (*Huangshan zhi* [1667], pp. 439–41).

16 東西宣歙池饒江信諸郡之山皆黃山之枝隴也 Qian reproduces here the text of the *Huangshan tujing*, but substitutes the term *zhilong* 枝隴 for the *zhimai* 肢脉 (veins or arteries) of the older text (*Huangshan tujing*, 1a–b). In geomantic terms, connections between mountains are an important part of sustaining a flow of vital energy between them. The term *zhilong* (sometimes written with 支 and 壟 or 龍; Qian himself uses 支 in Part VIII of this essay), which I have given here as "branches," is usefully thought of in more literal terms meaning connections between mounds or dragons (the *long* 龍 component of the character variants is significant here). On the relationship between mountains and dragons in traditional Chinese thought, see Hong-key Yoon, *Geomantic Relationships Between Culture and Nature in Korea* (Taipei: Orient Cultural Service, 1976), pp. 29–45. Yoon cites the Tang commentator Yang Yi 楊益 (Yang Yunsong 楊筠松): "Mount Kunlun 崑崙 is the backbone of the world. It sits right in the middle of the world, as if it were the backbone of man or the central beam of a house. From this central mass, four branch dragons stretch out into the world" (adapted from p. 33). For the Chinese text (unattributed), see Yi Ding 一丁, Yu Lu 雨露 and Hong Yong 洪涌, *Zhongguo gudai fengshui yu jianzhu xuanzhi* 中國古代風水與建築選址 (Shijiazhuang: Hebei kexue jishu chubanshe, 1996), p. 112. Yang's geomantic vision of Kunlun is something akin to the Yellow Mountain depicted here.

17 天都峰 Heavenly Capital Peak [定本 4; 新志 15–16; 導遊 132; 文化 71].

18 其峰曰天都天所都也亦曰三天子都 For a more detailed discussion of the various names of Heavenly Capital Peak, see Part IX. The issue of the relative heights of Heavenly Capital and the nearby Lotus Blossom 蓮花 has long been a contentious one, for a brief discussion of which see Li trans., *Travel Diaries of Hsü Hsia-k'o*, pp. 70–3. Xu Hongzu 徐弘祖 was one of the few travellers before the modern era who identified Lotus Blossom as the higher of the two, mostly, one feels, because he made it to both summits (Li Chi implies [71] that Qian Qianyi too was able to reach both summits, but this is clearly incorrect). The steepness and position of Heavenly Capital certainly give the illusion of its superior height when observed from several vantage points on the mountain, but this illusion is shattered when one reaches the top of either peak. The 1988 edition of the *Huangshan zhi* (31) ranks Heavenly Capital as the fifth highest peak on the mountain (at 1810 metres above sea level), with Lotus Blossom the first (at 1864 metres), a fact that somewhat undermines the subsequent imagery in Qian's account, but one should read the essay with the understanding that for Qian, the pre-eminence of Heavenly Capital Peak in both height and status was assumed.

another table in Yellow Mountain's imperial audience chamber. When the ancients established a capital, they would map out a square of a thousand *li* to be the imperial domain,[20] within which an essential element was a large river or some other great waterway to wash away the evil airs.[21] The waters of Yellow Mountain rush in together then separate and flow away towards the various prefectures. All of the waterways originate at Hot Springs,[22] so from the mountain the evil airs are washed a great distance indeed. Is it not appropriate then, that Yellow Mountain's highest peak be called Heavenly Capital?[23]

I started out from Shang Hill on the fifth day of the second month,[24]

---

19 扈者巋者岌者峘者嶧者蜀者 Qian draws here from the "Explanation of [Terms Related to] Mountains" 釋山 section of the *Erya* 爾雅, which reads: "Mountains that are low but large are called 'vast' 扈. Those that are small and crowded together are called 'bunched' 巋. When a small mountain extends 岌 higher than a large mountain it is called 'towering' 峘. Those that are joined are called 'connected' 嶧. Those that are independent are called 'lone' 蜀." (Xu ed., *Erya jinzhu*, p. 235.)

20 規方千里以為甸服 Qian borrows this phrase from *juan* 2 of the *Guoyu* 國語, which records King Xiang 襄 as saying: "When our former kings ruled the world, they would map out a square of a thousand *li* to be the imperial domain" 規方千里以為甸服 (*Guoyu* [Shanghai: *SBCK* edition], p. 14). The traditional constitutions of the various domains 服 had been set down in the "Yu gong" 禹貢 section of the *Shujing* 書經, which defines the imperial domain as five hundred *li* (五百里甸服), a length to be understood as extending in all four directions from the capital, giving a square of thousand-*li* sides. For explanatory notes on the *Shujing* text, including the possible origins of the term *dianfu* 甸服, see Legge trans., *Chinese Classics*, Volume 3 (1), pp. 142–51.

21 必有大川巨浸以流其惡 The need to wash away the evil airs of a capital had been established in the *Zuozhuan* 左傳, in which, during the commentary on the sixth year of the reign of Duke Cheng 成, Han Xianzi 韓獻子 of the Jin 晉 opines: "[At Xintian 新田] the soil is good and the water deep. It may be occupied without fear of disease. There are the Fen 汾 and the Kuai 澮 to carry away the evil airs 以流其惡." (Legge trans., *Chinese Classics*, Volume 5 (1), pp. 358–60; romanization altered.)

22 湯泉 Hot Springs [定本 22–3; 新志 63–7; 文化 135–6]. For clarity I have also used the name Hot Springs as a translation of 湯池. The springs are now more commonly referred to as 溫泉 or 硃砂泉.

23 謂之天都也不亦宜乎 In geomantic terms, the appropriate layout of watercourses was important not only for the successful placement of a capital (the metaphorical part of Qian's argument), but also, of course, for the health of the mountain itself. The Song scholar Hu Shunshen 胡舜申 (d. 1162?) discusses the importance of water in his *Dili xinfa* 地理新法: "The mountain is comparable to the human body, and the watercourses to the body's blood vessels. The matter of the growing or perishing of human bodies depends on the condition of the blood vessels. When blood is circulated around the body and flows in an orderly manner, a person is healthy and strong. However, in the opposite case, everyone is subject to disease or death" (Yoon, *Geomantic Relationships*, p. 50). There can be little doubt that Qian has once again drawn this image from the *Huangshan tujing*, which concludes with a detailed geomantic description of the flow of various waterways originating at Yellow Mountain (*Huangshan tujing*, 10a–12a).

24 余以二月初五日發商山 Shang 商 Hill is in Xiuning County, about ten kilometres southwest of modern Tunxi 屯溪. For a discussion of issues surrounding the dating of Qian's Yellow Mountain trip, see Chapter Four.

and on the seventh day I arrived at the Springs Cloister.[25] From Shang Hill to the prefectural seat is seventy *li*,[26] from the seat to the gate of Yellow Mountain is 120 *li*,[27] and from here to the Springs Cloister is another eight *li*.[28] Along this route there stands a temple called "Poplar Trunk," a terrace called "Rongcheng," a pond called "Long Pond," a ridge called "Stone Anvil," a rock called "Scentgrass Stone,"[29] a creek called "Fragrance Creek," and a hamlet called "Fragrance Hamlet."[30] Here the terrain is hard and steeply sloping, enclosed by cliffs and walls, bound by a trickling stream, overlooked by interlocking cliff banks. The people live in houses encircled by beautiful bamboo, and covered in fragrant grasses, with single-plank bridges leading up to their doors. The dredging has been neglected and the place has become so waterlogged that one has to lift up one's skirts to wade across, half shrouded in cloud and mist.

From Long Pond to the mountain gate, the hills encircle a valley, and the waters circle round and collect into a stream. The banks turn the waters down into the valley;[31] mountain and valley are like a hall and

---

25 初七日抵湯院 The Springs Cloister is a reference to the Auspicious Emblem Temple 祥符寺 (see below).

26 自商山至郡七十里 The prefectural seat here refers to the modern district of Huizhou 徽州 (in Ming times the entire Yellow Mountain area could be referred to as Huizhou).

27 自郡至山口一百二十里 The mountain gate 山口 (literally the "mouth of the mountain") is in the town of Tangkou 湯口 (literally the "mouth of the hot water"). There is, in fact, a town called Shankou 山口 between Huizhou and the Yellow Mountain Hot Springs, but I read this as a reference to the mountain entrance itself.

28 自郡至山口一百二十里至湯院又八里 Qian extracts this information again from the *Huangshan tujing* (1b): 自郡至山口一百二十里自山口至湯院又八里.

29 楊干寺 Poplar Trunk Temple [新志 220; 導遊 45]; 容成臺 Rongcheng Terrace [定本 21; 新志 93; 導遊 157]; 石碾嶺 Stone Anvil Ridge [定本 34]. 薌石 Scentgrass Stone [定本 29; 新志 51] boasts the four-character inscription by Wang Daokun (see Chapter Four).

30 其所逕寺曰楊干寺臺曰容成潭曰長潭嶺曰石碾石曰薌石溪曰芳溪村曰芳村 The various sites on the route from Huizhou to Tangkou had begun to be listed and described by travellers late in the previous century, an indication of the developing tourist culture in the area, and that the appropriate itinerary for the traveller was being prescribed in text. Qian draws here almost verbatim from the 1615 essay of Xie Zhaoshen 謝兆申 (*Huangshan zhi* [1667], pp. 489–94; *Huangshan zhi dingben*, pp. 247–52), the first of many such instances. Xie's *Xie Erbo xiansheng chuji* 謝耳伯先生初集 is said to be prefaced the thirteenth year of the Chongzhen 崇禎 reign (1640), although I have been unable to examine this work personally. It is quite possible, then, that a copy of Xie's works would have found its way to the desk of Qian Qianyi by 1642; certainly he draws heavily from Xie's account below as we shall see. Hereafter, references to Xie Zhaoshen's important essay are given as XZS, followed by a page reference to the *Huangshan zhi* (1667), which appears to be the more complete version of Xie's text.

31 縣長潭而山口山率環谷水率注溪谷窮復入一谷 From XZS (p. 489).

an embankment, circling each other while remaining independent.[32] The stream waters can shoot clear and straight like arrows, or else bubble and churn about like wheels,[33] and whether deep or shallow, patterned rocks can be seen lying at the bottom in disorderly profusion. For one hundred *li* around, the boundless firmament is resplendent in its bright colours, while the floating dust and the soaring filth is repelled by the cliffs; the foul air from the putrid world of men can never enter this space.

I asked a fellow traveller: "Do you understand Yellow Mountain? It is the great capital of the skies and the dwelling-place of the immortal Yellow Emperor. For two hundred *li* around there are the palaces and paths, where the many immortals come and go, and where the crowds of spirits rest, and among them there is a gate-keeping spirit, who can brush away the land, removing it from the sight of man. During my travels at Mount Supreme, before I had climbed to Heaven's Gate, and made it up to Sun-Gazing Peak, I had no understanding of the respect that is due to that great mountain.[34] Now, at the start of this journey, I am already respectful and pure of mind, silent and deferent; it is truly as if I had already made it to the summit of Heavenly Capital or Stone Gate Peak.[35] How then, could it be said that my coming on this trip has been in vain?"

On that day I bathed at the Hot Springs, and lodged for the evening at Peach Blossom Source Hermitage in the Elixir Valley.[36]

---

32   山與谷如堂如防旋相宮又相別也 A difficult line that relates back to the somewhat abstruse explanation of landforms provided in the *Erya* 爾雅 11: "A hill that resembles a hall 堂 is called dense 密; one that resembles an embankment 防 is called flourishing 盛 . . . a large hill that encircles 宮 a small hill is called a guardian 霍; a small hill independent 別 of a larger hill is called fresh 鮮." (Xu ed., *Erya jinzhu*, p. 236).

33   溪水清激如失或潰沸如輪 Qian draws again from XZS (p. 489): "[The waters] are pure and straight like flying arrows, or [churning] like spinning wheels" 其清澈如飛失或如旋輪.

34   未及登天門上日觀不知岱之尊也 Probably an allusion to Li Bai's 李白 ascent of Taishan, in which Heaven's Gate 天門 and Sun-Gazing 日觀 are the two peaks deemed appropriate for Li to begin his path to transcendence ("You Taishan liu shou" 遊泰山六首 in *Li Taibai quanji*, Volume 2, pp. 921–6; see my discussion in Chapter Four).

35   石門峰 Stone Gate Peak [定本 9; 新志 15; 導遊 83; 文化 68]. The reference to the two peaks, Heavenly Capital and Stone Gate, perhaps captures something of the theme of the early parts of Qian's essay, that Yellow Mountain is not only a numinous site in the Buddhist/Daoist tradition, but also one that accords with more orthodox Confucian ideals (especially evident in Qian's discussion of the siting of capitals). Stone Gate is a name with Confucian connotations (see *Lunyu* 論語 14.38; D. C. Lau trans., *The Analects* [Harmondsworth: Penguin Books, 1979], p. 130).

36   桃源菴 Peach Blossom Source Hermitage [定本 45–6; 新志 224; 導遊 66–7].

Part II

The area from the mountain gate to the mouth of the springs is the foot of Yellow Mountain, and this is the place at which the path upwards begins. The waters of the Hot Springs come from Amethyst Peak, dropping some 600 *ren* down into the Fragrant Spring Brook below.[37] At the mouth of the spring the waters bubble up steaming hot, but as the cold spring waters descend, the cool and the warm pool together, and as the waters spurt from the ground, their impurities are expelled. When I first got in, sweat flowed from my every pore, but almost before I could heave a sigh it was as if I had sobered from drunkenness, as if I had been delivered from a malarial fever.[38] After floating around for some time, I happened to recall the story of the Pure Nymph, the Jade Realized One,[39] and I put down a set of four

---

37 紫石峰 Amethyst Peak [定本 5; 新志 29–30; 導遊 72; 文化 78–9]; 香泉溪 Fragrant Spring Brook [導遊 135].

38 初浴汗蒸蒸溢毛孔已而愾然霍然如醒斯析如痁斯解 Dai Ao 戴澳 had recorded a similar experience of the Hot Springs in 1617: "When I first tested the waters they were too hot, but after a moment they were fine" 試之初似太熱項乃相宜 (*Huangshan zhi dingben*, p. 254).

39 愰然感素女玉真之事 The Jade Realized One 玉真 is a reference to Yang Guifei 楊貴妃 (original *ming* Yuhuan 玉環; 719–56), beautiful consort of the Tang Emperor Xuanzong 玄宗 (born Li Longji 李隆基; r. 713–56). Yang was originally married to the emperor's son, Prince Shou 壽 王 (born Li Mei 李瑁) before being sent to a nunnery, a process of purification that saw her adopt the sobriquet Taizhen 太真, and that was intended to lend legitimacy to her subsequent attachment to the emperor. Xuanzong had the Huaqing 華清 hot springs palace at Chang'an 長安 (modern Xi'an) reconstructed for Yang, because of which the latter is in literature frequently associated with bathing. The allusion to Yang, who was 34 years younger than Xuanzong, is almost certainly a reference to Liu Shi, herself some 36 years younger than Qian Qianyi. The Pure Nymph 素女 was a legendary divinity said to have been the Yellow Emperor's instructor in the sexual arts, and whose wisdom is preserved in the *Sunüjing* 素女經 (see Douglas Wile trans., *Art of the Bedchamber: The Chinese Sexual Yoga Classics Including Women's Solo Meditation Texts* [Albany: State University of New York Press, 1992]). One of the roles of the Pure Nymph was, as Keith McMahon notes, to bolster the sexual confidence of the emperor and to encourage him to have intercourse with younger women (*Misers, Shrews, and Polygamists: Sexuality and Male-Female Relations in Eighteenth-Century Chinese Fiction* [London: Duke University Press, 1995], p. 43), but as I can make no link between Yang and the Pure Nymph, or indeed find anything that might connect the latter to springs or bathing, I am inclined to read the 素女 of this line as attributive (i.e., referring to Yang herself). In any case the analogy is an interesting one — despite her beauty Yang's reign as consort was somewhat infamous, and tended to be associated with the emperor's neglect of affairs of state.

quatrains to mark the occasion.[40] After bathing I dried off in a pavilion, my kerchief, sandals and robes floating gracefully on the air, each beyond the dust of the world.

We headed west, where interlacing trees and bamboos conspired with pillars of cliff and rock to hide the way; it was truly as if there were no tracks here of man.[41] A walk of about half a *li* brought us to Mr She's Peach Blossom Source Hermitage,[42] before which the peaks Heavenly Capital, Blue Phoenix and Alms Bowl circle around like a folding screen.[43] To the left of the hermitage is White Dragon Pool,[44] the viscous water of which is a deep black.[45] Spurting against the great rocks, the waters let out a "pong"

---

40 作留題四絕句 For Qian's four quatrains, "Four Quatrains Composed Whist Bathing at the Hot Springs on the Fifth Day Following the Purification Ceremony" 禊後五日浴湯池留題四絕句, see *juan* 19 of the *Muzhai chuxueji* (*QMZQJ*, Volume 1, pp. 642–3). This passage raises the fascinating question of whether or not Liu Shi had any involvement in Qian's Yellow Mountain travels. Both Jonathan Chaves ("Yellow Mountain Poems," p. 467) and Ding Gongyi (*Wenxue sixiang*, p. 115) argue that Liu was present for this first part of the trip, as she composed a series of four quatrains (included in *juan* 19 of Qian's collection) that echoes the one to which Qian refers here. I am in no doubt that the allusion to Yang Guifei is a reference to Liu Shi, but I believe that there is enough external evidence to suggest that the pair separated before Qian reached the mountain proper (see Chapter Four). It should also be noted that the set of quatrains to which Qian refers here appears in Liu's collected works under the title "Four Quatrains Composed Whist Bathing at the Hot Springs below Yellow Mountain on the Fifth Day Following the Purification Ceremony *and Sent Off to Liu Shi*" 禊後五日浴黃山下湯池留題四絕句遙寄河東君 (*Liu Rushi ji* 145, my emphasis).

41 如無人逕 Probably an allusion to Wang Wei's 王維 "Passing the Temple of Collected Fragrance" 過香積寺, which opens: "Not knowing the way to the Temple of Collected Fragrance / I wander many *li* into cloud-bathed peaks. / Amongst the ancient trees, no tracks here of man" 不知香積寺數里入雲峰古木無人逕. See Zhao Diancheng 趙殿成 (1683–1756) ed., *Wang Youcheng ji jianzhu* 王右丞集箋注 (rpt.; Xianggang: Zhonghua shuju, 1972), Volume 1, pp. 131–2. For an alternative translation of this poem (rendered into "Visiting Hsiangchi Temple"), see G. W. Robinson trans., *Poems of Wang Wei* (Harmondsworth: Penguin Books, 1973), p. 94.

42 半里許佘氏桃源菴在焉 She Shusheng 佘書升 (*zi* Lunzhong 掄仲) was the late-Ming recluse credited with restoring the Peach Blossom Source Hermitage [定本 96].

43 青鸞峰 Blue Phoenix Peak [定本 5; 新志 23; 導遊 124–5; 文化 66]; 鉢盂峰 Alms Bowl Peak [定本 5; 新志 26; 導遊 76; 文化 53]. The *luan* 鸞 is a mythological bird described in the *Shanhaijing* 山海經 as resembling a pheasant with five-coloured stripes 狀如翟而五彩文, and was interpreted as an omen of peace (see Yuan Ke 袁珂 ed., *Shanhaijing jiaozhu* 山海經校注 [Shanghai: Guji chubanshe, 1980], p. 35). I have somewhat reductively rendered 青鸞 as "Blue Phoenix" to avoid the non-translation preferred by Strassberg ("luan-bird") in *A Chinese Bestiary: Strange Creatures from the Guideways Through Mountains and Seas* (Berkeley: University of California Press, 2002), p. 102.

44 白龍潭 White Dragon Pool [定本 25; 新志 83–4; 導遊 56; 文化 127].

45 水膏淳黛蓄 An adaptation of a phrase used in Liu Zongyuan's 柳宗元 "You Huangxi ji" 遊黃溪記, for which see Wu Wenzhi 吳文治 ed., *Liu Zongyuan ji* 柳宗元集 (Beijing: Zhonghua shuju, 1979), Volume 3, pp. 759–62. Qian draws heavily from Liu below, particularly in the middle sections of his essay.

sound,[46] spraying a fine drizzle over the lily magnolias, which glisten as bright as jade snow. Suddenly I heard a tapping on the bamboo fence, and found Shao Liangqing and Youqing of Haiyang, who had come from White Mount to pay me a call;[47] hearing the rustle of their footfall was a delight indeed.[48] In the dead of the night I lay listening to the crashing of overflowing waters, the noise of the stream competing with that of the rain, while surging waves splashed against each other.

The next morning I rose and sat in a small tower, watching the Heavenly Capital Peak waterfall trace its way through the variegated morning glow. Without warning the heavy rain began again, the wind whipping the waters up into a furious rage. As heaven and earth shook and rolled, the entire mountain was awash with white dragons, swinging their heads and flashing their tails, some wrenching sideways, some heaving onto their backs. While the waves of White Dragon Pool wrestled angrily, the trees in the forest crashed together, and even our tables and chairs were not spared a good shaking. The rains abated, but the spring waters seemed only to increase their rage, pounding against my chest like a pestle pounding a mortar. As the sun sank into the hills,[49] for a short while we discussed our travels.

Next to She's Hermitage are the Hot Springs, and from sunrise to sunset one can bathe, drink, draw water, wash one's hair, and prepare food all at this spot. In former times men would drink from chrysanthemum

---

46 水聲砰磅 An onomatope probably borrowed from Wang Zhijie 王之杰, who also uses the term 砰磅 to describe the sound at White Dragon Pool in his 1606 essay (*Huangshan zhi* [1667], pp. 452–4; *Huangshan zhi dingben*, pp. 221–4).

47 海陽邵梁卿幼青自白岳來訪 On the visit of Shao Liangqing 邵梁卿 and his nephew Youqing 幼青 see two prefaces by Qian in *QMZQJ*, Volume 2, pp. 934–6. The second of these is translated in Chapter Four.

48 足音跫然足樂也 An allusion to the "Xu Wugui" 徐无鬼 chapter of the *Zhuangzi* 莊子, which reads, in Burton Watson's translation: "A man who has fled into the wilderness, where goosefoot and woodbine tangle the little trails of the polecat and the weasel, and has lived there in emptiness and isolation for a long time, will be delighted if he hears so much as the rustle of a human footfall 聞人足音跫然而喜矣." (*The Complete Works of Chuang Tzu* [New York: Columbia University Press, 1968], p. 262). That all mention of the Shaos' visit is missing from LYM and WKQ, who omit entirely the line 俄聞籬落間剝啄海陽邵梁卿幼青自白岳來訪足音跫然足樂也, is somewhat puzzling given its appearance in all other texts. Although the frustrating lack of textual information in Li's collection precludes any definitive conclusions as to the reason for this excision, one cannot but notice here that the essay seems to flow better without this line, and I do not discount the possibility that it was originally inserted as an afterthought.

49 日下舂 Literally, "as the sun sank into Chong 舂 ('mortar') Mountain," referring to the mythical mountain into which the sun was thought to descend. See Ding Du's 丁度 (990–1053) Song-dynasty rhyming dictionary *Ji yun* 集韻 (rpt.; Taibei: Taiwan shangwu yinshuguan, 1965), Volume 1, p. 36 (平聲・鍾韻 section).

pools to gain strength, or drink wolfberry water for longevity.[50] But how can these be compared to this cinnabar spring, in which the Yellow Emperor bathed for three days, shedding his skin and renewing his hair?[51] For a thousand ounces of silver one can rent a hut in the Elixir Valley, and for two thousand one can purchase dried provisions. After several years of preparing elixirs, bathing and drinking at this spring, would not one's transcendence of this mortal world be guaranteed? Recently there was an official here who offered to sell a hut for three thousand ounces, and the many men who sought to acquire it fought amongst themselves. Any man who would turn his head from the chance to buy immortality for just three thousand ounces, would be laughable indeed.[52]

---

50   昔人飲菊潭而強飲杞水而壽 The waters of Chrysanthemum Pool 菊潭 (also known as Chrysanthemum Spring 泉) in Henan Province were reputed to have life-giving properties, a fact recorded in Li Shizhen's 李時珍 important *Bencao gangmu* 本草綱目 (rpt.; Ran Xiande 冉先德. [Beijing: Zhongguo guoji guangbo chubanshe, 1994], Volume 2, pp. 1039–40). Qian may well have drawn here from the brief introduction written by Su Shi 蘇軾 to his "Poetic Reply to [Tao Qian's 陶潛] Peach Blossom Source" 和桃花源詩, a somewhat self-contradictory essay in which Su refutes the argument that the people of Tao's record must have been immortal: "For generations the story of the Peach Blossom Source has been passed down, in the course of which it has become somewhat exaggerated. But all that Tao Yuanming [Tao Qian] had actually recorded was that "their ancestors fled here to escape the disorder of Qin rule," so the people whom the fisherman saw must have been the descendants of those, not the original people from Qin times, still living. Tao also says that the people "slaughtered some chickens to eat," and who has ever heard of an immortal slaughtering anything [for food]? From long ago comes the tale of the Chrysanthemum Stream 菊水 in Nanyang, the waters of which were sweet and fragrant. The thirty or so families that lived there drank from the stream and all lived long; some reached 120 or 130 years old. In the village of old men at Green Wall Mountain in the state of Shu, there are sometimes five generations seen together. The village is remote and the way there extremely difficult, so they never see any salt or vinegar, but in the stream there are many wolfberry trees 枸杞, with roots like dragons and snakes, and drinking these waters is what lets them live long 飲其水故壽." (*Su Dongpo quanji* 蘇東坡全集 [Beijing: Zhongguo shudian, 1986], Volume 2, pp. 86–7.)

51   軒轅浴之三日而伐皮易毛者乎 The story of the Yellow Emperor's soak in the Hot Springs is recorded in the *Huangshan tujing*, which cites the no longer extant *Zhou shu yiji* 周書異記 as its authority. The emperor is in fact supposed to have bathed for seven days (*Huangshan tujing* 2b: 黃帝至湯泉浸七日皴折故皮隨水而去), and Qian's "three days" here appears to be a mistake (in his corresponding poem the duration appears as seven days; see Poem #19, *QMZQJ*, Volume 1, pp. 653–4). For a similar version of the story (also giving seven days), see *Huangshan zhi dingben*, p. 100.

52   On the use of the term *jin* 金 for ounce of silver during the Ming period, "separating out the special things for which it was the appropriate currency from those ordinary things which could be paid for in more prosaic *liang* [兩]," see Clunas, *Superfluous Things*, p. 133 and pp. 177–81. As a price comparison, Qian acquired a rare Song-dynasty imprint of the two *Hanshu* 兩漢書 around 1620 for one thousand *jin* (or 1200 by another version, see Chapter One), while two thousand *jin* was the record price paid during the Ming era for a work of art, when the collector Xiang Yuanbian 項元汴 (*zi* Zijing 子京, *hao* Molin 墨林; 1525–90) purchased the *Zhanjin tie* 瞻近帖 by Wang Xizhi 王羲之.

Part III[53]

From Auspicious Emblem Temple[54] I crossed the stone bridge and proceeded north. Passing the Temple of Compassionate Radiance,[55] I walked for several *li*, passed by Cinnabar Hermitage and began my ascent.[56] To the east of this point stands Amethyst Peak, the fourth of Yellow Mountain's Thirty-six Peaks,[57] which connects up with Blue Phoenix and Heavenly Capital. Having passed by, I sought out the path that runs between the two peaks Alms Bowl and Old Man.[58] The feet of the peaks stand side by side, while the faces of their cliffs press in towards each other, and the more one looks the more it seems as though the two had been sculpted with a knife, for there is no visible crack between them. I continued along, hugging the cliff-wall, until all of a sudden a cave gaped open in front of me, light revealing the space before me, as if a gate had

---

53   Two annotated versions of this third section of the essay exist: BYC and NQX. For an alternative English translation of this section, see Strassberg trans., *Inscribed Landscapes*, pp. 315–6.

54   祥符寺 Auspicious Emblem Temple [定本 41; 新志 218; 導遊 60–1; 文化 177], the main structure at the Hot Springs area, was constructed in the Tang, but did not receive this name until the Xiangfu 祥符 period (1008–16) of the Song dynasty. As the oldest temple on the mountain, Auspicious Emblem, sometimes referred to as Springs Cloister 湯院 (see Part I) or the Hot Springs Temple 湯寺 (see Part V) receives much attention from Ming and Qing travellers, but situated close to the mountain gate, it features only as a resting point in Qian's narrative.

55   慈光寺 Temple of Compassionate Radiance [定本 41–2; 新志 220–1; 導遊 117–9; 文化 164–5] is discussed in more detail in Part VI, below.

56   度石橋而北蹄慈光寺行數里遡硃砂菴而上 A problematic line. Cinnabar Hermitage 硃砂菴 is, in fact, the former name of the Temple of Compassionate Radiance 慈光寺, a fact that seems to have been well known in the late Ming (several writers mention this, see for example Xu Hongzu's 徐弘祖 1616 essay: "[慈光] 寺舊名硃砂菴"; *Xu Xiake youji jiaozhu*, Volume 1, p. 19). MLS and LYM emend 菴 to 溪, resulting in the apparently more logical "crossed Cinnabar Stream" 遡硃砂溪. I remain uncomfortable with this solution, as the fact that "Cinnabar Hermitage" is repeated in the title of Qian's corresponding poem (#11) suggests a naming error rather than a textual corruption, in which case, "Cinnabar Stream" becomes impossible (one does not mistakenly call a stream a hermitage). I have therefore allowed the 菴 in the SBCK text to stand, but am reading it as a mistake by Qian. No editorial comment is offered in any of our texts on the issues pertaining to this character.

57   三十六峰之第四峰 Qian follows here the sequence of Yellow Mountain's "Thirty-six Peaks" recorded in the *Huangshan tujing*, for which see my note to Part IX, below.

58   老人峰 Old Man Peak [新志 25; 導遊 127–8; 文化 61] is one of the major landmarks of Yellow Mountain, frequently mentioned in the travel accounts of Ming and Qing scholars, although it is not included among the Thirty-six Peaks. The popularity of Old Man in the seventeenth century probably stemmed from its aesthetic qualities, with its bizarre form making it the perfect peak against which to view the spreading clouds. More recently, the fortunes of Old Man Peak have waned slightly; it is visible (only briefly) from the cable car but is now slightly removed from the main walking route up (or down) the mountain.

been broken down. For the traveller at Yellow Mountain, the real journey begins at this point.

After perhaps another *li*, I rested at Avalokiteśvara Crag,[59] which slopes upwards like a tilted umbrella.[60] I continued on past Old Man Peak, where the rock stands like an old man with hunched back.[61] On the overhanging cliffs there were many exceptional pines, splitting the rocks as they burst forth, and covering them with their tangled branches. As thick layers of white cloud began to engulf the pines, a monk said: "The clouds are about to spread into a sea, why not tarry here awhile to see it?" I took his advice, retiring to a pavilion that faces the peaks, and before my eyes, the hills and streams of the great landscape I had ascended the mountain to view, all became submerged in a great sea.

When rain is about to fall the clouds cluster and gather about the mountain; when the skies are about to clear the clouds disperse and return into the mountain. It is this gathering and dispersing around the hills and streams of this vast landscape that is called the "Spreading Sea."[62] The clouds first rose like floating cotton, circling around Old Man's waist and back, and in no time they had obscured him from head to toe. As they moved back and forth in disarray, the clouds pressed in on all sides,[63] overflowing into a great whirlpool. The sea had become cloud and the cloud had become a sea, the waves of which penetrated and crashed against each other, their forms like myriad towers and pavilions, like galloping horses, like junks, surging forth then sinking back; truly impossible to describe. The clouds lapped at my chest and brushed against my face, and with my body layered in cloud, I too had become an Old Man Peak! After some time, the clouds began to disperse, like waves rippling across water, an endless stream scattering in all directions; like a returning army of soldiers on horseback. Suddenly they were gone, leaving not the slightest trace. I cast an eye back to Old Man Peak, still hunched over, as if he were

---

59 觀音崖 Avalokiteśvara Crag [定本 19–20; 新志 90; 導遊 128]. On Avalokiteśvara, the Goddess of Mercy, see Chün-fang Yü's *Kuan-yin: The Chinese Transformation of Avalokiteśvara* (New York: Columbia University Press, 2001).

60 憩觀音崖崖攲立如側蓋 Qian draws this line from XZS (p. 491), replacing Xie's *yan* 巌 with *ya* 崖.

61 迳老人峰立石如老人傴僂 Another line from XZS (p. 491): 徑老人峰峰立石如鼇僂焉.

62 鋪海 The Spreading Sea [新志 58–62; 文化 139–40] of clouds (now usually referred to as 雲海), along with the springs, the rocks and the pines make up the famed Four Perfections of Yellow Mountain 黃山四絕.

63 迫遽廻合 A line from Liu Zongyuan's 柳宗元 "Yongzhou Longxingsi dongqiu ji" 永州龍興寺東丘記, for which see *Liu Zongyuan ji*, Volume 3, pp. 748–9. For H. C. Chang's translation of this passage, see my note to Part V, below.

respectfully receiving a guest.[64] Proceeding along the foot of Heavenly Capital I turned west, finally reaching Mañjuśrī Cloister,[65] at which I lodged for the evening.

From Avalokiteśvara Crag upwards, aged trees clog Yellow Mountain's paths, rocks are swathed in ancient vines, and green shoots of bamboo and flatsedge weave themselves together.[66] As the sun's rays pierce through the vegetation, a spring suddenly sprays in the air. Secluded and remote, it seems far removed from the world of man. The part of a mountain "before the summit is reached" is called the "verdure,"[67] and does such a name not truly describe this place? As I climbed Old Man Peak, the heavens extended out before me, while the Thirty-six Peaks pushed erratically up through the blanket of cloud below, and it seemed as if I had crossed over into another world.[68] It was only then that I truly understood Yellow Mountain.

Part IV

From down at Peach Blossom Source Hermitage, one can identify Heavenly Capital at the centre of all the peaks, but the form of the whole mountain is as smooth as a silk net, and nothing stands out above the rest. Now, however, that the clouds had risen to the middle of the peaks, they piled up in layers like a heap of clothes, a lush screen that separated each of the peaks, leaving Heavenly Capital towering above them all. I gained the top of the Old Man Peak gully, which runs along the foot of Heavenly Capital, grasping the high pines, and clambering up the rifts in the cliff walls, twisting upwards and hanging outwards. When I turned to look

---

64 回望老人峰傴僂如故若遲而肅客者 The image of Old Man Peak hunched over to receive a guest was probably borrowed from the 1618 essay of Qian's friend Yuan Zhongdao 袁中道 (*Huangshan zhi* [1667], pp. 463–4; *Huangshan zhi dingben*, pp. 258–60).

65 文殊院 Mañjuśrī Cloister [定本 44–5; 新志 230; 導遊 145–6; 文化 176] sat at the site between Lotus Blossom and Heavenly Capital Peaks now occupied by Jade Screen Tower 玉屏樓.

66 青竹綠莎蒙絡搖綴 A line from Liu Zongyuan's 柳宗元 "Zhi xiaoqiu xi Xiaoshitan ji" 至小丘西小石潭記: "the green trees and verdant vines weaved themselves together 蒙絡搖綴." See *Liu Zongyuan ji*, Volume 3, pp. 767–78.

67 山未及上日翠微. The reference here is to the definition provided in the *Erya* 爾雅: "[The part of a mountain] before the summit is reached [is called] the verdure" 未及上翠微. See Xu ed., *Erya jinzhu*, p. 235.

68 The sense of crossing 度 over into the world of the immortals is especially noticeable in this section of the essay, enhanced by the parallel crossings 度 at the beginning and here at the end.

again at Heavenly Capital, it was as if it stood alone,[69] peering out from behind a crown of hanging jewels. My esteem for this great peak was thus heightened even further.

I descended the ridge and started climbing again, finding a monk chiselling into the rock, the traces of his hatchet and chisel crisscrossed into the foot of the peak. There is a fissure in the stone wall here, and it is possible to enter the wall and follow the gap upwards. I proceeded thus for about a *li* [70] before Heavenly Capital started to disappear from view; as I climbed on, trying to keep it in sight meant losing my footing, but dragging my feet meant losing my view of the peak. At the end of the wall the rocks pile up together,[71] forming ladder steps that lead downwards. Watching a man descend by these steps is like watching water being drawn from a well; his body follows the rope deep down, and when he climbs back to the top, he emerges as if stepping out of the shaft.

I turned back and scaled the terrace on which sits Mañjuśrī Cloister,[72] the grand labour[73] of Pumen, the Master of Tranquillity.[74] The cloister backs into Folding Screen Peak, with an elephant to its left, and a lion to its right.[75] Two splayed pines shield the cloister like a feather canopy, and speckled with rocks, its surface looks like a patchwork kasāya.[76] There is

---

69 介而立 From XZS (p. 492). Part IV of Qian's account shows the most reliance on Xie Zhaoshen's essay.

70 歷緯里許 From XZS (p. 492).

71 壁絕石復上合 From XZS (p. 492).

72 折而陟臺是為文殊院 From XZS (p. 492): 折而陟臺是曰文殊之院.

73 荒度 A term originally employed in the *Shujing* 書經 to refer to the grand labours of Yu 禹, i.e., the labours associated with the regulation of the waters: "When [my son] Qi 啟 was wailing and weeping, I did not regard him, but kept planning with all my might my labour on the land" 啟呱呱而泣予弗子惟荒度土功 (Legge trans., *Chinese Classics*, Volume 3 (1), pp. 85; romanization altered).

74 On Pumen 普門, the Shaanxi monk who moved to Yellow Mountain in 1606, see Chapter Two. The name Pumen relates to *viśva*, the opening into all things, or the universality of the gate open to a Buddha. I am reading 安公 as an honorific term, as it seems always to be used with reference to Pumen.

75 院負疊嶂峰左象右獅 XZS (p. 492) has 院故負勝蓮之峰左擁石如象右擁石如獅. Qian substitutes Folding Screen 疊嶂 for Xie's Surpassing Lotus 勝蓮, and in Part IX (below) notes the general error of these two peaks being confused. The Mañjuśrī Cloister, of course, backs into Jade Screen Peak, and in terms of his placement of Folding Screen Peak, Qian's essay does not reconcile easily with any of the sources, ancient or modern. The elephant 象 and the lion 獅 are two rocks that sit on either side of the site of the Cloister. 疊嶂峰 Folding Screen Peak [定本 7; 新志 26; 導遊 222–3; 文化 55–6]; 象石 Elephant Rock [定本 31; 新志 38–9; 導遊 145]; 獅石 Lion Rock [定本 31; 新志 39; 導遊 144–5].

76 The kasāya 袈裟 is a form of traditional cassock worn by Buddhist monks, the name in Sanskrit reflecting the garment's variegated colour, which distinguished it from the white robes of ordinary people.

a path for one's feet above the terrace, but below, the ground drops away into emptiness.[77] Peach Blossom Peak stands at the foot of the supporting rocks, whence the Peach Blossom Spring originates.[78] To the terrace's east sits Heavenly Capital, like a pendant hanging upside down, to its west, Lotus Blossom flaunts its calyx,[79] and to its south it faces a vast open space.[80] Gazing out into the distance, I watched the floating mists; a rising haze of cyanic greens and violet blues, pierced by the rays of the setting sun as it made its way over the horizon. Before long the mist had collected and the haze gathered, so that now, in every direction the view was as one. In this hazy scene of setting sun there was no place to walk that was not submerged in a sea of cloud. In comparison to this, I could suddenly see the insignificance of the view at Old Man Peak, which had earlier left me feeling so pleased with myself.[81]

At the seating platform were two crows, circling and flapping around in the air.[82] A monk told me, "these are divine crows, and tomorrow they

---

77 二羅松如羽蓋面擁石如覆裂裳其上有趺跡其下下絕 From XZS (p. 492): 羅松二如蓋面擁石如覆裂裳其上有趺跡其下無臨地.

78 桃花峰居趺石之足桃花之湯出焉 From XZS (p. 492): 花峰麗焉峰故居趺石之足桃花之湯出焉. 桃花峰 Peach Blossom Peak [定本 5; 新志 27; 導遊 62; 文化 70].

79 其東則天都峰如旒倒垂其西則蓮華峰獻蕚焉 From XZS (492): 西則蓮華峰獻蕚焉……其東拱天都……如旒倒垂. 蓮華峰 (sometimes 花) Lotus Blossom Peak [定本 6; 新志 14–5; 導遊 151–3; 文化 61].

80 其東則天都峰如旒倒垂其西則蓮華峰獻蕚焉其南面曠如也 Final clause emended from the SBCK text's repetition of the western view (其西面曠如也), following MLS, LYM and WKQ, all of which read 南 for 西. A more accurate description would place Heavenly Capital to the southeast of the Cloister, Lotus Blossom to the northwest, and a view towards the southwest.

81 向所沾沾于老人峰者又存乎見少矣 Probably an allusion to the "Autumn Floods" 秋水 chapter of the Zhuangzi 莊子, which reads: "I sit here between heaven and earth as a little stone or a little tree sits on a huge mountain. Since I can see my own insignificance 方存乎見少, what reason would I have to pride myself?" (adapted from Watson trans., Complete Works of Chuang Tzu, p. 176). The spirit of the passage also echoes Liu Yuxi's 劉禹錫 (zi Mengde 夢得; 772–842) lament, voiced in the preface to his "On Nine Blossoms Mountain" 九華山歌: "In the past I esteemed Mount Splendour 華, and thought it the only truly exceptional mountain; I admired Mount Nüji 女几 and Mount Thorn 荊, and thought them the only truly beautiful mountains. Only now, having seen Nine Blossoms Mountain, do I regret the ease of my former words 始悼前言之容易也." See Tao Min 陶敏 and Tao Hongyu 陶紅雨 ed., Liu Yuxi quanji biannian jiaozhu 劉禹錫全集編年校注 (Changsha: Yuelu shushe, 2003), Volume 1, pp. 337–8. On his 1618 visit, Xu Hongzu 徐弘祖 was similarly impressed by the view from Mañjuśrī Terrace, describing it as "truly the most splendid sight on Yellow Mountain" 真黃山絕勝處 (Xu Xiake youji jiaozhu, Volume 1, p. 39).

82 坐臺有二鴉翔集 Emended to correct the SBCK text's 生臺, which Chaves, who translates this line (and follows Qian Zhonglian's 1985 edition of the Muzhai chuxueji) renders: "born on the terrace" ("Yellow Mountain Poems," p. 473, my emphasis). My emendation follows MLS, LYM and WKQ, creating the compound 坐臺, or seating terrace. I favour this solution as it accords with Qian's use of the term 座 [= 坐] to describe the Mañjuśrī Terrace in his corresponding poem (#12). Huang Xiyuan 黃習遠 (zi Bochuan 伯傳, hao Jiuge 儯閣), whose essay is dated 1613, also uses the name 文殊坐 for the site (Huangshan zhi [1667], pp. 480–3).

will act as your guides."[83] After feeding them, we sent them off with good wishes.

My bedchamber did not measure even a *gong* in length, and as the night air was still and crisp, the old monk and I pushed open the door and went out. In the faint moonlight, the blurred outlines of the Thirty-six Peaks could just be made out, but damp with the heavy dew,[84] my sandals and kerchief became soaked through, and, my spirit chilled and frozen to the bone,[85] I returned feeling sorry for myself. I had previously loved to sleep "rough" in the mountains, but compared to this, those nights were like sleeping in covered boudoirs, draughtless rooms, and chambers of polished stone, all adorned with damask canopies.[86] My *real* mountain life did not begin until this night.

---

83 僧言此神鴉也明日當為公先導 The presence of the divine crows 神鴉 [定本 60–1; 導遊 82], which act as guides for travellers, had been noted by Xu Chu 許楚 on his excursion of 1635 (*Huangshan zhi dingben*, p. 296).

84 零露瀼瀼 A phrase borrowed from the *Shijing* 詩經 (鄭風・野有蔓草), which James Legge translates thus: "On the moor is the creeping grass, / And how heavily is it loaded with dew! / There was a beautiful man, / Lovely, with clear eyes and fine forehead! / We met together accidentally, / And so my desire was satisfied. // On the moor is the creeping grass, / Heavily covered with dew 零露瀼瀼. / There was a beautiful man, / Lovely with clear eyes and fine forehead! / We met together accidentally, / And he and I were happy together." (*Chinese Classics*, Volume 4 [1], p. 147).

85 悽神寒骨 Qian borrows again here from Liu Zongyuan's "Zhi xiaoqiu xi Xiaoshitan ji," for which see *Liu Zongyuan ji*, Volume 3, pp. 767–8. Liu's passage, in Strassberg's translation, reads: "I sat down above the pond and was completely surrounded by bamboo and trees on all four sides. I felt solitary without anyone else there. The scene chilled my spirit and froze my bones 悽神寒骨. I became hushed, melancholy, and remote" (*Inscribed Landscapes*, p. 144).

86 其猶在曲屋突夏砥室羅幬之中乎 I read this line as an allusion to part of the "Zhao hun" 招魂 section of the *Chuci* 楚辭, which reads, in Hawkes' rendering:

> All the quarters of the world are full of harm and evil.
> Hear while I describe for you your quiet and reposeful home.
> High walls and deep chambers, with railings and tiered balconies;
> Stepped terraces, storied pavilions, whose tops look on the high mountains;
> Lattice doors with scarlet interstices, with carving on the square lintels;
> Draughtless rooms 突廈 for winter; galleries cool in summer;
> Streams and gullies wind in and out, purling prettily;
> A warm breeze bends the melilotus and sets the tall orchids swaying.
> Crossing the hall into the apartments, the ceilings and floors are vermilion,
> The chambers of polished stone 砥室, with kingfisher hangings on jasper hooks;
> Bedspreads of kingfisher seeded with pearls, all dazzling in brightness;
> Arras of fine silk covers the walls; damask canopies stretch overhead 羅幬 […].

See David Hawkes trans., *Ch'u Tz'ŭ: The Songs of the South* (London: Oxford University Press, 1959), pp. 105–6.

Part V

The day broke clear, and I left Mañjuśrī Cloister, with the backs of the divine crows disappearing ahead of me, and the two monks Zhaowei and Huankong following closely behind.[87] Wanting to avoid the treacherous Lotus Blossom Ravine,[88] we followed a bypath around to the right, but it turned out to be even more dangerous. Zhaowei supported my arms, while Huankong supported my feet, the three of us proceeding as if I were a jerboa being carried off by its mules.[89] We made our way thus for about three *li*, finally resting at Zhaowei's thatched hermitage. With Lotus Blossom Peak behind, and Heavenly Capital in front, the hermitage backs into a craggy peak; half concealed from the sky above, it overlooks a deep chasm, with the sun winding around below. In the shade of the thatched eaves, I sat on the white stones and took out one of Jiasui's painted fans to hand around, regretting that his staff and sandals were not there with me.

The two monks squatted on boulders, and described the most suitable way for us to continue our travels: from the Drinking Rocks Retreat we would continue three *li* to Thread of Heaven; come back about a *li* and descend the Hundred-Step Cloudladder.[90] After another *li*, we would climb to Great Pity Crest, and come out at a small newly cleared path, whence another three *li* would bring us to the Heavenly Sea Hermitage.[91] After lunching, walking northeast we would climb Level with Heaven

---

87 The monk Zhaowei 炤微 [定本 112], who lived below Lotus Blossom Peak, was a friend of Cheng Jiasui. The identity of the monk Huankong 幻空 is unknown to me.

88 蓮華溝 Lotus Blossom Ravine [定本 21; 導遊 150].

89 三人者蟨與駏蛩若也 An allusion to the "Daoyingxun" 道應訓 chapter of the *Huainanzi* 淮南子: "In the north there exists a beast by the name of *jue* 蟨 which has the front of a rat and the back of a hare. When it tries to run, it stumbles, and when it tries to walk, it falls. It often gathers sweet herbs to share with the *qiongqiong juxu* 蛩蛩駏驉, and whenever it is in trouble the *qiongqiong juxu* carries it off on its back." See *Huainanzi yizhu* 淮南子譯注, edited by Chen Guangzhong 陳廣忠 (Changchun: Jilin wenshi chubanshe, 1990), p. 564. In the *Shanhaijing*, the *qiongqiong juxu* is described as having the form of a horse, to which Guo Pu 郭璞 (*zi* Jingchun 景純; 276–324) adds that it can run one hundred *li* at a time (see *Shanhaijing jiaozhu*, pp. 246–7). Qian appears to have used *juqiong* 駏蛩 as two separate animals here, highlighting the confusion that appears to surround this animal in traditional sources (on which see Strassberg, *Chinese Bestiary*, p. 266, note 427). That the monk Zhaowei is expert at carrying visitors up the mountain is noted in the *Huangshan zhi dingben* (p. 112).

90 喝石居 Drinking Rocks Retreat [定本 55; 新志 231; 導遊 155] is the name of Zhaowei's thatched hermitage; 一線天 Thread of Heaven [新志 39; 導遊 142; 文化 106–7]; 百步雲梯 Hundred-Step Cloudladder [新志 104; 導遊 156; 文化 104].

91 大悲頂 Great Pity Crest [定本 45; 新志 229; 導遊 164; 文化 166] can be used to refer either to the monastic building (also called Great Pity Cloister 院) or to the peak on which it sits. 天海 Heavenly Sea [定本 48; 新志 227; 導遊 159–60] can similarly indicate either the name of the hermitage 菴 (my reading of this sentence) or the surrounding area.

Promontory, then five more *li* up Stalagmite Promontory.[92] At Start to Believe Peak we would turn and cross Scattered Blossom Dell, visit Seething Dragon Pine, pass Lions' Grove Monastery, climb Illumination Crest, and return to Heavenly Sea.[93] After a short rest, we would climb Alchemists' Terrace, then return.[94]

The sun had not yet reached its zenith, and the sky was like that of a clear autumn day; it seemed that Heaven itself was aiding me on this trip.[95] At lunchtime when we ate at Heavenly Sea, the divine crows flew out to greet us. We toured the mountain's sites, following the sequence laid out by the two monks,[96] and as the sun sank, the crows departed. Circling in the air as if to say goodbye, they returned to Heavenly Sea to lodge for the night.

Thread of Heaven is a steep and narrow set of rock walls, with water dashing down its sides like rain, and we hastened through. Where it records in the *Commentary* that under crags and cliffs, the ancients would take refuge from the wind and the rain, it refers to formations such as this.[97] The Cloudladder is located at the foot of Lotus Blossom Peak, a rock path cut out into over 700 steps. The steps are narrow in the tread and long in the rise, so one's feet drag along like ropes, and one's legs dangle as if being towed. Down or up one is hauled along, back feet waiting for front feet, front heels treading on back heels.[98] Glancing over the edge we trembled

---

92 平天矼 Level with Heaven Promontory [新志 102–3; 導遊 163]; 石筍矼 Stalagmite Promontory [導遊 97–8; 文化 86].

93 始信峰 Start to Believe Peak [新志 19; 導遊 92–3; 文化 69]; 散花塢 Scattered Blossom Dell [新志 106; 導遊 88–9; 文化 105]; 擾龍松 Seething Dragon Pine [定本 67; 新志 55; 導遊 90–1; 文化 114]; 師子林 Lions' Grove [定本 55; 新志 230; 導遊 104–5]; 光明頂 Illumination Crest [新志 15; 導遊 163; 文化 58].

94 煉丹臺 Alchemists' Terrace [定本 20; 新志 92; 導遊 161; 文化 94].

95 此游天所相也 Perhaps an allusion to the Duke Zhao 昭公 (Year Four) section of the *Zuozhuan* 左傳: "[The states] Jin 晉 and Chu 楚 depend on the aid of Heaven 天所相 for the superiority of one over the other" (Legge trans., *Chinese Classics*, Volume 5 (2), pp. 592–6; romanization altered). For a discussion of Qian's sense that he was assisted in his travels by a higher power, see Chapter Four.

96 次第游歷如二僧之云 Qian is, in fact, quite vague about the itinerary from this point onwards, and it is difficult to piece together with any certainty his route after leaving the Drinking Rocks Retreat. The route as set out by the two monks would have been a considerable undertaking. I am particularly disinclined to accept that Qian ever made it to Illumination Crest, for a discussion of which, see Chapter Four.

97 傳曰巖岑之下古人之所避風雨 Probably intended as an allusion to the entry on Duke Xi 僖公 (Year 32) found in the *Zuozhuan*: "At Yao there are two ridges. On the southern ridge is the grave of the sovereign Kao of the Xia dynasty; the northern is where King Wen took refuge from the wind and the rain" 其北陵文王之所避風雨也 (Legge trans., *Chinese Classics*, Volume 5 (1), pp. 220–1; romanization altered).

98 後趾須前趾前踵躡後踵 An echo of Wu Boyu's 吳伯與 (*zi* Fusheng 福生, *hao* Shimei 師每; *js.* 1613) description of the Cloudladder in 1611: "[A step] cannot completely fit one's feet, so the back foot must wait for the front foot to move before it can move" 不能全受足後趾俟前趾發乃可發 (*Huangshan zhi* [1667], pp. 446–50; *Huangshan zhi dingben*, pp. 236–40).

with fear, but, having mustered the nerve we descended, and only having reached the bottom did we congratulate each other for making it down safely.

Start to Believe Peak is not tall enough even to be the grandson of one of the Thirty-six Peaks.[99] It is really no more than a hillock, and yet it still retains all of the splendour of those various other peaks. From Lions' Grove Monastery we headed east, and came to two cliffs rising steeply together, their faces separated by about a *zhang*. From the fissure in the northern cliff protrudes a pine that reaches the southern cliff, which we grabbed to pull ourselves across.[100] We climbed to its summit, where sat another thatched hermitage, tilting to one side under the weight of the snow amassed on its roof. Looking down over the clouds and mists, one could see the tips of the peaks piercing through, and the most extraordinary sight of them all was the Stalagmite Promontory.

According to the *Topographical Classic*, after the Yellow Emperor and Master Fuqiu had ascended to the heavens,[101] "a pair of stalagmites was transformed into a pair of peaks, around a thousand *zhang* high."[102] But

---

99 始信峰于三十六峰不中為兒孫 Reading 中 as *zhòng* (in the sense of conforming, reaching). HM, MLS, LYM and WKQ prefer 之 to 不, presumably to solve the problem created by reading 中 as *zhōng*. I find this solution grammatically less plausible given that Start to Believe is not in fact one of the Thirty-six Peaks.

100 接引松 Receiving Pine [定本 67; 新志 54; 導遊 93; 文化 111], named for its outstretched branches receiving guests, had become a well known attraction for late-Ming and Qing travellers, see for example the accounts of Xu Hongzu 徐弘祖 (*Xu Xiake youji jiaozhu*, p. 21) and Wu Tingjian 吳廷簡 (*Huangshan zhi dingben*, p. 289), both of whom note the existence of a narrow bridge between the cliff faces, for which the pine acted as a rail. This conforms also with painted depictions of the pine. Qian's "pulling ourselves across" 援之以度 here seems to be something of an exaggeration.

101 黃帝浮丘公上昇之後 Master Fuqiu 浮丘公 was reputed to have assisted the Yellow Emperor in his ultimately successful quest for immortality.

102 圖經云黃帝浮丘公上昇之後雙石筍化成峰可高千丈 A line taken from the *Huangshan tujing*, which discusses the pair of stalagmites in its entry on Immortals Peak 仙人峰: "At the summit [of the peak] there are two stone men sitting facing each other that look as if they have been carved. According to the *Xianjizhu* 仙記注, Master Fuqiu and the Yellow Emperor passed by this place, and after they had ascended to the heavens, a pair of stalagmites were transformed into peaks about ten [see below] *zhang* high 上昇之後雙石筍化為峰可高十丈, believed to be the sacred traces of the two immortals. It is commonly said that the rock facing south is the Yellow Emperor, with a stone supporting his back and winding around like a jade imperial screen. The rock facing north is Master Fuqiu. The stone cliff underneath them is over 500 *ren* high, out of the reach of even the apes and monkeys. From the top of [the nearby] Amethyst Peak, one can see that they are just like two immortals sitting facing each other." (*Huangshan tujing*, 6a–b.) Given the characters' similar graphic forms it is conceivable that Qian's 千丈 (misquoting the *Huangshan tujing*'s 十丈; the *Xianjizhu* is also quoted as reading "ten" 十 in the *Huangshan zhi dingben*, p. 8) was the result of an error at the time of printing. However, all consulted versions including the *SBCK* text read 千丈, and it is entirely possible that Qian confused the two immortals with the great supporting rocks on which they sit. I have therefore decided against emendation of the text in this case, and have allowed Qian's 千丈 to stand.

here the stalagmites stand bunched together, no fewer than a hundred thousand. Exquisitely wrought, they shoot from the earth and plunge into the heavens, connecting and splitting into so many eccentric mutations, these could never be measured merely in *zhang*. When the ghosts and spirits were put to work by the Creator of All Things,[103] breaking up the heavens, ploughing the earth into pasture, and boring into the organs of Chaos,[104] were not these the very tools they used? Looking out across ten thousand *ren*, the hills of Xuanzhou and Chiyang were like tiny ripples on the floor of the great valley, no larger than piles of grain in a garner. From up high they appeared like fortified garrison posts, their empty hills echoing with the voices of men. Beyond stood Verdant Peak and the Pine Valley,[105] the north-western limits of Yellow Mountain.

Standing reverently before the Alchemists' Terrace is Alchemists' Peak.[106] Verdant, Flew Here, and the other peaks,[107] each with a position of power not below that of the others, close in towards the terrace as imperial guards. Sloping outwards, they fall in together like the teeth of a comb, or pieces lined up on a chess board, as if they had been sculpted with a blade, as if they had been erected as a line of wooden pickets. This is the place that was chosen by the Yellow Emperor as his private dwelling, and as such it is guarded by spirits. Foolish men who have not bothered to

---

103 造物者 On the concept of the Creator of All Things, see Edward H. Schafer's "The Idea of Created Nature in T'ang Literature," *Philosophy East and West* 15 (1965): 153–60. Schafer cites several writers who speculate about the existence and purpose of the Creator (the "Fashioner of Creatures" in Schafer's terms), including Han Yu 韓愈, Li Bai 李白 and Liu Zongyuan 柳宗元. See also Yuan Mei's 袁枚 opinion on the Creator's methods in his 1782 essay "Yellow Dragon Mountain" 遊黃龍山記, in Strassberg trans., *Inscribed Landscapes*, pp. 403–5.

104 鑿混沌之肺腑 The reference here is to the story of Chaos (*Hundun* 混沌) as described in the 應帝王 chapter of the *Zhuangzi* 莊子: "The emperor of the South Sea was called Shu 儵 [Brief], the emperor of the North Sea was called Hu 忽 [Sudden], and the emperor of the central region was called Hundun [Chaos]. Shu and Hu from time to time came together for a meeting in the territory of Hundun, and Hundun treated them very generously. Shu and Hu discussed how they could repay his kindness. 'All men,' they said, 'have seven openings so they can see, hear, eat, and breathe. But Hundun alone doesn't have any. Let's trying [*sic*] boring him some!' 嘗試鑿之. Every day they bored another hole, and on the seventh day Hundun died." (Watson trans., *Complete Works of Chuang Tzu*, p. 97; romanization altered.) On the concept of Chaos in Chinese mythology, see Yuan Ke's 袁珂 *Zhongguo gudai shenhua* 中國古代神話 (Beijing: Zhonghua shuju, 1960), pp. 30–1 and Anne Birrell's *Chinese Mythology: An Introduction* (Baltimore: John Hopkins University Press, 1993), pp. 98–100.

105 翠微峰 Verdant Peak [定本 8; 新志 23; 導遊 228–9; 文化 54; Cahill gives 薇 for 微 in "Huang Shan Paintings," p. 250]; 松谷 Pine Valley [導遊 220–1; 文化 106].

106 煉丹峰 Alchemists' Peak [定本 4; 新志 15; 導遊 160–1; 文化 61].

107 In modern times Flew Here Peak 飛來峰 is usually interpreted as a reference to the famous Flew Here Rock 石 [導遊 113–5; 文化 91], but to the seventeenth-century traveller the rock sat on the peak, as Min Linsi noted in 1679 [定本 31]. That Qian does not go on to describe the remarkable Flew Here Rock is to me a strong indication that he never made it to Illumination Crest (see Chapter Four).

learn this are laying down boards and constructing buildings here — these should be swept away by the irresistible gales,[108] or burnt in the flames of the *kalpa* fires;[109] they surely cannot outlast the present reign. The Thirty-six Peaks stand scattered out to all sides, opened up like the petals of a lotus, with Alchemists' Terrace nestled in their centre as the flower's heart. The terrace itself is square, and wide enough to hold ten thousand men.[110] It is sheer on three sides, and looking over the front edge into nothingness,[111] I found myself having to back up and lie supine, my feet paralysed with fear and unable to be lifted,[112] while my head felt dizzy for some time afterwards.

From the Springs Temple upwards,[113] climbing this mountain means pushing back the undergrowth,[114] and treading narrow and secluded ways. The view here may be said to belong to the confined type. But from Mañjuśrī Cloister on, the hills are stripped bare, stretching unimpeded up towards the heavens; this view belongs to the open type.[115] As my eyes

---

108 剛風 This appears to be a Buddhist/Daoist term, perhaps related to *jingang* 金剛 (Skt. *vajra*) meaning diamond, and by extension, indestructibility, or else meant as a reference to the *kalpa* gales, one of the calamities that brings about the end of the world (see next).

109 劫火 In traditional Buddhist cosmography, the term *kalpa* 劫 refers to the time that must elapse between the creation of the world and its recreation. This period is divided into a four-stage cycle (the four *kalpas*) of formation 成, continuance 住, decline 壞 and disintegration 空, each of which is divided again into twenty small *kalpas* (one of which is of approximately sixteen million years' duration). The *kalpa* fires 劫火, the *kalpa* floods 劫水 and the *kalpa* gales 劫風 are the three great calamities 災 that bring about the end of the world at the final stage of the *kalpa* of decline.

110 臺方廣可置萬人 An observation borrowed from Tang Binyin's 湯賓尹 1612 essay: 最方以廣其上可置萬人者鍊丹臺也 (*Huangshan zhi* [1667], pp. 474–9; *Huangshan zhi dingben*, pp. 241–6).

111 三面剷削前臨無地 Drawn from Wang Zhijie's 王之杰 1608 observation: 三面剷削前臨堊塈者 (*Huangshan zhi* [1667], pp. 454–5; *Huangshan zhi dingben*, pp. 224–7).

112 足蹜蹜不能舉 Probably an allusion to *Lunyu* 論語 10.5: "[When Confucius held the jade tablet] his expression was solemn as though in fear and trembling, and his feet were constrained 足蹜蹜 as though following a marked line." (Lau trans., *Analects*, p. 102.)

113 自湯寺而上 The Springs Temple refers here to Auspicious Emblem Temple 祥符寺.

114 自湯寺而上披蒙茸 Probably borrowed from Su Shi's 蘇軾 famous "Latter Ode to Red Cliff" 後赤壁賦: "I gathered up my robes and stepped onto the bank, finding my footing up the steep slope and pushing back the undergrowth 披蒙茸" (Stephen Owen trans., *An Anthology of Chinese Literature: Beginnings to 1911* [New York: W. W. Norton and Co., 1996], p. 676).

115 自湯寺而上⋯⋯蓋奧如也自文殊院而上⋯⋯蓋曠如也 An explicit reference to the aesthetic theory articulated by Liu Zongyuan in his "Yongzhou Longxingsi dongqiu ji (*Liu Zongyuan ji*, Volume 3, pp. 748–9): "Those in quest of interesting scenery take delight chiefly in two types of view: the expanse and spaciousness of the open view, and the immediate impact and hidden mysteries of the confined view 遊之适大率有二曠如也奧如也如斯而已. Where the ground rises steeply over potential obstructions or breaks through thick vegetation to give an impression of vast space and distance, it is suited to the open view. Where a hillock or mound intrudes or shrubs and undergrowth lie in concealment to offer unexpected scenes at every turn 迫遽廻合 [the phrase used by Qian in Part III], the spot is more suited to the confined view." (H. C. Chang trans., *Chinese Literature 2: Nature Poetry* [Edinburgh: Edinburgh University Press, 1977], p. 123.)

followed the rays of the setting sun along the Stalagmite Promontory and Alchemists' Terrace, my thoughts became muddled and my spirit waned,[116] and as I examined my innermost self, those spiritual regions and strange realms gradually revealed themselves to my soul. How do I know that in the time it takes to lift and lower the head,[117] this scene will not be taken away in the blink of an eye, or carried off on someone's back in the middle of the night?[118] How do I know that my body is really here, and that the mounds and valleys, the heaped dust and accumulated dirt of the world are not already so remote as to be lost to me? And how can I know that these places on which I now sit, and these lands in which I now roam, are not illusory? It is said that "the bases of the five mountains rested on

---

116 意迷精爽 Reading *shuang* 爽 in the sense of *sang* 喪 (loss), to accord with the text of the "King Mu of Zhou" 周穆王 chapter of the *Liezi* 列子, the source of the allusion here. For the relevant passage, see below.

117 俛仰之間 A phrase that takes its origins from the *Zhuangzi* 莊子: [The mind's] heat is that of burning fire, its coldness that of solid ice, its swiftness such that, in the time it takes to lift and lower the head 俛仰之間, it has twice swept over the four seas and beyond." (Watson trans., *Complete Works of Chuang Tzu*, p. 116.)

118 夜半有負之而趨者與 An allusion to a somewhat abstruse passage from *juan* 6 (大宗師) of the *Zhuangzi* 莊子, which Watson renders into: "You hide your boat in the ravine and your fish net in the swamp and tell yourself that they will be safe. But in the middle of the night a strong man shoulders them and carries them off 夜半有力者負之而走, and in your stupidity you don't know why it happened." (*Complete Works of Chuang Tzu*, pp. 80–1.) Watson follows the suggestion of the commentator Yu Yue 俞樾, reading *shan* 汕 (fishing basket) for *shan* 山 (mountain), thus solving the problematic concealment of a mountain in a swamp (for this and other commentaries on the passage see Guo Qingfan's 郭慶藩 (1844–96?) *Zhuangzi jishi* 莊子集釋 [rpt.; Wang Xiaoyu 王孝魚 ed., Beijing: Zhonghua shuju, 1961], Volume 1, pp. 243–6). The "powerful one" 有力者 however, seems more likely to refer to the Creator (i.e., 造物者) than "a strong man," and this indeed is how Qian seems to have interpreted the passage, using it here to illustrate the myriad transformations and the inherent instability of landscape. This is also the way the passage is explained in *juan* 7 of the tenth-century Buddhist sūtra *Zongjinglu* 宗鏡錄, which, like Qian, uses the term *qu* 趨 here in place of *zou* 走, suggesting that this work may in fact have been the source of Qian's allusion. The *Zongjinglu* is a collection of sayings, hymns and translations compiled by the monk Yanshou 延壽 (904–75), noted for his advocacy of pluralism in Buddhist teaching, and who recommended the harmonization of the Chan and Pure Land Schools. An important text in the late-Ming period, the *Zongjinglu* appears in the works of men such as Yuan Hongdao (see McDowall trans., *Four Months of Idle Roaming*, p. 10), and its absence from the listings of the Tower of Crimson Clouds library is taken by Cao Rong 曹溶 as evidence of the incompleteness of that catalogue (see Chapter One). The sūtra is the 2016th work of the Chinese Buddhist canon 大藏經, reproduced in volume 48 of the *Taishō shinshū daizōkyō* 大正新修大藏經, edited by Takakusu Junjirō 高楠順次郎 and Watanabe Kaigyoku 渡邊海旭 (Tōkyō: Taishō issaikyō kankōkai, 1924–32). For an interesting instance of the term "powerful one" 有力者 being used to describe Qian himself (by Mao Yi 毛扆 [*zi* Fuji 斧季; 1640–1713] citing his father Mao Jin 毛晉) see Xiaofei Tian's *Tao Yuanming and Manuscript Culture: The Record of a Dusty Table* (Seattle: University of Washington Press, 2005), pp. 45–6.

nothing";[119] perhaps I too, am supported by nothing, and am really hurtling through space.[120] I am but a man of flesh, burdened with this decaying body, and travelling to this Pure City, this Purple Star, has ruffled my very soul. How will I be able to let go of the magician's sleeve, and bravely seek to return to my own world?[121] King Zhuang of Chu once said: "You

---

119 如所謂五山之根無所連著者 Qian draws directly from the "Tangwen" 湯問 chapter of the *Liezi* 列子, a passage to which he refers again in Part VII. See Yang Bojun 楊伯峻 ed., *Liezi jishi* 列子 集釋 (Beijing: Zhonghua shuju, 1979), pp. 151–2, a passage translated by A. C. Graham thus: "Within [the deep ravine] there are five mountains, called Daiyu, Yuanjiao, Fanghu, Yingzhou and Penglai [. . .] The men who dwell there are all of the race of immortal sages 所居之人皆 仙聖之種, who fly, too many to be counted, to and from from [*sic*] one mountain to another in a day and a night 一日一夕飛相往來者不可數焉. Yet the bases of the five mountains used to rest on nothing 而五山之根無所連著; they were always rising and falling, going and returning, with the ebb and flow of the tide, and never for a moment stood firm." (A. C. Graham trans., *The Book of Lieh-tzǔ* [London: John Murray, 1960], p. 97; romanization altered.) Richard Strassberg notes that the search for "paradisical isles" in the Gulf of Bohai is recorded in the *Shiji* 史記: "Ever since the times of Kings Wei [r. 356–320 BCE] and Xuan [r. 319–301 BCE] of Qi and King Zhao [r. 311–279 BCE] of Yan, expeditions were dispatched to the three divine islands of Penglai, Fangzhang, and Yingzhou. They were said to lie in the Gulf of Bohai not far beyond where men dwelled. Unfortunately, whenever anyone approached them, winds would arise and blow his boat off course." (*Chinese Bestiary*, pp. 204–5.)

120 吾亦將馮空而碩虛與 I read Qian's use of *yun xu* 碩虛 (hurtling through space) as significant here, alluding again to the "King Mu of Zhou" chapter of the *Liezi* (in some versions of which, *yun* 碩 is given as *yun* 殞; see *Liezi jishi*, p. 93). For the relevant passage, see next.

121 以游乎清都紫微余心蕩焉夫安得不執化人之袪懼而求還也與 The line, and several lines from earlier in this section of the essay form an allusion to the "King Mu of Zhou" chapter of the *Liezi* (*Liezi jishi*, pp. 90–4): "Not long afterwards, [the magician] invited the King to come with him on an excursion. He soared upwards, with King Mu clinging to his sleeve 執化人 之袪, and did not stop until they were in the middle sky. There they came to the magician's palace. It was built with gold and silver, and strung with pearls and jades; it stood out above the clouds and the rain, and one could not tell what supported it underneath. In the distance it looked like a congealed cloud. All that the eye observed and the ear listened to, the nose inhaled and the tongue tasted, were things unknown in the world of men. The King really believed that he was enjoying 'the mighty music of the innermost heaven', in the Pure City or the Purple Star 清都紫微, the palaces where God dwells. When he looked down, his own palaces and arbours were like rows of clods and heaps of brushwood.

When it seemed to the King that he had lived there twenty or thirty years without thinking of his own country, the magician again invited him to accompany him on an excursion. They came to a place where they could not see the sun and moon above them, nor the rivers and seas below them. Lights and shadows glared, till the King's eyes were dazzled and he could not look; noises echoed towards them, till the King's ears hummed and he could not listen. Every member and organ loosened in terror, his thoughts ran riot and his spirits waned 意迷精喪 [see above]; and he asked the magician to let him go back 請化人求還. The magician gave him a push, and the King seemed to meteor through space 王若碩虛焉 [see above].

When he awoke, he was sitting as before in his own palace, and his own attendants waited at his side. He looked in front of him; the wine had not yet cooled, the meats had not yet gone dry. When the King asked where he had been, his courtiers answered:

'Your majesty has only been sitting here absorbed in something.'"

See Graham trans., *Book of Lieh-tzǔ*, pp. 62–3. In broader terms one can read Qian's entire passage as an echo of the general theme of this *Liezi* story — the *shenyou* 神遊, or journey of the spirit.

prepared to receive me at Unyielding Terrace, which faces south towards Provender Hill, overlooks the Ambler, and has the Yangzi to its left and the Huai to its right. The pleasure of such a place would be enough to make a man forget even death.[122] I fear that after spending time there it would not be possible to return."[123] My roaming this mountain is a pleasure indeed, but such is the pleasure that I do not dare to stay for too long.

Part VI

Rising at daybreak, I found the wind gusty and unruly.[124] We selected the way of the Cloudladder, where the wind blew against our faces, pushing us backwards, and then at our backs, knocking us prostrate. Hurled backwards and forwards, it felt as if I were being lifted by the armpits; I have never known wind to be of such strength. The end of the Cloudladder is the foot of Lotus Blossom Peak, the path resembles the stem of a lotus,[125] bending around and concealing itself in the belly of the peak. Where the steps end, the path bursts back out of the peak's belly; climbing is like following the lotus root up to its double stage of petals. As the wind became

---

122 其樂忘死 The punctuation added to LYM and WKQ is incorrect here, closing off the quotation too early and thus erroneously attributing the next line, "I fear that after spending time there it would not be possible to return" 恐留之而不能反 to Qian himself. This line is part of the original *Huainanzi* 淮南子 text (see next). In the case of the annotated WKQ text this error is all the more negligent given that the passage from the *Huainanzi* is correctly cited (WKQ, p. 109 and p. 173).

123 楚莊王日子具于強臺南望料山以臨方皇左江右淮其樂忘死恐留之而不能反 An allusion to the "Daoyingxun" chapter of the *Huainanzi*, in which, justifying his failure to attend a feast, King Zhuang of Chu 楚莊王 says (Chinese given where original text differs from Qian's citation): "I heard that 吾聞 you had prepared to receive me at Unyielding Terrace. Now this Unyielding Terrace 強臺者 faces south towards Provender Hill, overlooks the Ambler, and has the Yangzi to its left, and the Huai to its right. The pleasure of such a place would be enough to make a man forget even death. Such pleasure cannot be enjoyed by a man of my shallow morals 若吾德薄之人不可以當此樂也; I fear that after spending time there it would not be possible to return." See *Huainanzi yizhu*, p. 564. For a short account of the reign of King Zhuang (r. 613–591 BC), see *juan* 40 of the *Shiji* 史記 (Volume 5, pp. 1699–1703), and Barry B. Blakeley's treatment of this account in "Chu Society and State: Image versus Reality," in Constance A. Cook and John S. Major ed., *Defining Chu: Image and Reality in Ancient China* (Honolulu: University of Hawai'i Press, 1999), pp. 51–66 (63–4).

124 晨起風蓬蓬然 Probably borrowed from Wu Boyu 吳伯與 (1611), who uses the phrase at Alchemists' Peak (*Huangshan zhi* [1667], pp. 446–50; *Huangshan zhi dingben*, pp. 236–40).

125 徑如荷莖 From XZS (p. 493).

ever more severe, I was no longer able to drag myself upwards against it, so I sat cross-legged against a rock, and waited for the other climbers to arrive. We followed the path back down, but I longed to turn back, and every time we passed a rock or a pine my head would turn as if I had caught sight of an old friend. A monk said: "Amongst the Thirty-six Peaks there is not one from which it is easy to part. Why not hasten to the Temple of Compassionate Radiance, where one can call upon all of the various peaks, while one's hand never leaves the railing?"

Compassionate Radiance is situated on a branch ridge of Heavenly Capital, nestled up against Peach Blossom and Lotus Blossom Peaks. Cinnabar, Blue Phoenix and Amethyst Peaks stand on its left,[126] while to its right, Folding Screen and Cloud Gate Peaks are both poised facing outwards.[127] Pumen, the Master of Tranquillity, who had previously established a monastery at Bracing Mountain,[128] achieved a vision of Yellow Mountain while at meditation, and so from Bracing Mountain moved to this site.[129] When he entered the gates of the capital,[130] with powerful resolve and in touch with the unfathomable realms, the Empress Dowager Cisheng opened up the imperial treasury to the shaven-headed ones,[131] and presented them with purple robes, pennants and staffs.[132] The Emperor

---

126 硃砂峰 Cinnabar Peak [定本 5; 新志 28; 導遊 123; 文化 78].

127 寺踞天都之隴枕桃花蓮華二峰左則硃砂青鸞紫石右則疊嶂雲門竝外翼焉 From XZS (p. 489). 雲門峰 Cloud Gate Peak [定本 9; 新志 21; 導遊 240–1].

128 普門安公者縛禪清凉山中 For 縛禪 I am reading *fu* 縛 (tie, bind, fetter) in the sense of *jie* 結 (tie, knot, weave), which carries with it an idea of construction. Bracing Mountain (Qingliangshan 清凉山) refers here to Wutaishan 五臺山 in Shanxi, one of the four great Buddhist mountains in China, and from which Pumen and several other early seventeenth-century monks at Yellow Mountain had arrived. The name "Bracing" had been used since ancient times in reference to its unusually cold weather; the eleventh-century gazetteer *Guang Qingliang zhuan* 廣清涼傳 compiled by the monk Yanyi 延一 recorded that ice was present even during summer (cited in Mary Anne Cartelli's "On a Five-Colored Cloud: The Songs of Mount Wutai," *Journal of the American Oriental Society* 124 (4) (2004): 735–57 [738]). On the cult of Mañjuśrī at Five Terraces Mountain, see Shinohara Koichi's "Literary Construction of Buddhist Sacred Places: *The Record of Mt. Lu* by Chen Shunyu," *Asiatische Studien* 53 (4) (1999): 937–64.

129 遂縣清涼徙焉 According to the *Huangshan zhi dingben* (p. 41), Pumen moved to Yellow Mountain in the *bingwu* 丙午 year of the reign of the Wanli Emperor (1606).

130 比入都門 Pumen is said to have left the mountain to travel to the capital in search of funding for his grand Yellow Mountain project during the 38th year (1610) of the Wanli reign (*Huangshan zhi* [1988], p. 233).

131 慈聖皇太后 On the patronage of Buddhist projects by the Empress Dowager Cisheng (1546–1614) see Chapter Two.

132 賜紫衣幡杖 On the gifts presented by the imperial palace to the Yellow Mountain monks, see *Huangshan zhi* (1988), p. 233.

Shenzong bestowed a name-tablet inscribed with the words "Compassionate Radiance,"[133] and issued a decree of protection and support.[134]

Today the temple houses the set of sūtras that Cisheng had adorned as a gift from the imperial house.[135] There is a four-faced gold Buddha figure,[136] in seven layers, with each layer containing four Venerated Ones, making twenty-eight of these in total. Each Venerated One sits on a Lotus Blossom Throne,[137] and each throne boasts seven depictions of the Bodhisattva Cundi among its leaves.[138] On each leaf there sits a Buddha, and of these there could not be fewer than ten thousand. All of this was put into effect by Cisheng and the imperial palaces.[139]

Prior to the construction of his four-faced hall, Pumen crafted a model of it out of wood. Within its four corners and four beams not even the most

---

133   神宗賜寺額曰慈光 The name *Ciguang* 慈光 implies the compassion both of the Empress Dowager as mother of the Ming state, and of the Buddha.

134   神宗賜寺額曰慈光降敕護持 The gazetteers disagree over the exact dates here. According to the *Huangshan zhi dingben* (p. 41), the tablet was bestowed in the autumn of the *xinhai* 辛亥 year (1611). The *Huangshan zhi* (1988) dates the tablet (p. 233) to the spring of the 40th year of the Wanli reign (1612), with the gifts of robes and staffs coming the following year. About the decree Qian is fairly vague here, it seems that Compassionate Radiance was officially designated as a temple for the protection of the dynasty, so that there would have been an understanding that prayers and readings would be performed regularly for the health of the state in general and individuals in the imperial family in particular, in exchange for the financial support the temple received. The Qing traveller Huang Zhaomin 黃肇敏 dates this designation to the 36th year of the Wanli reign (1608), but this cannot be correct ("Huangshan jiyou" 黃山紀遊, reproduced in Lao Yian 勞亦安 ed., *Gujin youji congchao* 古今遊記叢鈔 [Taibei: Zhonghua shuju, 1961], Volume 3, pp. 13–41).

135   慈聖所欽賜裝池也 Qian uses the slightly obscure term 裝池 here, which probably accounts for the variation between the texts. LYM prefers 裝滲, while in its reprinting of this omitted section, the *Huangshan zhi dingben* (pp. 41–2) prefers 裝潢. All three compounds denote here the preparation of volumes into a decorated boxed set. According to the *Huangshan zhi dingben* (p. 41), the set filled 678 cases 函.

136   四面金像 The figure seems to have been a depiction of the four-faced Vairocana 四面毘盧遮那, a form of the Buddha related to the sun, the all-pervasive spiritual body of Buddha-truth.

137   Emended to 像七層層四尊凡二十有八尊有蓮花坐 following LYM and WKQ. The original *SBCK* text reads 層有蓮花坐, a grammatically plausible alternative, which would give seven thrones. I am assuming that each of the *zun* 尊 (Venerated Ones) would have sat on its own Lotus Blossom Throne, giving a total of 28 (a reading supported both by Huang Zhaomin's 黃肇敏 account [*Gujin youji congchao*, Volume 3, p. 21], and Min Linsi's paraphrasing of Qian's passage [*Huangshan zhi dingben*, p. 42]). I am therefore reading 尊 for 層.

138   準提 The Bodhisattva Cundi was traditionally represented with eighteen arms and three eyes, one of Avalokiteśvara's 觀音 retinue. She is associated with Marīcī 摩利支, in Daoist terms the Queen of Heaven 天后.

139   慈聖及兩宮所施造也 Chou Tao-chi (*DMB*, Volume 1, pp. 856–9) notes that the patronage of Buddhist temples by the Empress Dowager Cisheng was opposed on financial grounds by Grand Secretary Zhang Juzheng 張居正. In his essay, Xie Zhaoshen actually records a conversation he had with Pumen about the construction of this Buddha figure (*Huangshan zhi* [1667], pp. 489–90; *Huangshan zhi dingben*, p. 248).

trifling detail was neglected,[140] and this model is still stored here today.[141] Pumen single-handedly created the monastic presence on this mountain,[142] establishing here the burning lamp.[143] At that time, as the imperial palaces bestowed their compassionate favour, this temple bulged with treasures from within the four seas,[144] truly transporting the heavenly realm of Tushita down to this world of man.[145] The transformation of a wasteland of thorn and brushwood into a Buddha-realm was a marvellous achievement indeed.

These days, with military unrest daily more worrying, and famines raging year after year, the tolling of the great fish bells has all but ceased,[146] and there is barely even enough coarse grain to go around. Recalling the drums and bells that would ring out from the Palace of Eternal Faith,[147] and counting up the monasteries that once stood in Luoyang,[148] one cannot but

---

140 普門將構四面殿手削木為式四阿四霤不失毫髮 A good example of the gradual development of a descriptive tradition relating to the mountain. Qian's description as usual owes much to that of Xie Zhaoshen, who describes the corners and beams of the model shown to him by Pumen (XZS, pp. 489–90). Qian's own text seems also to have had a more direct influence on Huang Zhaomin 黃肇敏, who reproduces Qian's line almost verbatim: 擬構四佛殿手削木為式四阿四霤 不失累黍 (Gujin youji congchao, Volume 3, p. 22).

141 普門安公者……今藏弆焉 This entire passage is missing from MLS, but is reproduced in juan 2 of the Huangshan zhi dingben, pp. 41–2. There is some slight variation between Qian's text and the text that appears in Min's gazetteer (as in the case of the term 裝潢, noted above). According to Xie Zhaoshen, Pumen's model was "no more than four feet tall" 高不盈四尺 (XZS, pp. 489–90).

142 普門隻手開山 MLS reads 普門安公隻手開山, a transmission error probably caused by the extraction of the preceding passage (which begins 普門安公者).

143 燼然建立 Establishing the burning lamp, that is, the light that allows us to overcome our ignorance of the Buddha and his teachings.

144 四海之物力充牣 Reading 四海 as 四海之內, i.e., from all over the empire.

145 移兜率于人間 In Buddhist cosmography Tushita 兜率 is the realm in which Maitreya, the Bodhisattva who will be the next Buddha, waits for his coming. This idea was evidently a favourite of Qian's, as it appears in slightly altered forms in several other essays in the Muzhai chuxueji (see QMZQJ, Volume 3, pp. 1718, 1721, 1724 and 1743).

146 鐘魚 The great wooden fish (also 魚板 or 木魚) were traditionally used in monasteries to announce meal times. In the case of bronze bells at least, it is possible to read the decline here quite literally; monastic bells were prone to being confiscated by the Ming state to make weapons during protracted military campaigns (see Brook, Confusions of Pleasure, pp. 156–7).

147 長信 The Palace of Eternal Faith served as the residence of the Empress Dowager during Han times. Among writings on the palace, see Li Bai's 李白 poem "Changxingong" 長信宮 (Li Taibai quanji, Volume 2, pp. 1173–4).

148 數伽藍于雒陽 A reference to Yang Xuanzhi's 楊衒之 (d. 555? CE) Luoyang qielan ji 洛陽伽藍 記 [Account of Monasteries in Luoyang], completed in 547 CE. The city of Luoyang was the Northern Wei capital between 493 and 534 CE, and, at its peak, was home to over a thousand Buddhist monasteries, the positions and histories of which were later recorded by Yang. For full translations of this important text, see W. F. J. Jenner's Memories of Loyang: Yang Hsüan-chih and the Lost Capital (493–534) (Oxford: Clarendon Press, 1981) and Yi-t'ung Wang trans., A Record of Buddhist Monasteries in Lo-yang (Princeton: Princeton University Press, 1984).

sigh for one's own ruined and disordered age. Such, indeed, was the cause of Li Gefei's lament over the famous gardens.[149]

Pumen's stūpa sits at the rear of the Temple of Compassionate Radiance. The white rocks have all been worn down;[150] rinsed smooth by a stream of floating peach blossoms that winds its way around in front of the stūpa. In comparison to this, one can see that the graveyards of the world of man, with their tomb mounds that look like Mount Qilian, are truly contemptible.[151]

---

149 斯李文叔之所以致慨于名園也 A reference to Li Gefei's 李格非 (*zi* Wenshu 文叔; 1041?–1101) *Luoyang mingyuan ji* 洛陽名園記 [Account of Famous Gardens in Luoyang], written in 1095, a treatment of nineteen celebrated gardens of the former capital, to which Li adds the following important commentary (in Philip Watson's rendering): "Luoyang lies at the centre of the world. It holds the strategic pass between Mount Yao and Min Lake, and sits astride the access point to Qin and Long; and was the old stamping ground of Zhao and Wei. So it is a place that is bound to be contended over from all quarters. When the situation in the world is normal, then this all ceases, but if there are disturbances Luoyang is the first to experience war. This is why I hold that the prosperity or decline of Luoyang is an indication of whether the world is well governed or in chaos. For in the Zhenguan (627–49) and Kaiyuan (713–41) periods of the Tang dynasty there were reputed to have been more than a thousand residences and palaces built by senior ministers and imperial relatives in the Eastern Capital (of Luoyang). When chaos and disruption set in, and these continued in the miseries of the Five Dynasties (907–60), the lakes and pools, bamboos and trees were trampled by the carriages of war, and abandoned to become a wasteland. The high pavilions and great gazebos were consumed in smoke and fire and turned to ashes. They were annihilated and destroyed with the Tang dynasty itself, and not a wrack remained. That is why I hold that the rise and fall of these gardens is an indication of the prosperity or decline of Luoyang. So if the good government or chaos of the world may be known since they are indicated by the prosperity or decline of Luoyang; and if the prosperity or decline of Luoyang may be known since they are indicated by the rise and fall of its gardens, then my writing of this Record of Famous Gardens has surely been to some purpose." ("Famous Gardens of Luoyang, by Li Gefei: Translation with Introduction," *Studies in the History of Gardens and Designed Landscapes* 24 (1) (2004): 38–54. For an alternative translation of this passage, see Stanislaus Fung's "Longing and Belonging in Chinese Garden History," in Michel Conan ed., *Perspectives on Garden Histories* (Washington DC: Dumbarton Oaks, 1999), pp. 205–19. The implication here is clearly that the condition and number of Buddhist monasteries on Yellow Mountain may similarly be used as an index for measuring the health of the Ming state, currently in a period of decline. This passage is the closest Qian comes to commenting on the contemporary social and political landscape; in general the essay remains fairly detached.

150 白石鑿鑿 A phrase borrowed from the *Shijing* 詩經 (唐風・揚之水), which begins: "Spray rises from those waters; / The white rocks are rinsed." 揚之水白石鑿鑿 (Arthur Waley trans., *The Book of Songs* [New York: Grove Press, 1960], p. 70).

151 人世牛眼馬鬣起冢象祁連者方斯薐如亦可感也 Mount Qilian 祁連山 is a vast mountain range that stretches over Gansu and Qinghai Provinces, an area associated with the ancient race of Xiongnu 匈奴 (*qilian* is Mongolian for Heaven). I read the comparison here as referring to the large and perhaps gaudy grave mounds back in the world of man, a contrast to the elegant simplicity of the monk's stūpa. Elsewhere Qian uses the same simile to contrast with his descriptions of other tombs, for which see *QMZQJ*, Volume 2, pp. 1491; Volume 3, pp. 1553, 1694 and 1949.

On this evening, I once again bathed at the Hot Springs, and lodged at Peach Blossom Source Hermitage. The mountain monk who had accompanied me could not bring himself to stay,[152] and as he solemnly took his leave, I sent word to Heavenly Capital, Lotus Blossom and the other peaks, just as the men of Wu say "I will be waiting for word of thee."[153] Wang Zemin of the Yuan era wrote, "Lodging at the Springs Temple, I heard the sound of the birds, chirping away as if echoing each other in song, now *presto*, now *largo*. This bird is called the Mountain Singing Thrush, and off the mountain, there is not one to be seen."[154] I was just then experiencing my own "Southern Shore parting,"[155] so when I heard them I felt a tug at my wretched heartstrings. I bade farewell to Yellow Mountain, and it took a day's effort to return home.

Part VII

When I arrived to ascend this mountain, I first bathed at the Hot Springs and rested at the Peach Blossom Source Hermitage. That night brought heavy rain, and seated in the small tower at White Dragon Pool I was able to follow the progress of the waters as they fell from Heavenly Capital Peak. The rains abated and I began my ascent, with the dense cloud vapours still filling the air, so that as I reached Old Man Peak I could turn

---

152 山僧相送不忍舍 That is, the monk was unwilling to spend too long off the mountain proper, the Hot Springs and the Peach Blossom Source Hermitage being found down in the foothills.

153 如吳人語念相聞也 The *Song shu* 宋書 records the phrase "I'll be waiting for word of thee" 念相聞 as having originated with Zhang Fu 張敷 (*zi* Jingyin 景胤), who used it when parting. (*Song shu* [rpt.; Beijing: Zhonghua shuju, 1974], Volume 5, p. 1396.)

154 元人汪澤民曰宿湯寺聞啼禽聲若歌若答節奏疾徐名山樂鳥下山咸無有 The relevant passage of Wang Zemin's 汪澤民 essay reads (Chinese given where different from that quoted in Qian's text): "At night 夜 I heard the sound of the birds, an extremely strange sound 聲甚異, as if echoing each other in song, now *presto*, now *largo*. This bird is called the Mountain Singing Thrush, and off the mountain, there is not one to be seen." (*Huangshan zhi* [1667], pp. 433–5; *Huangshan zhi dingben*, pp. 205–7.) Min Linsi makes use of parts of Wang's essay in the "Birds" section of the *Huangshan zhi dingben* (p. 60). Jiang Guan 江瓘 also makes use of Wang's words "as if echoing each other in song" 若歌若答 in his 1548 essay (*Huangshan zhi* [1667], pp. 437–9; *Huangshan zhi dingben*, pp. 209–12). 山樂鳥 Mountain Singing Thrush (*Garrulax Poecilorhynchus*) [新志 162–3; 文化 23].

155 南浦之別 A phrase that originates from a line in the *Chuci* 楚辭 (九歌·河伯): "Eastward you journey, with hands stately folded, / Bearing your fair bride to the southern harbour 送美人兮南浦" (Hawkes trans., *Songs of the South*, p. 42). The 南浦, which I have rendered into "Southern Shore," had become a well-known symbol of separation, in this context continuing Qian's metaphor of the various peaks being friends, from whom he must reluctantly part.

and watch the Spreading Sea. Then for three days I roamed this mountain, while the firmament remained boundless and clear, and as on a crisp mid-autumn morning, one could take in a thousand *li* with one glance. In the past, every traveller who climbed Yellow Mountain in spring or summer had the vapours and mists press in all around him, and he could never make out more than a *zhang* from his face. The mountain monks all sighed with wonder at the clear skies that greeted us, something they had never seen before. No sooner had I left the mountain, than the heavy rains returned to saturate everything through, and seeing this, my companions and I congratulated each other even more.[156]

Afterwards, a traveller asked me: "Did you take pleasure in travelling at Yellow Mountain?" I replied, "I took pleasure indeed, but this was not 'travel'." As far as prominence is concerned amongst the Thirty-six Peaks, none can compare with Heavenly Capital and Lotus Blossom. Leaving Fragrance Hamlet, one sees Lotus Blossom Peak standing alone,[157] and reaching White Dragon Pool one sees Heavenly Capital standing right in the centre like a screen. But then one climbs to the Temple of Compassionate Radiance, nestled in between Heavenly Capital and Lotus Blossom, and sees that the separate are in fact connected, introducing themselves like lodgers in an inn.[158] When one rests at Mañjuśrī Cloister, Heavenly Capital arches in from the east like a banner, while Lotus Blossom perches on the right, like a flower unfurling its petals; from here the faces of the two peaks are seen in full. Continuing on, one starts in a new direction, while the shapes of the peaks, like reflections plucked from a mirror, change with every step one takes, their twisting faces becoming the *profils perdus* one could never glimpse by sitting still and merely looking them up and down. The effect of movement cannot be replicated, so there can be no idleness in this type of travel.

Men of former times would say that those gathering medicinal herbs could reach the summit of Heavenly Capital with three days worth of

---

156 甫出山雨復大作淋灕霑溼同游者更相慶也 An echo of an earlier experience described by Wu Tingjian 吳廷簡, for which, see my discussion in Chapter Four.

157 出芳村則蓮花峰離立 Adapted from XZS (p. 489): 是日芳村出村則蓮華諸峰突立.

158 離而又屬顧若宿留 Drawn from two separate lines in Han Yu's 韓愈 important "Nanshan shi" 南山詩, a poem of 102 couplets, for which see Qu Shouyuan 屈守元 and Chang Sichun 常思春 ed., *Han Yu quanji jiaozhu* 韓愈全集校注 (Chengdu: Sichuan daxue chubanshe, 1996), Volume 1, pp. 321–50. For the last phrase I have used the translation of A. C. Graham found in his *Poems of the Late T'ang* (Harmondsworth: Penguin Books, 1965), pp. 77–9.

wrapped provisions.[159] Then, during the reign of the Wanli Emperor, the monks Pumen and Kuoan made the climb one after the other,[160] and their stone stūpas, flags and lanterns still stand there imposingly today. Is it, then, that only those beyond this decaying flesh and these rotting bones can scale these heights, up to which Heaven has not provided a way?[161]

It is said that "Stone Gate is the central peak of Blackmount."[162] The Yellow Mountain Tower in She Prefecture looks north towards this peak, in the contours of which runs a split that resembles a great gate. A poet of the Tang dynasty once said: "In idle moments I rest against the vermilion balustrade gazing to the northwest, / The only fitting name for this is Stone Gate Tower."[163] So the height and shape of Stone Gate Peak has been seen since Tang times from the tower in She Prefecture, but no traveller ever went to investigate, and now even the mountain monks do not know this peak's exact location. Can this really be called "travel"?

---

159 昔人言採藥者裹三日糧達天都頂 Wang Zemin 汪澤民 records in his essay a conversation with a monk, who tells him: "Heavenly Capital Peak is the particularly high one [of a group of three peaks]. At the top there are many well-known medicinal herbs, and those who collect them wrap up provisions and ascend, reaching the summit in three days" 採者裹糧以上三日達峰頂 (*Huangshan zhi* [1667], pp. 433–5; *Huangshan zhi dingben*, pp. 205–7). In his 1548 essay, Jiang Guan 江瓘 also repeats Wang's observation (*Huangshan zhi* [1667], pp. 437–9; *Huangshan zhi dingben*, pp. 209–12).

160 闊菴 Kuoan [定本 106; 新志 234; 導遊 119] is said to have assisted Pumen in the founding of the monasteries built during the Wanli period.

161 夫獨非腐肉朽骨而遂如天之不可升耶 The entry in the *Huangshan zhi dingben* (p. 106) records that Pumen and Kuoan said of the difficult Heavenly Capital: "Man originally had no desire to climb [this peak], but now that a will exists it must be satisfied, so how could Heaven not provide the steps upwards 何天之不可階升?"

162 石門為黟山之中峰 A reference to the *Huangshan tujing* (8a): "[Peak] Number 24: Stone Gate Peak is the central peak of Blackmount" 第二十四石門峰即黟山之中峰. That Qian leaves the name Yishan 黟山 here reinforces my feeling that he intends the line to be read as a quote, and I have translated and punctuated it as such. It is possible, also, that this first use of Yellow Mountain's former name represents Qian's increasing understanding of the landscape, accompanying the slightly more reflective mood that characterises this seventh section of the essay.

163 歙郡黃山樓北瞰此峰峰勢中坼若巨門唐人有詩曰閒倚朱欄西北望只宜名作石門樓 A reference to a poem by Yu Dehui 于德晦 (*fl.* 840?–855?), for which see *Huangshan zhi dingben*, p. 370. Qian also makes use of the rather lengthy title of the poem ("In She Prefecture There is a Yellow Mountain Tower, which Looks North Towards Yellow Mountain, in the Contours of which Runs a Split that Resembles the Form of a Great Gate, So I Composed this Poem to Mark it" 歙郡有黃山樓北瞰黃山山勢中坼若巨門狀因題一絕). Yu's original line uses the name "Great 巨 Gate Tower," and for this reason HM, MLS, LYM, WKQ and LQS all prefer 巨 to 石, correcting Qian's misquotation. Such a solution, however, is possible only if one ignores the argument of the passage, which requires the identification of the "Stone" Gate Tower as early as the Tang period. I have therefore allowed the 石門樓 of the *SBCK* text to stand as Qian's error. Yu's poem does not appear in the *Quan Tang shi* 全唐詩, but is included in *juan* 6 of Wang Zhongmin 王重民, Sun Wang 孫望 and Tong Yangnian 童養年 ed., *Quan Tang shi waibian* 全唐詩外編 (Beijing: Zhonghua shuju, 1982), Volume 1, pp. 133–4.

To *travel* at Yellow Mountain, one would have to wrap up provisions, pull on a pair of grass sandals, and pass away the months and the years with just the mountain monks and the fuel gatherers for travelling companions. Only then might one truly grasp the character of the hills and streams, and know fully the contours of the ridges and peaks.[164] Even then, though, the steepest cliff walls, the stalactite caves, the violet beds of cloud and their azure pillows, the places where the Wild Man drinks,[165] and where Master Ruan sings,[166] would be inaccessible. The peach blossoms flutter as large as fans, the pine flowers wave like banners, the bamboo leaves sit like brimmed hats, and the lotus flowers drift like boats, but one who has not held to an ascetic life will never encounter them.

On the summits of the Thirty-six Peaks, where the vegetation has disappeared without trace, even the gibbons and birds tremble with fear; only those who drive a wind carriage or ride a cloud chariot can reach

---

164 游兹山者必當裏餱糧曳芒屨經年累月與山僧樵翁為伴侶庶可以攬山川之性情窮峰巒之形勝 This sense of the need to spend time learning to understand the mountain seems a reaction against the "recumbent travel" 臥遊 associated with Zong Bing, frequently invoked by Ming travellers (see for example Wu Rixuan's 吳日宣 1609 essay: ["At rest – literally, "sitting or reclining" – "one can visit the various splendours" 可坐臥以覽諸勝; *Huangshan zhi* (1667), pp. 466–71, *Huangshan zhi dingben*, pp. 227–31], and marks something of a shift in the essay, where previously the emphasis had been on the more spiritual aspects of the journey. It echoes Wang Siren's 王思任 praise of the painter Lü Dalai 呂大來, who was said to have "fully understood the personalities [of the various peaks of Nanmingshan 南明山] over the course of the days and years" ("Nanming jiyou xu" 南明紀遊序 in *Wang Jizhong xiaopin*, pp. 174–5), and anticipates Shitao's claim that Yellow Mountain was his teacher, and he the mountain's friend (*Enlightening Remarks on Painting*, Richard E. Strassberg trans. [Pasadena: Pacific Asia Museum, 1989], p. 19).

165 毛人之所飲 Attached to the entry on Stone Gate Peak in the *Huangshan tujing* (8a) is the story that a "wild man" (literally: "hairy man" 毛人) was found and killed at the foot of the peak during the reign of the Dali 大曆 Emperor of the Tang (766–79). The possibility of a wild man roaming around the more inaccessible peaks of Yellow Mountain is hinted at in a few early works, but for some the term seems to refer to the "immortal apes" 仙猿 seldom seen by men, and listed in the "Animals" section of the *Huangshan zhi dingben*, which records that the white ape was dubbed the "snowman" 雪翁 by the monk Pumen (p. 61). Occasional sightings are recorded in the existing essays – Huang Ruheng 黃汝亨 saw one at Lotus Blossom Peak in 1610: "There was an ape as [white as] snow" 有猿如雪 (*Huangshan zhi* [1667], pp. 459–63; *Huangshan zhi dingben*, pp. 232–6) and Yang Bu 楊補 saw one in 1632: "There was a white rock that looked like a man – the monk told me it was an ape" 白石如人僧曰猿也 (*Huangshan zhi dingben*, pp. 277–85).

166 阮公之所歌 The *Huangshan tujing* notes that the seventeenth peak of Yellow Mountain was given the name Ascension 上昇, after a certain Master Ruan 阮公 ascended to the heavens from its summit, giving rise to the "sounds of immortal music" 仙樂之聲 that have been heard there ever since (6b). Late-Ming readers may have interpreted this as a reference to the famous Daoist whistler Ruan Ji 阮籍 (*zi* Sizong 嗣宗; 210–63), said also to be an expert at playing the zither, although I have been unable to find any textual evidence to support this association.

them.[167] The *Book of Liezi* tells of those five mountains across the seas, "the men who dwell on which are all of the race of immortal sages, who fly, too many to be counted, back and forth between the mountains in a day and a night."[168] How do I know that a race of "immortal sages" is not flying back and forth between these Thirty-six Peaks, just as if they were walking the crisscrossed paths between fields? If one day I retire to Peach Blossom Source Hermitage, bathe morning and night at the Hot Springs and live out my life in asceticism, then, perhaps, the spirit of Yellow Mountain might permit me to put on my travelling shoes once again.

Part VIII

The extraordinary sights of Yellow Mountain are its springs, its clouds and its pines. Of extraordinary ponds, there is none to match the White Dragon Pool, and of extraordinary springs, there is none to match the Hot Springs. Both of these are situated in the foothills of Yellow Mountain. The waters of Peach Blossom Source flow down into Hot Springs, and the waters of Milky Water Source and White Cloud Stream flow east into Peach Blossom Stream;[169] indeed, all of the Twenty-four Streams flow down and

---

167 唯乘飆輪駕雲車可以至焉 The cloud chariot was traditionally considered to be a vehicle used by the immortals. One is reminded here of Mary Wollstonecraft's (1759–97) observation in her 1797 essay "On Poetry, And Our Relish for the Beauties of Nature": "The imagery of the ancients seems naturally to have been borrowed from surrounding objects and their mythology. When a hero is to be transported from one place to another, across pathless wastes, is any vehicle so natural, as one of the fleecy clouds on which the poet has often gazed, scarcely conscious that he wished to make it his chariot?" (Janet Todd and Marilyn Butler ed., *The Works of Mary Wollstonecraft: Volume 7* [London: William Pickering, 1989], p. 8). Wollstonecraft anticipated by some 20 years Shelley's declaration: "O that a chariot of cloud were mine! / I would sail on the waves of the billowy wind / To the mountain peak and the rocky lake" (Neville Rogers ed., *The Complete Poetical Works of Percy Bysshe Shelley: Volume 2* [Oxford: Clarendon Press, 1975], p. 316).

168 列子言海外五山所居之人皆仙聖之種一日一夕飛相往來者不可數 Qian draws again directly from the *Liezi* 列子, returning to the passage to which he alluded in Part V, on this occasion citing his source (*Liezi jishi*, pp. 151–2). For a translation of the relevant passage in full, see above.

169 桃源溪水流入湯泉乳水源白雲溪東流入桃花溪 For the direction of watercourses Qian has borrowed again from the *Huangshan tujing*, which tells us: "Below Peach Blossom Peak is Peach Blossom Source and Peach Blossom Stream 有桃花源桃花溪 ... In the third month ... the Stream turns red with blossoms as it flows into the Hot Springs" 水紅流入湯泉 (4a), and later: "Milky Water Source's waters taste like milk, and drop down into White Cloud Stream 乳水源味如乳下有布下水落白雲溪 ... the waters [of which] flow east into Peach Blossom Stream" 水向東流入桃花溪 (5a). 桃花源 Peach Blossom Source [定本 11]; 桃花溪 Peach Blossom Stream [定本 15; 新志 78; 導遊 55; 文化 125–6]; 乳水源 Milky Water Source [定本 12; 新志 76; 導遊 240]; 白雲溪 White Cloud Stream [新志 78–9; 導遊 166].

converge at Yellow Mountain's foot.[170] In the hollows of the mountain it is water that fills its belly,[171] and the waters that shoot out and connect with each other always do so from the belly downwards, so there are springs to be found on the mountain's lower slopes, but none on its upper slopes.

Yellow Mountain is so extremely high that thunder-showers occur in its lower regions.[172] The gathering and dispersing of cloud, the scattering and returning of cloud, all occurs around the mountain's waist. Whenever one observes Heavenly Capital and the other peaks, clouds rise to their waists like belts, but they can never reach the summits. After a while, one is enclosed on all sides, and the lower parts of the peaks are screened by cloud and mist, while all the time their crests remain beyond the reach of the cloud. The clouds that form the Spreading Sea fill the eyes like a rising tide, then suddenly they scatter, like startled ducks or fleeing hares. From the upper regions of Yellow Mountain's peaks, which protrude above the cloud, the firmament seems boundless, as the clouds have nothing to which they can attach themselves.

From the Springs Temple upwards, Yellow Mountain is covered with pines and well-known trees, the juniper, the yew, the cedar and the catalpa,[173] entwined with vines and covered in flatsedge,[174] with everything hidden in the shade of luxuriant foliage.[175] When one climbs Old Man

---

170 二十四溪皆流注山足 For Yellow Mountain's Twenty-four Streams 二十四溪, see *Huangshan zhi dingben*, pp. 14–7.

171 山空中水實其腹 An interesting way of phrasing this idea — probably meant as a playful allusion to Book 1 of the *Daodejing* 道德經: "In governing the people, the sage empties their minds but fills their bellies 實其腹, weakens their wills but strengthens their bones." (D. C. Lau trans., *Tao Te Ching* [Harmondsworth: Penguin Books, 1963], p. 59.)

172 山極高則雷雨在下 The *Huangshan tujing* notes (1a–1b) that: "This mountain is tall enough to brush the heavens and touch the sun . . . [so] thunder showers occur in its lower regions" 雷雨在下.

173 檜柜梗楠 From Jiang Guan 江瓘, who lists these four trees in sequence in his own 1548 essay (*Huangshan zhi* [1667], pp. 437–9; *Huangshan zhi dingben*, pp. 209–12; the latter erroneously reads 梗 for 柜).

174 山皆直松名材……藤絡莎被 From Wang Zemin 汪澤民 (substituting only *cai* 材 for Wang's *sha* 杉 [firs], and inserting Jiang Guan's four trees — see previous note). See *Huangshan zhi* (1667), pp. 433–5; *Huangshan zhi dingben*, pp. 205–7.

175 幽蔭薈蔚 From Liu Zongyuan's 柳宗元 "Yongzhou Longxingsi dongqiu ji" (*Liu Zongyuan ji*, Volume 3, pp. 748–9): "I then had ornamental plants and rocks laid out in criss-cross patterns all over the mound. The ground was now a carpet of green grass, and the trees provided shade and seclusion" 幽蔭薈蔚. (Chang trans., *Nature Poetry*, pp. 123–4.)

Peak,[176] one finds on the overhanging cliffs many strange pines,[177] all protruding from the faces of the rocks. From there on, there is no tree that is not a pine, and no pine that is not exceptional.[178] There are those with trunks no larger than a man's shin, but with roots that twist and coil across a whole *mu*. There are those with roots no longer than a *zhang*, but with branches luxuriant and wide-reaching enough to provide shade for the adjacent paths. There are those that follow the cliffs across gullies, their boughs extending as though suspended in mid-air. There are those that penetrate the fissures in the cliff rocks, bursting out as if they were growing horizontally. There are those that flicker and wave like delicate feather canopies, and those that writhe about like powerful flood dragons. There are those that lie near to the ground, then rise, only to fall back to the ground again. There are those that run sideways, are cut off, and then turn to the side once more.

To the left of the Mañjuśrī Cloister, behind the Cloudladder, the hill drops sharply away, and is covered with pines. Bending this way and that, circling around and back again, they bow to passing travellers, and are a particularly remarkable sight. At the northern cliff of Start to Believe Peak, a pine stretches out towards the southern cliff, allowing travellers to pull themselves across by its branches. This tree is commonly referred to as the "Receiving Pine." To its west a great rock stands like a screen, and with it sits a pine, about three *chi* high, but with branches that stretch for a *mu*. Its twisted trunk bores into the rock face and bursts out again, fracturing the stone from top to bottom and creating a crack that runs down its centre. The branches of this tree intertwine and grab at each other; it is known as the "Seething Dragon Pine."

---

176 陡老人峰 Yang Qinghua's partial translation of Part VIII (Yu, "Sensuous Art," pp. 28–30) begins here and ends at 蔚為奇觀也 (but omits the lines 文殊院之左雲梯之背山形下絕皆有松踞之倚傾還會與人俛仰此尤奇也). As previously noted, Yang's translation unfortunately ignores the context of the extract, and as such its true sense is lost. This first group of characters, for example, is translated as "The top of Old Man Peak was gained," disregarding the purpose of the text — Qian's active narrative ended at Part VI, while here he reflects more generally on a peak he has described in Part III. On the distinction between the narrative and lyric voices in Qian's essay, see Chapter Four.

177 陡老人峰懸崖多異松 From XZS (p. 491).

178 無樹非松無松不奇 Even today various forms of the phrase "No tree is not a pine, no rock is without a pine, and no pine is not exceptional" 無樹非松無石不松無松不奇 are used to describe the pines on Yellow Mountain, although its precise origin is unknown. Wu Rixuan 吳日宣 had noted in 1609, "Every peak boasts trees, while every tree is a pine" 每峰必樹每樹必松 (*Huangshan zhi* [1667], pp. 466–71, *Huangshan zhi dingben*, pp. 227–31). Xu Hongzu 徐弘祖 is so impressed with the pines on his 1616 visit that he exclaims, "Who would have expected that this extraordinary mountain had on its slopes something equally extraordinary?" 不意奇山中又有此奇品也 (*Xu Xiake youji jiaozhu*, Volume 1, p. 19).

At the peaks of Stalagmite Promontory and the Alchemists' Terrace the rocks stand up proudly, connected neither by ridge nor mound of earth. Every rock is crowned by a single pine, like a pin on a head of hair, or a canopy sitting above its carriage. Viewed from afar, they look like the tiny blades of shepherd's purse, pointing this way and that into the clouds. So remarkable, so extraordinary is the scene, that words alone could never describe it.

The Yellow Mountain pines need no earth, and take no more than the bare rock as their soil, while their trunks and bark are also all made from stone. Nourished by rain and clouds, and battered by frost and snow, these pines date back to the very birth of heaven and earth, and flourished throughout the days of antiquity. They really belong with the legendary ointments and jades, with the elixirs and herbs of immortality, for they are certainly no ordinary trees. To think that there are those who want to hack down these trees and shove them into dishes for their own amusement — is this not the vilest of practices?[179]

To the east of the Cloudladder wriggles a long prostrate pine, once hobbled by a thunderbolt. Spanning several dozen *zhang*, its scales and mane writhe about helplessly, and everyone who passes pities its present state.[180] When I saw it, however, I laughed, saying: "The Creator of All Things directed this piece of theatre, obstructing and bending the pine as He saw fit. In centuries to come, who knows what kind of extraordinary sight all these forks and bends will have created? The flower sellers of

179 顧欲斫而取之作盆盎近玩不亦陋乎 Feng Mengzhen 馮夢禎 had noted in 1605 that a market existed for Yellow Mountain pines for this purpose, observing that collectors would buy them "for their [miniature] dish scenes" 以充盆景 (*Huangshan zhi* [1667], pp. 450–2; *Huangshan zhi dingben*, pp. 215–7). The twisted, gnarled character of Yellow Mountain pines made them particularly prized for use in bonsai arrangements, as noted by the Qing writer Shen Fu 沈 復 (*zi* Sanbai 三白, *hao* Meiyi 梅逸; b. 1763), who remarked of a visit to Renli 仁里, Anhui: "We went into the temple and found that the pots of flowers and fruits that had been placed in the main worship hall and the courtyard had been selected for their unique natural shapes 盡以蒼老古怪為佳, instead of having been trimmed and pruned. Most were pines from Yellow Mountain." (Leonard Pratt and Chiang Su-hui trans., *Six Records of a Floating Life* [Harmondsworth: Penguin Books, 1983], p. 115.) See also H. L. Li's *Chinese Flower Arrangement* (Mineola: Dover Publications, 2002), pp. 64–5.
180 鱗鬣偃蹇怒張過者惜之 The use of verbs and adjectives pertaining to dragons to describe the pines occurs frequently in seventeenth-century prose and poetry, Wu Rixuan's 吳日宣 1609 observation being fairly typical: "The pine's branches writhe about, twisting and bending like an old dragon" 松枝偃蹇卷曲如老龍 (*Huangshan zhi* [1667], pp. 466–71, *Huangshan zhi dingben*, pp. 227–31). The *Huangshan zhi* (1988) lists four famous pines at Yellow Mountain with "dragon" 龍 in their names (pp. 52–7), including the great Seething Dragon 擾龍 mentioned above.

Wu take old flowering plum branches, bend them, bind them, and at the first sign of spring, show them off as being especially peculiar among their arrangements. Has not this pine simply had its branches bent in the same way by the Creator?"[181] A thousand years from now, there is bound to be someone who will verify these words of mine and laugh about it.

Part IX

The Thirty-six Peaks of Blackmount were all carefully recorded in the *Topographical Classic*,[182] but these days, scholars and officials are unable to settle on all of their names, while monks and shepherds are unable to point out all of their locations. Those peaks that are known, such as Heavenly Capital, Lotus Blossom, Alchemists' and Cinnabar, number no more than ten or so. Stone Man Peak has been mistaken for Old Man Peak,[183] Cloud Gate Peak for Scissors Peak,[184] Folding Screen Peak for Surpassing Lotus Peak, and then there is that tiny mound of earth that has simply assumed

---

181 茲松也其亦造物之折枝也與 The Yellow Mountain pine/flowering plum 梅 comparison would later be taken up by Zhang Dai 張岱: "[Western Creek] is a most secluded spot, with many ancient flowering plums with dwarf trunks. Twisted and bent, they greatly resemble Yellow Mountain pines. Enthusiasts come here and buy the very smallest trees to put in their dishes as miniature scenes." 以作小景 (Xia and Cheng ed., *Taoan mengyi / Xihu mengxun*, p. 269).

182 黟山三十六峰詳載圖經 The *Huangshan tujing* records Yellow Mountain's "Thirty-six Peaks" as follows: (1) Alchemists' 煉丹峰; (2) Heavenly Capital 天都峰; (3) Blue Phoenix 青鸞峰; (4) Amethyst 紫石峰; (5) Alms Bowl 鉢盂峰; (6) Peach Blossom 桃花峰; (7) Cinnabar 硃砂峰; (8) Lions' 獅子峰; (9) Lotus Blossom 蓮花峰; (10) Stone Man 石人峰; (11) Amidst the Clouds 雲際峰; (12) Folding Screen 疊障峰; (13) Fuqiu 浮坵峰; (14) Rongcheng 容成峰; (15) Yellow Emperor 軒轅峰 [after the original name (*ming*) of the emperor]; (16) Immortals 仙人峰; (17) Ascension 上昇峰; (18) Clear Pool 青潭峰; (19) Verdant 翠微峰; (20) Immortals' Capital 仙都峰; (21) Gazing at Immortals 望仙峰; (22) Ninth Dragon 九龍峰; (23) Sacred Spring 聖泉峰; (24) Stone Gate 石門峰; (25) Chess Rock 棊石峰; (26) Stone Pillar 石柱峰; (27) Cloud Gate 雲門峰; (28) Waterfall 布水峰; (29) Stone Bed 石床峰; (30) Rosy Cloud 丹霞峰; (31) Beyond the Clouds 雲外峰; (32) Pine Forest 松林峰; (33) Violet Cloud 紫雲峰; (34) Lotus 芙蓉峰; (35) Flying Dragon 飛龍峰, and (36) Precious Stone 采石峰. My preferred edition (Anhui, 1935) of the *Huangshan tujing* text omits (20) Immortals' Capital 仙都峰 from the sequence (19 is followed by 21), and I have supplemented the list by consulting the new Xianzhuang shuju 線裝書局 edition (*Zhonghua shanshuizhi congkan* 中華山水志叢刊 [Beijing, 2004], Volume 15, pp. 229–39). The *Huangshan zhi dingben*'s listing of the peaks is an identical sequence.

183 石人峰 Stone Man Peak [定本 7; 新志 29; 導遊 169–70; 文化 68].

184 雲門峰謁為剪刀 At least two of Qian's predecessors had noted this confusion – Feng Mengzhen 馮夢禎 in 1605: "Cloud Gate has two cliffs that seem to form a gate, through which the clouds move. It is commonly called Scissors Peak" 雲門者兩山如門雲通其中俗名剪刀峰 (*Huangshan zhi* [1667], pp. 450–2; *Huangshan zhi dingben*, pp. 215–7), and Zhu Bao 朱苞 (*zi* Yijiu 以九, *hao* Ban'an 半庵) in 1630: "The peak is commonly referred to as Scissors Peak, but upon investigation of the chronicles and gazetteers, I found it to be called Cloud Gate" 俗呼為剪刀峰之傳志則稱為雲門 (*Huangshan zhi dingben*, pp. 260–6).

the name — Start to Believe Peak. There is a poem by Li Bai titled "On Seeing Wen the Recluse Back to Yellow Mountain's White Goose Peak,"[185] but today this peak is not listed as one of the Thirty-six. Those that are part of the Thirty-six Peaks are all at least seven hundred *ren* high, while the numerous other peaks that rise to only two or three hundred *ren* are not accorded this placement,[186] and White Goose Peak may well be one of these others.[187]

When the Master of Tranquillity Pumen fulfilled the destiny afforded him in his vision by establishing the Mañjuśrī Cloister,[188] he gave the ridge behind Old Man Peak the name Three Contemplations Ridge.[189] After

---

185 李太白有詩送溫處士歸黃山白鵝峰 For the poem, "Song Wen chushi gui Huangshan Baiefeng jiuju" 送溫處士歸黃山白鵝峰舊居 (the final two characters are omitted by Qian here) see *Li Taibai quanji*, Volume 2, pp. 770–3 (the poem is also included in *Huangshan zhi dingben*, p. 367). It is interesting to note that Li refers in his poem to thirty-two peaks, rather than the now famous Thirty-six. 白鵝峰 White Goose Peak [新志 17; 導遊 86–7; 文化 53].

186 其外諸峰高二三百仞者不與焉 The *Huangshan tujing* appends the following note to its descriptions of the Thirty-six Peaks: "The heights of the Thirty-six Peaks given here are the measurements from their ridges 脊 upwards, and follow the *Shanhaijing*'s standard that one *ren* 仞 is equal to eight *chi* 尺. Apart from these Thirty-six, the numerous other peaks that rise to only two or three hundred *ren* high 諸峰高二三百仞者, and the myriad cliffs, caves, streams and springs that are not mentioned in the classics or biographies, are not recorded here" (10a). See also my discussion in Chapter Two.

187 李太白有詩送溫處士歸黃山白鵝峰今不在三十六峰之列蓋三十六峰皆高七百仞以上其外諸峰高二三百仞者不與焉白鵝峰或亦諸峰之一也 Wang Qi cites these lines, emended slightly, as part of his annotations to Li Bai's poem (*Li Taibai quanji*, Volume 2, pp. 770), but with a spurious attribution to Qian Baichuan 錢百川 (*zi* Dongzhi 東之, *hao* Hanzhai 寒齋), in what I interpret to be a fascinating example of the wide-reaching effects of Qing censorship policies during the eighteenth century. The 1977 editor of the collection notes in the Publisher's Introduction 出版說明 (pp. 9–10) that the first (1758) version of Wang's preface acknowledged that Qian Qianyi's commentaries on Du Fu had informed his own study of Li Bai's poetry, but that in the subsequent edition (1761), Qian's name had been removed. It seems likely that the attribution of Qian Qianyi's comments to Qian Baichuan was the product of an expedient alteration made during the publication of the later edition of the text, on which the present Zhonghua shuju edition is based. Although many corrections are said to have been made to the text during the preparation of the 1977 edition, this spurious attribution is one point of interest that seems to have gone unnoticed.

188 自普門安公乘宿夢因緣闢文殊院 Paraphrasing XZS (p. 492): 是曰文殊院蓋普師乘宿夢闢焉.

189 三觀嶺 The entry in the *Huangshan zhi dingben* (p. 33) records the origin of the name Three Contemplations 三觀 thus: "Pumen said, "To the east this ridge looks upon Mañjuśrī Cloister. The contemplation of Mañjuśrī is the contemplation of wisdom 智觀. To the northwest it looks upon Great Pity Crest. The contemplation of Avalokiteśvara is the contemplation of pity 悲觀. And to the west, it looks upon Samantabhadra Hall 普賢殿. The contemplation of Samantabhadra is the contemplation of resolve" 願觀 [Samantabhadra was said to be the Bodhisattva of ten resolves 十大願]. He therefore fixed [the ridge] with the name Three Contemplations." See also 新志 99; 文化 86.

this, those sites that had been given names — such as Illumination Crest, Heavenly Sea and Lions' Grove — became numerous, all taking their names in accordance with the wishes of the Mañjuśrī Cloister monks. After Pumen had established his monastery, the people of Huizhou began to use Yellow Mountain to seduce tourists, and the carriages now pass each other in an endless procession to and from the mountain.[190] Wherever the tourists go every tree has a carved tablet, and every cliff face has been inscribed with a name.[191] The green peaks and the white rocks have suffered the grief of having their skin stripped and faces branded,[192] and indeed, in the future even the Thirty-six Peaks will lose the ability to protect their former selves.

The crest of Yellow Mountain is referred to as the "Sea," and the *li* or so from Level with Heaven Promontory around to Alchemists' Peak is called "Sea Gate." Around Illumination Crest is the "Anterior Sea," while Lions' Grove marks the "Posterior Sea," which stretches out for perhaps several *li*. If it were the height and sheerness of this mountain that caused its lowlands to be called "seas," then would not the top of Splendour Mountain, "enclosed by high cliffs, one stunning ridge rising above the last,"[193] be called "Splendour Sea"? Or if it were the rising vapours, filling the eyes with waves of cloud that have been called a "sea," then would not the cloud at Mount Supreme, "pounding the rocks and rising, pressing together in a tiny mass"[194] be called the "Supreme Sea"? To call a mountain

---

190 普門開山之後徽人以黃山媚客輲車輴軒至止相望 MLS omits Qian's clause about the "seduction" of tourists (徽人以黃山媚客), a somewhat unflattering description that Min perhaps felt inapposite to the purpose of his gazetteer.

191 所至輙樹眉顏額磨厓題名 For a list of the inscriptions on Yellow Mountain, some of which are no longer extant, see *Huangshan zhi* (1988), pp. 107–25.

192 青峰白石有剝膚黥面之憂 Qian borrows here from an essay by Yuan Hongdao 袁宏道 (*Yuan Hongdao ji jianjiao*, Volume 1, pp. 457–9): "The Buddha speaks of every evil deed receiving retribution . . . What crimes have the green hills and the white rocks committed, that their faces are branded and their skin slashed 青山白石有何罪過無故黥其面裂其膚? The practice is truly inhumane." See my discussion in Chapter Four.

193 華山之頂高嵓四合重嶺秀起 A direct quote from the "Huashan ji" 華山記, an otherwise unknown work cited in *juan* 7 of the *Yiwen leiju* 藝文類聚, compiled by Ouyang Xun 歐陽詢 around the year 620 (rpt.; Wang Shaoying 汪紹楹 ed. [Shanghai: Guji chubanshe, 1982], Volume 1, p. 132).

194 泰山之雲觸石而出膚寸而合 A direct quote from *juan* 5 of the *Gongyang zhuan* 公羊傳, a commentary on the *Chunqiu* 春秋. See He Xiu's 何休 (129–182 CE) *Chunqiu Gongyang jingzhuan jiegu* 春秋公羊經傳解詁 (rpt.; Shanghai: *SBCK* edition), p. 47. The phrase also appears in *juan* 13 of the *Huainanzi* 淮南子 (*Huainanzi yizhu*, p. 661).

a sea, and to call a sea yellow, are errors that have no canonical basis. These should be excised from all texts, so that the spirit of Yellow Mountain may be cleansed through.

Ever since it was recorded in the *Classic of Mountains and Seas* and in the *Classic of Waterways*[195] that Three Heavenly Sons Screen is also called Three Heavenly Sons Capital,[196] the compilers of the gazetteers have held many varied and conflicting views.[197] There was one commentator who made sense of it all by saying that "Leading Mountain acts as the head, Blackmount acts as the spine, and Great Screen Mountain acts as the rump,"[198] and this, indeed, is how it appears. Wu Shixian, an old man from Xin'an, says: "The highest peak of Yellow Mountain is called Three Heavenly Sons Capital, and in every direction it is protected by a screen. In the Wu District there is a Three Heavenly Sons Screen, which is the southern screen. Hermitage Mountain is also called Three Heavenly Sons Screen, so this is the western screen. In Jixi County there is Great Screen,

---

195 山海經水經 The punctuation added in LYM and WKQ (《山海經・水經》) is rather misleading here, suggesting that the *Shuijing* 水經 is a part of the *Shanhaijing* 山海經, which is not only incorrect but also ignores Qian's reference to authorship below. The *Shuijing* now exists only as part of Li Daoyuan's 酈道元 (*zi* Shanchang 善長; d. 527) annotations, *Shuijing zhu* 水經注 (on the separation of text and commentary in this work, see Hu Shih's "A Note on Ch'üan Tsu-wang, Chao I-ch'ing and Tai Chên: A Study of Independent Convergence of Research as Illustrated in Their Works on the *Shui-ching chu*," in *ECCP*, pp. 970–82).

196 自山海經水經紀三天子鄣亦曰三天子都 The relevant passage in the *Shanhaijing* 山海經 occurs in the "Eastern Regions Within the Seas" 海內東經 chapter, and reads: "The River Lu 廬 comes out of Three Heavenly Sons Capital 三天子都 and enters the Yangzi west of Peng Marsh 彭澤. One author says that [Three Heavenly Sons Capital] is [Three] Heavenly Sons Screen 一曰天子鄣." (*Shanhaijing jiaozhu*, p. 332.) The *Shuijing* 水經 records the following entry: "The waters of the River Lu 廬 come out of Three Heavenly Sons Capital 三天子都, flow north through the west of Peng Marsh County 彭澤縣, and continue north into the Yangzi," while Li Daoyuan's appended commentary refers to the passage (above) in the *Shanhaijing* (Tan Shuchun 譚屬春 and Chen Aiping 陳愛平 ed., *Shuijing zhu* 水經注 [Changsha: Yuelu shushe, 1995], p. 575).

197 地志家紛紛聚訟 For a sense of the scholarly reaction to this passage by various annotators, see *Shanhaijing jiaozhu*, pp. 268, 332–4 and 458–9. The many variant interpretations evident in the sixteenth and seventeenth-century essays I have examined as part of the present study point to general confusion as to the precise meaning of these passages.

198 有疏通之者曰率山為首黟山為背大鄣為尻 The commentary referred to here is unknown to me, but resembles in theme an essay written in the early sixteenth century by Wang Xun 汪循, in which these three mountains are identified as being of the same branch. See "You Shuaishan ji" 遊率山記 in *Gujin youji congchao*, Volume 3, pp. 26–9. By contrast, in his 1532 essay, Wang Xuanxi 汪玄錫 sees Great Screen and Leading Mountain to be one and the same 大鄣山又名率 山 (*Huangshan zhi* [1667], pp. 435–6; *Huangshan zhi dingben*, pp. 208–9).

which is the northeast screen. So Heavenly Capital acts as the capital for the sons of Heaven, while Leading Mountain, Hermitage Mountain and Great Screen act as that capital's screens. This is what was meant by the commentaries of both Bo Yi and Sang Qin,[199] and by the historical anecdotes of Blackmount."

Wu Shixian is indeed the most extraordinary of men.[200] He dwells in a little four-walled[201] nest of books,[202] and when he sees a wealthy man from

---

199 此伯益桑欽之疏義 Authorship of the *Shanhaijing* 山海經 was conventionally ascribed to Yu Yu 禹 and his assistant Yi 益 (*fl.* c. 2000 BCE; later usually Bo Yi 伯益 as Qian has it here, the term *bo* 伯 probably originally being meant as a title), after this view was put forward by the Han editor of the text, Liu Xiu 劉秀 (Liu Xin 劉歆; 53 BCE–23 CE). Bo Yi is a somewhat problematic figure in Chinese history, problematic because he seems to have become at some point a fusion of at least two distinct figures, for a discussion of which see Birrell's *Chinese Mythology*, pp. 58–9, and the brief note in James Legge's translation of the *Shujing* 書經 in his *Chinese Classics*, Volume 3 (1), p. 46. For English translations and more extensive treatments of the authorship of the text, see Anne Birrell trans., *The Classic of Mountains and Seas* (Harmondsworth: Penguin Books, 1999), pp. xxxviii–xlii, and Strassberg's *Chinese Bestiary*, pp. 3–13. The Han scholar Sang Qin 桑欽 (*zi* Junchang 君長) was traditionally considered to be the author of the *Shuijing* 水經, although this view is no longer held.

200 時憲振奇人也 Probably an allusion to the "Heaven and Earth" 天地 chapter of the *Zhong shuo* 中說, a work apparently compiled by the disciples of Wang Tong 王通 (*zi* Zhongyan 仲淹, posthumous *hao* Wenzhongzi 文中子; 580–617): "Someone asked about Yang Xiong 揚雄 and Zhang Heng 張衡. The Master [Wang Tong] said: 'They were the extraordinary men of ancient times 古之振奇人也. Their thought was exhaustive and their speech was deliberate.'" (Zheng Chunying 鄭春穎 ed., *Wenzhongzi Zhong shuo yizhu* 文中子中說譯注 [Haerbin: Heilongjiang renmin chubanshe, 2002], p. 42.)

201 所居環堵 A reference to the *Zhuangzi* 莊子 (庚桑楚 chapter), which reads: "[Master Gengsang said:] I have heard that the Perfect Man dwells corpse-like in his little four-walled room 尸居環堵之室, leaving the hundred clans to their uncouth and uncaring ways, not knowing where they are going, where they are headed." (Watson trans., *Complete Works of Chuang Tzu*, pp. 248–9.) The phrase came to be synonymous with the poor but virtuous scholar, most famously used by Tao Qian 陶潛 in his "Wuliu xiansheng zhuan" 五柳先生傳: "the walls of his bare rooms 環堵蕭然 no longer afforded shelter from wind or sun" (*Tao Yuanming ji*, pp. 175–6).

202 巢書 An allusion to Lu You's 陸游 (*zi* Wuguan 務觀, *hao* Fangweng 放翁; 1125–1210) "book nest" 書巢, described by Lu in his essay "Account of the Book Nest" 書巢記: "Within [my room], whether set out on shelves, ranged in front of them, or propped on the bed, whichever way you look, it's all books. Whether I'm eating, drinking, moving about or in repose, even moaning in illness or sighing with depression, I'm always amongst my books. No guests or visitors reach me, my wife and children see nothing of me; I'm even unaware of the variations in wind and rain, or thunder and hail. And when, in the midst of all this, I want to get up I'm surrounded by a wild disorder of books, like piles of dry twigs, to such an extent that I can't go anywhere. Then I always laugh at myself and say: "Isn't this what I'd call 'a nest'?" (Philip Watson trans., "Prose Writings of Lu You," *Renditions* 62 [2004]: 7–23 [10]). For the original essay, see *juan* 18 of *Lu Fangweng quanji* 陸放翁全集 (Taibei: Heluo tushu chubanshe, 1975), pp. 105–6.

Xi'nan,[203] he spits in his face and sends him off.[204] I was but a traveller in Xin'an, and yet the people of Xin'an did not know this man's name. It is for this reason that I have chosen to use Shixian's words to complete my account of Yellow Mountain.

---

203 Xi'nan 溪南 and Xin'an 新安 are two distinct districts of old Huizhou.

204 見溪南富人則唾面去之 This line has been excised entirely from MLS; once again it was probably considered inappropriate for the gazetteer context. LYM, rather curiously, prefers 不喜見富人 (" . . . and he doesn't like seeing wealthy men"). The most famous articulation of concerns about the wealthy merchants of Huizhou had come, of course, from Zhang Tao 張濤, compiler of the *Shexian zhi* 歙縣志 of 1609, in which he lamented: "One man in a hundred is rich, while nine out of ten are impoverished. The poor cannot stand up to the rich who, though few in number, are able to control the majority. The lord of silver rules heaven and the god of copper cash reigns over the earth. Avarice is without limit, flesh injures bone, everything is for personal pleasure, and nothing can be let slip. In dealings with others, everything is recompensed down to the last hair. The demons of treachery stalk." (Brook, *Confusions of Pleasure*, pp. 238–9.) The original essay is reprinted in the 1995 edition of the *Shexian zhi* (p. 798).

Conclusion

In the fourth month of the *guimao* 癸卯 year of the Qianlong reign (1783), long after the calamity of 1644 had passed from living memory, the 67-year-old poet Yuan Mei was crossing one of Yellow Mountain's terraces when he came across an ancient pine 古松:

> Its roots grew towards the east; its body fell to the west, while its head faced south, plunging into a rock and emerging from its other side. This rock seemed to be alive and hollow, so that the pine was able to conceal itself within and become one with the rock. The pine seemed afraid of Heaven, not daring to grow upwards, so while it was ten arm spans around, it was barely two feet tall. There were so many other pines of this sort that it was impossible to record them all.[1]

Among the men of his generation, Yuan was the chief inheritor of Gongan values of literary self-expression, and would certainly have read many of the late-Ming essays we have examined here. But travellers in Yuan's world did not need an anthology to recognize the eccentric, serpentine pines that lived in symbiosis with the rocks; by then they had become so much a part of Yellow Mountain lore that it would have been unimaginable to write of them in any other way. The fact that a pine did not dare 不敢 to grow upwards would not have raised an eyebrow among Qian Qianyi and his seventeenth-century contemporaries, but it would certainly have surprised Jing Hao, who, centuries earlier, knew the pine to grow straight and true, "with the virtuous air of a gentleman." Perhaps the clearest indication that Yellow Mountain pines had now been written into élite consciousness is the fact that Yuan Mei describes just one example before moving on to the next stop on his itinerary, as if a detailed description of their now easily recognizable forms had become somewhat redundant.

This study has examined a number of written and visual representations of Yellow Mountain produced mainly during the seventeenth century. I have argued that a far more useful understanding of the *youji* under discussion here is achieved by reading this landscape not so much as an empirically verifiable fact, but as a product of a system of representational practices that developed within the specific social, political, cultural and economic context of late-Ming Jiangnan. Qian Qianyi's essay of 1642 is a narrative of self-realization through ascent, an engagement with a landscape that takes the form of religious pilgrimage, while remaining grounded in orthodox Confucian philosophy. For Qian, Yellow Mountain is a site that can best be understood through text, and he presents the landscape always within the context of his literary heritage. Deliberate emphasis, ambiguity and exclusion are part of the narrative; the story of Qian's engagement with the landscape as presented in "Account of My Travels at Yellow Mountain" differs from that found elsewhere in the *Muzhai chuxueji*, in verse, in preface and in colophon. The writings of previous travellers inform and direct Qian's gaze, and his essay is as much an engagement with a representational tradition as it is an account of neutral observation.

Perhaps the greatest and most fascinating challenge to a reading of Qian's Yellow Mountain essay as a kind of first-hand and objective record is the extent to which the language of his text draws from the writings of others, a fact not immediately obvious to the modern reader of the text in unpunctuated form. A close analysis of the essay reveals significant debts to the works of Qian's literary forefathers, and we need to remind ourselves here that although we might require the help of punctuation and annotations to recognize an allusion to a Daoist text, Qian's contemporary readers, for the most part, did not. Just as at the other side of the Eurasian continent, John Milton (1608–74), whose life also spanned the Ming-Qing transition, could assume that readers of his epic poem would identify Adam's pentametered confession "She gave me of the tree, and I did eat" as being cut from *Genesis* 3:12,[2] so too could Qian know that his own unacknowledged borrowings from Wang Wei, Su Shi or the *Zhuangzi* would be recognized by his peers. Recognition of literary allusions was crucial — not incidental — to the reader's experience of these men's works, and in this sense at least, the heavily annotated form in which I have presented Qian's essay above probably approximates for the modern reader the experience of a seventeenth-century literatus more closely than would the text on its own.

In the final page of the introduction to his anthology of travel writing, Richard Strassberg notes that by the end of the Song period, "a number of influential texts had emerged to form a canon, while the important sites of literary pilgrimage had been mapped and inscribed."[3] This study has attempted to highlight the extent to which travel writing, and indeed, the travel experience itself, was for the late-Ming man-of-letters an engagement with those inscriptions. Recording an appropriate response to a landscape inevitably involved responding to the works of one's literary forefathers, and the *youji* of the period are cluttered with descriptions and expressions cut from centuries of collected writings. At Hengshan 衡山 Xu Hongzu "recall[s] 憶 Li Bai's lines about the sun glistening on the snow of the Five Peaks and blossoms floating over Dongting," a "recollection" cut verbatim from Zhang Juzheng's experience at the same spot.[4] Qian's observation that "two splayed pines shield [Mañjuśrī] Cloister like a feather canopy, and speckled with rocks, its surface looks like a patchwork kasāya" (Part IV) comes straight from the essay of his late friend Xie Zhaoshen. Such instances force us to allow the concept of authorship a more collaborative connotation than it is usually afforded in post-Renaissance Western scholarship, but it is also worth noting here that Qian's Yellow Mountain is partly composed not only by other people, but in many cases *of other landscapes*. Where Qian describes the waters of White Dragon Pool with a line from Liu Zongyuan (Part II), originally written centuries earlier about a site thousands of *li* away, Yellow Mountain becomes part of a complex web of written heritage spanning both time and space.

What we are working towards here is a recognition of the extent to which Qian's text is *textile* in Roland Barthes' sense, and that the narrative is made up of linguistic units that are *déjà lu* (already read),[5] an idea that has gained traction across a number of disciplines. Simon Pugh's understanding of landscape and its representations as "'readable' like any other cultural form,"[6] is taken up in a thoughtful recent study of mountains in Western culture by Robert Macfarlane, who argues that "we read landscapes . . . in the light of our own experience and memory, and that of our shared cultural memory."[7] But the metaphor of reading can only be useful here if it is understood as an *active* process of engagement with a text, rather than a passive acceptance of something pre-existing. Jing Hao knew that representation required selection 取 by the viewer, an idea articulated more recently by another art historian, John Berger, who argued that "to look is an act of choice."[8] I am inclined to think that it is more constructive to understand this Yellow Mountain as a landscape *written* by Qian, through a process in which, as Chu-tsing Li notes of visual arts, "referring to the past for models did not mean a simple process of copying or imitating; rather, the idea of transformation was seen as part of the artist's creative act."[9]

The Yellow Mountain that has been at the centre of this study is a story essentially written by (and for) a small number of élite males, all educated under the same system and all working out of the relatively insular world of late-Ming Jiangnan. While this region undoubtedly included some of the Ming state's largest and most important cities, recent scholarship reminds us that there was also a Ming world on the other side of the Yangzi, and I am acutely aware that my study has been necessarily narrow in terms of its geographical focus.[10] Similarly, if I have said little about what this landscape may or may not have represented for pilgrims, monks, women, innkeepers, porters or chairbearers of the period, it is because, sadly, the absence of literary evidence would make such a study almost impossible. The essays of men such as Qian Qianyi have survived in the public sphere, sometimes against the odds, precisely because their authors held such standing in the world of letters to which they belonged. In an important recent study, W. J. T. Mitchell urges us to think not about what landscape is, but what it *does* in terms of its role as an instrument of cultural power,[11] an approach that might usefully be applied to the way we think about landscape in late imperial China. Imperial rites and inscriptions at mountains had acted as powerful symbols of political authority for centuries before Qian Qianyi ever set foot on Yellow Mountain, and of course, the Kangxi Emperor would later use the landscape of early Qing Nanjing for the same purpose, as Jonathan Hay reminds us.[12] A part of what the present study has attempted to show is that in their privileged ability to experience, interpret and represent landscape in their own terms, men such as Qian Qianyi played an equally important, if slightly more subtle, role in the maintenance of cultural authority in seventeenth-century Jiangnan society.

The story of Yellow Mountain did not, of course, end with Yuan Mei's visit in 1783, although its popularity did fall into decline soon after the turn of the nineteenth century. Its twentieth-century rediscovery (again assisted by infrastructural development) saw the landscape reinvented once again, and the ways in which various competing representations of Yellow Mountain have been complicit in its redefinition as a nationalistic symbol of "Chineseness" might well provide a fruitful area of future scholarship. But while its meaning has shifted, Yellow Mountain does retain something of its late-Ming self. The exceptional 奇 pines are still exceptional, and the bizarre 怪 rocks are still bizarre; visible reminders of seventeenth-century aesthetic sensibilities, and linguistic traces of one landscape's debt to the late-Ming world.

Epilogue

Last year I journeyed to Yellow Mountain, and [later], without measuring myself 不自量度, I recorded my travels over an entire fascicle. Afterwards I greatly regretted doing so . . . and now, I have written this to register my regret, and to counsel those others of this world who love to travel.

Qian Qianyi, "Introduction to Drafts of My Travels in Eastern Yue" 越東遊草引 (1642)[1]

Qian would not have long to dwell on his literary excess. The late-Ming world that he and his peers had known was moving inexorably towards its ignominious collapse, and even on the mountain itself it had been noticeable that "the tolling of the great fish bells ha[d] all but ceased." For the educated élite, the transfer to Qing rule would prove difficult, and for Qian, the resulting posthumous denunciation by the Qianlong Emperor, and censorship of his literary works, would threaten to erase completely his place in the literary canon. "Now Qian Qianyi is already dead . . ." the emperor fumed in 1769,

> . . . and his bones have long ago rotted away. We will let him be. But his books remain, an insult to right doctrines, and a violation of [the principles of] loyalty. How can we permit them to exist and be handed down any longer? They must early be done away with. Now therefore let every governor-general and governor see to it that all the bookshops and private libraries in his jurisdiction produce and send [to the yamen] his [collected

works]. In addition let orders be despatched to small villages, country hamlets, and out of the way regions in mountain fastnesses for the same purpose. The time limit for this operation is two years. Not a volume must escape the burning.[2]

Fortunately for us, this challenge, the greatest yet to Qian Qianyi's inscription into the peaks of Yellow Mountain, ultimately proved unsuccessful.

Appendix A
A Note on the Text

Qian Qianyi's own preface to his "Account of My Travels at Yellow Mountain" 游黄山記 is dated the first month of the *renwu* 壬午 year (1642). If we date the trip itself to the third month of the previous year, then there was an interval of ten months between the journey and the composition of the preface to the essay. While it is possible that the preface was written long after the composition of the rest of the essay, Qian's reference to his "cold window" 寒窗 does suggest that the preface date (i.e. the first month of the year) applies to the entire prose account.

The completed essay in ten parts (including preface) was first published in the *Muzhai chuxueji*, the 110-*juan* collection of Qian's early writings compiled by his friend and pupil Qu Shisi. This collection is almost universally ascribed to the *guiwei* 癸未 year (1643), after Qu Shisi's preface, which bears that date.[1] There is though, considerable evidence to suggest that the project was enlarged after the setting of the table of contents, and that the collection on which presently existing editions are based was not finally completed until the *jiashen* 甲申 year (1644).[2] The preface to the collection written by Cao Xuequan 曹學佺 (*zi* Nengshi 能始, *hao* Shicang 石倉; 1574–1647) is certainly dated 1644, and even allowing for the possibility of its being pre-dated, the collection contains at least one poem written at the start of that year.[3] This poem is attached to *juan* 20下, not mentioned in the table of contents, and sadly no longer evident in Qian Zhonglian's 錢仲聯 Shanghai guji chubanshe 上海古籍出版社 editions (in which 20上 and 20下 are combined). Qu Shisi's preface refers to 100 *juan* only, while the copy later made by Wang Shimin 王時敏 (*zi* Xunzhi 遜之, *hao* Yanke 烟客; 1592–1680) was said to have been based on a manuscript of the same size, suggesting that this was the scope of the original collection as at the ninth month of 1643 (the date of the Qu preface).[4]

At present the *Muzhai chuxueji* exists in two forms. Around the year 1675, Qian's great-great-nephew Qian Zeng 錢曾 (*zi* Zunwang 遵王, *hao* Yeshiweng 也是翁; 1629–1700?) produced an annotated edition, in twenty fascicles, of the poems contained in the *Muzhai chuxueji*, titled *Muzhai chuxueji shizhu* 牧齋初學集詩註 [Annotated Poetry from the *Muzhai chuxueji*].[5] Censorship of Qian Qianyi's works following the Qianlong Emperor's eighteenth-century edicts resulted in a gap of more than two hundred years before, in the second year of the Xuantong 宣統 reign (1910), the original Qu edition and the Qian Zeng commentaries were brought together to form a single text by Xue Fengchang 薛鳳昌 (*zi* Gongxia 公俠, *hao* Suihanzhai 邃漢齋; 1876–1943) at the Suihanzhai 邃漢齋, and published as part of the *Muzhai quanji* 牧齋全集 [Complete Works from Shepherd's Studio], a collection that also included the *Muzhai youxueji* and the *Toubiji* 投筆集 [Abandoned Brush Collection; containing those poems written after 1658 but not included in the *Muzhai youxueji*]. This edition was published by Shanghai's Wenming shuju 文明書局, and reprinted in 1925. Meanwhile, the Shangwu yinshuguan 商務印書館 published a facsimile reprint of the original Qu edition as part of the first series 初編 (1919–22) of the *Sibu congkan* 四部叢刊 collection, ignoring the commentaries by Qian Zeng and the later Suihanzhai synthesis text.

When the Shanghai guji chubanshe brought out a new edition of *Muzhai chuxueji* in 1985, the editor Qian Zhonglian used the Suihanzhai edition as his base text 底本, apparently consulting the *Sibu congkan* edition to make further emendations.[6] This text was republished without alteration in the Shanghai guji chubanshe edition of *Qian Muzhai quanji* 錢牧齋全集 (*QMZQJ*) that appeared in 2003.[7]

For the copy-text (see Appendix B) of my translation of "You Huangshan ji" I have taken the version found in the *SBCK* edition of the *Muzhai chuxueji* (Volume 3, pp. 483–90) as my principal authority, as it is the most readily accessible facsimile reprint of the original Ming edition. The Shanghai guji chubanshe editions, being based on the Suihanzhai synthesis text, have had more opportunity to be altered in transmission, and the inclusion of the Qian Zeng commentaries is in any case unnecessary here, as the prose essays of the *Muzhai chuxueji* were never annotated. I have made some emendations on the basis of reference to the alternative texts (b–j):

(a) **SBCK:** The text of "You Huangshan ji" found in the *Sibu congkan* edition of *Muzhai chuxueji* (Shanghai: Shangwu yinshuguan), Volume 3, pp. 483–90 (see Figure 13). The *Muzhai chuxueji* also appears as Volumes 114–5 of the

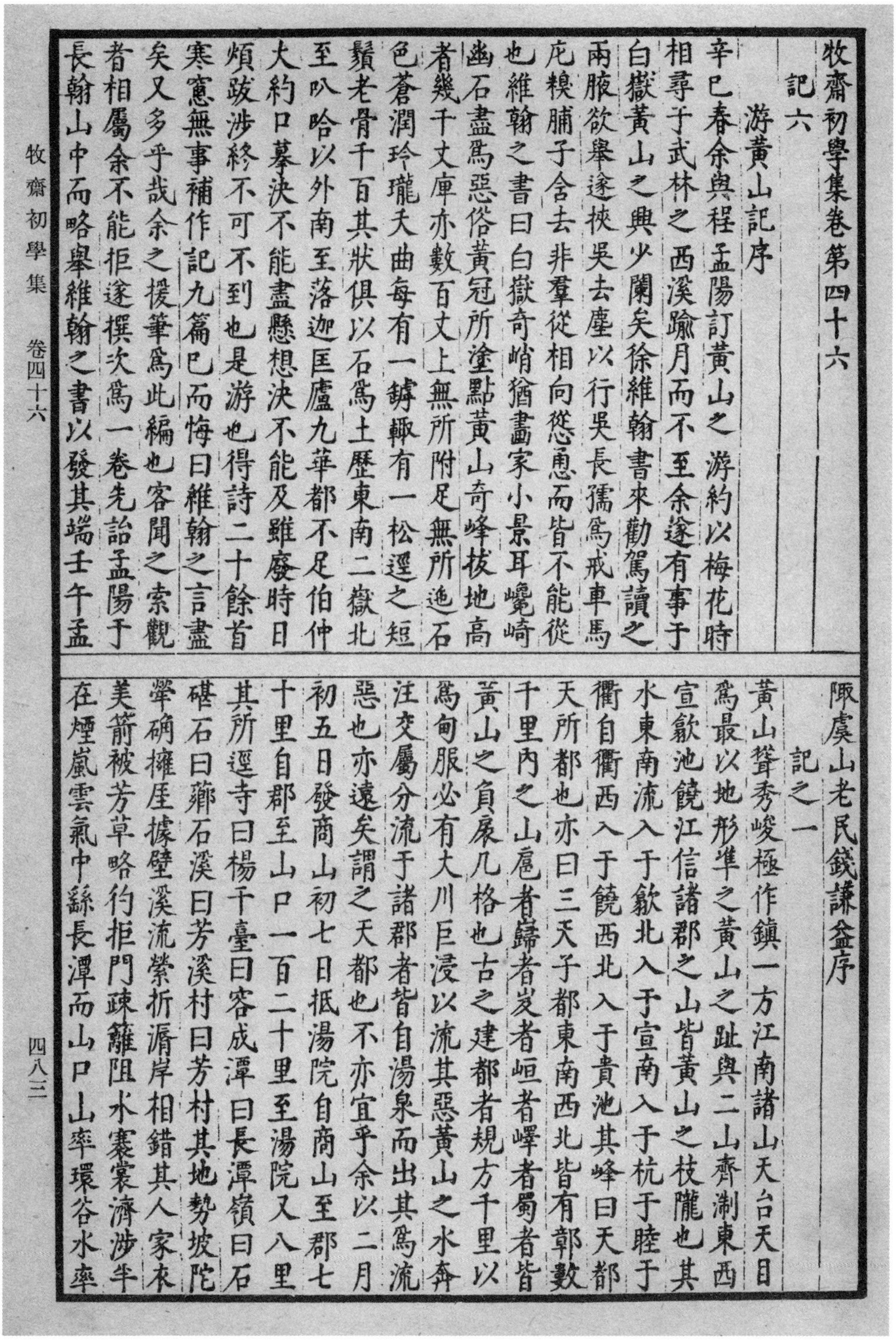

牧齋初學集卷第四十六

記六

游黃山記序

辛巳春余與程孟陽訂黃山之游約以梅花時相尋于武林之西溪踰月而不至余遂有事于白嶽黃山之興少闌矣徐維翰書來勸駕讀之兩腋欲舉遂挾吳去塵以行吳長孺爲戒車馬庀糗糒子含去非羣從相向慫恿而皆不能從也維翰之書曰白嶽奇峭猶畫家小景耳巉崎幽石盡爲惡俗黃冠所塗點黃山奇峰拔地高者幾千丈庳亦數百丈上無所附足無所過石色蒼潤玲瓏夭曲每有一罅輒有一松逕之短鬚老骨千百其狀俱以石爲土歷東南二嶽北至叺哈以外南至落迦匡廬九華都不足伯仲大約口摹決不能盡懸想決不能及雖廢時日煩跋涉終不可不到也是游也得詩二十餘首寒窻無事補作記九篇已而悔曰維翰之言盡矣又多乎哉余之援筆爲此編也客聞之索觀者相屬余不能拒遂撰次爲一卷先詒孟陽于長翰山中而略舉維翰之書以發其端壬午孟陬虞山老民錢謙益序

記之一

黃山聳秀峻極作鎮一方江南諸山天台天目爲最以地形準之黃山之趾與二山齊淛東西宣歙池饒江信諸郡之山皆黃山之枝隴也其水東南流入于歙北入于宣南入于杭于睦于衢自衢西入于饒西北入于貴池其峰曰天都天所都也亦曰三天子都東南西北皆有鄣數千里內之山扈者歸者岌者峘者嶧者蜀者皆黃山之負扆几格也古之建都者規方千里以爲甸服必有大川巨浸以流其惡黃山之水奔注交屬分流于諸郡者皆自湯泉而出其爲流惡也亦遠矣謂之天都也不亦宜乎余以二月初五日發商山初七日抵湯院自商山至郡七十里自郡至山口一百二十里至湯院又八里其所逕寺曰楊干臺曰容成潭曰長潭嶺曰石磋石曰鄉石溪曰芳溪村曰芳村其地勢坡陀犖确擁厓據壁溪流縈折潳岸相錯其人家衣美蔚被芳草略彴拒門疎籬阻水褰裳濟涉半在煙嵐雲氣中緜長潭而山口山率環谷水率

牧齋初學集　卷四十六　四八三

Figure 13: Opening page of Qian Qianyi's 錢謙益 (1582–1664) "You Huangshan ji" 游黃山記, *Muzhai chuxueji* 牧齋初學集, *Sibu congkan* 四部叢刊 (初編) edition (3: 483). Shanghai: Shangwu yinshuguan, 1919–22.

Siku jinhui shu congkan 四庫禁燬書叢刊 series (Beijing: Beijing chubanshe, 2000), another facsimile reprint of the Qu Shisi edition, identical to the *SBCK* text, although the quality of reproduction in the *SBCK* version is far superior.

(b) **SHZ:** The text of "You Huangshan ji" found in the Suihanzhai 邃漢齋 edition of *Muzhai quanji* (Shanghai: Wenming shuju, 1910). The collection spans 40 volumes, of which the first 24 make up the *Muzhai chuxueji*. This edition brings together the original Ming text and annotations made by Qian Zeng to the 20 *juan* of poetry.

(c) **QZL:** The text of "You Huangshan ji" found in Qian Zhonglian ed., *Qian Muzhai quanji* (Shanghai: Guji chubanshe, 2003), Volume 2, pp. 1147–59. The first three volumes are an exact reprint (including pagination) of the *Muzhai chuxueji* (Shanghai: Guji chubanshe, 1985) in three volumes. Based on (and in the case of this essay, identical to) the 1910 Suihanzhai text, but with punctuation added.

(d) **HM:** The text of "You Huangshan ji" found in the 1667 edition of the *Huangshan zhi* 黃山志, compiled by the monk Hongmei 弘眉 (rpt.; Beijing: Xianzhuang shuju, 2004), pp. 500–6. An error with this reprint unfortunately seems to have resulted in the omission of a section of Parts II–III, which should appear between pages 501 and 502.

(e) **MLS:** The text of "You Huangshan ji" included in the 1679 gazetteer *Huangshan zhi dingben* 黃山志定本, compiled by Min Linsi 閔麟嗣 (rpt.; Shanghai: Anhui congshu bianyinchu, 1935), Volume 7, pp. 18b–32b. The original text is reputed to have been replete with errors, which were corrected for the 1686 edition, on which the 1935 version is based. The version of the essay in the new Xianzhuang shuju 線裝書局 edition of this gazetteer (Beijing, 2004, pp. 360–7) is likewise a facsimile reprint of this text. The reproduced and reformatted 1990 edition of this gazetteer (Hefei: Huangshan shushe) is unreliable, and has not been considered for the present purpose.

(f) **LYM:** The text of "You Huangshan ji" included in Li Yimang 李一氓 ed., *Ming Qing ren you Huangshan jichao* 明清人遊黃山記鈔 (Hefei: Anhui renmin chubanshe, 1983), pp. 40–52, which seems to have been based on the HM text.

(g) **WKQ:** The text of "You Huangshan ji" included in Wang Keqian's 王克謙 anthology, *Lidai Huangshan youji xuan* 歷代黃山遊記選 (Hefei: Huangshan shushe, 1988), pp. 102–29. This work represents the only attempt to annotate Qian's essay in its entirety, although a number of deficiencies exist, particularly its failure to identify people mentioned. This text seems to have been based on the LYM text, and these two versions show the most variance with the *SBCK* text.

(h) **BYC:** The text of Parts III and VIII of "You Huangshan ji" included and annotated in Bei Yunchen 貝運辰 ed., *Lidai youji xuan* 歷代遊記選 (Changsha: Hunan renmin chubanshe, 1980), pp. 289–97.

(i) **NQX:** The text of Parts III and VIII of "You Huangshan ji" included and annotated in Ni Qixin 倪其心 ed., *Zhongguo gudai youji xuan* 中國古代遊記選 (Beijing: Zhongguo youji chubanshe, 1985), Volume 2, pp. 255–64.

(j) **LQS:** The text of Parts VII and VIII of "You Huangshan ji" included in the 1988 edition of the *Huangshan zhi* 黃山志 edited by Lü Qiushan 呂秋山 et al. (Hefei: Huangshan shushe), pp. 319–21.

I have left the copy-text unpunctuated, and in the translation above I have generally ignored the various attempts at punctuation offered by the editors of the alternative texts, except in cases in which erroneous punctuation leads to a reading of the text I can show conclusively to be impossible. Where two texts contain different possible forms of the same character (for example, *zhang* [障 and 嶂], *Shizilin* [師子林 and 獅子林]), the *SBCK* version has been preferred, and these cases are not identified in the text below (my reference for such variants is the *Hanyu da cidian* 漢語大詞典 [*pujiben* 普及本; Shanghai: Hanyu da cidian chubanshe, 2000]; those not listed as interchangeable [同 or 通] are given as variants). For a useful discussion of this type of textual variant see Endymion Wilkinson's *Chinese History: A Manual* [Revised and Enlarged] (Cambridge, MA: Harvard University Press, 2000), pp. 417–26. One interesting observation that arises from comparing this type of variant is that no text (with the exception of simplified versions) shows any internal consistency in its choice of characters, so multiple forms of characters such as *yue* (岳 and 嶽), *an* (庵 and 菴), *you* (游 and 遊), *feng* (峰 and 峯) and *hua* (華 and 花), appear throughout individual texts. As always, where this occurs, the form of the character present at that specific point in the *SBCK* text has been retained.

Of the genuine variants found the majority fall under one of the following identifiable categories:[8]

(a) Substitutions of similar graphic forms: e.g. BYC reads 丈 for 文 (Part III); LYM reads 北 for 比 (Part VI).

(b) Substitutions due to similarities in sound: e.g. LYM reads 費 for 廢 (Preface); WKQ reads 紋 for 文 (Part III).

(c) Substitutions to improve the sense of the text: e.g. LYM reads 滲 for 池 in the unusual compound 裝池 (Part VI).

(d) Excisions of text where those lines are reproduced elsewhere: e.g. MLS omits the lines 普門塔在寺後白石鑿鑿桃花流水圍繞塔前人世牛眼馬鬣起冢象祁連者方斯蔑如亦可感也 and reproduces them in another part of the gazetteer (Part VI).

(e) Excisions of text where those lines are inappropriate or taboo: e.g. MLS omits the line 徽人以黃山媚客 (Part IX); the omission of all mention of Shao Liangqing 邵梁卿 and Youqing 幼青 in LYM may also be an occurrence of this (Part II).

(f) Misplacement of text after an excision: e.g. MLS omits a passage beginning with 普門安公者, and then erroneously begins the following passage with 普門安公隻手開山 (Part VI).

(g) Inversion of characters: e.g. QZL inverts the characters 枝扶 to produce the phrase 而扶枝疎蔽道旁, thus breaking up the compound 扶疎 (Part VIII).

(h) Inversion of characters and reading phrases to improve the sense of the text: e.g. MLS and LYM invert 百千 to produce the more pleasing 千百 in the phrase 千百年 (Part VIII).

Many of the character variants found in the different texts are minor and become obscured in translation, and these, with the exception of those of particular interest, have been included only in the following appendix, rather than as annotations to the translated text. The focus of the present study is unapologetically literary, and in the absence of an annotated critical edition of the *Muzhai chuxueji*, any attempt at a definitive textual analysis, starting with manuscripts, would fall well beyond the scope of this project. Nevertheless, the establishment of the stable copy-text is a critical foundation on which the present study is based, and the variants present in the consulted texts do, one feels, have much to say about the writing and editorial processes of late imperial China.

The accidental or deliberate alteration of texts during their transmission has, of course, been a concern for generations of literary critics. The Tang calligrapher Li Yangbing's 李陽冰 (*zi* Shaowen 少溫; *fl.* 765–80) call for the creation of a set of stone classics, which "a hundred generations hence would still require no additions or erasures 無所損益,"[9] is an early instance of recorded anxiety over the accuracy of important texts that would only deepen as the decades passed. Song critics such as Ye Mengde 葉夢德 (*zi* Shaoyun 少蘊, *hao* Shilin 石林; 1077–1148) were already lamenting that from the late tenth century on, the woodblocks used by the ever-expanding print industry were riddled with errors: "But that generation accepted woodblock texts as correct, while the manuscripts of collectors have been lost with every passing day, and so the errors can never be corrected."[10] By the Wanli period, Chen Jiru was complaining that after several rounds of correction and reprinting, a manuscript on which he was working still contained two or three typographical errors for every hundred characters 魯魚帝虎百有二三.[11]

Five decades on, Fredson Bowers' (1905–91) famous lament that the existing texts of most of the great works of English literature are now "inexcusably corrupt" should still serve as a sobering warning.[12] While the pejorative analysis of textual variance implied by the term "corrupt" is perhaps not a particularly useful way to approach the issue (particularly in the Chinese tradition),[13] the fact that we still read works of literature from editions that contain no textual analysis or that have been emended without editorial comment, cannot but give pause to the literary critic (or indeed, to the critic of visual arts, as James Fenton reminds us).[14] But despite such warnings, I admit to feeling some surprise on finding that of the ten distinct versions of Qian Qianyi's "You Huangshan ji" I consulted during this study, only two (SHZ and QZL) are identical, while to date no editor has provided any evidence of having consulted more than one version of the text, or documented any emendation made. I have for the present study completed this lengthy but crucial process myself, but one imagines that the production of an annotated critical edition of Qian's collected works (particularly the hitherto neglected prose) will be a vital prerequisite to further advances in the field.[15]

Appendix B
游黃山記
錢謙益 (1582–1664) 著

Preface 序

辛巳春余與程孟陽訂黃山之游約以梅花時相尋于武林之西溪踰月而不至〔1〕
余遂有事于白嶽黃山之興少闌矣徐維翰書來勸駕讀之兩腋欲舉遂挾吳去塵以行
吳長孺爲戒車馬〔2〕庀糇脯子含去非羣從相向慫恿而皆不能從也維翰之書曰白
嶽奇峭猶畫家小景耳巉崎幽石盡爲惡俗黃冠所塗點黃山奇峰拔地高者幾千丈庳
亦數百丈土無所附足無所迤石色蒼潤玲瓏夭曲每有一罅輒有一松迤之短鬣老骨
千百其狀以石爲土歷東南二嶽北至叭哈以外南至落迦匡廬九華都不足伯仲大
約口摹決不能盡懸想決不能及雖廢時日〔3〕煩跋涉終不可不到也是游也得詩
二十餘首寒窶無事補作記九篇已而悔曰維翰之言盡矣又多乎哉余之援筆爲此編
也客聞之索觀者相屬余不能拒遂撰次爲一卷先詒孟陽〔4〕于長翰山中而略舉維
翰之書以發其端壬午孟陬虞山老民錢謙益序

〔1〕踰月而不至 [MLS: 踰月不至].
〔2〕吳長孺爲戒車馬 [HM, LYM, WKQ: 吳長孺爲駕車馬].
〔3〕雖廢時日 [LYM, WKQ: 雖費時日].
〔4〕先詒孟陽 [HM, MLS, LYM, WKQ: 先貽孟陽].

Part I 記之一

黃山聳秀峻極作鎮一方江南諸山天台天目爲最以地形準之黃山之趾與二山齊溯
東西宣歙池饒江信諸郡之山皆黃山之枝隴也其水東南流入于歙北入于宣南入于

杭于睦于衢自衢西入于饒西北入于貴池其峰曰天都天所都也亦曰三天子都東南
西北皆有鄣數千里内之山扈者歸者岌者岠者嶧者蜀者皆黃山之負扆几格也古之
建都者規方千里以爲甸服必有大川巨浸以流其惡黃山之水奔注交屬分流于諸郡
者皆自湯泉而出其爲流惡也亦遠矣謂之天都也不亦宜乎余以二月初五日發商山
初七日抵湯院自商山至郡七十里自郡至山口一百二十里〔1〕至湯院又八里其所
遶寺曰楊干臺曰容成潭曰長潭嶺曰石磡石曰鄉石溪曰芳溪〔2〕村曰芳村其地勢
坡陀犖确擁厓據壁溪流縈折滑岸相錯其人家衣美箭被芳草略约拒門疏籬阻水塞
裳濟涉半在煙嵐雲氣中繇長潭而山口山率環谷水率注溪谷窮復入一谷山與谷如
堂如防旋相宮又相別也溪水清激如失或濆沸如輪文石錯落深淺見底百里之内天
容沕寥雲物鮮華游塵飛埃望厓却反人世腥腐穢濁之氣無從至焉余語同游者曰子
知黃山乎是天中之都會而軒轅之洞府也二百里内〔3〕皆離宮閣道羣真之所往來
百神之所至止殆有神物司啓閉給糞除于此地而人未之見也吾嘗游岱矣未及登天
門上日觀不知岱之尊也今吾之至于斯也肅然而清悄然而恐怳然如在天都石門之
上余之兹游也而豈徒哉是日浴于湯池宿藥谷之桃源菴

〔1〕自郡至山口一百二十里 [MLS: 自郡至山口百二十里].
〔2〕溪曰芳溪 [SHZ, QZL: 溪曰方溪].
〔3〕二百里内 [WKQ: 二百里之內].

Part II 記之二

自山口至湯口山之麓也登山之遶於是始湯泉之流自紫石峰六百仞縣布其下有香
泉溪泉口濆沸蒸熱冷泉下注涼溫齊和瀵尾涌出穢濁迸去初浴汗蒸蒸溢毛孔已而
悚然霍然如醒斯析如痟斯解拍浮久之怳然感素女玉真之事〔1〕作留題四絕句浴
罷風于亭巾屨衣袂飄飄然皆塵外物也折而西竹樹交加崖石撐柱蒙籠羃歷如無人
遶行半里許余氏桃源菴在焉菴之前天都青鸞鉢盂諸峰回合如屏障其左則白龍潭
水膏渟黛蓄噴薄巨石水聲硡磅微雨霡霂辛夷焰簪皎如玉雪俄聞籬落間剝啄海陽
邵梁卿幼青自白岳來訪足音跫然足樂也〔2〕午夜聞衝撞彌急溪聲雨聲澎湃錯互
〔3〕晨起坐小樓視天都峰瀑布〔4〕痕爛斑椵駮俄而雨大至風水發作天地掀簸
漫山皆白龍掉頭捽尾拖倒拔白龍潭水鼓怒觸搏林木轟磕几席震掉雨止泉益怒
呀呷撞胸如杵在臼日下舂少閒乃相與商游事焉〔5〕余氏菴傍湯池朝夕浴于斯飲
于斯汲于斯以斯池爲湯沐焉服食焉皆可也昔人飲菊潭而強飲杞水而壽況丹砂之
泉軒轅浴之三日而伐皮易毛者乎以千金賃藥谷之廬以二千金庀糧糒治藥物沐飲
于斯者數年登真度世可執券而取也今有進賢冠于此曰賣之三千金人爭攘臂而
求之以三千金買一仙人則掉頭不顧此可爲一笑者也

〔1〕玉真 [LYM, WKQ: 玉貞].
〔2〕俄聞籬落間剝啄海陽邵梁卿幼青自白岳來訪足音跫然足樂也 [Omitted in
    LYM, WKQ].

〔３〕澎湃錯互 [LYM, WKQ: 澎湃錯亘].
〔４〕視天都峰瀑布 [WKQ: 觀天都峰瀑布].
〔５〕少間乃相與商游事焉 [LYM, WKQ: 少間乃商游事焉].

Part III 記之三

縣祥符寺度石橋而北踰慈光寺行數里逕硃砂菴〔１〕而上其東曰紫石峰三十六峰之第四峰與青鸞天都皆崒山也過此取道鉢盂老人兩峰之閒峰趾相迮兩崖合沓彌望削成不見罅縫捫壁而往呀然洞開軒豁呈露如闢門闔登山者蓋發軔于此〔２〕里許憩觀音崖崖歆立如側蓋逕老人峰立石如老人傴僂縣厓多奇松裂石迸出糾枝覆蓋白雲蓬蓬冒松起僧曰雲將鋪海盍少待諸遂憩於囬峰之亭登山極望山河大地皆海也天將雨則雲族而聚于山〔３〕將晴則雲解而歸于山山山河大地其聚其歸皆所謂鋪海也雲初起如冒絮盤旋老人腰脊閒〔４〕俄而滅頂及足〔５〕却迎凌亂迫邅廻合瀰漫匼匝海亦雲也雲亦海也穿漏盪摩如百千樓閣如奔馬如風檣奔踊卻會不可名狀盪胸撲面身在層雲中亦一老人峰也久之雲氣解駮如浪文水勢〔６〕絡繹四散又如歸師班馬倏忽崩潰〔７〕窅然不可復跡矣回望老人峰傴僂如故若遲而肅客者緣天都趾而西至文殊院宿焉黃山自觀音厓〔８〕而上老木揩徑〔９〕壽藤冒石青竹綠莎蒙絡搖綴日景乍穿〔１０〕飛泉忽灑陰沉窅窱非復人世山未及上曰翠微其此之謂乎升老人峰天宇恢廓雲物在下三十六峰糸錯涌現〔１１〕怳怳然又度一世矣吾至此而後乃知黃山也〔１２〕

〔１〕逕硃砂菴 [MLS, LYM, WKQ: 逕硃砂溪].
〔２〕登山者蓋發軔于此 [NQX: 登山者皆發軔于此].
〔３〕雲族而聚于山 [LYM, WKQ: 雲簇而聚于山].
〔４〕盤旋老人腰脊閒 [LYM, WKQ: 盤旋于老人腰脊閒].
〔５〕俄而滅頂及足 [BYC, NQX: 俄而没頂及足].
〔６〕如浪文水勢 [LYM, WKQ: 如浪紋水勢. BYC: 如浪丈水勢].
〔７〕倏忽崩潰 [LYM, WKQ: 倏忽奔潰. BYC: 倏然崩潰].
〔８〕觀音厓 [WKQ: 觀音巖].
〔９〕老木揩徑 [NQX: 老木楷徑].
〔１０〕日景乍穿 [LYM, WKQ, BYC, NQX: 日影乍穿].
〔１１〕三十六峰糸錯涌現 [MLS: 三十六峰糸錯涌見].
〔１２〕吾至此而後乃知黃山也 [LYM, WKQ: 吾至此而乃知黃山也].

Part IV 記之四

憩桃源菴指天都爲諸峰之中峰山形絡繹未有以殊異也雲生峰腰層疊如裼衣焉雲氣翁翳峰各離立天都乃巋然于諸峰矣立老人峰沿磵上皆緣天都之趾援危松攀巘壁或折而陛或縣而度旋觀天都如冕而垂如介而立際向之所見尊嚴有加焉下嶺復上僧方鑿石斧鑿之痕與趾相錯也石壁斷裂人從石罅中上歷罅里許天都逐罅而走甫瞪目而踵已失也甫曳踵而目又失也壁絕石復上合乃梯而下人之下如汲井身則其絚也汲既深〔1〕絚穴地而出又從井幹中上也折而陟臺是爲文殊院普門安公所荒度也院負疊嶂峰左象右獅二羅松如羽蓋〔2〕㢤擁石如覆袈裟其上有趺跡其下下絕桃花峰居趺石之足桃花之湯出焉其東則天都峰〔3〕如旒倒垂其西則蓮華峰獻蕚焉〔4〕其南面曠如也〔5〕指點凝望浮煙蠹靄青葱紺碧穿漏于夕陽平楚之閒已而煙凝靄積四望如一暮景夕嵐無往而非雲海向所沾沾于老人峰者又存乎見少矣坐臺有二鴉〔6〕翔集僧言此神鴉也明日當爲公先導〔7〕與之食祝而遣之寢室不滿一弓夜氣肅冽與老僧推戶而起三十六峰微茫浸月魄中零露瀼瀼霑涇巾屨悽神寒骨峭愴而返故好山栖野宿〔8〕以此方之其猶在曲屋突夏砥室羅幬之中乎余之山居而宿焉者自茲夕始也

〔1〕汲既深 [WKQ: 級既深].
〔2〕二羅松如羽蓋 [WKQ: 二羅松如蓋].
〔3〕其東則天都峰 [MLS: 其東則天都諸峰].
〔4〕蓮華峰獻蕚焉 [LYM, WKQ: 蓮華獻蕚焉].
〔5〕Emended to 其南面曠如也 following MLS, LYM, WKQ [*SBCK*, HM, SHZ, QZL: 其西面曠如也].
〔6〕Emended to 坐臺有二鴉 following MLS, LYM, WKQ [*SBCK*, HM, SHZ, QZL: 生臺有二鴉].
〔7〕明日當爲公先導 [HM, LYM, WKQ: 明日當與公先導].
〔8〕余故好山栖野宿 [WKQ: 余故好山野栖宿].

Part V 記之五

清曉出文殊院神鴉背行而先炤微幻空兩僧從焉避蓮華溝險從支逕右折險益甚炤微肘掖余臂幻空踵受余趾三人者鹽與駏蛩若也行三里許憩炤微茆菴菴背蓮花面天都負山厱嵓蔽虧雲漢俯視洞壑日車在下陰茆薝藉白石出孟陽畫扇傳觀惜不與偕杖屨也二僧踞盤石疏記所宜游者曰緜喝石居三里至一線天再折一里許〔1〕下百步雲梯又一里上大悲頂出新闢小徑三里許達天海飯訖東北行上平天矼五里上石筍矼轉始信峯經散花塢看擾龍松過師子林上光明頂復歸天海少憩登煉丹臺而還日未亭午天氣如清秋大游天所相也食時飯天海神鴉却而迎焉次第游歷如二僧之云〔2〕日夕鴉去迴翔如顧別乃返天海宿焉一線天石壁峭陿水旁激如雨疾趨過之傳曰巖岑之下古人之所避風雨謂此也雲梯當蓮華峰之趾磴道歷七百級磴陿而

級長踵曳如絙脛垂如汲〔3〕下上攀援後趾須前趾前踵躡後踵旁瞰股栗作氣而後下乃相慶脫于險也始信峰于三十六峰不中爲兒孫〔4〕一部婁耳而頗踞諸峰之勝餘師子林束折兩厓陡立相去丈許北厓裂罅處一松被南厓援之以度陟其巔〔5〕苮菴欹傾積雪揹拄俯視雲氣諸峰矗出其最奇石笋矼也圖經云黃帝浮丘公上昇之後雙石笋化成峰可高十丈今石笋攢立不啻千百嵌空突起拔地插天鈎連坼裂譎詭化貿亦不可以丈計豈造物者役使鬼神破碎虛空穿大地爲苑囿鑿混沌之肺腑以有此也起視大壑却立萬仞指點宣州池陽堆皺疊摺纍如囷廩馮高臨下如限堵墻堆阜虛落人語殷殷過此則翠微松谷黃山西北之境盡矣煉丹臺之前拱立相向者煉丹峰也翠微飛來諸峰各負勢不相下胥俛爲環衞崩厓倚傾櫛比基布若削劒戟若樹儲胥軒轅相宅之地故有神物護訶安人不察設版築室宜其蕩剛風而焚劫火不終朝而輒毀也〔6〕三十六峰側影旁軼敷花如蔿苔丹臺藏貯其中如的中之薏臺方廣可置萬人三面劖削前臨無地却行偃卧足蹐蹐不能舉〔7〕目胸眩者久之余之登茲山也自湯寺而上披蒙茸歷幽仄蓋奧如也自文殊院而上指削成邐雲漢蓋曠如也及遵石笋丹臺觀夕陽望光景意迷精爽默自循省靈區異境顯顯心目安知俛仰之間不將一瞬遷改〔8〕夜半有負之而趨者與安知吾身在此而市朝陵谷堆壘聚塊者不已窅然若喪與又安知吾所坐之處所游之地〔9〕非幻化爲之如所謂五山之根無所連著者而吾亦將馮空而磧虛與余肉人也載朽腐之軀以游乎清都紫微余心蕩焉夫安得不執化人之袪懼而求還也與楚莊王曰子具于強臺南望料山以臨方皇左江右淮其樂忘死恐雷之而不能反吾之於此山所以游焉而樂樂焉而不敢以久雷也

〔1〕再折一里許 [MLS: 再折里許].

〔2〕如二僧之云 [LYM, WKQ: 如二僧云].

〔3〕脛垂如汲 [HM: 脛垂如級].

〔4〕始信峰于三十六峰不中爲兒孫 [HM, MLS, LYM, WKQ: 始信峰于三十六峰之中爲兒孫].

〔5〕陟其巔 [SHZ, QZL: 陟其嶺].

〔6〕不終朝而輒毀也 [MLS: 不終朝輒毀也].

〔7〕足蹐蹐不能舉 [HM, MLS, LYM, WKQ: 足縮縮不能舉].

〔8〕不將一瞬遷改 [HM, LYM, WKQ: 不將一瞬遷改].

〔9〕所游之地 [MLS: 所臨之地].

Part VI 記之六

晨起風蓬蓬然取道雲梯囿風逆上負風而仆仆而起兩腋若有人相扶不知其爲風力也盡雲梯則爲蓮華峰之趾徑如荷莖紆迴藏峰腹中磴窮穿峰腹而出如緣荷本上重臺也〔1〕風愈厲逆曳不得上乃據石趺坐以俟登陟者巡途而下欲前復却一松一石低廻如故人僧曰三十六峰處處惜別盖早至慈光寺招邀諸峰與執手欄楯間乎寺踞天都之隴枕桃花蓮華二峰〔2〕左則硃砂青鸞紫石右則疊嶂雲門立外翼焉普門安公者縛禪清凉山中定中見黃山遂繇清凉徙焉比入都門〔3〕願力冥感〔4〕慈聖

皇太后頒内帑爲薙髮賜紫衣幡杖神宗賜寺額曰慈光降敕護持今寺尊奉藏經慈聖所欽賜裝池也〔5〕四面金像像七層層四尊凡二十有八尊有蓮花坐〔6〕坐有七準提居葉中一葉一佛佛不啻萬計慈聖及兩宮所施造也普門將搆四面殿手削木爲式四阿四嚮不失毫髮今藏弆焉〔7〕普門隻手開山〔8〕熾然建立當其時兩宮之慈恩加被四海之物力充牣移兜率于人間化榛莽爲佛土何其盛也軍興日煩饑饉洊至鍾魚寥落糠覈不繼追鼓鐘于長信〔9〕數伽藍于雒陽蓋不勝滄海劫灰之嘆焉斯李文叔之所以致慨于名園也普門塔在寺後白石鑿鑿桃花流水圍繞塔前人世牛眼馬鬣起冢象祁連者方斯蔑如亦可感也〔10〕是夕再浴湯池宿桃源菴〔11〕山僧相送不忍舍鄭重而別寄語天都蓮花諸峰如吳人語念相聞也元人汪澤民曰宿湯寺聞啼禽聲若歌若答節奏疾徐名山樂鳥下山咸無有余方有南浦之別聞之悽然感余心焉既與黄山別遂窮日之力以歸

〔1〕如緣荷本上重臺也 [LYM, WKQ: 如緣荷本而上重臺也].
〔2〕枕桃花蓮華二峰 [MLS: 桃花蓮華二峰].
〔3〕比入都門 [LYM, WKQ: 北入都門].
〔4〕願力冥感 [LYM, WKQ: 顧力冥感].
〔5〕慈聖所欽賜裝池也 [LYM, WKQ: 慈聖所欽賜裝滲也].
〔6〕Emended to 凡二十有八尊有蓮花坐 following LYM, WKQ [*SBCK*, HM, SHZ, QZL: 凡二十有八層有蓮花坐].
〔7〕普門安公者縛禪清凉山中定中見黄山遂繇清凉徙焉比入都門願力冥感慈聖皇太后頒内帑爲薙髮賜紫衣幡杖神宗賜寺額曰慈光降敕護持今寺尊奉藏經慈聖所欽賜裝池也四面金像像七層層四尊凡二十有八尊有蓮花坐坐有七準提居葉中一葉一佛佛不啻萬計慈聖及兩宮所施造也普門將搆四面殿手削木爲式四阿四嚮不失毫髮今藏弆焉 [Omitted in MLS].
〔8〕普門隻手開山 [MLS: 普門安公隻手開山].
〔9〕追鼓鐘于長信 [WKQ: 追鐘鼓于長信].
〔10〕普門塔在寺後白石鑿鑿桃花流水圍繞塔前人世牛眼馬鬣起冢象祁連者方斯蔑如亦可感也 [Omitted in MLS].
〔11〕宿桃源菴 [WKQ: 宿桃桃源菴].

Part VII 記之七

余之登山也浴湯池〔1〕憩桃源菴夜半大雨坐白龍潭小樓看天都峰瀑布雨止登山雲氣猶滃鬱登老人峰看鋪海山行三日天宇軒豁〔2〕如高秋蕭辰一望千里每春夏登山煙嵐偪塞不辨尋丈山僧嘆詫得未曾有〔3〕甫出山雨復大作淋灕霑溼同游者更相慶也客曰黄山之游樂乎余應之曰樂則樂矣游則未也三十六峰之最著者莫如天都蓮花出芳村則蓮花峰離立抵白龍潭則天都正中如屏陟慈光寺踞天都而枕蓮花離而又屬顧若宿留憩文殊院天都東拱若幡幢之建立蓮花右翊若瓣花之披敷兩峰之面目畢見矣自兹以往偭背易嚮步武換形如鏡中取影横見倒出〔4〕非坐卧俯

仰不能髣髴而茲遊未遑也昔人言採藥者裹三日糧達天都頂萬曆閒普門闢菴相繼
登陟石塔龕燈儼然在焉夫獨非腐肉朽骨而遂如天之不可升耶石門爲黟山之中峰
歙郡黃山樓北瞰此峰峰勢中坼若巨門唐人有詩曰閒倚朱欄西北望只宜名作石門
樓〔5〕則石門之高峻唐時郡樓見之而游人無復過問即山僧亦莫知所在此可以名
游耶游茲山者〔6〕必當裹餱糧曳芒屨經年累月與山僧樵翁爲伴侶庶可以攬山川
之性情窮峰巒之形勝然而霞城乳竇紫床碧枕毛人之所飲阮公之所歌未可以津逮
也桃花如扇松花如纛竹葉如笠蓮葉如舟非鍊形度世之人未易遘也〔7〕三十六峰
之巓樵蘇絕跡猿鳥悚慄唯乘颮輪〔8〕駕雲車可以至焉列子言海外五山所居之人
皆仙聖之種一日一夕飛相往來者不可數吾安知仙聖之人不往來於三十六峰之閒
如東阡北陌乎〔9〕吾將買山桃源朝夕浴于湯池鍊形度世然後復理游屐焉山靈其
許我哉

〔1〕浴湯池 [LQS: 浴場池].
〔2〕天宇軒豁 [HM: 天雨軒豁].
〔3〕山僧嘆詫得未曾有 [HM: 山僧嘆詫未得曾有].
〔4〕橫見倒出 [HM, LYM, WKQ, LQS: 橫見側出].
〔5〕只宜名作石門樓 [HM, MLS, LYM, WKQ, LQS: 只宜名作巨門樓].
〔6〕游茲山者 [HM: 茲游山者].
〔7〕未易遘也 [LYM, WKQ, LQS: 未易覯也].
〔8〕唯乘颮輪 [LYM, WKQ, LQS: 惟乘颮輪].
〔9〕如東阡北陌乎 [HM, LYM, WKQ, LQS: 如東阡北陌者乎].

Part VIII 記之八

山之奇以泉以雲以松水之奇莫奇于白龍潭〔1〕泉之奇莫奇于湯泉皆在山麓桃源
溪水流入湯泉乳水源白雲溪東流入桃花溪二十四溪皆流注山足山空中水實其腹
水之激射奔注皆自腹以下故山下有泉而山上無泉也山極高則雷雨在下雲之聚而
出旅而歸皆在腰膂閒每見天都諸峰雲生如帶不能至其冢久之瀪然四合雲氣蔽翳
其下而峰頂故在雲外也鋪海之雲彌望如海忽焉迸散〔2〕如鳧驚兔逝山高出雲外
天宇曠然雲無所附麗故也湯寺以上山皆直松名材檜榅楩楠〔3〕藤絡莎被幽陰薈
蔚陟老人峰懸崖多異松負石絕出過此以往無樹非松無松不奇有幹大如脛而根蟠
屈以畝計者〔4〕有根只尋丈而枝扶疏蔽道旁者〔5〕有循厓度壑因依如懸度者
〔6〕有穿罅冗縫〔7〕崩迸如側生者有幢幢如羽葆者〔8〕有矯矯如蛟龍者有臥
而起起而復臥者有橫而斷斷而復橫者也〔9〕文殊院之左〔10〕雲梯之背山形下
絕皆有松踞之倚傾還會與人俛仰此尤奇也始信峰之北厓一松被南厓援其枝以度
俗所謂接引松也其西巨石屏立一松高三尺許廣一畝曲幹撐石厓而出自上穿下石
爲中裂糾結摎拏所謂擾龍松也石筍矼鍊丹臺峰石特出離立無支隴無贅阜一石一
松如首之有笄如車之有蓋參差入雲遙望如薺奇矣詭矣不可以名言矣松無土以石
爲土其身與皮幹皆石也滋雲雨殺霜雪〔11〕句喬元氣甲拆太古殆亦金膏水碧上

藥靈草之屬非凡草木也顧欲斫而取之作盆盎近玩不亦陋乎度雲梯而柬有長松夭
矯雷劈之仆地橫亘數十丈〔12〕鱗鬣偃蹇怒張過者惜之余笑曰〔13〕此造物者
爲此戲劇逆而折之使之更百千年〔14〕不知如何槎枒輪囷〔15〕蔚爲奇觀也吳
人賣花者揀梅之老枝屈折之約結之獻春則爲瓶花之尤異者以相夸焉茲松也其亦
造物之折枝也與千年而後必有微吾言而一笑者〔16〕

〔1〕莫奇于白龍潭 [WKQ: 莫奇于百龍潭].
〔2〕忽焉迸散 [HM, MLS, LYM, WKQ, LQS: 忽然迸散].
〔3〕檜榧梗楠 [SHZ, QZL: 檜榧梗楠].
〔4〕而根蟠屈以畝計者 [LYM, WKQ, LQS: 而根盤屈以畝計者].
〔5〕而枝扶疎蔽道旁者 [SHZ, QZL: 而扶枝疎蔽道旁者].
〔6〕因依如懸度者 [BYC: 因於于懸度者].
〔7〕有穿罅冗縫 [LYM, WKQ LQS: 有穿罅穴縫].
〔8〕有幢幢如羽葆者 [LQS: 布幢幢如羽葆者].
〔9〕Emended to 斷而復橫者也, a synthesis of SHZ, QZL [斷而復橫也] and
　　all other texts [斷而復橫者].
〔10〕文殊院之左 [LYM, WKQ, LQS: 文殊之左].
〔11〕殺霜雪 [LQS: 殺霜雨].
〔12〕橫亘數十丈 [LQS: 橫旦數十丈].
〔13〕余笑曰 [MLS: 余曰].
〔14〕使之更百千年 [MLS, LYM, WKQ, LQS: 使之更千百年].
〔15〕不知如何槎枒輪囷 [NQX: 不知如何杈枒輪囷].
〔16〕必有微吾言而一笑者 [BYC: 必有徵無吾言而一笑者].

Part IX 記之九

黟山三十六峰詳載圖經學士大夫不能悉其名而山僧牧子不能指其處所知者天都
蓮花煉丹硃砂十餘峰而已石人峰謔爲老人雲門峰謔爲剪刀疊嶂峰謔爲勝蓮又有
以培塿而冒峰名者始信峰也李太白有詩送溫處士歸黃山白鵞峰今不在三十六峰
之列蓋三十六峰皆高七百仞以上其外諸峰高二三百仞者不與焉白鵞峰或亦諸峰
之一也自普門安公乘宿夢因緣闢文殊院命老人峰背一嶺曰三觀嶺於是命名者紛
如〔1〕曰光明頂曰天海曰師子林皆傳會文殊院而名也普門開山之後徽人以黃山
媚客〔2〕輶車軿軒至止相望所至輒樹眉顏額磨厓題名青峰白石有剝膚黥面之憂
三十六峰亦將不能保其故吾矣山之巓曰海子縣平天矼循煉丹峰里許名曰海門光
明頂爲前海師子林爲後海修廣可數里如以茲山峻絕目其平衍處爲海則華山之頂
高崌四合重嶺秀起不名之曰華海如以雲生之候彌望雲浪目之曰海〔3〕則泰山之
雲觸石而出膚寸而合不名之曰岱海以海名山以黃名海紕繆不典當一切鐫削爲山
靈一洗之也自山海經水經紀三天子鄣亦曰三天子都地志家紛紛聚訟有疏通之者
曰率山爲首黟山爲背大鄣爲尻似矣新安老生吳時憲曰黃山有最高峰曰三天子都

東西南北皆有部〔4〕婺有三天子部南部也匡廬亦稱三天子部西部也績溪有大部
東北部也天都爲天子都率山匡廬大部爲天子都之部此伯益桑欽之疏義而黟山之
掌故也時憲振奇人也所居環堵巢書其中見溪南富人則唾面去之〔5〕余遊新安新
安人無能舉其姓名者矣故余作黄山記以時憲之言終焉

〔1〕於是命名者紛如 [HM: 於是欲名者紛如].
〔2〕徽人以黄山媚客 [Omitted in MLS].
〔3〕目之曰海 [LYM, WKQ: 目之爲海].
〔4〕東西南北皆有部 [LYM, WKQ: 東南西北皆有部].
〔5〕見溪南富人則唾面去之 [Omitted in MLS; HM: 見溪南富人則唾面而去之;
    LYM, WKQ: 不喜見富人].

Notes

Introduction

1 Rpt.; Wang Bomin 王伯敏 ed., in *Zhongguo hualun congshu* 中國畫論叢書 (Beijing: Renmin meishu chubanshe, 1963). Among the many alternative translations of this treatise see that of Stephen H. West ("A Record of the Methods of the Brush"), in Pauline Yu, Peter Bol, Stephen Owen and Willard Peterson ed., *Ways with Words: Writing about Reading Texts from Early China* (Berkeley: University of California Press, 2000), pp. 202–13. West renders this passage into: "If it is the visible pattern of a thing — seize its visible pattern; if it is the essential substance of a thing — seize its essential substance. One cannot seize on visible pattern and make it essential substance." (204)

2 E. H. Gombrich, "The Renaissance Theory of Art and the Rise of Landscape," in *idem*, *Norm and Form: Studies in the Art of the Renaissance* (London: Phaidon Press, 1966), pp. 107–21 (116–7). See also *Art and Illusion: A Study in the Psychology of Pictorial Representation* (London: Phaidon Press, 1959).

3 Jacques Barzun, *From Dawn to Decadence — 1500 to the Present: 500 Years of Western Cultural Life* (London: HarperCollins, 2000), p. 72.

4 René Magritte, "La Ligne de vie," cited in Sarah Whitfield, *Magritte* (London: South Bank Centre, 1992), p. 62.

5 James Hargett, *On the Road in Twelfth Century China: The Travel Diaries of Fan Chengda (1126–1193)* (Stuttgart: Franz Steiner Verlag, 1989), p. 2. See also Hargett's entry, "*Yu-chi wen-hsüeh*," ICTCL, Volume 1, pp. 936–9.

6 Julian Ward, *Xu Xiake (1587–1641): The Art of Travel Writing* (Richmond: Curzon, 2001), p. 125.

7 Craig Clunas, *Fruitful Sites: Garden Culture in Ming Dynasty China* (London: Reaktion Books, 1996). The best critical treatment of Clunas' study of which I am aware is the review article by Mark Jackson, "Landscape/Representation/Text: Craig Clunas's *Fruitful Sites* (1996)," *Studies in the History of Gardens and Designed Landscapes* 19 (3/4) (1999): 302–13.

8 W. J. T. Mitchell, "Editor's Note: The Language of Images," *Critical Inquiry* 6 (3) (1980): 359–62.

9   Simon Schama, *Landscape and Memory* (London: HarperCollins, 1995), p. 61.

10 Simon Coleman and John Elsner, *Pilgrimage Past and Present: Sacred Travel and Sacred Space in World Religions* (London: British Museum Press, 1995), p. 212.

11 D. W. Meinig, "The Beholding Eye: Ten Versions of the Same Scene," in *idem* ed., *The Interpretation of Ordinary Landscapes: Geographical Essays* (Oxford: Oxford University Press, 1979), pp. 33–48 (34).

12 David Hawkes trans., *The Story of the Stone (Volume One: The Golden Days)* (Harmondsworth: Penguin Books, 1973), pp. 324–5. For the original text, see Cao Xueqin and Gao E 高鶚, *Hongloumeng* (rpt.; Beijing: Renmin wenxue chubanshe, 1998), Volume 1, p. 217.

13 *Shanchuan xiuli de Zhongguo* 山川秀麗的中國 [*di si jie "Hanyu qiao" shijie daxuesheng Zhongwen bisai wenda tiji* 第四屆 "漢語橋" 世界大學生中文比賽問答題集] (Shanghai: Huadong shifan daxue chubanshe, 2005), p. 15. On the Four Perfections of Yellow Mountain, see Chapter Four.

14 *Huangshan tujing*, reprinted as Volume 1 of the *Anhui congshu* 安徽叢書 Series 5 (Shanghai: Anhui congshu bianyinchu, 1935). This important work will be discussed in Chapter Two. Pine trees are mentioned in this text only in the entry on Pine Forest Peak 松林峰 (9b).

15 Jing, "Bifa ji." This passage is treated in Stephen H. West, Stephen Owen, Martin Powers and Willard Peterson's "*Bi fa ji*: Jing Hao, 'Notes on the Method for the Brush,'" in Yu et al. ed., *Ways with Words*, pp. 202–44. See also Powers' "When is a Landscape like a Body?" in Wen-hsin Yeh ed., *Landscape, Culture, and Power in Chinese Society* (Berkeley: University of California Press, 1998), pp. 1–22.

16 Huang Zongxi, "Sijiu lu" 思舊錄, in Shen Shanhong 沈善洪 ed., *Huang Zongxi quanji* 黃宗羲全集 (Hangzhou: Zhejiang guji chubanshe, 2005), Volume 1, p. 377.

17 Luther Carrington Goodrich, *The Literary Inquisition of Ch'ien-Lung* (New York: Paragon Book Reprint Corp., 1966), pp. 102–3 (romanization altered).

18 A number of new studies have appeared since I began working on this project, and one that I have not yet had the opportunity to read is Yang Lianmin's 楊連民 *Qian Qianyi shixue yanjiu* 錢謙益詩學研究 (Beijing: Shehui kexue wenxian chubanshe, 2007). I am also acutely aware that I have barely scraped the surface of the astonishing number of articles about all aspects of Qian Qianyi that have been published in the journals of the major Chinese universities over the past two decades, for a useful list of which, see Ding Gongyi's 丁功誼 *Qian Qianyi wenxue sixiang yanjiu* 錢謙益文學思想研究 (Shanghai: Guji chubanshe, 2006), pp. 259–61.

19 Brian R. Dott, *Identity Reflections: Pilgrimages to Mount Tai in Late Imperial China* (Cambridge, MA: Harvard University Press, 2004).

20 Partial translations of the essay into English appear in Richard E. Strassberg's *Inscribed Landscapes: Travel Writing from Imperial China* (Berkeley: University of California Press, 1994), pp. 315–6 [Part III] and in Yang Qinghua's rendition of Yu Kwang-chung's "The Sensuous Art of the Chinese Landscape Journal," in Stephen C. Soong and John Minford ed., *Trees on the Mountain: An Anthology of New Chinese Writing* (Hong Kong: Chinese University Press, 1986), pp. 23–40 [a partial translation of Part VIII]. The essay appears in annotated form in Wang Keqian 王克謙 ed., *Lidai Huangshan youji xuan* 歷代黃山遊記選 (Hefei: Huangshan shushe, 1988), pp. 102–29 [the complete essay, but with considerable deficiencies, including a failure to identify people or the majority of literary allusions, erroneous punctuation etc.]; Bei Yunchen 貝運辰 ed., *Lidai youji xuan* 歷代遊記選 (Changsha: Hunan renmin chubanshe, 1980), pp. 289–97 [Parts III and VIII only], and Ni Qixin 倪其心 ed., *Zhongguo gudai youji xuan* 中國古代遊記選 (Beijing: Zhongguo youji chubanshe, 1985), Volume 2, pp. 255–64 [also Parts III and VIII]. The trip and its resulting writings are mentioned briefly in Gao Zhangcai's 高章采

Guanchang shike 官場詩客 (Xianggang: Zhonghua shuju, 1991), pp. 162–6, Ding Gongyi's *Wenxue sixiang*, pp. 111–8, and in three studies by Pei Shijun 裴世俊: *Sihai zongmeng wushi nian: Qian Qianyi zhuan* 四海宗盟五十年：錢謙益傳 (Beijing: Dongfang chubanshe, 2001), p. 95; *Qian Qianyi guwen shoutan* 錢謙益古文首探 (Ji'nan: Qilu shushe, 1996), pp. 100–2 and *Qian Qianyi shige yanjiu* 錢謙益詩歌研究 (Ningxia: Ningxia renmin chubanshe, 1991), pp. 95–103, a discussion that seems to draw heavily on the editor's introduction to Li Yimang 李一氓 ed., *Ming Qing ren you Huangshan jichao* 明清人遊黃山記鈔 (Hefei: Anhui renmin chubanshe, 1983), although it is not attributed as such (see especially Pei's comment on the transformations of the seasons, p. 98). See also Chen Yinke, [Chen Yinque] 陳寅恪, *Liu Rushi biezhuan* 柳如是別傳 (Shanghai: Guji chubanshe, 1980), Volume 2, pp. 613–34.

21 See, for example, Susan Sontag's *On Photography* (New York: Farrar, Strauss and Giroux, 1977).

22 Adele Austin Rickett trans., *Wang Kuo-wei's Jen-chien Tz'u-hua: A Study in Chinese Literary Criticism* (Hong Kong: Hong Kong University Press, 1977), p. 71.

Chapter 1

1 Martin Heijdra notes that "while the number of officials hovered between 25,000 and 40,000, the number of degree holders [had] increased from 100,000 to 550,000 [by the end of the Ming]." ("The Socio-Economic Development of Rural China during the Ming," in Denis Twitchett and Frederick W. Mote ed., *The Cambridge History of China Volume 8: The Ming Dynasty, 1368–1644, Part 2* [Cambridge: Cambridge University Press, 1998], pp. 417–578 [561]).

2 Timothy Brook, *The Confusions of Pleasure: Commerce and Culture in Ming China* (Berkeley: University of California Press, 1998), p. 173. On some of the factors contributing to the decline of the imperial courier system, see Hoshi Ayao, "Transportation in the Ming Dynasty," *Acta Asiatica* 38 (1980): 1–30.

3 See in particular: Craig Clunas, *Superfluous Things: Material Culture and Social Status in Early Modern China* (Cambridge: Polity Press, 1991); Brook, *Confusions of Pleasure*; Wai-yee Li, "The Collector, the Connoisseur, and Late-Ming Sensibility," *T'oung Pao* 81 (4/5) (1995): 269–302.

4 Clunas, *Superfluous Things*, p. 108.

5 Clunas, *Superfluous Things*, p. 137.

6 Brook, *Confusions of Pleasure*, p. 220. On Ming sumptuary restrictions, see also Craig Clunas' "Regulation of Consumption and the Institution of Correct Morality by the Ming State," in Chun-chieh Huang and Erik Zürcher ed., *Norms and the State in China* (Leiden: E. J. Brill, 1993), pp. 39–49. I do not mean to suggest here that the relaxation of sumptuary laws was on its own responsible for the changing concepts of taste and fashion in late-Ming society, which was of course a product of a wide range of influences. In terms of aesthetic qualities of visual arts, for example, Chu-tsing Li notes that in contrast to other periods, by the late Ming "very few painters were attached to the court, which meant that neither the emperor nor his court served as an arbiter of contemporary taste." ("The Artistic Theories of the Literati," in *idem* and James C. Y. Watt ed., *The Chinese Scholar's Studio: Artistic Life in the Late Ming Period* [New York: Thames and Hudson, 1987], pp. 14–22 [14].)

7 Hilary J. Beattie, *Land and Lineage in China: A Study of T'ung-ch'eng County, Anhwei, in the Ming and Ch'ing Dynasties*, cited in Clunas, *Superfluous Things*, p. 155.

8   Brook, *Confusions of Pleasure*, p. 238.

9   Jonathan Hay, *Shitao: Painting and Modernity in Early Qing China* (Cambridge: Cambridge University Press, 2001), p. 19.

10   Timothy Brook, "Communications and Commerce," in Twitchett and Mote ed., *Cambridge History of China Volume 8*, pp. 579–707 (581).

11   Clunas, *Superfluous Things*, p. 146.

12   "I once visited a friend in Jiaxing, and noted that when entertaining guests the household used silver braziers and golden spittoons. Every guest had a set of golden dish and dish-stand, and a great golden cup with a pair of *chi* dragons. Each set contained about 15 or 16 *liang*. I passed the night there, and the next morning washed my face in a silver basin chased with plum blossom. The hangings, curtains and bed clothes were all of brocaded gauze, and my sight was assaulted to the point where I could not close my eyes all night. I have heard that the family even has incense-burners of gold, making them the richest family in Jiangnan, and at the same time the acme of common vulgarity incapable of being outdone." See Craig Clunas, "Some Literary Evidence for Gold and Silver Vessels in the Ming Period (1368–1644)," in Michael Vickers ed., *Pots and Pans: A Colloquium on Precious Metals and Ceramics in the Muslim, Chinese and Graeco-Roman Worlds, Oxford, 1985* (Oxford Studies in Islamic Art III, Oxford: Oxford University Press, 1986), pp. 83–7 (86).

13   Sandi Chin and Cheng-chi (Ginger) Hsü, "Anhui Merchant Culture and Patronage," in James Cahill ed., *Shadows of Mt. Huang: Chinese Painting and Printing of the Anhui School* (Berkeley: University Art Museum, 1981), pp. 19–24 (21).

14   Chin and Hsü, "Anhui Merchant Culture," p. 22.

15   Li, "The Collector," pp. 275–6.

16   English-language studies of Ming printing and publishing include: K. T. Wu, "Colour Printing in the Ming Dynasty," *T'ien Hsia Monthly* 11 (1) (1940): 30–44, and "Ming Printing and Printers," *Harvard Journal of Asiatic Studies* 7 (1942–43): 203–60; Francesca Bray, *Technology and Society in Ming China (1368–1644)* (Washington DC: American Historical Association, 2000), pp. 7–17, and Chow Kai-wing, "Writing for Success: Printing, Examinations and Intellectual Change in Late Ming China," *Late Imperial China* 17 (1) (1996): 120–57.

17   Books were also a collectable commodity, of course, on which see Brook's *Confusions of Pleasure*, pp. 167–72, Clunas' *Superfluous Things* and "Books and Things: Ming Literary Culture and Material Culture," *Chinese Studies* (London: British Library Occasional Paper #10, 1988), pp. 136–42.

18   Richard Vinograd, *Boundaries of the Self: Chinese Portraits, 1600–1900* (Cambridge: Cambridge University Press, 1992), pp. 28–67; Craig Clunas, "Artist and Subject in Ming Dynasty China," *Proceedings of the British Academy 105: 1999 Lectures and Memoirs* (Oxford: Oxford University Press, 2000), pp. 43–72.

19   Yang Ye trans., *Vignettes from the Late Ming: A Hsiao-p'in Anthology* (Seattle: University of Washington Press, 1999), pp. xviii.

20   Ye, *Vignettes from the Late Ming*, pp. xviii–xix.

21   Ye, *Vignettes from the Late Ming*, pp. xviii.

22   Chen Jiru, "Wenyu xu" 文娛序, in Hu Shaotang 胡紹棠 ed., *Chen Meigong xiaopin* 陳眉公小品 (Beijing: Wenhua yishu chubanshe, 1996), pp. 24–6. The punctuation given in this annotated edition of the text ascribes this dating to Zheng Yuanxun, while Ye's translation ascribes the line to Chen Jiru himself.

23   Robert E. Hegel, "*Vignettes from the Late Ming: A Hsiao-p'in Anthology* by Yang Ye," reviewed in *Journal of Asian and African Studies* 37 (1) (March 2002): 116–8. Statements that similarly downplay the rhetorical function of late-Ming *xiaopin*

abound; see, for example, Yin Gonghong 尹恭弘 (*Xiaopin gaochao yu wan Ming wenhua* 小品高潮與晚明文化 [Beijing: Huawen chubanshe, 2001]): "Only the late-Ming *xiaopin* was able to throw off the bonds of didacticism [that had characterized the prose of earlier periods] and give free expression to the desires of the [author's] heart" 縱心而談 (2).

24 Lu Shusheng, "Yanshi ji," in Shi Zhicun 施蟄存 ed., *Wan Ming ershijia xiaopin* 晚明二十家小品 (Shanghai: Shanghai shudian, 1984), pp. 18–9. This essay is translated as "Inkslab Den" in Ye's anthology (pp. 12–3).

25 Ye's only comment here is of Lu Shusheng's *xiaopin* in general: "Rich in literary allusions, Lu's vignettes often breathe a sense of humour and a cheerful appreciation of life's little pleasures" (*Vignettes from the Late Ming*, p. 11).

26 Gu Qiyuan, *Lanzhen caotang ji* 嬾真草堂集 cited in Qianshen Bai, *Fu Shan's World: The Transformation of Chinese Calligraphy in the Seventeenth Century* (Cambridge, MA: Harvard University Press, 2003), p. 19; Bai leaves the term *qi* untranslated throughout his discussion.

27 Bai, *Fu Shan's World*, p. 19. "It was precisely its vagueness," Bai continues, "that opened the term up to innumerable possibilities." (pp. 19–20) Similarly, in her thoughtful treatment of the term *yi* 異 [strange], Judith T. Zeitlin notes the difficulty of defining an idea that is "a cultural construct created and constantly renewed through writing and reading" (*Historian of the Strange: Pu Songling and the Chinese Classical Tale* [Stanford: Stanford University Press, 1993], p. 6).

28 Bai, *Fu Shan's World*, p. 19.

29 Judith T. Zeitlin, "The Petrified Heart: Obsession in Chinese Literature, Art, and Medicine," *Late Imperial China* 12 (1) (1991): 1–26, and *Historian of the Strange*, pp. 62–97.

30 Duncan Campbell, "Qi Biaojia's 'Footnotes to Allegory Mountain': Introduction and Translation," *Studies in the History of Gardens and Designed Landscapes* 19 (3/4) (1999): 243–71 (247). See also Joanna F. Handlin-Smith's "Gardens in Ch'i Piao-chia's Social World: Wealth and Values in Late-Ming Kiangnan," *Journal of Asian Studies* 51 (1) (1992): 55–81 (59–64).

31 Zhang Dai, "Qi Zhixiang pi," 祁止祥癖 in Xia Xianchun 夏咸淳 and Cheng Weirong 程維榮 ed., *Taoan mengyi / Xihu mengxun* 陶庵夢憶 / 西湖夢尋 (Shanghai: Guji chubanshe, 2001), pp. 72–3.

32 Alfred Gell, "Newcomers to the World of Goods: Consumption among the Muria Gonds," in Arjun Appadurai ed., *The Social Life of Things: Commodities in Cultural Perspective* (Cambridge: Cambridge University Press, 1986), pp. 110–38 (112).

33 For an extension of this idea into the realms of landscape art during the Yuan-Ming transition, see Richard Vinograd, "Family Properties: Personal Context and Cultural Pattern in Wang Meng's *Pien* Mountains of 1366," *Ars Orientalis* 13 (1982): 1–29: "The predominant subjects of Yuan scholar-amateur landscape were, for the most part, not merely generally notable sites or famed scenic spots, but rather local mountains and streams, regional vistas, studio environs, and villa settings which were closely tied to the artist or recipient or both by bonds of ownership, personal association or family history." (p. 11, romanization altered)

34 The handscroll exists today in two versions, one in the Ogawa Family Collection, Kyoto, and the other in the Honolulu Academy of Arts (known as *Changjiang jixue* 長江積雪 [The Yangzi River after Snow]). There is considerable debate over the authenticity of the two scrolls, which, in the present context, I have chosen to ignore. The work and its provenance are superbly treated in Wen Fong's "Rivers and Mountains after Snow (Chiang-shan hsüeh-chi), Attributed to Wang Wei (AD 699–759)," *Archives of Asian Art* 30 (1976–77): 6–33, in which Fong asserts the primacy of the Ogawa version. This version is also reproduced in Naitō Torajirō's 內

藤虎次郎 (1866–1934) *Shina kaiga shi* 支那繪畫史 (rpt.; Kanda Kiichirō 神田喜一郎 and Naitō Kenkichi 內藤乾吉 ed., *Naitō Konan zenshū* 內藤湖南全集 [Tōkyō: Chikuma shobō, 1969–1976], Volume 13) as plates 24 and 25. Michael Sullivan's plate 97 (*Chinese Landscape Painting – Volume II: The Sui and Tang Dynasties* [Berkeley: University of California Press, 1980]) is labelled as the Ogawa scroll but appears to be another work.

35   Adapted from Fong, "Rivers and Mountains," p. 14.

36   Adapted from Fong, "Rivers and Mountains," p. 15.

37   Fong, "Rivers and Mountains," p. 12, citing Wang Shimin 王時敏 (1592–1680). *QRSM* (Volume 2, p. 1084) records a Cheng Jiahua 程甲化 as having the sobriquet (*zi* 字) Jibai 季白, although this Cheng is given as being from Putian 莆田 (Fujian) rather than from Xin'an.

38   A reference to the Zhang Hua 張華 biography in the *Jin shu* 晉書 (rpt.; Beijing: Zhonghua shuju, 1974), in which two swords are uncovered in the ground at Fengcheng (Volume 4, p. 1075).

39   Qian Qianyi, "Ba Dong Xuanzai yu Feng Kaizhi chidu" 跋董玄宰與馮開之尺牘, in *Muzhai chuxueji* 85 (*QMZQJ*, Volume 3, pp. 1788–9). The original version, which differs slightly from that published in the *Muzhai chuxueji*, is reproduced (without translation) as an appendix to Fong's "Rivers and Mountains." Qian actually calls the painting *Jiangshan jixue* 江山霽雪, although this fact goes unmentioned by Fong. The original text is dated the *renwu* 壬午 year of the Chongzhen reign (1642).

40   Harriet T. Zurndorfer, *Change and Continuity in Chinese Local History: The Development of Hui-chou Prefecture, 800 to 1800* (Leiden: E. J. Brill, 1989), pp. 225–8.

41   Chin and Hsü, "Anhui Merchant Culture," p. 23.

42   Arjun Appadurai, "Introduction: Commodities and the Politics of Value," in *idem* ed., *Social Life of Things*, pp. 3–63 (38).

43   Xu Hongzu (1586–1641) is one man who does complain frequently of such difficulties in the diaries of his great travels in the southwest (see Ward, *Xu Xiake*). Such long and remote journeys were, however, very much the exception among late-Ming travellers.

44   The 1570 edition of *Yitong lucheng tuji* was republished in 1635 as *Tianxia shuilu lucheng* 天下水陸路程 (rpt.; Yang Zhengtai 楊正泰 ed., Taiyuan: Shanxi renmin chubanshe, 1992).

45   Clunas, *Superfluous Things*, p. 13.

46   Huang Liuhong, *Fuhui quanshu* 福惠全書 cited in Brook, "Communications and Commerce," pp. 624–5.

47   Sung Ying-hsing, *T'ien-kung K'ai-wu: Chinese Technology in the Seventeenth Century*, translated by E-tu Zen Sun and Shiou-chuan Sun (London: Pennsylvania State University Press, 1966), p. xiii (romanization altered). Francesca Bray notes in her study that "[m]any key features of Ming transport technology, such as the magnetic compass, ships built with watertight compartments, and canal locks, were already in use by the Song. The Ming was remarkable less for the invention of new technologies than for their wide dissemination as commerce advanced, population grew, and China's internal and external trading links were consolidated." (*Technology and Society*, p. 19)

48   Yuan Hongdao, "Dongdongting" 東洞庭, in Qian Bocheng 錢伯城 ed., *Yuan Hongdao ji jianjiao* 袁宏道集箋校 (Shanghai: Guji chubanshe, 1981), Volume 1, pp. 163–4.

49   Stephen McDowall trans., *Four Months of Idle Roaming: The West Lake Records of Yuan Hongdao (1568–1610)* (Wellington: Asian Studies Institute Translation Paper #4, 2002), p. 1.

50   Dante Alighieri, *The Comedy of Dante Alighieri: Cantica I: Hell [l'Inferno]*, translated by Dorothy L. Sayers (Harmondsworth: Penguin Books, 1949), p. 235.

51 Hong Mei 弘眉 comp., *Huangshan zhi* 黃山志 (1667), reprinted in *Zhonghua shanshuizhi congkan (shanzhi juan)* 中華山水志叢刊 (山志卷) (Beijing: Xianzhuang shuju, 2004), Volume 15, pp. 241–574 (471–4). This work will be discussed in Chapter Two.

52 Robyn Davidson, "Introduction," in *idem* ed., *The Picador Book of Journeys* (London: Picador, 2001), pp. 1–7 (3).

53 Of wrong sorts of traveller there were of course many, most famously articulated in Wang Siren's 王思任 (*zi* Jizhong 季重, *hao* Suidong 遂東; 1575–1646) "Jiyou yin" 紀遊引, for which see Li Wu 李嗚 ed., *Wang Jizhong xiaopin* 王季重小品 (Beijing: Wenhua yishu chubanshe, 1996), pp. 138–9.

54 Hargett, *On the Road*, p. 44.

55 Strassberg, *Inscribed Landscapes*, p. 56.

56 James M. Hargett, "Some Preliminary Remarks on the Travel Records of the Song Dynasty (960–1279)," *Chinese Literature: Essays, Articles, Reviews* 7 (1/2) (July 1985): 67–93 (70).

57 W. Jackson Bate, *The Burden of the Past and the English Poet* (Cambridge, MA: Harvard University Press, 1970), p. 4.

58 Michel Butor, "Le voyage et l'écriture" in *idem*, *Répertoire IV* (Paris: Minuit, 1974), pp. 9–29.

59 Tian Rucheng, *Xihu youlanzhi* (rpt.; Shanghai: Guji chubanshe, 1998). Yuan draws from this work in his "Fourth Record of West Lake" 西湖四 (see McDowall trans., *Four Months of Idle Roaming*, pp. 4 and 15).

60 Brook, "Communications and Commerce," p. 625.

61 McDowall trans., *Four Months of Idle Roaming*, pp. 3–9.

62 Paul Fussell, *Abroad: British Literary Traveling Between the Wars* (Oxford: Oxford University Press, 1980), pp. 40–1.

63 Alan Brien, "Tourist Angst," *The Spectator* (July 31, 1959): 133.

64 Gu Yanwu, *Rizhilu jishi* 日知錄集釋, Huang Rucheng 黃汝成 ed. (rpt.; Shijiazhuang: Huashan wenyi chubanshe, 1990), Volume 1, pp. 473–5.

65 Brook, *Confusions of Pleasure*, p. 174.

66 Dean MacCannell, *The Tourist: A New Theory of the Leisure Class* (New York: Schocken Books, 1976), p. 10.

67 S. A. M. Adshead, "The Seventeenth Century General Crisis in China," *Asian Profile* 1 (2) (1973): 271–80 (272).

68 A more complete listing of Qian Qianyi's known sobriquets is found in *QRSM*, Volume 2, p. 926. For biographical details, see the entry by L. Carrington Goodrich and J. C. Yang in *ECCP*, pp. 148–50 and that by Ming-shui Hung in *ICTCL*, Volume 1, pp. 277–9. For more extensive treatments of Qian's life, see Pei, *Sihai zongmeng*; Chen, *Liu Rushi biezhuan* and Jin Hechong 金鶴沖, *Qian Muzhai xiansheng nianpu* 錢牧齋先生年譜, reprinted in *QMZQJ*, Volume 8, pp. 930–52. Jin's study was also reprinted along with three other *nianpu* (chronological biographies) of Qian by Ge Wanli 葛萬里, Pengcheng tuishi 彭城退士 and Zhang Lianjun 張聯駿 in *Beijing tushuguan cang zhenben nianpu congkan* 北京圖書館藏珍本年譜叢刊 (Beijing: Beijing tushuguan chubanshe, 1999) 64: 559–720. In addition to those already noted, literary studies of Qian's works in Chinese include: Li Qing 李慶, "Qian Qianyi: Ming mo shidafu xintai de dianxing" 錢謙益：明末士大夫心態的典型, *Fudan xuebao* 復旦學報 [*sheke ban* 社科版] (1989) (1): 37–43; Sun Zhimei 孫之梅, *Qian Qianyi yu Ming mo Qing chu wenxue* 錢謙益與明末清初文學 (Ji'nan: Qilu shushe, 1996); Cai Yingyuan 蔡營源, *Qian Qianyi zhi shengping yu zhushu* 錢謙益之生平與著述 (Miaoli: Fuhua shuju, 1977), which also includes a useful *nianpu*; Liu Zuomei 柳作梅, "Wang Shizhen yu Qian Qianyi zhi shilun" 王士禎 [*sic*] 與錢謙益之詩論, *Shumu jikan* 書目季刊 2 (3) (1968): 41–9; Hu Youfeng 胡幼峰, *Qing chu Yushanpai shilun* 清初虞山派

詩論 (Taibei: Guoli bianyiguan, 1994), and Zhu Dongrun 朱東潤, "Shu Qian Qianyi zhi wenxue piping" 述錢謙益之文學批評, in *idem*, *Zhongguo wenxue piping lunji* 中國文學批評論集 (Shanghai: Kaiming shudian, 1947), pp. 76–95 (and reprinted in *idem*, *Zhongguo wenxue lunji* 中國文學論集 [Beijing: Zhonghua shuju, 1983], pp. 71–89). Zhu erroneously dates Qian's birth to the fourth year of the Longqing reign (1570), and his subsequent discussion is somewhat hindered by this mistake (p. 79). For studies in English, see: Hellmut Wilhelm, "Bibliographical Notes on Ch'ien Ch'ien-i," *Monumenta Serica* 7 (1942): 196–207; Jonathan Chaves, "The Yellow Mountain Poems of Ch'ien Ch'ien-i (1582–1664): Poetry as *Yu-chi*," *Harvard Journal of Asiatic Studies* 48 (2) (1988): 465–92; K. L. Che, "Not Words But Feelings — Ch'ien Ch'ien-I [*sic*] (1582–1664) on Poetry," *Tamkang Review* 6 (1) (1975): 55–75, and Chi-hung Yim [嚴志雄], *The Poetics of Historical Memory in the Ming-Qing Transition: A Study of Qian Qianyi's (1582–1664) Later Poetry* (Unpublished PhD thesis: Yale University, 1998). As I write, Yim's monograph, *The Poet-Historian Qian Qianyi* (Routledge, 2009) has yet to be released.

69 Sun, *Ming mo Qing chu wenxue*, p. 14; Pei, *Shige yanjiu*, p. 14. For the Qian family tree, see Cai, *Shengping yu zhushu*, p. 6.

70 Sun Zhimei argues that fostering the development of a network of political, social and literary connections during Qianyi's early life, such as his introduction to Gu Xiancheng 顧憲成 (*zi* Shushi 叔時, *hao* Xiaoxin 小心; 1550–1612) at age 15 *sui*, was one of the most significant roles his father Shiyang played in Qianyi's upbringing (*Ming mo Qing chu wenxue*, pp. 26–7).

71 Cai, *Shengping yu zhushu*, pp. 6–10. In his "Sijiu lu," Huang Zongxi erroneously refers to Qianyi's son as Qian Sunyi 孫貽, a conflation of *ming* 名 and *zi* 字 (*Huang Zongxi quanji*, Volume 1, p. 378).

72 Lynn A. Struve, *The Ming-Qing Conflict, 1619–1683: A Historiography and Source Guide* (Ann Arbor: Association for Asian Studies, 1998), p. 64.

73 Goodrich, *Literary Inquisition*, p. 104 (romanization altered).

74 On the *Siku quanshu* project, see *ICTCL*, Volume 1, pp. 247–9 and R. Kent Guy, *The Emperor's Four Treasuries: Scholars and the State in the Late Ch'ien-lung Era* (Cambridge, MA: Harvard University Press, 1987).

75 On the transmission of Qian's writings despite the efforts of the Qianlong Emperor, see Wilhelm, "Bibliographical Notes," pp. 196–8: "One would think that a nation-wide persecution such as this might have resulted in a serious loss of literary material, but actually Qianlong's inquisition was a failure. All the more important writings of Qian have outlived this persecution, and those which have been lost succumbed not to political but to natural calamities" (romanization altered).

76 The best treatment of the reception of Qian Qianyi's writings following the Qianlong era is Kang-i Sun Chang's "Qian Qianyi and His Place in History," in Wilt L. Idema, Wai-yee Li and Ellen Widmer ed., *Trauma and Transcendence in Early Qing Literature* (Cambridge, MA: Harvard University Press, 2006), pp. 199–218. Chang cites among others Zhao Yuan 趙園, who refers to Qian as "one who lost his integrity" 失節者 (*Ming Qing zhi ji shidafu yanjiu* 明清之際士大夫研究, cited on p. 199).

77 See Jonathan D. Spence and John E. Wills, Jr. ed., *From Ming to Ch'ing: Conquest, Region and Continuity in Seventeenth-Century China* (New Haven: Yale University Press, 1979).

78 In addition to those below see: Hongnam Kim, *The Life of a Patron: Zhou Lianggong (1612–1672) and the Painters of Seventeenth-Century China* (New York: China Institute in America, 1996); Ho Koon-piu, "Should We Die as Martyrs to the Ming Cause? Scholar-officials' Views on Martyrdom during the Ming-Qing Transition," *Oriens Extremus* 37 (2) (1994): 123–51; Tom Fisher, "Loyalist

Alternatives in the Early Ch'ing," *Harvard Journal of Asiatic Studies* 44 (1984): 83–122; Wing-ming Chan, "The Early-Qing Discourse on Loyalty," *East Asian History* 19 (2000): 27–52; and Lawrence D. Kessler, "Chinese Scholars and the Early Manchu State," *Harvard Journal of Asiatic Studies* 31 (1971): 179–200.

79 Tobie Meyer-Fong, "Making a Place for Meaning in Early Qing Yangzhou," *Late Imperial China* 20 (1) (1999): 49–84 (52). "From the vantage point of the 1660s . . ." she continues, "the range of options was far more nuanced than a simple trichotomy of 'romantics,' 'stoics,' and 'martyrs' would allow" [in reference to Frederic Wakeman, Jr., "Romantics, Stoics, and Martyrs in Seventeenth-Century China," *Journal of Asian Studies* 43 (4) (1984): 631–65]. Elsewhere, Meyer-Fong notes of the new age, "the (re)creation of a new, broadly inclusive community of elites, in some cases along the lines of preconquest friendship networks, preceded, and even facilitated, political accommodation that gradually took place between Han elites and the new Qing order" ("Packaging the Men of Our Times: Literary Anthologies, Friendship Networks, and Political Accommodation in the Early Qing," *Harvard Journal of Asiatic Studies* 64 (1) (2004): 5–56 [6]). On relationships between scholars of the early Qing, see Xie Zhengguang 謝正光 [Andrew Hsieh], *Qing chu shiwen yu shiren jiaoyou kao* 清初詩文與士人交遊考 (Nanjing: Nanjing daxue chubanshe, 2001).

80 Gu Yanwu was one man who refused contact with Qian during the early Qing on moral grounds. See Frederic Wakeman, Jr., *The Great Enterprise: The Manchu Reconstruction of Imperial Order in Seventeenth-Century China* (Berkeley: University of California Press, 1985), Volume 2, pp. 718–20 and p. 879, n. 86.

81 Bai, *Fu Shan's World*. Qian Qianyi's continued contact with Huang Zongxi, who had actively resisted the Manchu takeover of southern China until 1649 (*ECCP*, pp. 351–4), is one argument for a more cautious approach to his life and career during the early Qing.

82 On Qian's collaboration with the Qing government and the issue of his involvement in anti-Qing resistance movements, see in particular: Jin, *Qian Muzhai xiansheng nianpu*, pp. 938–52; Jerry Dennerline, *The Chia-ting Loyalists: Confucian Leadership and Social Change in Seventeenth-Century China* (New Haven: Yale University Press, 1981), pp. 266–8; Chen, *Liu Rushi biezhuan*, Volume 3, and Wai-yee Li, "Heroic Transformations: Women and National Trauma in Early Qing Literature," *Harvard Journal of Asiatic Studies* 59 (2) (1999): 363–443 (395–408).

83 Qian Qianyi, "Ke *Gushi tanyuan* mulu hou xu" 刻《古史談苑》目錄後序, in *Muzhai chuxueji* 74 (*QMZQJ*, Volume 3, pp. 1636–8). This work is now housed in the National Central Library 中央圖書館 in Taiwan (Cai, *Shengping yu zhushu*, p. 39).

84 On this group, see John W. Dardess, *Blood and History in China: The Donglin Faction and its Repression, 1620–1627* (Honolulu: University of Hawai'i Press, 2002).

85 Nelson I. Wu, "Tung Ch'i-ch'ang (1555–1636): Apathy in Government and Fervor in Art," in Arthur F. Wright and Denis Twitchett ed., *Confucian Personalities* (Stanford: Stanford University Press, 1962), pp. 260–93.

86 Cai, *Shengping yu zhushu*, p. 45.

87 On Gongan literary thought, see in particular: two studies by Chih-p'ing Chou, "The Poetry and Poetic Theory of Yüan Hung-tao (1568–1610)," *Tsing-Hua Journal of Chinese Studies* (New Series) 15 (1/2) (1983): 113–42, and *Yüan Hung-tao and the Kung-an School* (Cambridge: Cambridge University Press, 1988); Ren Fangqiu 任訪秋, *Yuan Zhonglang yanjiu* 袁中郎研究 (Shanghai: Guji chubanshe, 1983); Martine Vallette-Hémery, *Yuan Hongdao (1568–1610): théorie et pratique littéraires* (Paris: Mémoires de l'Institut des Hautes Études Chinoises, 1982); Zhang Guoguang 張國光 and Huang Qingquan 黃清泉 ed., *Wan Ming wenxue gexinpai*

Gongan san Yuan yanjiu 晚明文學革新派公安三袁研究 (Wuhan: Huazhong shifan daxue chubanshe, 1987), and two studies by Jonathan Chaves, "The Expression of Self in the Kung-an School: Non-Romantic Individualism," in Robert E. Hegel and Richard C. Hessney ed., *Expressions of Self in Chinese Literature* (New York: Columbia University Press, 1985), pp. 123–50, and "The Panoply of Images: A Reconsideration of the Literary Theories of the Kung-an School," in Susan Bush and Christian Murck ed., *Theories of the Arts in China* (Princeton: Princeton University Press, 1983), pp. 341–64. Qian's friend Cheng Jiasui is discussed in Chapter Four.

88 On the concept of *xingling*, see James J. Y. Liu, *The Art of Chinese Poetry* (London: Routledge, 1962), pp. 70–6.

89 Yuan Hongdao, "Liu Yuanding shi xu" 劉元定詩序, *Yuan Hongdao ji jianjiao*, Volume 3, pp. 1528–9.

90 Qian Qianyi, "Shu Qu Youzhong shijuan" 書瞿有仲詩卷, in *Muzhai youxueji* 47 (*QMZQJ*, Volume 6, pp. 1557–9). The *Muzhai youxueji* 牧齋有學集 [Collected Further Scholarship from Shepherd's Studio] of 1664 was the second published collection of Qian's works.

91 Qian Qianyi, "Huang Tingbiao Ren'an shi xu" 黃庭表忍菴詩序, in *Muzhai youxueji* 20 (*QMZQJ*, Volume 5, pp. 846–7). For more extensive examinations of Qian's literary theories in relation to those of the Gongan School, see Sun, *Ming mo Qing chu wenxue*, pp. 123–39 and pp. 257–79, Hu, *Yushanpai shilun*, pp. 44–9, Lynn A. Struve, "Huang Zongxi in Context: A Reappraisal of His Major Writings," *Journal of Asian Studies* 47(3) (1988): 474–502 and Che, "Not Words But Feelings," pp. 60–1.

92 On the compilation of the *Liechao shiji*, see Sun, *Ming mo Qing chu wenxue*, pp. 342–58, Yim, *Poetics of Historical Memory*, pp. 235–41, and Meyer-Fong, "Packaging the Men of Our Times," pp. 18–21.

93 Qian Qianyi, "Yaohuangji xu" 姚黃集序, in *Muzhai chuxueji* 29 (*QMZQJ*, Volume 2, pp. 885–6). See also Zheng Yuanxun, "Yingyuan ziji" 影園自記, translated by Duncan Campbell as *A Personal Record of My Garden of Reflection* (Wellington: Asian Studies Institute Translation Paper #5, 2004).

94 Qian Qianyi, "Ti Du Canglüe ziping shiwen" 題杜蒼略自評詩文, in *Muzhai youxueji* 49 (*QMZQJ*, Volume 6, pp. 1594–5).

95 Qian Qianyi, "Jiangyin Li Guanzhi qishi xu" 江陰李貫之七十序, in *Muzhai chuxueji* 37 (*QMZQJ*, Volume 2, pp. 1026–7).

96 The most extensive treatment of Qian's library to date is Jian Xiujuan's 簡秀娟 *Qian Qianyi cangshu yanjiu* 錢謙益藏書研究 (Taibei: Hanmei tushu, 1991). See also Chen, *Liu Rushi biezhuan*, Volume 2, pp. 820–32. The destruction of the Tower of Crimson Clouds collection is related in a colophon by another twice-serving official, Cao Rong 曹溶: "Not long after he had travelled north [to take up office] he [Qian] returned home on the pretext of ill health, taking up residence in Red Bean Mountain Estate 紅豆山莊. Turning to his book collection, he began again to bring order to it, mending those books that needed repair, making copies of those that needed copying, at the same time sorting the collection into various categories. He then had the whole collection housed upstairs in the Tower of the Crimson Clouds, in seventy-three large bookcases. With evident joy, he would survey his collection, exclaiming: 'I may well have been reduced to poverty in my old age but I'm certainly rich in terms of my books!' Ten or so days later his young daughter was playing upstairs in the tower with her wet-nurse in the middle of the night when, as the wick of the lamp was being trimmed, it fell amidst a pile of papers and caught fire. Downstairs, Qian Qianyi arose with a start, but by that time the flames already lit up the sky and the tower was beyond saving. He fled outside. Before long, both the tower itself and the books that it had once housed had been

reduced to ashes." Cao Rong, "Jiangyunlou cangshu mu tici" 絳雲樓藏書目題詞, appended to the *Jiangyunlou shumu* 絳雲樓書目 (see publication details below), pp. 321–2, translated by Duncan Campbell in "The Moral Status of the Book: Huang Zongxi in the Private Libraries of Late Imperial China," *East Asian History* 32/33 (2006/2007): 1–24 (17).

97 Cai, *Shengping yu zhushu*, p. 102.

98 Niu Xiu, "Hedongjun" 河東君, reproduced in Fan Jingzhong 范景中 and Zhou Shutian 周書田 ed., *Liu Rushi shiji* 柳如是事輯 (Hangzhou: Zhongguo meishu xueyuan chubanshe, 2002), pp. 13–7.

99 Duncan Campbell, "Cao Rong (1613–85) on Books: Loss, Libraries and Circulation," unpublished seminar paper delivered to the Department of History, University of Otago (10 May 2006), p. 10. For Tu Lien-chê's biography of Cao, see *ECCP*, p. 740.

100 The *Jiangyunlou shumu* is published as part of the *Xuxiu siku quanshu* 續修四庫全書 collection (Shanghai: Guji chubanshe, 2002), Volume 920, pp. 319–424, a facsimile reprint of the 1820 edition housed at the Beijing Library. The catalogue is a rather eclectic document, frequently omitting details such as the compiler or number of volumes in a work, but clearly placing importance on the period of the imprint. Cao Rong notes that Qian "would only list in his catalogue the older imprints of works," and cites glaring omissions (such as the *Zongjinglu* 宗鏡錄) as evidence for the document's incompleteness ("Jiangyunlou cangshu mu tici," p. 322). I am inclined to think that the catalogue tells us more about the way in which Qian Qianyi wanted to present himself as a collector than about the actual holdings of the library.

101 "A book that has once been part of the collection of a famous person and which carries both his seal and his handwriting seems to have a much enhanced ancient fragrance 古香 about it" (cited in Gu Huizhi 谷輝之 ed., *Liu Rushi shiwen ji* 柳如是詩文集 [Beijing: Xinhua shudian, 1996], p. 243).

102 Qian Qianyi, "Ba Songban Zuozhuan" 跋宋版左傳, in *Muzhai chuxueji* 85 (*QMZQJ*, Volume 3, p. 1780).

103 Cao, "Jiangyunlou cangshu mu tici," p. 322. On some of the other avenues of élite consumption enjoyed by Qian (such as tea, wine and music), see Li, "Xintai de dianxing."

104 Campbell, "Moral Status of the Book," p. 16.

105 Qian Qianyi, "Da Shanyin Xu Bodiao shu" 答山陰徐伯調書, in *Muzhai youxueji* 39 (*QMZQJ*, Volume 6, pp. 1346–9).

106 Qian Qianyi, "Da Du Canglüe lunwen shu" 答杜蒼略論文書, in *Muzhai youxueji* 38 (*QMZQJ*, Volume 3, pp. 1306–9).

107 Qian Qianyi, "Du Du xiaojian" 讀杜小箋, in *Muzhai chuxueji* 106–10 (*QMZQJ*, Volume 3, pp. 2153–2219). The full study (i.e. including that completed after the publication of the *Muzhai chuxueji*) is reprinted as *Qian zhu Du shi* 錢注杜詩 (Shanghai: Guji chubanshe, 1979) in two volumes. Some decades ago William Hung (*Tu Fu: China's Greatest Poet* [Cambridge, MA: Harvard University Press, 1952]) raised questions over the authenticity of Qian's edition of Du Fu's works: "Qian Qianyi (1582–1664) was a man of masterly erudition, persuasive literary ability, and rather doubtful character . . . In my judgement, the so-called Wu Ruo text with its fine display of variant readings — a hand copy of which was in the possession of Qian alone, but was nowhere to be found shortly after his time — was a clever forgery made by plagiarising a plagiarist's edition of 1204 and by putting in a number of additions and alterations. Circumstantial evidence seems to point to Qian himself as the forger" (pp. 13–5, romanization altered). The commentary is nonetheless an extraordinary insight into Qian's literary thought, and

would certainly repay further scholarship. For a useful preliminary study, see Zhang Jipei 張繼沛, "Qian Qianyi jian Du zhi yaozhi ji qi jituo" 錢謙益箋杜之要旨及其寄託, in *Lianhe shuyuan sanshi zhounian jinian lunwenji* 聯合書院三十周年紀念論文集 (Xianggang: Zhongwen daxue chubanshe, 1986), pp. 215–34. The two most comprehensive treatments of the work of which I am aware are Hao Runhua's 郝潤花 Qian zhu Du shi *yu shishi huzheng fangfa* 《錢注杜詩》與詩史互証方法 (Hefei: Huangshan shushe, 2000), and Chan Che-shan's 陳芷珊 lengthy *Qian jian Du shi yanjiu* 錢箋杜詩研究 (Unpublished PhD thesis: The University of Hong Kong, 2005).

108 "Publisher's Introduction" 出版説明 to Wang Qi ed., *Li Taibai quanji* 李太白全集 (rpt.; Beijing: Zhonghua shuju, 1977), pp. 9–10.

109 *Jiangyunlou shumu*, pp. 323–5.

110 James C. Y. Watt, "The Literati Environment," in Li and Watt ed., *The Chinese Scholar's Studio*, pp. 1–13 (1).

111 Qian Qianyi, "Xinke Shisanjing zhushu xu" 新刻十三經注疏序, in *Muzhai chuxueji* 28 (*QMZQJ*, Volume 2, pp. 850–2).

112 For biographical details on Liu, see the entry by Fang Chao-ying in *ECCP*, pp. 529–30, and that by Beata Grant in *ICTCL*, Volume 2, pp. 107–9. For a more extensive treatment of Liu's life and work in addition to Chen's *Liu Rushi biezhuan*, see Bian Min 卞敏, *Liu Rushi xinzhuan* 柳如是新傳 (Hangzhou: Zhejiang renmin chubanshe, 1997).

113 Shen Qiu 沈虯, "Hedongjun ji" 河東君記, reprinted in Fan and Zhou ed., *Liu Rushi shiji*, pp. 18–20.

114 "Thus did I hear" 如是我聞 is a conventional phrase in Buddhist texts.

115 Brook, *Confusions of Pleasure*, p. 230.

116 Dorothy Ko, *Teachers of the Inner Chambers: Women and Culture in Seventeenth-Century China* (Stanford: Stanford University Press, 1994); Zhang Hongsheng 張宏生 ed., *Ming Qing wenxue yu xingbie yanjiu* 明清文學與性別研究 (Nanjing: Jiangsu guji chubanshe, 2002); Wai-yee Li, "The Late Ming Courtesan: Invention of a Cultural Ideal," in Ellen Widmer and Kang-i Sun Chang ed., *Writing Women in Late Imperial China* (Stanford: Stanford University Press, 1997), pp. 46–73; Kang-i Sun Chang, *The Late-Ming Poet Ch'en Tzu-lung: Crises of Love and Loyalism* (New Haven: Yale University Press, 1991). See also Robyn Hamilton, "The Pursuit of Fame: Luo Qilan (1755–1813?) and the Debates about Women and Talent in Eighteenth-Century Jiangnan," *Late Imperial China* 18 (1) (1997): 39–71.

117 Niu Xiu's description of the literary partnership between Qian and Liu is a typically male-fantasist image: "In old age, Qian's obsession with reading and with books became even more pronounced and as he went about his editing and his checking of textual variants it was only Liu Shi that he would ever consult. Whenever the slightest furrow crossed his brow or his brush paused as it plied its way down the page, Liu Shi would immediately leap to her feet and proceed upstairs to consult some book or other and although the volumes were stacked as high as the rafters she would soon return with a particular volume of a specific book and would open it up *to point with her slender fingers* to precisely the right passage, never once making a mistake." (Niu, "Hedongjun," translated in Campbell, "Cao Rong (1613–85) on Books," p. 13 [my emphasis].)

118 Qian Qianyi, "Xinsi yuanri" 辛巳元日 and Liu Shi, "Yuanri ciyun" 元日次韻, in *Muzhai chuxueji* 18 (*QMZQJ*, Volume 1, pp. 622–3).

Chapter 2

1   The *Erya* 爾雅 lists the Five Marchmounts 五嶽 as follows: Tai 泰 in the east; Hua 華 in the west; Huo 霍 in the south; Heng 恒 in the north, and Song 嵩 in the centre. Beginning in the Sui period (581–618), Mount Heng 衡, originally recognized as the Southern Marchmount, began to regain that title once again at the expense of Mount Huo. See Xu Chaohua 徐朝華 ed., *Erya jinzhu* 爾雅今注 (Tianjin: Nankai daxue chubanshe, 1987), p. 238. For a useful discussion of the development of this system, see Aat Vervoorn's "Cultural Strata of Hua Shan, the Holy Peak of the West," *Monumenta Serica* 39 (1990–91): 1–30 (esp. pp. 1–13). I follow here Edward H. Schafer's translation of the term *yue* 嶽 as "Marchmount," explained in his *Pacing the Void: T'ang Approaches to the Stars* (Berkeley: University of California Press, 1977): "My version is based on the ancient belief that these numinous mountains stood at the four extremities of the habitable world, the marches of man's proper domain, the limits of the ritual tour of the Son of Heaven. There was, of course, a fifth — a kind of axial mount in the center of the world" (6).

2   See the "Shun dian" 舜典 chapter of the *Shujing*, rendered into English in James Legge trans., *The Chinese Classics* (rpt.; Hong Kong: Hong Kong University Press, 1960), Volume 3 (1), pp. 29–51.

3   Sima Qian 司馬遷, *Shiji* (rpt.; Beijing: Zhonghua shuju, 1959), Volume 4, pp. 1355–1404. For a rare first-hand account of these rituals, see the essay by Ma Dibo 馬第伯 entitled "Feng shan yiji" 封禪儀記, in Strassberg's *Inscribed Landscapes*, pp. 57–62.

4   John Hay, *Kernels of Energy, Bones of Earth: The Rock in Chinese Art* (New York: China House Gallery, 1985), pp. 59–60.

5   Robert E. Harrist, Jr., "Reading Chinese Mountains: Landscape and Calligraphy in China," *Orientations* (Dec 2000): 64–9 (65–6). On the rejection of the traditional *feng* and *shan* sacrifices by the Qing emperors, see Dott, *Identity Reflections*, pp. 150–81. Dott cites among other sources a poem composed by the Kangxi Emperor: "I desire, with close officials, to venerate true government; / there is no longer any need for gold seals and jade covers." (179)

6   John Lagerwey ("The Pilgrimage to Wu-tang Shan" in Susan Naquin and Chün-fang Yü ed., *Pilgrims and Sacred Sites in China* [Berkeley: University of California Press, 1992], pp. 293–332) notes that Daoists "were never entirely successful in pressing this claim, and of the five only Huashan and Taishan, albeit in very different manner [*sic*], play a significant and ongoing role in Daoist religious history" (328 n18, romanization altered).

7   Brook, "Communications and Commerce," p. 629.

8   Brook, "Communications and Commerce," p. 630.

9   Zhang Dai, "Xihu xiangshi" 西湖香市, in Xia and Cheng ed., *Taoan mengyi / Xihu mengxun*, pp. 109–10.

10   In an important study, James Robson ("The Polymorphous Space of the Southern Marchmount [Nanyue 南嶽]: An Introduction to Nanyue's Religious History and Preliminary Notes on Buddhist-Daoist Interaction," *Cahiers d'Extrême-Asie* 8 [1995]: 221–64) cautions against the definitive categorization of sites as uniquely Buddhist or Daoist, showing that the history of Mount Heng 衡 was informed by its involvement with a number of competing religious traditions. See also Vervoorn, "Cultural Strata," p. 23.

11   Guo Xi, "Shanshui xun" 山水訓 in *Linquan gaozhi ji* 林泉高致集, translated as "Advice on Landscape," in Victor Mair, Nancy S. Steinhardt and Paul R. Goldin ed., *Hawai'i Reader in Traditional Chinese Culture* (Honolulu: University of Hawai'i Press, 2005), pp. 380–7.

12   Min Linsi 閔麟嗣 comp., *Huangshan zhi dingben* (Hefei: Huangshan shushe, 1990), pp. 80–115. This important gazetteer is discussed later in this chapter.

13   *Huangshan zhi* (1667), pp. 457–9.

14   For a note on the term *tujing* 圖經, which "by the Ming dynasty . . . had become somewhat archaic," see Timothy Brook, *Geographical Sources of Ming-Qing History* (Ann Arbor: Center for Chinese Studies, University of Michigan, 2002), p. 4.

15   Paul W. Kroll, "Verses from on High: The Ascent of T'ai Shan," in Shuen-fu Lin and Stephen Owen ed., *The Vitality of the Lyric Voice: Shih Poetry from the Late Han to the T'ang* (Princeton: Princeton University Press, 1986), pp. 167–216 (pp. 186–9).

16   Michael Loewe, *Faith, Myth and Reason in Han China* (Indianapolis: Hackett Publishing Company, 1994), pp. 130–6.

17   Anne Swann Goodrich, *The Peking Temple of the Eastern Peak*, cited in Joseph P. McDermott's "The Making of a Chinese Mountain, Huangshan: Politics and Wealth in Chinese Art," *Asian Cultural Studies* 17 (1989): 145–76 (153). See also Naquin and Yü, "Introduction: Pilgrimage in China," in *idem* ed., *Pilgrims and Sacred Sites*, pp. 1–38 (17). On religious toponyms at Daoist mountains, see Thomas Hahn's "The Standard Taoist Mountain and Related Features of Religious Geography," *Cahiers d'Extrême-Asie* 4 (1988): 145–56.

18   The Yuan scholar Wang Zemin 汪澤民, who is introduced later in this chapter, notes the year of his acquisition of the text, the *wuxu* 戊戌 year of the Dade 大德 reign (1298), but provides no other details (*Huangshan zhi dingben* 207). Qian Qianyi, as we will see, makes frequent use of the *Huangshan tujing* in the composition of his own essay, although the only work pertaining to Yellow Mountain listed in the *Jiangyunlou shumu* (345) is "Huangshan Lushan er tu" 黃山盧山二圖 [Maps of Yellow Mountain and Hermitage Mountain].

19   *Huangshan tujing* 1a. My rendering of Huangshan 黃山 as Yellow Mountain (in the singular) throughout this study is based on the way the name is used by the authors on whose essays I focus here, with *shan* 山 as a single entity consisting of a group of *feng* 峰 [peaks]. Strassberg, not unreasonably, renders the name into "Yellow Emperor Mountain" (see his *Inscribed Landscapes*) based on its supposed etymology, but the degree to which the character *Huang* 黃 would have suggested *Huangdi* 黃帝 [Yellow Emperor] to a late-Ming reader is unclear. To my mind, the fact that so many seventeenth-century travellers feel the need to record the origins of the name in their essays, and the fact that uncertainty remains in the minds of some scholars as to this story's legitimacy, argues against Strassberg's extrapolative translation.

20   *Huangshan zhi* 黃山志 (Hefei: Huangshan shushe, 1988), p. 2.

21   *Huangshan zhi* (1988), p. 2.

22   Zhao Fang, "Song Chen Dabo you Huangshan huanshi xu" 送陳大博遊黃山還詩序, in *Huangshan zhi dingben*, pp. 172–3.

23   *Huangshan zhi* (1988) 2; *Lie xian zhuan*, traditionally ascribed to Liu Xiang 劉向 (original *ming* Gengsheng 更生, *zi* Zizheng 子政; 79?–6 BCE), (rpt.; Shanghai: Guji chubanshe, 1990), p. 23. Many scholars in the seventeenth century seem to have preferred the name "Yellow Sea" 黃海 for the mountain, and we find this used particularly in titles and colophons of paintings produced during the early Qing period. Xie Zhaoshen 謝兆申 attributes the name "Yellow Sea" to his friend Pan Zhiheng 潘之恒 (*Huangshan zhi dingben* 247; for Pan's essay on the subject, see *Huangshan zhi* (1667), pp. 479–80). About this name too there is an element of ambiguity — some travellers at least seem to have taken it to refer to a specific site on the mountain rather than the entire range (see, for example, Wang Zhijie's 王之杰 essay in *Huangshan zhi* (1667), pp. 454–5; *Huangshan zhi dingben*, pp. 224–7).

24   *Huangshan zhi dingben*, p. 373.

25 Far more difficult to quantify, but even more important in the present context, is the extent to which their observations and experiences of the peaks were informed by the names handed down to Ming and Qing scholars, a theme to which I shall return later.

26 In this respect at least, the definitive listing and mapping in the 1988 edition of the *Huangshan zhi* of all of Yellow Mountain's peaks and their heights is somewhat problematic in my view, implying (at least in the case of the original 36) a thousand-year continuity in the relationship between name and site that, as Qian shows us, is more than a little misleading. After the naming of White Goose Peak in Li Bai's eighth-century poem, it disappears, omitted from the *Huangshan tujing*'s listing of the Thirty-six Peaks, to which is appended the following note: "Apart from these thirty-six, the numerous other peaks that rise to only two or three hundred *ren* high 諸峰高二三百仞者, and the myriad cliffs, caves, streams and springs that are not mentioned in the classics or biographies are not recorded here" (*Huangshan tujing* 10a). Qian Qianyi, as we will see in his essay, draws on this explanation and suggests that Li Bai's peak might be too small to be listed, while less than half a century later, Min Linsi appends to his entry on White Goose Ridge 嶺 the comment that in his poem Li Bai [erroneously] called the ridge a peak (*Huangshan zhi dingben*, p. 33). By 1988, however, White Goose Peak "is located to the east of White Goose Ridge . . . and stands at 1768 metres above sea level," a height that ranks it ninth of all the peaks (82 are identified) in Yellow Mountain (*Huangshan zhi* [1988], p. 17).

27 Wang Xuanxi 汪玄錫 refers in his essay of 1532 to the fact that the Huizhou locals held different opinions as to what exactly constituted "Yellow Mountain" ("Huangshan youji" 黃山遊記, in *Huangshan zhi dingben*, pp. 208–9).

28 Observing the economic landscape in *Wuzazu* 五雜俎, Xie Zhaozhe 謝肇淛 claimed: "The rich men of the empire in the regions south of the Yangzi are from Xin'an . . . The great merchants of Huizhou have made fisheries and salt their occupation, and have amassed fortunes amounting to one million taels of silver." See Ping-ti Ho, "The Salt Merchants of Yang-chou: A Study of Commercial Capitalism in Eighteenth-Century China," *Harvard Journal of Asiatic Studies* 17 (1954): 130–68 (143, romanization altered).

29 Huang, *Yitong lucheng tuji*, p. 246.

30 One can also trace the boom in the Yellow Mountain region by the number of successful *jinshi* candidates in She 歙 County: a total of 188 during the whole of the Ming, of which a disproportionately high 89 date from the Wanli period or later (i.e. after 1573). See *Shexian zhi* 歙縣志 (Beijing: Zhonghua shuju, 1995), pp. 505–14.

31 Yang Erzeng, "Huangshan tushuo" 黃山圖說, in *Hainei qiguan*, reprinted in *Zhongguo gudai banhua congkan erbian* 中國古代版畫叢刊二編 (Shanghai: Guji chubanshe, 1994), Volume 8.

32 Wang Qi, *Sancai tuhui* (rpt.; Shanghai: Guji chubanshe, 1985), p. 273. For a partial reproduction and discussion of this work in English, see John A. Goodall's *Heaven and Earth: Album Leaves from a Ming Encyclopaedia: San-ts'ai t'u-hui, 1610* (Boulder: Shambhala, 1979).

33 References to this work in the present study (excluding that used for the textual analysis of Qian Qianyi's essay; see Chapter Five) are to the Huangshan shushe edition (Hefei, 1990), which at the time I began working on Yellow Mountain was the most easily accessible edition. The recently published Xianzhuang shuju edition (*Zhonghua shanshuizhi congkan* 中華山水志叢刊 [Beijing: 2004] 16: 133–532), also based on the 1686 edition, became available to me too late to be used, but appears to be a far more reliable text, and should now become the standard edition of this work.

34   *Huangshan zhi dingben*, p. 5.

35   The exact date of this work is uncertain. Evidently there were two versions produced, the first compiled by Wang Shihong with the help of Wu Song 吳菘 and Wu Zhantai 吳瞻泰 (*zi* Dongyan 東巖, *hao* Genzhai 艮齋; 1657–1735) after 1679 (the date of Min Linsi's work), the second edition revised by Wang Yuanzhi 汪遠志 and Wang Shuqi 汪樹琪 and published no earlier than 1691. The revised edition, upon which the presently existing edition is based (*Anhui congshu* 安徽叢書 Series 5 [Shanghai: Anhui congshu bianyinchu, 1935], Vols. 10–15), contains a preface by Huang Zongxi dated the *xinwei* 辛未 year (1691). Huang also composed a preface to Wang Shihong's poetry, "Wang Fuchen shixu" 汪扶晨詩序, which seems not to have been included in the gazetteer (see *Huang Zongxi quanji*, Volume 10, pp. 86–8). The 1988 edition of the *Huangshan zhi* gives 1686 as the original date of publication (p. 247). Brook (*Geographical Sources*, p. 85) refers to a 1691 edition only, but erroneously dates *Huang Zongxi*'s preface to 1631 (i.e. the previous *xinwei* year). For arguments against the possibility of a "definitive" Yellow Mountain gazetteer, see the prefaces to this collection. For a complete listing of Yellow Mountain gazetteers of the Ming and Qing, see Brook, *Geographical Sources* under She 歙, pp. 84–6.

36   Anlan Chaogang comp., *Huangshan Cuiweisi zhi* (rpt.; Yangzhou: Jiangsu guangling guji keyinshe, 1996).

37   The *Huangshan song shi pu* appeared in Zhang Chao 張潮 (b. 1650) ed., *Zhaodai congshu* 昭代叢書, first published in 1697 (ed. Yang Fuji 楊復吉 [1747–1820] rpt.; Shanghai: Guji chubanshe, 1990), Volume 1, pp. 52–4.

38   Most of the discussion that follows is based on the essays found in either the *Huangshan zhi* (1667) or the *Huangshan zhi dingben*. Of these, the latter is more reliable in terms of its chronological arrangement. Li Yimang's rather inaptly named *Ming Qing ren you Huangshan jichao*, which somewhat bizarrely includes two essays from the Song and Yuan periods, is a shorter collection of the most important of these essays, in some cases in slightly alternative versions. Li also includes the two essays by Xu Hongzu which are missing from the previous collections. Alternative versions of some essays also appear in the Jiangnan 江南 section of Wu Qiushi 吳秋士 ed., *Tianxia mingshan youji* 天下名山遊記 (Shanghai: Zhongying shudian, 1936). See also Wang ed., *Lidai Huangshan youji xuan*, and for poetry, Huang Songlin 黃松林 ed., *Huangshan gujin youlan shi xuan* 黃山古今遊覽詩選 (Hefei: Huangshan shushe, 1989).

39   *Huangshan zhi* (1667), p. 433; *Huangshan zhi dingben*, p. 204.

40   *Huangshan zhi* (1667), pp. 433–5; *Huangshan zhi dingben*, pp. 205–7.

41   *Huangshan zhi* (1667), p. 435; *Huangshan zhi dingben*, p. 207.

42   *Huangshan zhi* (1667), pp. 435–6; *Huangshan zhi dingben*, pp. 208–9.

43   For the Yellow Mountain poems of Jia Dao, see *Huangshan zhi dingben*, pp. 369–70.

44   *Huangshan zhi* (1667), pp. 437–9; *Huangshan zhi dingben*, pp. 209–12.

45   James Cahill, "Huang Shan Paintings as Pilgrimage Pictures," in Naquin and Yü ed., *Pilgrims and Sacred Sites*, pp. 246–92 (252).

46   *Huangshan zhi* (1667), pp. 439–41.

47   *Huangshan zhi* (1667), pp. 444–6; *Huangshan zhi dingben*, pp. 212–4. Although Xie himself, as his name implies, was born in Hangzhou. For a brief biography of this man (by Leon Zolbrod and L. Carrington Goodrich), see *DMB*, Volume 1, pp. 546–50.

48   Brook, *Geographical Sources*, pp. 35–6.

49   Zhu Huirong 朱惠榮 ed., *Xu Xiake youji jiaozhu* 徐霞客遊記校注 (Kunming: Yunnan renmin chubanshe, 1985), Volume 1, pp. 17–23 and 39–42. For a

translation and short discussion of Xu's two essays, see Li Chi trans., *The Travel Diaries of Hsü Hsia-k'o* (Hong Kong: Chinese University Press, 1974), pp. 67–83. See also Fang Chao-ying's biography of Xu in *ECCP*, pp. 314–6, Ward, *Xu Xiake* and Andrea Riemenschnitter, "Traveler's Vocation: Xu Xiake and His Excursion to the Southwestern Frontier," in Nicola Di Cosmo and Don J. Wyatt ed., *Political Frontiers, Ethnic Boundaries, and Human Geographies in Chinese History* (London: RoutledgeCurzon, 2003), pp. 286–323.

50 *Huangshan zhi dingben*, p. 97. Qian Qianyi is said to have urged the great bibliophile Mao Jin to publish the collection in the early Qing, although this proved unsuccessful, and the *Xu Xiake youji* was not published until the Qianlong era (see Chaves, "Yellow Mountain Poems," pp. 465–6).

51 The fact that in his Yellow Mountain essay Qian Qianyi himself does not mention Xu's successful ascent of Heavenly Capital certainly accords with Chang Chun-shu's view that when he wrote his biography of Xu, Qian had not yet seen the *Xu Xiake youji* (Chang, "An Annotated Bibliography on Hsü Hsia-k'o," cited in Chaves, "Yellow Mountain Poems," p. 465). For Qian's biography of Xu, "Xu Xiake zhuan" 徐霞客傳, see *QMZQJ*, Volume 3, pp. 1593–6.

52 *Huangshan zhi* (1667), pp. 455–6; *Huangshan zhi dingben*, p. 215.

53 *Huangshan zhi* (1667), pp. 450–2; *Huangshan zhi dingben*, pp. 215–7.

54 For Pan's essays, see *Huangshan zhi* (1667), pp. 479–80.

55 See, for example, the 1610 essay of Zou Kuangming (*Huangshan zhi* [1667], pp. 471–4).

56 The number of named monastic buildings on Yellow Mountain that date back to the early seventeenth century (see *Huangshan zhi* [1988], pp. 218–32) is a strong indication that this period was one of high religious activity, although literary conventions dictate that monks still feature only infrequently in the travel accounts of the age.

57 On the Empress Dowager Cisheng, see the entry by Chou Tao-chi in *DMB*, Volume 1, pp. 856–9.

58 See Else Glahn's biography of Fudeng in *DMB*, Volume 1: 462–6, and Ray Huang, *1587: A Year of No Significance: The Ming Dynasty in Decline* (New Haven: Yale University Press, 1981), pp. 14–5.

59 Chün-fang Yü, *The Renewal of Buddhism in China: Chu-hung and the Late Ming Synthesis* (New York: Columbia University Press, 1981), p. 154.

60 McDermott, "Making of a Chinese Mountain," p. 157.

61 It seems likely also that imperial support of Pumen and his monks should have created an interest in the mountain among those outside of the Huizhou region, investing the landscape with empire-wide political and cultural importance, although the relatively small number of extant written accounts by seventeenth-century visitors from further afield argues against this.

62 Bai, *Fu Shan's World*, p. 128.

63 In aesthetic terms, there are clear parallels here between the formalistic ideals of the late Ming and those of the Romantic movements in the West. This can be seen particularly in the interest shown during both periods in the kinds of grotesque forms that would not have conformed to earlier aesthetic ideals. The types of dense cloud forms that late-Ming travellers found so fascinating at Yellow Mountain and that would have their praises sung by the Western Romantics, existed, of course, long before they began to attract popular attention. Three years after Qian Qianyi visited Yellow Mountain, the diarist John Evelyn (1620–1706) described his crossing the Alps into Italy in a particularly "late-Ming" fashion: "As we ascended, we enter'd a very thick, soled and darke body of Clowds, which look'd like rocks at a little distance, which dured us for neere a mile going up; they were dry misty

Vapours hanging undissolved for a vast thicknesse, & altogether both obscuring the Sunn & Earth, so as we seemed to be rather in the Sea than the Clowdes, till we having pierc'd quite through, came into a most serene heaven, as if we had been above all human Conversation, the Mountaine appearing more like a greate Iland, than joynd to any other hills; for we could perceive nothing but a Sea of thick Clowds rowling under our feete like huge Waves . . ." (E. S. de Beer ed., *The Diary of John Evelyn* [Oxford: Clarendon Press, 1955], Volume 2, pp. 207–8). The diary, significantly, was not published until 1818, the height of Romanticism in the West, and a period that also boasts works of visual art that (in a thematic sense at least) would not be out of place in early seventeenth-century Jiangnan, or indeed, at Yellow Mountain. See, for example, Caspar David Friedrich's (1774–1840) *Der Wanderer über dem Nebelmeer* of 1818 (Hamburg: Kunsthalle).

64   *Huangshan zhi* (1667), pp. 471–4.

65   *Huangshan zhi* (1667), pp. 452–5; *Huangshan zhi dingben*, pp. 221–7.

66   *Huangshan zhi* (1667), pp. 459–63; *Huangshan zhi dingben*, pp. 232–6.

67   *Huangshan zhi* (1667), pp. 489–94 in five parts; *Huangshan zhi dingben*, pp. 247–52 (in a condensed form).

68   *Huangshan zhi dingben*, pp. 253–8.

69   *Huangshan zhi* (1667), pp. 474–9; *Huangshan zhi dingben*, pp. 241–6.

70   *Huangshan zhi* (1667), pp. 433–5; *Huangshan zhi dingben*, pp. 205–7.

71   *Huangshan zhi* (1988), pp. 218–32.

72   *Huangshan zhi* (1988), pp. 232–40.

73   Nor can this golden age of Buddhism on the mountain, and indeed, throughout China during the Wanli reign, be attributed to state financial support alone. The Buddhist revival in the late Ming, as Chün-fang Yü reminds us, was one of a range of developments that characterized "the general intellectual and religious dynamism of the period" (see "Ming Buddhism," in Twitchett and Mote ed., *Cambridge History of China Volume 8*, pp. 893–952).

74   *Huangshan zhi dingben*, pp. 266–77.

75   For Yang's essay, see *Huangshan zhi dingben*, pp. 277–85.

76   It is possible, in fact, that the name of the tree was given incorrectly, as no such pine appears listed in the standard reference works, including the important early Qing catalogue by Min Linsi, *Huangshan song shi pu* (1697).

77   *Huangshan zhi* (1667), pp. 512–8; *Huangshan zhi dingben*, pp. 286–94.

78   For a note on the practice, see Kroll, "Verses from on High," pp. 201–2. Kroll's discussion is based on Li Bai's ascent of Taishan: "At Heaven's Gate, one long whistle I give / And from a myriad *li* the clear wind comes 天門一長嘯 / 萬里清風來" (200). See also Paul Demiéville's "La Montagne dans l'art littéraire chinois," in *France-Asie/Asia* 20 (1) (1965): 7–32: "le sifflement (*xiao*) était une pratique taoïste à laquelle on attribait une sorte d'efficacité cosmique" (18, romanization altered), and Susan E. Nelson's "The Piping of Man," in Wu Hung and Katherine R. Tsiang ed., *Body and Face in Chinese Visual Culture* (Cambridge, MA: Harvard University Press, 2005), pp. 283–310.

79   *Huangshan zhi* (1667), p. 466.

80   See Qian's Poem #14, "Chushiri cong Wenshuyuan guo Heshian dao Yixiantian xia Baibu Yunti jing Lianhuafeng qi Tianhai" 初十日從文殊院過喝石菴到一綫天下百步雲梯逕蓮華峰憩天海 (*QMZQJ*, Volume 1, pp. 648–9). For a note on my system of numbering Qian's Yellow Mountain poems, see Chapter Four.

81   *Huangshan zhi dingben*, pp. 294–7.

Chapter 3

1   Craig Clunas, *Pictures and Visuality in Early Modern China* (London: Reaktion Books, 1997), p. 83.
2   Ye, *Vignettes from the Late Ming*, p. 16.
3   McDermott, "Making of a Chinese Mountain," pp. 161–3. See also Hay, *Shitao*, pp. 42–6.
4   One can trace the shift in scholarly approach to this issue in treatments of the life and career of the calligrapher Fu Shan, who, according to his 1944 biography by C. H. Ts'ui and J. C. Yang (*ECCP*, pp. 260–2) "never wrote or painted for money, preferring to rely on his wide knowledge of medicine, and his practical ability as a physician to make a living." Qianshen Bai's recent study is a much more extensive and sophisticated treatment of artistic practice during the Ming-Qing transition, showing clearly that Fu, in his own words, "suffer[red] the burden of writing calligraphy for an income" (*Fu Shan's World*, p. 86). For other recent critical examinations of the role of the marketplace in late-imperial art production and consumption, see James Cahill, *The Painter's Practice: How Artists Lived and Worked in Traditional China* (New York: Columbia University Press, 1994); Hay, *Shitao*; and Craig Clunas, *Elegant Debts: The Social Art of Wen Zhengming, 1470–1559* (London: Reaktion Books, 2004).
5   Chin and Hsü, "Anhui Merchant Culture," p. 23; Ellen Johnston Laing, "Sixteenth-Century Patterns of Art Patronage: Qiu Ying and the Xiang Family," *Journal of the American Oriental Society* 111 (1) (1991): 1–7.
6   Qian Qianyi, "Ba Qian Hou Hanshu" 跋前後漢書, in *Muzhai chuxueji* 85 (*QMZQJ*, Volume 3, pp. 1780–1) and "Shu jiu cang Song diao liang Hanshu hou" 書舊藏宋雕兩漢書後, in *Muzhai youxueji* 46 (*QMZQJ*, Volume 6, pp. 1529–30). In the former Qian gives the original purchase price as 1000 *jin* 金, but in the latter this has increased to 1200 *jin*.
7   It was noticeable that both of the two major recent exhibitions of Yellow Mountain art, "Dreams of Yellow Mountain: Landscapes of Survival in Seventeenth-Century China" (Metropolitan Museum of Art, New York, September 2003–February 2004) and "Yellow Mountain: China's Ever-Changing Landscape" (Arthur M. Sackler Gallery, Washington DC, May–August 2008) concentrated on post-1644 works.
8   Julia Andrews and Haruki Yoshida, "Theoretical Foundations of the Anhui School," in Cahill ed., *Shadows of Mt. Huang*, pp. 34–42 (34).
9   Adapted from Andrews and Yoshida, "Theoretical Foundations," p. 34.
10 James Cahill, "Introduction," in *idem* ed., *Shadows of Mt. Huang*, pp. 7–15 (10).
11 McDermott, "Making of a Chinese Mountain," pp. 157–61.
12 Susan Bush and Hsio-yen Shih ed., *Early Chinese Texts on Painting* (Cambridge, MA: Harvard University Press, 1985), p. 224.
13 Craig Clunas makes the point that "élite theory, and in particular its counter-representational rhetoric, only begins to make some kind of sense when we consider that it operated in a climate of picture-making that was in the main entirely '*within* representation,' satisfying customers who required images for reasons very different from those proposed by the theorists whose views had come to seem normative by the present century." See *Pictures and Visuality*, p. 45.
14 Clunas, *Pictures and Visuality*, p. 109.
15 McDermott, "Making of a Chinese Mountain," p. 150. This work is reproduced as Figure 2 圖二 in Zhou Wu 周蕪 ed., *Huipai banhuashi lunji* 徽派版畫史論集 (Hefei: Anhui renmin chubanshe, 1983).
16 Clunas, *Pictures and Visuality*, p. 36.
17 Cahill ("Huang Shan Paintings," p. 273) cites the anonymous handscroll on silk (his Figures 6.3 and 6.4) in the Museum of Fine Arts, Boston (MFA) as the earliest

known extant painting of Yellow Mountain. The work bears the spurious signature of Xu Ben 徐賁 (1335–93?), although as Cahill notes, a dating by style would place it in the early sixteenth century. This date would still make it the earliest extant Yellow Mountain painting, if indeed that were its subject, but an examination of the entire work, particularly the scene to the far left of the scroll, argues against this. The MFA now identifies the work (08.87) as *Yandangshan zhenxing tujuan* 雁蕩山真形圖卷 [The True Form of Geese Pond Mountain].

18 Cahill, "Huang Shan Paintings," pp. 286–8.

19 Both series are reproduced in full in Xu Hongquan's 許宏泉 *Dai Benxiao* 戴本孝 (Shijiazhuang: Hebei jiaoyu chubanshe, 2002), pp. 130–57.

20 Hui Zou, "The *Jing* of a Perspective Garden," *Studies in the History of Gardens and Designed Landscapes* 22 (4) (2002): 293–326 (298–300).

21 Clunas, *Fruitful Sites*, p. 98.

22 Wang Xinyi, "Guitianyuan ju ji" 歸田園居記 cited in Clunas, *Fruitful Sites*, pp. 98–100.

23 Clunas, *Fruitful Sites*, pp. 100–1. For a discussion of the concept, see Wai-kam Ho's "The Literary Concepts of 'Picture-like' (*Ju-hua*) and 'Picture-Idea' (*Hua-i*) in the Relationship between Poetry and Painting," in Alfreda Murck and Wen C. Fong ed., *Words and Images: Chinese Poetry, Calligraphy, and Painting* (New York: Metropolitan Museum of Art, 1991), pp. 359–404, and on the idea of "pictorialism" in the novel *Hongloumeng*, see Xiao Chi's *The Chinese Garden as Lyric Enclave: A Generic Study of the Story of the Stone* (Ann Arbor: Center for Chinese Studies, Michigan University, 2001), pp. 177–89.

24 Zhao Nong 趙農 ed., *Yuan ye tushuo* 園冶圖説 (Ji'nan: Shandong huabao chubanshe, 2003), p. 217.

25 Yuan Mei, "Suiyuan wuji" 隨園五記 in Wang Yingzhi 王英志 ed., *Yuan Mei quanji* 袁枚全集 (Nanjing: Jiangsu guji chubanshe, 1993), Volume 2, p. 208. See also my translation of this essay, in "In Lieu of Flowers: The Transformation of Space and Self in Yuan Mei's (1716–1798) Garden Records," *New Zealand Journal of Asian Studies* 3 (2) (2001): 136–49 (147–9).

26 Yi-fu Tuan describes the West Lake landscape thus: "The landscapes surrounding the lake, and the lake itself, are largely artificial. The natural scene of the Hangzhou area was a deltaic flat, sluggishly drained by a few streams. Out of the flat alluvium, islands of bedrock obtrude. When the streams were dammed, perhaps as early as the first century AD, a lake collected behind the dyke so that the basic elements of the Chinese landscape — mountains juxtaposed against alluvial banks and water — were formed" (*China* [Chicago: Aldine-Atherton, 1969], pp. 124–5, romanization altered).

27 Li Rihua, *Weishuixuan riji* 味水軒日記 (rpt.; Tu Youxiang 屠友祥 ed. Shanghai: Yuandong chubanshe, 1996), pp. 130–1.

28 McDowall trans., *Four Months of Idle Roaming*, p. 5.

29 *Huangshan zhi dingben*, p. 289.

30 Yi-fu Tuan, *Topophilia: A Study of Environmental Perception, Attitudes and Values* (Englewood Cliffs, NJ: Prentice-Hall, 1974), p. 133. See also Tuan's "Foreword" to Kenneth Robert Olwig's *Landscape, Nature, and the Body Politic: From Britain's Renaissance to America's New World* (Madison: University of Wisconsin Press, 2002), pp. xi–xx.

31 The Republican-era scholar Lu Xun 魯迅 (original name Zhou Shuren 周樹人, *zi* Yucai 豫才; 1881–1936) later referred to what he called the "ten-sight disease," which, he claimed, "reached epidemic proportions in the Qing dynasty" (Lu, "More Thoughts on the Collapse of Leifeng Pagoda," in Yang Xianyi and Gladys Yang trans., *Selected Works* [Beijing: Foreign Languages Press, 1980], Volume 2, pp. 113–8).

32 Ho, "Literary Concepts," p. 366.

33 Cahill, "Huang Shan Paintings," p. 281.

34 Gao Juhan 高居翰 [James Cahill], "Lun Hongren *Huangshan tuce* de guishu" 論弘仁《黃山圖冊》的歸屬, *Duoyun* 朵雲 9 (1985): 108–24. The album is usually attributed to Hongren. Based on an analysis of seals and brush technique, Cahill argues that the album, painted by Xiao, may have been modelled on an earlier, and no longer extant, album by Hongren. For an alternative view, see Xu Bangda 徐邦達, "*Huangshan tuce* zuozhe kaobian" 《黃山圖冊》作者考辨, in the same volume of *Duoyun*: 125–9.

35 Hsu Wen-Chin, "Images of Huang-shan in Shih-t'ao's Paintings," *National Palace Museum Bulletin* [Taipei] 27 (1/2) (1992): 1–37 (5–6).

36 Shitao, *Dadizi tihua bashi* 大滌子題畫跋詩, edited by Wang Yichen 汪繹辰 (rpt.; Shanghai: Renmin meishu chubanshe, 1987), p. 23.

37 *Mei Qing Huangshan tuce* 梅清黃山圖冊 (rpt.; Shanghai: Renmin meishu chubanshe, 1980).

38 Clunas, *Pictures and Visuality*, p. 114.

39 Cahill, "Huang Shan Paintings," p. 253.

40 McDermott's claim ("Making of a Chinese Mountain," p. 148) that "[Yellow Mountain] prose accounts of the late Ming and Qing rarely repeat the description or emotional reaction of earlier travellers" loses its validity when one examines in detail the development of the prose tradition surrounding the site. Essays of the period, on the contrary, seem to build on existing literature in ever more complex ways as appropriate responses become standardized.

41 Qian Qianyi, "Nanjing guozijian chajiu Fenggong muzhiming" 南京國子監察酒馮公墓誌銘, in *Muzhai chuxueji* 51 (*QMZQJ*, Volume 2, pp. 1299–1302).

42 Qian Qianyi, "Zhang Muhuang ruren muzhiming" 張母黃孺人墓誌銘, in *Muzhai chuxueji* 59 (*QMZQJ*, Volume 2, pp. 1441–4).

43 Qian Qianyi, "Zhuijian wangyou Suian Xie Erbo shu" 追薦亡友綏安謝耳伯疏, in *Muzhai chuxueji* 81 (*QMZQJ*, Volume 3, pp. 1733–4). Xie is also mentioned in the biography 行狀 [Record of Conduct] of Guan Zhidao 管志道 (*zi* Dengzhi 登之, *hao* Dongming 東溟; 1536–1608) Qian composed in 1628, "Huguang tixing anchasi qianshi jinjie chaolie dafu Guangong xingzhuang" 湖廣提刑按察司僉事晉階朝列大夫管公行狀, in *Muzhai chuxueji* 49 (*QMZQJ*, Volume 2, pp. 1252–67).

44 Qian Qianyi, "Ming chushi Yang jun Wubu muzhiming" 明處士楊君無補墓誌銘, in *Muzhai youxueji* 32 (*QMZQJ*, Volume 6, pp. 1165–6).

45 Cai, *Shengping yu zhushu*, pp. 34–5.

46 Qian Qianyi, "He Wen sili shice xu" 賀文司理詩冊序 (for Wenli) in *Muzhai chuxueji* 35 (*QMZQJ*, Volume 2, pp. 999–1000) and "Wu Mucheng ruren qishi xu" 吳母程孺人七十序 (for Dazhen), in *Muzhai chuxueji* 38 (*QMZQJ*, Volume 2, pp. 1052–3).

47 The second appendix (pp. 279–86) to Cai's *Shengping yu zhushu* provides a list of Qian's known associates (over 900 are listed), although its value is limited somewhat by its use of sobriquets (*zi*) rather than given names (*ming*), and the fact it provides no references. Cai lists Pan Jingsheng (i.e. Pan Zhiheng) as another acquaintance of Qian.

48 Fung uses the term in reference to garden writing and garden making, for which see "Word and Garden in Chinese Essays of the Ming Dynasty: Notes on Matters of Approach," *Interfaces: Image, texte, language* 11–12 (June 1997): 77–90.

Chapter 4

1 Chaves, "Yellow Mountain Poems," p. 468. Chaves' total of 25 accords with Li Chi's assessment (*Travel Diaries of Hsü Hsia-k'o*, p. 71). *Juan* 19 of the *Muzhai chuxueji* ("Dongshan shiji" 東山詩集 2) actually contains a total of 32 poems: 25 Yellow Mountain poems composed by Qian; a set of four quatrains by Liu Shi that respond to those of Qian numbered #2–5, and three further poems composed by Qian in the days following his descent off the mountain proper. I would be inclined to include the final three poems in any discussion of the set, particularly as they involve a visit to Cheng Jiasui, an important metaphorical presence in the journey. For convenience, I have adopted Chaves' system of numbering the poems (a chronological sequence from the beginning of the *juan* but excluding the four by Liu Shi).

2 Chaves, "Yellow Mountain Poems," pp. 468–70: "The very fact that the first group of poems by Qian on his trip to the Yellow Mountains can be said to have a 'dynamic' aspect, being replete with verbs descriptive of the poet's movement through the landscape, is an indication of how far Qian has gone in moving *shi* poetry in the direction of the *youji* genre" (romanization altered). Craig Clunas, who draws on the discussion in Michel de Certeau's *The Practice of Everyday Life*, identifies a similar distinction between the "map" and the "tour" in his treatment of Ming garden accounts, for which see *Fruitful Sites*, p. 141.

3 Taken out of context, this change in voice is perhaps more difficult to discern. The only existing translation (of which I am aware) of any section of Parts VII–IX is by Yang Qinghua (whose translation is of Yu Kwang-chung's "Sensuous Art"), in which Yu cites the passage (making up approximately half of Part VIII) as part of a discussion of descriptions of pine trees in travel essays. Removed from its original context, the passage is rendered by Yang into a sequential narrative, beginning with "The top of Old Man Peak was gained." With the narrative having ended at Part VI, Qian is here reflecting more generally on a site he visited in Part III, and I therefore render the line into "When one climbs Old Man Peak . . ." (see Chapter Five).

4 One might also read significance in the number of sections to the essay — nine — a mirror perhaps of the traditional nine divisions of the ordered empire, as set out in the "Tribute of Yu" 禹貢 section of the *Shujing*.

5 Cheng Jiasui, *Ougengtang ji* 耦耕堂集, cited in Chen, *Liu Rushi biezhuan*, Volume 1, pp. 221–2.

6 Qian Qianyi, *Liechao shiji xiaozhuan* 列朝詩集小傳 (Shanghai: Guji chubanshe, 1959), Volume 2, pp. 576–9.

7 Cheng, *Ougengtang ji*, cited in Chen, *Liu Rushi biezhuan*, Volume 1, pp. 221–2.

8 Chen, *Liu Rushi biezhuan*, Volume 2, pp. 615–31.

9 My edition of Liu Shi's collected works is Zhou Shutian 周書田 and Fan Jingzhong 范景中 ed., *Liu Rushi ji* 柳如是集 (Hangzhou: Zhongguo meishu xueyuan chubanshe, 1999). An alternate edition of the poems Qian and Liu composed together during this period may be found in Zhou Fagao 周法高 ed., *Qian Muzhai Liu Rushi yishi ji Liu Rushi youguan ziliao* 錢牧齋柳如是佚詩及柳如是有關資料 (Taibei: self-published, 1978).

10 Accepting on face value the date of the trip given in Qian's essay was, indeed, an error that I myself made when this project was in its early stages [see my "Qian Qianyi's (1582–1664) Reflections on Yellow Mountain," *New Zealand Journal of Asian Studies* 7 (2) (2005): 134–52].

11 Keith Hazelton, *A Synchronic Chinese-Western Daily Calendar, 1341–1661 A.D.* (Revised ed.; Minneapolis: Ming Studies Research Series, University of Minnesota, 1985), p. 301.

12 Following the preface date, James Cahill incorrectly dates the trip itself to 1642 ("Huang Shan Paintings," p. 277).

13 Pei-yi Wu, *The Confucian's Progress: Autobiographical Writings in Traditional China* (Princeton: Princeton University Press, 1990), pp. 95–9. In his *Haunted Journeys: Desire and Transgression in European Travel Writing* (Princeton: Princeton University Press, 1991), Denis Porter asserts that "the most interesting writers of nonfictional travel books have managed to combine explorations in the world with self-exploration." (5)

14 Michelle Yeh, *Modern Chinese Poetry: Theory and Practice Since 1917* (New Haven: Yale University Press, 1991), p. 8.

15 Hans H. Frankel, "The Contemplation of the Past in T'ang Poetry," in Arthur F. Wright and Denis Twitchett ed., *Perspectives on the T'ang* (New Haven: Yale University Press, 1973), pp. 345–65, and *The Flowering Plum and the Palace Lady: Interpretations of Chinese Verse* (New Haven: Yale University Press, 1976), pp. 113–27. The French critic Roland Barthes similarly observes ("The Eiffel Tower," in *The Eiffel Tower and other Mythologies*, translated by Richard Howard [New York: Hill and Wang, 1979], pp. 3–18) that "to perceive Paris from above is infallibly to imagine a history; from the top of the [Eiffel] Tower, the mind finds itself dreaming of the mutation of the landscape which it has before its eyes; through the astonishment of space it plunges into the mystery of time . . ." (11)

16 *Yuan Hongdao ji jianjiao*, Volume 1, pp. 457–9. In a recent study, Judith Zeitlin highlights a significant distinction between writing on walls and writing on cliff faces, an important consideration here, as Qian Qianyi's various collections are replete with poems written on walls 題壁. See Zeitlin, "Disappearing Verses: Writing on Walls and Anxieties of Loss," in *idem* and Lydia H. Liu ed., *Writing and Materiality in China: Essays in Honor of Patrick Hanan* (Cambridge, MA: Harvard University Press, 2003), pp. 73–132.

17 Pei-yi Wu, "An Ambivalent Pilgrim to T'ai Shan in the Seventeenth Century," in Naquin and Yü ed., *Pilgrims and Sacred Sites*, pp. 65–88 (77).

18 Ward, *Xu Xiake*, p. 177.

19 Kathlyn Maurean Liscomb, *Learning from Mount Hua: A Chinese Physician's Illustrated Travel Record and Painting Theory* (Cambridge: Cambridge University Press, 1993), pp. 36–7.

20 Fang Bao, "You Yandang ji" 遊雁蕩記 in *Fang Wangxi xiansheng quanji* 方望溪先生全集 (Shanghai: *SBCK* edition), Volume 1, p. 211. This essay is also translated in Strassberg's *Inscribed Landscapes*, pp. 400–1.

21 *Huangshan zhi* (1667), pp. 512–6; *Huangshan zhi dingben*, pp. 286–90.

22 *Huangshan zhi* (1988), pp. 107–25.

23 Helen Leach, *Cultivating Myths: Fiction, Fact and Fashion in Garden History* (Auckland: Random House, 2000), pp. 97–8.

24 *Huangshan zhi dingben*, p. 247.

25 *Huangshan zhi dingben*, p. 29. For Wang's travel essay, see *Huangshan zhi* (1667), pp. 441–4.

26 Sun Yiyuan 孫一元 (*zi* Taichu 太初; 1484–1520), "Huangshan ge er shou" 黃山歌二首 (*Huangshan zhi dingben*, pp. 413–4).

27 Yuan Mei, "You Huangshan ji" 遊黃山記 in *Yuan Mei quanji*, Volume 2, pp. 514–5. The translation is that of Strassberg, for which see *Inscribed Landscapes*, pp. 406–10.

28 On life-expectancy in the Ming dynasty, see Heijdra's "Socio-Economic Development," pp. 435–7.

29 *Liu Rushi ji*, p. 145. Chaves ("Yellow Mountain Poems," p. 467) and Ding (*Wenxue sixiang*, p. 115) speculate that the inclusion of these quatrains in Liu's collected

works and the fact that she composed a corresponding set of her own indicates her presence at the hot springs, for a discussion of which, see my note to Part II of Qian Qianyi's essay.

30 The praise of Yellow Mountain at the expense of White Mount had already become fairly common by Qian's time. Most memorably perhaps, Huang Ruheng claims in his essay of 1610 (*Huangshan zhi* [1667], pp. 459–63; *Huangshan zhi dingben*, pp. 232–6) that to compare the two was like comparing Yi Guang 夷光 (a famous courtesan, also known as Xi Shi 西施) with the Luo River Nymph 洛神 (a mythical divinity).

31 Wu notes the broad range of meanings encompassed by the term *xue* 學, but leaves it untranslated (*Confucian's Progress*, pp. 96–7). In choosing here to render the concept into "self-cultivation" I particularly have in mind the brief note appended to his recent translation of the *Daxue* 大學 by Andrew Plaks, who explains: "The educational process enjoined by the second word *xue* through its paradigm of moral fulfilment in every phase of human capacity is of an order that can only partially and misleadingly be expressed in the narrow sense of the English 'learning'. Rather, the word *xue* in Confucian discourse covers a full spectrum of personal accomplishment from the active to the contemplative spheres, centring [*sic*] upon the core concept of the perfection of the individual character, a notion that precisely matches the scope and meaning of the central idea of 'self-cultivation'." (Plaks trans., *Ta Hsüeh* and *Chung Yung [The Highest Order of Cultivation and On the Practice of the Mean]* [London: Penguin Books, 2003], p. 3 [romanization altered]). For further discussion of the life as journey metaphor, see Riemenschnitter, "Traveler's Vocation." Wu gives 贊 for 讚 in the name Deng Yi*zan*, which I believe to be an error.

32 Naquin and Yü, "Introduction: Pilgrimage in China," pp. 11–2.

33 Timothy Brook, *Praying for Power: Buddhism and the Formation of Gentry Society in Late-Ming China* (Cambridge, MA: Harvard University Press, 1993), p. 353.

34 Timothy Brook, "At the Margin of Public Authority: The Ming State and Buddhism," in *idem*, *The Chinese State in Ming Society* (London: RoutledgeCurzon, 2005), pp. 139–57, and *Praying for Power*.

35 Qian had apparently been particularly influenced by the monk Deqing 德清 (*zi* Chengyin 澄印, *hao* Hanshan 憨山; 1546–1623). See Sun, *Ming mo Qing chu wenxue*, pp. 203–42.

36 Brook, *Praying for Power*, p. 65.

37 Huang, *Year of No Significance*, p. 8.

38 Gu, *Rizhilu jishi*, Volume 2, pp. 823–4.

39 Li Rihua, *Zitaoxuan zazhui* 紫桃軒雜綴, cited in Watt, "Literati Environment," p. 6.

40 Qian Zhongshu argues against Qian Qianyi's being a devout Buddhist, claiming that the latter's conversion to Buddhism later in life was intended as penance for his betrayal of the Ming ruling house. For this position and a convincing argument against it, see Xie Zhengguang [Andrew Hsieh] 謝正光, "Qian Qianyi fengfo zhi qianhou yinyuan ji qi yiyi" 錢謙益奉佛之前後因緣及其意義, in *Qinghua daxue xuebao* 清華大學學報 [*zhexue shehui kexue ban* 哲學社會科學版] 3 (21) (2006): 13–30.

41 On pilgrimage at Taishan, see Dott, *Identity Reflections*, pp. 79–100 and Wu, "Ambivalent Pilgrim." Although, of course, the relative inaccessibility and lesser spiritual significance of Yellow Mountain suggests that any organized pilgrimage activity would have occurred on a much smaller scale than it did at Taishan.

42 Wu, "Ambivalent Pilgrim," p. 66: "There have been hardly any accounts of a pilgrimage by the participants themselves if we define such an account as a prose narrative in which the author describes *unambiguously* his participation in a sequence of events that he himself *explicitly* recognises as a pilgrimage." See also, pp. 82–5.

43 In this respect I am inclined to feel that Julian Ward overstates somewhat the

significance of Buddhism in the travel diaries of Xu Hongzu, whose "desire for the company of monks" (*Xu Xiake*, p. 173) while on his journeys seems better understood as typical of the educated men of his age.

44   McDermott, "Making of a Chinese Mountain," p. 146.

45   Ward, *Xu Xiake*, p. 177.

46   Cahill, "Huang Shan Paintings," p. 277. On the applicability of the concept of the Sublime to Chinese literary and aesthetic theory, see Kin-yuen Wong's "Negative-Positive Dialectic in the Chinese Sublime," in Ying-hsiung Chou ed., *The Chinese Text: Studies in Comparative Literature* (Hong Kong: Chinese University Press, 1986), pp. 119–58, and Rickett trans., *Jen-chien Tz'u-hua*, pp. 13–7.

47   Robert MacFarlane, *Mountains of the Mind: A History of a Fascination* (London: Granta Books, 2003), p. 158.

48   Ge Hong, *Baopuzi neipian* 抱朴子內篇, translated in Kroll's "Verses from on High," p. 168.

49   Naquin and Yü, "Introduction: Pilgrimage in China," p. 27.

50   Ann Bermingham, "Reading Constable," in Simon Pugh ed., *Reading Landscape: Country — City — Capital* (Manchester: Manchester University Press, 1990), pp. 97–120 (101–2).

51   Jonathan Rée, *Philosophical Tales: An Essay on Philosophy and Literature* (London: Methuen, 1987), p. 67.

52   Li Bai, "You Taishan liu shou" 遊泰山六首, in *Li Taibai quanji*, Volume 2, pp. 921–6. For an excellent discussion of this set of poems in the context of the literary depiction of Taishan, see Kroll's "Verses from on High."

53   For a discussion of which, see Naquin and Yü, "Introduction: Pilgrimage in China," pp. 11–2.

54   *Huangshan zhi* (1667), pp. 512–8; *Huangshan zhi dingben*, pp. 286–94.

55   Qian Qianyi, "Shierri fa Taoyuanan chu Tangkou jing Fangcun di Qiankou" 十二日發桃源菴出湯口逕芳村抵濬口 (*QMZQJ*, Volume 1, pp. 652–3).

56   *Xu Xiake youji jiaozhu*, Volume 1, p. 22.

57   Sima, *Shiji*, Volume 1, p. 242 and Volume 4, pp. 1366–7.

58   Dwight C. Baker, *T'ai Shan: An Account of the Sacred Eastern Peak of China*, cited in Dott, *Identity Reflections*, p. 55 (romanization altered).

59   *Kangxi qiju zhu* 康熙起居注, translated by Dott in *Identity Reflections*, p. 171 (adapted).

60   Li, "You Taishan liu shou," pp. 925–6; Kroll, "Verses from on High," pp. 212–5.

61   Dott, *Identity Reflections*, pp. 90–1.

62   Alan Morinis, "Introduction," in *idem* ed., *Sacred Journeys: The Anthropology of Pilgrimage* (Westport: Greenwood Press, 1992), pp. 1–28 (10).

63   Morinis, "Introduction," pp. 13–4.

64   MacCannell, *The Tourist*, pp. 42–3.

65   See Pierre Francastel, "Problèmes de la sociologie de l'art," in Georges Gurvitch ed., *Traité de sociologie* Tome II (Paris: Presses universitaires de France, 1960), pp. 278–96 (284).

66   *Huangshan zhi* (1667), p. 434; *Huangshan zhi dingben*, p. 206.

67   *Huangshan zhi dingben*, p. 275.

68   *Mengzi* 孟子, 7A.24. For an English rendition of this passage, see D. C. Lau trans., *Mencius* (Harmondsworth: Penguin Books, 1970), p. 187.

69   *Huangshan zhi dingben*, p. 257.

70   Alan J. Berkowitz, "The Moral Hero: A Pattern of Reclusion in Traditional China," *Monumenta Serica* 40 (1992): 1–32.

71   For a useful list of secondary literature dealing with Chinese eremitic traditions, see Alan J. Berkowitz, "Reclusion in Traditional China: A Selected List of References," *Monumenta Serica* 40 (1992): 33–46.

72   *Huangshan zhi dingben*, p. 45.

73   Tao Qian, "Taohuayuan ji" 桃花源記, in Lu Qinli 逯欽立 ed., *Tao Yuanming ji* 陶
      淵明集 (Beijing: Zhonghua shuju, 1979), pp. 165–7. On Tao and the development
      of the Chinese eremitic tradition, see A. R. Davis, "The Narrow Lane: Some
      Observations on the Recluse in Traditional Chinese Society," *East Asian History* 11
      (1996): 33–44.

74   James was referring to the travels of Edith Wharton (1862–1937); cited in Julian
      Barnes' *Something to Declare* (London: Picador, 2002), p. 67. Even the car in which
      the Whartons travelled was fitted, in her husband's words, with "every known
      accessorie and comfort" (R. W. B. Lewis, *Edith Wharton: A Biography* [New York:
      Harper and Row, 1975], p. 177).

75   Ye Mengzhu 葉夢珠, *Yueshi bian* 閱世編 (rpt.; Lai Xinxia 來新夏 ed.; Shanghai: Guji
      chubanshe, 1981), p. 153; *Shexian zhi*, p. 108.

76   Brook, *Confusions of Pleasure*, p. 237.

77   Steven D. Carter, "Bashō and the Mastery of Poetic Space in *Oku no hosomichi*,"
      Journal of the American Oriental Society 120 (2) (2000): 190–8 (191).

78   Handlin-Smith, "Ch'i Piao-chia's Social World," p. 66.

79   The idea of the garden in the West likewise carries a connotation of paradise, of
      course, most obviously discernable from the etymological derivation of the latter
      from its post-classical Latin form *paradisus*, originating from the ancient Greek
      παράδεισος, a Persian enclosed park, orchard, or pleasure ground, from the Old
      Iranian *pairidaēza*, meaning enclosure (*Oxford English Dictionary*).

80   There is a further parallel evident here between the *youji* and landscape art of both
      China and the West, in that we are frequently aided in our readings of landscape
      paintings by additional information, such as (in the case of Constable, for example)
      the personal communications of the artist. See Bermingham, "Reading Constable."
      Readings of Joyce's (1882–1941) novel *Ulysses* were likewise often filtered through
      the author's letters, and subsequent editions were of course informed by his own
      compilation of lists of errata (see Jeri Johnson, "Composition and Publication
      History," in *idem* ed., *Ulysses: The 1922 Text* [Oxford: Oxford University Press,
      1993], pp. xxxviii–lvi).

81   See Duncan Campbell trans., *Notes Made Whilst Travelling and at Repose (Book
      One)* (Wellington: Asian Studies Institute Translation Paper #2, 1999), p. 1.

82   Qu Shouyuan 屈守元 ed., *Hanshi waizhuan jianshu* 韓詩外傳箋疏 (Chengdu: Bashu
      shushe, 1996), p. 656.

83   Chaves, "Yellow Mountain Poems," pp. 471–2.

84   Yim, *Poetics of Historical Memory*. See also Chen Bo 辰伯 (Wu Han 吳晗 [1909–
      69]), "Qian Muzhai zhi shixue" 錢牧齋之史學, in *Wenshi zazhi* 文史襍誌 4 (7/8)
      (1944): 57–9.

85   See Susan Sontag, "A Poet's Prose," in *idem*, *Where the Stress Falls: Essays* (London:
      Vintage, 2003), pp. 3–9.

86   Qian Qianyi, "Shao Youqing shicao xu" and "Shao Liangqing shicao xu," in
      QMZQJ, Volume 2, pp. 934–6. The second of these is in fact undated, but as they
      appear together it seems reasonable to assume that they were both composed in
      the twelfth month of 1641 (the date on the first piece).

87   A kind of mystical stone bridge spanning 20 to 30 *zhang* between two peaks is
      recorded in the *Huangshan tujing* (10a) as having been seen in the Kaiyuan 開元
      reign of the Tang (713–42) but never found again.

88   Reading *gong* 公 for *xi* 溪. On Master Ruan 阮公, see Chapter Five.

89   According to the *Huangshan tujing*, the Green Ox 青牛 was once seen at Verdure
      Temple 翠微寺 (7a). The Green Ox is the creature on the back of which Laozi 老子
      is traditionally said to have flown (*Lie xian zhuan*, p. 3).

90 On the Wild Man 毛人 of Yellow Mountain, see Chapter Five.

91 For Qian's poem, "Sanyue qiri fa Qiankou jing Yanggansi yu Shizhenling chu Fangcun di Xiangfusi" 三月七日發灊口徑楊干寺踰石磴嶺出芳村抵祥符寺 (Poem #1), see *QMZQJ*, Volume 1, pp. 641–2.

92 Qian, "Sanyue qiri," in *QMZQJ*, Volume 1, pp. 641–2.

93 Julia Kristeva, Σημειωτική *[Sēmeiōtikē]: Recherches pour une sémanalyse* (Paris: Éditions du Seuil, 1969), p. 146.

Chapter 5

1 I borrow here, of course, the words of Don Quixote (or rather, the words of his translator). See Miguel de Cervantes Saavedra, *The Ingenious Hidalgo Don Quixote de la Mancha*, John Rutherford trans. (London: Penguin Books, 2000), p. 915.

2 See John Minford's "Pieces of Eight: Reflections on Translating *The Story of the Stone*," in Eugene Eoyang and Lin Yao-fu ed., *Translating Chinese Literature* (Bloomington: Indiana University Press, 1995), pp. 178–203.

Conclusion

1 Yuan, "You Huangshan ji," in *Yuan Mei quanji*, Volume 2, pp. 514–5.

2 John Milton, *Paradise Lost* (rpt.; Alastair Fowler ed., 2nd edition [revised], Harlow: Pearson, 2007), p. 547.

3 Strassberg, *Inscribed Landscapes*, p. 56.

4 Li trans., *Travel Diaries of Hsü Hsia-k'o*, p. 264, n. 43 (romanization altered); Zhang Juzheng, "You Hengyue ji" 遊衡嶽記, in Zhang Shunhui 張舜徽 ed., *Zhang Juzheng ji* 張居正集 (Wuhan: Hubei renmin chubanshe, 1987), Volume 3, pp. 541–6.

5 Roland Barthes, *S/Z* (Paris: Éditions du Seuil, 1970), pp. 22–7.

6 Simon Pugh, "Introduction: Stepping out into the Open," in *idem* ed., *Reading Landscape*, pp. 1–6 (2–3).

7 Macfarlane, *Mountains of the Mind*, pp. 18–9.

8 John Berger, *Ways of Seeing* (Harmondsworth: Penguin Books, 1972), p. 8.

9 Li, "Artistic Theories," p. 18.

10 Roger V. Des Forges, *Cultural Centrality and Political Change in Chinese History: Northeast Henan in the Fall of the Ming* (Stanford: Stanford University Press, 2003).

11 W. J. T. Mitchell, "Introduction," in *idem* ed., *Landscape and Power* (Chicago: University of Chicago Press, 1994), pp. 1–4.

12 Jonathan Hay, "Ming Palace and Tomb in Early Qing Jiangning: Dynastic Memory and the Openness of History," *Late Imperial China* 20 (1) (1999): 1–48 (17).

Epilogue

1 *Muzhai chuxueji* 34 (*QMZQJ*, Volume 2, pp. 927–8).

2 Goodrich, *Literary Inquisition*, pp. 102–3 (romanization altered).

Appendix A

1   Qu Shisi, "Muzhai xiansheng Chuxueji mulu hou xu" 牧齋先生初學集目錄後序, in *Muzhai chuxueji* (*SBCK* edition, Volume 1, pp. 26–7; *QMZQJ*, Volume 1, pp. 52–4) and in *Qu Shisi ji* 瞿式耜集 (Shanghai: Guji chubanshe, 1981), pp. 303–5. Among 1643 datings of the collection, see the *SBCK* edition, Volume 1: reverse title page; *QMZQJ*, Volume 1, pp. 1–9; *ECCP*, p. 149; *ICTCL*, Volume 1, p. 278 and Karl Lo, *A Guide to the Ssŭ Pu Ts'ung K'an* (Lawrence: University of Kansas Libraries, 1965), p. 38. Goodrich (*Literary Inquisition*, p. 106, n. 20) bizarrely claims that the work was "completed in 1621 and printed in 1643."

2   Cai, *Shengping yu zhushu*, pp. 218–9; Wilhelm, "Bibliographical Notes," p. 199.

3   Qian Qianyi, "Jiashen yuanri" 甲申元日, in *Muzhai chuxueji* (*SBCK* edition, Volume 2, p. 225; *QMZQJ*, Volume 1, p. 743).

4   Pan Zhonggui 潘重規, *Qian Qianyi toubiji jiaoben* 錢謙益投筆集校本, cited in Cai, *Shengping yu zhushu*, p. 157. The preface written by Cheng Jiasui, "Muzhai xiansheng chuxueji xu" 牧齋先生初學集序, dated the winter of 1643, also refers to a 100-*juan* collection (*QMZQJ*, Volume 3, pp. 2224–5).

5   For a short biography of Qian Zeng, see that by Tu Lien-chê in *ECCP*, pp. 157–8.

6   Qian Zhonglian, "Chuban shuoming" 出版説明, in *QMZQJ*, Volume 1, p. 4.

7   On the problematic textual transmission issues concerning the *Muzhai youxueji*, see Zhu Zejie's 朱則杰 "Qian Qianyi Liu Rushi congkao" 錢謙益柳如是叢考 in *Zhejiang daxue xuebao* 浙江大學學報 [*renwen shehui kexue ban* 人文社會科學版] 32 (5) (2002): 13–8.

8   I am indebted here to the work of Susan Cherniack, who, in her extensive treatment of Song textual criticism, documents many more types of textual error found in classical Chinese literature, and from which my brief list here is adapted. See the appendix (pp. 102–25) to her "Book Culture and Textual Transmission in Sung China," *Harvard Journal of Asiatic Studies* 54 (1994): 5–125.

9   Li Yangbing, "Shang Li dafu lun guzhuan shu" 上李大夫論古篆書, in *juan* 81 of Yao Xuan 姚鉉 (*zi* Baozhi 寶之; 968–1020) ed., *Tang wen cui* 唐文粹, first printed in 1039 (rpt.; Shanghai: *SBCK* edition), p. 540. Even the use of stone was not enough to prevent the alteration of texts though, as Wang Anshi discovered in 1054. Finding a stele at Baochanshan 襃禪山 (also called Huashan 華山), Wang is surprised to read the character *hua* 花 instead of *hua* 華, suggesting an alteration in the name based on confusion over homophones: "When I considered the fallen stele, I felt sorry that such an ancient inscription had not been preserved, that later generations have misinterpreted what it transmits and none could identify the correct name." See Wang, "You Baochanshan ji" 遊襃禪山記 in Ning Bo 寧波, Liu Lihua 劉麗華 and Zhang Zhongliang 張中良 ed., *Wang Anshi quanji* 王安石全集 (Changchun: Jilin renmin chubanshe, 1996), pp. 872–3. The translation is that of Richard Strassberg, for which see *Inscribed Landscapes*, pp. 175–7.

10 Cherniack, "Book Culture and Textual Transmission," p. 49.

11 Chen Jiru, *Taiping qinghua* 太平清話 (rpt.; Shanghai: Shangwu yinshuguan, 1936), p. 40. For a more recent Western example of concern about inaccurate textual transmission, one need look no further than James Joyce: "Since the completion of *Ulysses* I feel more and more tired but I have to hold on till all the proofs are revised. I am extremely irritated by all those printer's errors. Working as I do amid piles of notes at a table in a hotel I cannot possibly do this mechanical part with my wretched eye and a half. Are these to be perpetuated in future editions? I hope not." (Letter of November 1921, cited in Jack P. Dalton's "The Text of *Ulysses*," in Fritz Senn ed., *New Light on Joyce from the Dublin Symposium* [Bloomington: Indiana University Press, 1972], pp. 99–119 [118 n. 35].)

12 Fredson Bowers, *Textual and Literary Criticism* (London: Cambridge University Press, 1959), p. 4.

13 I am inclined to think that the pejorative evaluation of textual variance that characterizes the Greg/Bowers approach to textual criticism is a fairly unhelpful one in most contexts, and its advocates continually fail to engage adequately with the arguments not only of the New Critics (see especially W. K. Wimsatt and Monroe C. Beardsley's "The Intentional Fallacy," in Wimsatt's *The Verbal Icon: Studies in the Meaning of Poetry* [Kentucky: Kentucky University Press, 1954], pp. 3–18), but also with those, like D. F. McKenzie, who see text production as a social process (see "The Sociology of a Text: Orality, Literacy and Print in Early New Zealand," *The Library*, Sixth Series 6 [4] [1984]: 333–65). In a Chinese context, Susan Cherniack's claim that "the traditional interpretation of Confucius's textual work as an act of transmission suggests that the Chinese understanding of transmission includes a concept of collaborative authorship that is excluded from the modern Western term" ("Book Culture and Textual Transmission," p. 17) is important here, as is her observation, that Song editors often explained emendations by the fact that a text "did not conform with human nature" 不近人情 or was "unreasonable" 無理 (p. 87). That our understanding of Qian Qianyi's text will be greatly enhanced if we view variants as products of social and historical contexts (rather than "inexcusable corruptions"), can easily be seen in the case of excisions made from the MLS texts, where Qian's words seem to have been deemed detrimental to the promotional purposes of the gazetteer.

14 "If we were to put on miraculous spectacles that allowed us to detect every piece of retouching on an Old Master painting, a trip to any of our great galleries would give us a shock." See James Fenton, "Vandalism and Enlightenment" (Review of "Enlightenment: Discovering the World in the Eighteenth Century," an exhibition at the British Museum), *New York Review of Books* 51 (3): August 12, 2004: 51.

15 In this regard, the Shanghai guji chubanshe's 2003 edition of the *Qian Muzhai quanji* has been something of a disappointment, the vast majority of the *Muzhai chuxueji* having been reprinted without annotation or other scholarly appendage.

Selected Bibliography

Geographical and Topographical Sources

Gu She shanchuan tu 古歙山川圖. 1758. Rpt.; *Zhongguo gudai banhua congkan erbian* 中國古代版畫叢刊二編. Shanghai: Guji chubanshe, 1994.

Hainei qiguan 海內奇觀. 1609. Yang Erzeng 楊爾曾 comp. Rpt.; *Zhongguo gudai banhua congkan erbian* 中國古代版畫叢刊二編. Shanghai: Guji chubanshe, 1994.

Huangshan Cuiweisi zhi 黃山翠微寺志. 1691. Anlan Chaogang 安懶超綱 comp. Rpt.; Yangzhou: Jiangsu guangling guji keyinshe, 1996.

Huangshan lingyaolu 黃山領要錄. 1774. Wang Hongdu 汪洪度 comp. Rpt.; *Zhonghua shanshuizhi congkan* 中華山水志叢刊. Beijing: Xianzhuang shuju, 2004.

Huangshan song shi pu 黃山松石譜. 1697. Min Linsi 閔麟嗣 comp. Zhang Chao 張潮 ed., *Zhaodai congshu* 昭代叢書. Rpt.; Shanghai: Guji chubanshe, 1990.

Huangshan tujing 黃山圖經. Song dynasty. Rpt.; *Anhui congshu* 安徽叢書 Series 5. Shanghai: Anhui congshu bianyinchu, 1935.

——. Rpt.; *Zhonghua shanshuizhi congkan* 中華山水志叢刊. Beijing: Xianzhuang shuju, 2004.

Huangshan zhi 黃山志. 1667. Hongmei 弘眉 comp. Rpt.; *Zhonghua shanshuizhi congkan* 中華山水志叢刊. Beijing: Xianzhuang shuju, 2004.

Huangshan zhi 黃山志. 1771. Zhang Peifang 張佩芳 comp. Rpt.; *Zhonghua shanshuizhi congkan* 中華山水志叢刊. Beijing: Xianzhuang shuju, 2004.

Huangshan zhi 黃山志. 1988. Lü Qiushan 呂秋山 et al. comp. Hefei: Huangshan shushe.

Huangshan zhi dingben 黃山志定本. 1686. Min Linsi 閔麟嗣 comp. Rpt.; *Anhui congshu* 安徽叢書 Series 5. Shanghai: Anhui congshu bianyinchu, 1935.

——. Rpt.; Hefei: Huangshan shushe, 1990.

——. Rpt.; *Zhonghua shanshuizhi congkan* 中華山水志叢刊. Beijing: Xianzhuang shuju, 2004.

Huangshan zhi xuji 黃山志續集. 1691?. Wang Shihong 汪士鋐 comp. Rpt.; *Anhui congshu* 安徽叢書 Series 5. Shanghai: Anhui congshu bianyinchu, 1935.

Mingshan tu 名山圖. 1633. Rpt.; *Zhongguo gudai banhua congkan erbian* 中國古代版畫叢刊二編. Shanghai: Guji chubanshe, 1994.

Sancai tuhui 三才圖會. 1609?. Wang Qi 王圻 comp. Rpt.; Shanghai: Guji chubanshe, 1985.

Shexian zhi 歙縣志. 1995. Beijing: Zhonghua shuju.

Xihu youlanzhi 西湖遊覽志. 1547. Tian Rucheng 田汝成 comp. Rpt.; Shanghai: Guji chubanshe, 1998.

Yitong lucheng tuji 一統路程圖記. 1570. Huang Bian 黃汴 comp. Rpt.; *Tianxia shuilu lucheng* 天下水陸路程. Yang Zhengtai 楊正泰 ed. Taiyuan: Shanxi renmin chubanshe, 1992.

Zhongguo lishi dituji 中國歷史地圖集 [Volume 7]. 1975. Beijing: Zhonghua ditu xueshe chubanshe.

Other Sources

Adshead, S. A. M. "The Seventeenth Century General Crisis in China," *Asian Profile* 1 (2) (1973): 271–80.

Andrews, Julia and Haruki Yoshida. "Theoretical Foundations of the Anhui School," in James Cahill ed., *Shadows of Mt. Huang: Chinese Painting and Printing of the Anhui School*, pp. 34–42. Berkeley: University Art Museum, 1981.

Appadurai, Arjun ed. *The Social Life of Things: Commodities in Cultural Perspective*. Cambridge: Cambridge University Press, 1986.

Bai, Qianshen. *Fu Shan's World: The Transformation of Chinese Calligraphy in the Seventeenth Century*. Cambridge, MA: Harvard University Press, 2003.

Barnes, Julian. *Something to Declare*. London: Picador, 2002.

Barthes, Roland. *S/Z*. Paris: Éditions du Seuil, 1970.

———. *The Eiffel Tower and Other Mythologies*. Richard Howard trans. New York: Hill and Wang, 1979.

Barzun, Jacques. *From Dawn to Decadence – 1500 to the Present: 500 Years of Western Cultural Life*. London: HarperCollins, 2000.

Bate, W. Jackson. *The Burden of the Past and the English Poet*. Cambridge, MA: Harvard University Press, 1970.

Bei Yunchen 貝運辰 ed. *Lidai youji xuan* 歷代遊記選. Changsha: Hunan renmin chubanshe, 1980.

Berger, John. *Ways of Seeing*. Harmondsworth: Penguin Books, 1972.

Berkowitz, Alan J. "The Moral Hero: A Pattern of Reclusion in Traditional China," *Monumenta Serica* 40 (1992): 1–32.

———. "Reclusion in Traditional China: A Selected List of References," *Monumenta Serica* 40 (1992): 33–46.

Bermingham, Ann. "Reading Constable," in Simon Pugh ed., *Reading Landscape: Country – City – Capital*, pp. 97–120. Manchester: Manchester University Press, 1990.

Bian Min 卞敏. *Liu Rushi xinzhuan* 柳如是新傳. Hangzhou: Zhejiang renmin chubanshe, 1997.

Bickford, Maggie. *Bones of Jade, Soul of Ice: The Flowering Plum in Chinese Art*. New Haven: Yale University Art Gallery, 1985.

———. *Ink Plum: The Making of a Chinese Scholar-Painting Genre*. Cambridge: Cambridge University Press, 1996.

Birrell, Anne. *Chinese Mythology: An Introduction*. Baltimore: Johns Hopkins University Press, 1993.

———. trans. *The Classic of Mountains and Seas*. Harmondsworth: Penguin Books, 1999.

Blakeley, Barry B. "Chu Society and State: Image versus Reality," in Constance A. Cook and John S. Major ed., *Defining Chu: Image and Reality in Ancient China*, pp. 51–66. Honolulu: University of Hawai'i Press, 1999.

Bloom, Harold. *The Anxiety of Influence: A Theory of Poetry*. New York: Oxford University Press, 1973.

Bowers, Fredson. *Textual and Literary Criticism*. London: Cambridge University Press, 1959.

Bray, Francesca. *Technology and Society in Ming China (1368–1644)*. Washington DC: American Historical Association, 2000.

Brien, Alan. "Tourist Angst," *The Spectator* (July 31, 1959): 133.

Brook, Timothy. *Praying for Power: Buddhism and the Formation of Gentry Society in Late-Ming China*. Cambridge, MA: Harvard University Press, 1993.

———. "Communications and Commerce," in Denis Twitchett and Frederick W. Mote ed., *The Cambridge History of China Volume 8: The Ming Dynasty, 1368–1644, Part 2*, pp. 579–707. Cambridge: Cambridge University Press, 1998.

———. *The Confusions of Pleasure: Commerce and Culture in Ming China*. Berkeley: University of California Press, 1998.

———. *Geographical Sources of Ming-Qing History*. Ann Arbor: Center for Chinese Studies, University of Michigan, 2002.

———. *The Chinese State in Ming Society*. London: RoutledgeCurzon, 2005.

Burkus-Chasson, Anne. "'Clouds and Mists That Emanate and Sink Away': Shitao's Waterfall on Mount Lu and Practices of Observation in the Seventeenth Century," *Art History* 19 (2) (1996): 169–90.

Bush, Susan. "Tsung Ping's Essay on Painting Landscape and the 'Landscape Buddhism' of Mount Lu," in *idem* and Christian Murck ed., *Theories of the Arts in China*, pp. 132–64. Princeton: Princeton University Press, 1983.

Bush, Susan and Hsio-yen Shih ed. *Early Chinese Texts on Painting*. Cambridge, MA: Harvard University Press, 1985.

Butor, Michel. "Le voyage et l'écriture," in *idem*, *Répertoire IV*, pp. 9–29. Paris: Minuit, 1974.

Cahill, James. *Chinese Painting*. New York: Rizzoli International, 1977.

———. ed. *Shadows of Mt. Huang: Chinese Painting and Printing of the Anhui School*. Berkeley: University Art Museum, 1981.

———. "Huang Shan Paintings as Pilgrimage Pictures," in Susan Naquin and Chün-fang Yü ed., *Pilgrims and Sacred Sites in China*, pp. 246–92. Berkeley: University of California Press, 1992.

———. *The Painter's Practice: How Artists Lived and Worked in Traditional China*. New York: Columbia University Press, 1994.

———. *See also* Gao Juhan 高居翰.

Cai Yingyuan 蔡營源. *Qian Qianyi zhi shengping yu zhushu* 錢謙益之生平與著述. Miaoli: Fuhua shuju, 1977.

Campbell, Duncan. "Qi Biaojia's 'Footnotes to Allegory Mountain': Introduction and Translation," *Studies in the History of Gardens and Designed Landscapes* 19 (3/4) (1999): 243–71.

———. "Cao Rong (1613–85) on Books: Loss, Libraries and Circulation." Unpublished seminar paper delivered to the Department of History, University of Otago (10 May 2006).

———. "The Moral Status of the Book: Huang Zongxi in the Private Libraries of Late-Imperial China," *East Asian History* 32/33 (2006/2007): 1–24.

Cao Xueqin. *The Story of the Stone (Volume One: The Golden Days)*. David Hawkes trans. Harmondsworth: Penguin Books, 1973.

Cao Xueqin 曹雪芹 and Gao E 高鶚. *Hongloumeng* 紅樓夢. Rpt.; two volumes. Beijing: Renmin wenxue chubanshe, 1998.

Carrington Goodrich, Luther. *The Literary Inquisition of Ch'ien-Lung*. New York: Paragon Book Reprint Corp., 1966.

———. ed. *Dictionary of Ming Biography 1368–1644*. Two volumes. New York: Columbia University Press, 1976.

Cartelli, Mary Anne. "On a Five-Colored Cloud: The Songs of Mount Wutai," *Journal of the American Oriental Society* 124 (4) (2004): 735–57.

Carter, Steven D. "Bashō and the Mastery of Poetic Space in *Oku no hosomichi*," *Journal of the American Oriental Society* 120 (2) (2000): 190–8.

Cass, Victoria. *Dangerous Women: Warriors, Grannies, and Geishas of the Ming*. Lanham: Rowman and Littlefield, 1999.

Cervantes Saavedra, Miguel de. *The Ingenious Hidalgo Don Quixote de la Mancha*. John Rutherford trans. London: Penguin Books, 2000.

Chan Che-shan 陳芷珊. *Qian jian Du shi yanjiu* 錢箋杜詩研究. Unpublished PhD thesis: The University of Hong Kong, 2005.

Chan, Wing-ming. "The Early-Qing Discourse on Loyalty," *East Asian History* 19 (2000): 27–52.

Chang, H. C. trans. *Chinese Literature 2: Nature Poetry*. Edinburgh: Edinburgh University Press, 1977.

Chang, Kang-i Sun. *The Late-Ming Poet Ch'en Tzu-lung: Crises of Love and Loyalism*. New Haven: Yale University Press, 1991.

———. "Qian Qianyi and His Place in History," in Wilt L. Idema, Wai-yee Li and Ellen Widmer ed., *Trauma and Transcendence in Early Qing Literature*, pp. 199–218. Cambridge, MA: Harvard University Press, 2006.

Chaves, Jonathan. "The Panoply of Images: A Reconsideration of the Literary Theories of the Kung-an School," in Susan Bush and Christian Murck ed., *Theories of the Arts in China*, pp. 341–64. Princeton: Princeton University Press, 1983.

———. "The Expression of Self in the Kung-an School: Non-Romantic Individualism," in Robert E. Hegel and Richard C. Hessney ed., *Expressions of Self in Chinese Literature*, pp. 123–50. New York: Columbia University Press, 1985.

———. "The Yellow Mountain Poems of Ch'ien Ch'ien-i (1582–1664): Poetry as *Yu-chi*," *Harvard Journal of Asiatic Studies* 48 (2) (1988): 465–92.

Che, K. L. "Not Words But Feelings — Ch'ien Ch'ien-I [*sic*] (1582–1664) on Poetry," *Tamkang Review* 6 (1) (1975): 55–75.

Chen Bo 辰伯 [Wu Han 吳晗]. "Qian Muzhai zhi shixue" 錢牧齋之史學, *Wenshi zazhi* 文史襍誌 4 (7/8) (1944): 57–9.

Chen Chuanxi 陳傳席. *Zhongguo shanshuihua shi* 中國山水畫史 [*xiudingben* 修訂本]. Tianjin: Renmin meishu chubanshe, 2001.

Chen Guangzhong 陳廣忠 ed. *Huainanzi yizhu* 淮南子譯注. Changchun: Jilin wenshi chubanshe, 1990.

Chen Jiru 陳繼儒. *Taiping qinghua* 太平清話. Rpt.; Shanghai: Shangwu yinshuguan, 1936.

———. *Chen Meigong xiaopin* 陳眉公小品. Hu Shaotang 胡紹棠 ed. Beijing: Wenhua yishu chubanshe, 1996.

Chen Yinke [Chen Yinque] 陳寅恪. *Liu Rushi biezhuan* 柳如是別傳. Three volumes. Shanghai: Guji chubanshe, 1980.

Cherniack, Susan. "Book Culture and Textual Transmission in Sung China," *Harvard Journal of Asiatic Studies* 54 (1994): 5–125.

Chin, Sandi and Cheng-chi (Ginger) Hsü. "Anhui Merchant Culture and Patronage," in James Cahill ed., *Shadows of Mt. Huang: Chinese Painting and Printing of the Anhui School*, pp. 19–24. Berkeley: University Art Museum, 1981.

Chou, Chih-p'ing. "The Poetry and Poetic Theory of Yüan Hung-tao (1568–1610)," *Tsing-Hua Journal of Chinese Studies* (New Series) 15 (1/2) (1983): 113–42.

———. *Yüan Hung-tao and the Kung-an School*. Cambridge: Cambridge University Press, 1988.

Chow Kai-wing. "Writing for Success: Printing, Examinations and Intellectual Change in Late Ming China," *Late Imperial China* 17 (1) (1996): 120–57.

Clayton, Jay and Eric Rothstein ed. *Influence and Intertextuality in Literary History*. Madison: University of Wisconsin Press, 1991.

Clunas, Craig. "Some Literary Evidence for Gold and Silver Vessels in the Ming Period (1368–1644)," in Michael Vickers ed., *Pots and Pans: A Colloquium on Precious Metals and Ceramics in the Muslim, Chinese and Graeco-Roman Worlds, Oxford, 1985*, pp. 83–7. Oxford Studies in Islamic Art III. Oxford: Oxford University Press, 1986.

———. "Books and Things: Ming Literary Culture and Material Culture," *Chinese Studies*, pp. 136–42. London: British Library Occasional Paper #10, 1988.

———. *Superfluous Things: Material Culture and Social Status in Early Modern China*. Cambridge: Polity Press, 1991.

———. "Regulation of Consumption and the Institution of Correct Morality by the Ming State," in Chun-chieh Huang and Erik Zürcher ed., *Norms and the State in China*, pp. 39–49. Leiden: E. J. Brill, 1993.

———. *Fruitful Sites: Garden Culture in Ming Dynasty China*. London: Reaktion Books, 1996.

———. *Pictures and Visuality in Early Modern China*. London: Reaktion Books, 1997.

———. "Artist and Subject in Ming Dynasty China," in *Proceedings of the British Academy 105: 1999 Lectures and Memoirs*, pp. 43–72. Oxford: Oxford University Press, 2000.

———. *Elegant Debts: The Social Art of Wen Zhengming, 1470–1559*. London: Reaktion Books, 2004.

Coleman, Simon and John Elsner. *Pilgrimage Past and Present: Sacred Travel and Sacred Space in World Religions*. London: British Museum Press, 1995.

Dalton, Jack P. "The Text of *Ulysses*," in Fritz Senn ed., *New Light on Joyce from the Dublin Symposium*, pp. 99–119. Bloomington: Indiana University Press, 1972.

Dante Alighieri. *The Comedy of Dante Alighieri: Cantica I: Hell [l'Inferno]*. Dorothy L. Sayers trans. Harmondsworth: Penguin Books, 1949.

Dardess, John W. *Blood and History in China: The Donglin Faction and its Repression, 1620–1627*. Honolulu: University of Hawai'i Press, 2002.

Davidson, Robyn ed. *The Picador Book of Journeys*. London: Picador, 2001.

Davis, A. R. "The Narrow Lane: Some Observations on the Recluse in Traditional Chinese Society," *East Asian History* 11 (1996): 33–44.

Demiéville, Paul. "La Montagne dans l'art littéraire chinois," *France-Asie/Asia* 20 (1) (1965): 7–32.

Dennerline, Jerry. *The Chia-ting Loyalists: Confucian Leadership and Social Change in Seventeenth-Century China*. New Haven: Yale University Press, 1981.

Des Forges, Roger V. *Cultural Centrality and Political Change in Chinese History: Northeast Henan in the Fall of the Ming*. Stanford: Stanford University Press, 2003.

Ding Du 丁度. *Ji yun* 集韻. Rpt.; five volumes. Taibei: Taiwan shangwu yinshuguan, 1965.

Ding Gongyi 丁功誼. *Qian Qianyi wenxue sixiang yanjiu* 錢謙益文學思想研究. Shanghai: Guji chubanshe, 2006.

Dott, Brian R. *Identity Reflections: Pilgrimages to Mount Tai in Late Imperial China*. Cambridge, MA: Harvard University Press, 2004.

Du Fu 杜甫. *See under* Qian Qianyi.

Evelyn, John. *The Diary of John Evelyn*. E. S. de Beer ed. Six volumes. Oxford: Clarendon Press, 1955.

Fan Jingzhong 范景中 and Zhou Shutian 周書田 ed. *Liu Rushi shiji* 柳如是事輯. Hangzhou: Zhongguo meishu xueyuan chubanshe, 2002.

Fang Bao 方苞. *Fang Wangxi xiansheng quanji* 方望溪先生全集. Rpt.; two volumes. Shanghai: *SBCK* edition.

Fang Xuanling 房玄齡. *Jin shu* 晉書. Rpt.; ten volumes. Beijing: Zhonghua shuju, 1974.

Fenton, James. "Vandalism and Enlightenment" (Review of "Enlightenment: Discovering the World in the Eighteenth Century," an exhibition at the British Museum), *New York Review of Books* 51 (3): August 12, 2004: 51.

Fisher, Tom. "Loyalist Alternatives in the Early Ch'ing," *Harvard Journal of Asiatic Studies* 44 (1984): 83–122.

Fong, Wen. "Rivers and Mountains after Snow (Chiang-shan hsüeh-chi), Attributed to Wang Wei (AD 699–759)," *Archives of Asian Art* 30 (1976–77): 6–33.

Francastel, Pierre. "Problèmes de la sociologie de l'art," in Georges Gurvitch ed., *Traité de sociologie* (Tome II), pp. 278–96. Paris: Presses universitaires de France, 1960.

Frankel, Hans H. "The Contemplation of the Past in T'ang Poetry," in Arthur F. Wright and Denis Twitchett ed., *Perspectives on the T'ang*, pp. 345–65. New Haven: Yale University Press, 1973.

———. *The Flowering Plum and the Palace Lady: Interpretations of Chinese Verse*. New Haven: Yale University Press, 1976.

Fung, Stanislaus. "Word and Garden in Chinese Essays of the Ming Dynasty: Notes on Matters of Approach," *Interfaces: Image, texte, language* 11–12 (June 1997): 77–90.

———. "Longing and Belonging in Chinese Garden History," in Michel Conan ed., *Perspectives on Garden Histories*, pp. 205–19. Washington DC: Dumbarton Oaks, 1999.

Fussell, Paul. *Abroad: British Literary Traveling Between the Wars*. Oxford: Oxford University Press, 1980.

Gao Juhan 高居翰 [James Cahill]. "Lun Hongren *Huanshan tuce* de guishu" 論弘仁《黃山圖冊》的歸屬, *Duoyun* 朵雲 9 (1985): 108–24.

Gao Zhangcai 高章采. *Guanchang shike* 官場詩客. Xianggang: Zhonghua shuju, 1991.

Ge Wanli 葛萬里. *Muzhai xiansheng nianpu* 牧齋先生年譜. Rpt.; *Beijing tushuguan cang zhenben nianpu congkan* 北京圖書館藏珍本年譜叢刊 (Beijing: Beijing tushuguan chubanshe, 1999) 64: 559–86.

Gell, Alfred. "Newcomers to the World of Goods: Consumption among the Muria Gonds," in Arjun Appadurai ed., *The Social Life of Things: Commodities in Cultural Perspective*, pp. 110–38. Cambridge: Cambridge University Press, 1986.

Gombrich, E. H. *Art and Illusion: A Study in the Psychology of Pictorial Representation*. London: Phaidon Press, 1959.

———. *Norm and Form: Studies in the Art of the Renaissance*. London: Phaidon Press, 1966.

Goodall, John A. *Heaven and Earth: Album Leaves from a Ming Encyclopaedia: San-ts'ai t'u-hui, 1610*. Boulder: Shambhala, 1979.

Graham, A. C. trans. *The Book of Lieh-tzŭ*. London: John Murray, 1960.

———. *Poems of the Late T'ang*. Harmondsworth: Penguin Books, 1965.

Gu Yanwu 顧炎武. *Rizhilu jishi* 日知錄集釋. Huang Rucheng 黃汝成 ed. Rpt.; two volumes. Shijiazhuang: Huashan wenyi chubanshe, 1990.

Guan Xihua 管錫華. *Jiaokanxue* 校勘學. Hefei: Anhui jiaoyu chubanshe, 1991.

Guo Qingfan 郭慶藩. *Zhuangzi jishi* 莊子集釋. Rpt.; Wang Xiaoyu 王孝魚 ed. Three volumes. Beijing: Zhonghua shuju, 1961.

Guo Xi. "Advice on Landscape," John Hay, Victor H. Mair, Susan Bush and Hsio-Yen Shih trans., in Mair, Nancy S. Steinhardt and Paul R. Goldin ed., *Hawai'i Reader in Traditional Chinese Culture*, pp. 380–7. Honolulu: University of Hawai'i Press, 2005.

Guoyu 國語. Rpt.; Shanghai: *SBCK* edition.

Guy, R. Kent. *The Emperor's Four Treasuries: Scholars and the State in the Late Ch'ien-lung Era*. Cambridge, MA: Harvard University Press, 1987.

Hahn, Thomas. "The Standard Taoist Mountain and Related Features of Religious Geography," *Cahiers d'Extrême-Asie* 4 (1988): 145–56.

Hamilton, Robyn. "The Pursuit of Fame: Luo Qilan (1755–1813?) and the Debates about Women and Talent in Eighteenth-Century Jiangnan," *Late Imperial China* 18 (1) (1997): 39–71.

Han Yu 韓愈. *Han Yu quanji jiaozhu* 韓愈全集校注. Qu Shouyuan 屈守元 and Chang Sichun 常思春 ed. Five volumes. Chengdu: Sichuan daxue chubanshe, 1996.

Handlin-Smith, Joanna F. "Gardens in Ch'i Piao-chia's Social World: Wealth and Values in Late-Ming Kiangnan," *Journal of Asian Studies* 51 (1) (1992): 55–81.

Hanyu da cidian 漢語大詞典 [*pujiben* 普及本]. Shanghai: Hanyu da cidian chubanshe, 2000.

Hao Runhua 郝潤花. Qian zhu Du shi *yu shishi huzheng fangfa* 《錢注杜詩》與詩史互証方法. Hefei: Huangshan shushe, 2000.

Hargett, James M. "Some Preliminary Remarks on the Travel Records of the Song Dynasty (960–1279)," *Chinese Literature: Essays, Articles, Reviews* 7 (1/2) (July 1985): 67–93.

———. *On the Road in Twelfth Century China: The Travel Diaries of Fan Chengda (1126–1193)*. Stuttgart: Franz Steiner Verlag, 1989.

Harrist, Robert E. Jr. "Reading Chinese Mountains: Landscape and Calligraphy in China," *Orientations* (Dec 2000): 64–9.

Hassam, Andrew. " 'As I Write': Narrative Occasions and the Quest for Self-Presence in the Travel Diary," *Ariel* 21 (4) (1990): 33–48.

Hawkes, David trans. *Ch'u Tz'ŭ: The Songs of the South*. London: Oxford University Press, 1959.

Hay, John. *Kernels of Energy, Bones of Earth: The Rock in Chinese Art*. New York: China House Gallery, 1985.

———. "Boundaries and Surfaces of Self and Desire in Yuan Painting," in *idem* ed., *Boundaries in China*, pp. 124–70. London: Reaktion Books, 1994.

Hay, Jonathan. "Ming Palace and Tomb in Early Qing Jiangning: Dynastic Memory and the Openness of History," *Late Imperial China* 20 (1) (1999): 1–48.

———. *Shitao: Painting and Modernity in Early Qing China*. Cambridge: Cambridge University Press, 2001.

Hazelton, Keith. *A Synchronic Chinese-Western Daily Calendar, 1341–1661 A.D.* Revised edition; Minneapolis: Ming Studies Research Series, University of Minnesota, 1985.

He Pingli 何平立. *Chongshan linian yu Zhongguo wenhua* 崇山理念與中國文化. Ji'nan: Qilu shushe, 2001.

He Xiu 何休. *Chunqiu Gongyang jingzhuan jiegu* 春秋公羊經傳解詁. Rpt.; Shanghai: *SBCK* edition.

Hegel, Robert E. "*Vignettes from the Late Ming: A Hsiao-p'in Anthology* by Yang Ye" (review), *Journal of Asian and African Studies* 37 (1) (March 2002): 116–8.

Heijdra, Martin. "The Socio-Economic Development of Rural China during the Ming," in Denis Twitchett and Frederick W. Mote ed., *The Cambridge History of China Volume 8: The Ming Dynasty, 1368–1644, Part 2*, pp. 417–578. Cambridge: Cambridge University Press, 1998.

Ho Koon-piu. "Should We Die as Martyrs to the Ming Cause? Scholar-officials' Views on Martyrdom during the Ming-Qing Transition," *Oriens Extremus* 37 (2) (1994): 123–51.

Ho, Ping-ti. "The Salt Merchants of Yang-chou: A Study of Commercial Capitalism in Eighteenth-Century China," *Harvard Journal of Asiatic Studies* 17 (1954): 130–68.

Ho, Wai-kam. "The Literary Concepts of 'Picture-like' (*Ju-hua*) and 'Picture-Idea' (*Hua-i*) in the Relationship between Poetry and Painting," in Alfreda Murck and Wen C. Fong ed., *Words and Images: Chinese Poetry, Calligraphy, and Painting*, pp. 359–404. New York: Metropolitan Museum of Art, 1991.

Hoshi Ayao. "Transportation in the Ming Dynasty," *Acta Asiatica* 38 (1980): 1–30.

Hsu Wen-Chin. "Images of Huang-shan in Shih-t'ao's Paintings," *National Palace Museum Bulletin* [Taipei] 27 (1/2) (1992): 1–37.

Hu Shouwei 胡守為 ed. Liu Rushi biezhuan *yu guoxue yanjiu* 《柳如是別傳》與國學研究. Hangzhou: Zhejiang renmin chubanshe, 1995.

Hu Youfeng 胡幼峰. *Qing chu Yushanpai shilun* 清初虞山派詩論. Taibei: Guoli bianyiguan, 1994.

Huang, Ray. *1587: A Year of No Significance: The Ming Dynasty in Decline*. New Haven: Yale University Press, 1981.

Huang Songlin 黃松林 ed. *Huangshan gujin youlan shi xuan* 黃山古今遊覽詩選. Hefei: Huangshan shushe, 1989.

———. *Huangshan daoyou daquan* 黃山導遊大全. Hefei: Huangshan shushe, 1993.

Huang Zongxi 黃宗羲. *Huang Zongxi quanji* 黃宗羲全集. Shen Shanhong 沈善洪 ed. 12 volumes. Hangzhou: Zhejiang guji chubanshe, 2005.

Hucker, Charles O. *A Dictionary of Official Titles in Imperial China*. Stanford: Stanford University Press, 1985.

Hummel, Arthur W. ed. *Eminent Chinese of the Ch'ing Period*. Two volumes. Washington DC: Government Printing Office, 1943–44.

Hung, William. *Tu Fu: China's Greatest Poet*. Cambridge, MA: Harvard University Press, 1952.

Hurvitz, Leon. "Tsung Ping's Comments on Landscape Painting," *Artibus Asiae* 32 (1970): 146–56.

Jackson, Mark. "Landscape/Representation/Text: Craig Clunas's *Fruitful Sites* (1996)," *Studies in the History of Gardens and Designed Landscapes* 19 (3/4) (1999): 302–13.

Jenner, W. F. J. *Memories of Loyang: Yang Hsüan-chih and the Lost Capital (493–534)*. Oxford: Clarendon Press, 1981.

Jian Xiujuan 簡秀娟. *Qian Qianyi cangshu yanjiu* 錢謙益藏書研究. Taibei: Hanmei tushu, 1991.

Jin Hechong 金鶴沖. *Qian Muzhai xiansheng nianpu* 錢牧齋先生年譜, in Qian

Zhonglian 錢仲聯 ed., *Qian Muzhai quanji* 錢牧齋全集, Volume 8, pp. 930–52. Shanghai: Guji chubanshe, 2003.

Jing Hao 荊浩. "Bifa ji" 筆法記. Rpt.; Wang Bomin 王伯敏 ed., in *Zhongguo hualun congshu* 中國畫論叢書. Beijing: Renmin meishu chubanshe, 1963.

———. "A Record of the Methods of the Brush." Stephen H. West trans., in Pauline Yu, Peter Bol, Stephen Owen and Willard Peterson ed., *Ways with Words: Writing about Reading Texts from Early China*, pp. 202–13. Berkeley: University of California Press, 2000.

Johnson, Jeri. "Composition and Publication History," in idem ed., *Ulysses: The 1922 Text*, pp. xxxviii–lvi. Oxford: Oxford University Press, 1993.

Kerridge, Richard. "Ecologies of Desire: Travel Writing and Nature Writing as Travelogue," in Steve Clark ed., *Travel Writing and Empire: Postcolonial Theory in Transit*, pp. 164–82. London: Zed Books, 1999.

Kessler, Lawrence D. "Chinese Scholars and the Early Manchu State," *Harvard Journal of Asiatic Studies* 31 (1971): 179–200.

Kim, Hongnam. *The Life of a Patron: Zhou Lianggong (1612–1672) and the Painters of Seventeenth-Century China*. New York: China Institute in America, 1996.

Ko, Dorothy. *Teachers of the Inner Chambers: Women and Culture in Seventeenth-Century China*. Stanford: Stanford University Press, 1994.

Kristeva, Julia. *Σημειωτική [Sēmeiōtikē]: Recherches pour une sémanalyse*. Paris: Éditions du Seuil, 1969.

Kroll, Paul W. "Verses from on High: The Ascent of T'ai Shan," in Shuen-fu Lin and Stephen Owen ed., *The Vitality of the Lyric Voice: Shih Poetry from the Late Han to the T'ang*, pp. 167–216. Princeton: Princeton University Press, 1986.

Lagerwey, John. "The Pilgrimage to Wu-tang Shan," in Susan Naquin and Chün-fang Yü ed., *Pilgrims and Sacred Sites in China*, pp. 293–332. Berkeley: University of California Press, 1992.

Laing, Ellen Johnston. "Sixteenth-Century Patterns of Art Patronage: Qiu Ying and the Xiang Family," *Journal of the American Oriental Society* 111 (1) (1991): 1–7.

Lao Yian 勞亦安 ed. *Gujin youji congchao* 古今遊記叢鈔. Six volumes. Taibei: Zhonghua shuju, 1961.

Lau, D. C. trans. *Tao Te Ching*. Harmondsworth: Penguin Books, 1963.

———. trans. *Mencius*. Harmondsworth: Penguin Books, 1970.

———. trans. *The Analects*. Harmondsworth: Penguin Books, 1979.

Lazzaro, Claudia. *The Italian Renaissance Garden: From the Conventions of Planting, Design, and Ornament to the Grand Gardens of Sixteenth-Century Central Italy*. New Haven: Yale University Press, 1990.

Leach, Helen. *Cultivating Myths: Fiction, Fact and Fashion in Garden History*. Auckland: Random House, 2000.

Legge, James trans. *The Chinese Classics*. Five volumes. Rpt.; Hong Kong: Hong Kong University Press, 1960.

Lewis, R. W. B. *Edith Wharton: A Biography*. New York: Harper and Row, 1975.

Li Bai 李白. *Li Taibai quanji* 李太白全集. Wang Qi 王琦 ed. Rpt.; three volumes. Beijing: Zhonghua shuju, 1977.

Li, Chu-tsing. "The Artistic Theories of the Literati," in *idem* and James C. Y. Watt ed., *The Chinese Scholar's Studio: Artistic Life in the Late Ming Period*, pp. 14–22. New York: Thames and Hudson, 1987.

Li, Chu-tsing and James C. Y. Watt ed. *The Chinese Scholar's Studio: Artistic Life in the Late Ming Period*. New York: Thames and Hudson, 1987.

Li Daoyuan 酈道元. *Shuijing zhu* 水經注. Rpt.; Tan Shuchun 譚屬春 and Chen Aiping 陳愛平 ed. Changsha: Yuelu shushe, 1995.

Li, Hui-lin. "Mei Hua: A Botanical Note," in Maggie Bickford, *Bones of Jade, Soul of Ice: The Flowering Plum in Chinese Art*, pp. 245–50. New Haven: Yale University Art Gallery, 1985.

———. *Chinese Flower Arrangement*. Mineola: Dover Publications, 2002.

Li Jiahong 李家宏 ed. *Huangshan lüyou wenhua da cidian* 黃山旅遊文化大辭典. Hefei: Zhongguo kexue jishu daxue chubanshe, 1994.

Li Qing 李慶. "Qian Qianyi: Ming mo shidafu xintai de dianxing" 錢謙益：明末士大夫心態的典型, *Fudan xuebao* 復旦學報 [*sheke ban* 社科版] (1989) (1): 37–43.

Li Rihua 李日華. *Weishuixuan riji* 味水軒日記. Rpt.; Tu Youxiang 屠友祥 ed. Shanghai: Yuandong chubanshe, 1996.

Li Shizhen 李時珍. *Bencao gangmu* 本草綱目. Rpt.; Ran Xiande 冉先德 ed. Four volumes. Beijing: Zhongguo guoji guangbo chubanshe, 1994.

Li, Wai-yee. "The Collector, the Connoisseur, and Late-Ming Sensibility," *T'oung Pao* 81 (4/5) (1995): 269–302.

———. "The Late Ming Courtesan: Invention of a Cultural Ideal," in Ellen Widmer and Kang-i Sun Chang ed., *Writing Women in Late Imperial China*, pp. 46–73. Stanford: Stanford University Press, 1997.

———. "Heroic Transformations: Women and National Trauma in Early Qing Literature," *Harvard Journal of Asiatic Studies* 59 (2) (1999): 363–443.

Li Yimang 李一氓 ed. *Ming Qing ren you Huangshan jichao* 明清人遊黃山記鈔. Hefei: Anhui renmin chubanshe, 1983.

———. ed. *Ming Qing huajia Huangshan huace* 明清畫家黃山畫冊. Hefei: Anhui meishu chubanshe, 1985.

Liscomb, Kathlyn Maurean. *Learning from Mount Hua: A Chinese Physician's Illustrated Travel Record and Painting Theory*. Cambridge: Cambridge University Press, 1993.

Liu, James J. Y. *The Art of Chinese Poetry*. London: Routledge, 1962.

Liu Shi 柳是. *Liu Rushi shiwen ji* 柳如是詩文集. Gu Huizhi 谷輝之 ed. Beijing: Xinhua shudian, 1996.

———. *Liu Rushi ji* 柳如是集. Zhou Shutian 周書田 and Fan Jingzhong 范景中 ed. Hangzhou: Zhongguo meishu xueyuan chubanshe, 1999.

Liu Xiang 劉向 attrib. *Lie xian zhuan* 列仙傳. Rpt.; Shanghai: Guji chubanshe, 1990.

Liu Yuxi 劉禹錫. *Liu Yuxi quanji biannian jiaozhu* 劉禹錫全集編年校注. Tao Min 陶敏 and Tao Hongyu 陶紅雨 ed. Two volumes. Changsha: Yuelu shushe, 2003.

Liu Zongyuan 柳宗元. *Liu Zongyuan ji* 柳宗元集. Wu Wenzhi 吳文治 ed. Four volumes. Beijing: Zhonghua shuju, 1979.

Liu Zuomei 柳作梅. "Wang Shizhen yu Qian Qianyi zhi shilun" 王士稹 [*sic*] 與錢謙益之詩論, *Shumu jikan* 書目季刊 2 (3) (1968): 41–9.

Lo, Karl. *A Guide to the Ssŭ Pu Ts'ung K'an.* Lawrence: University of Kansas Libraries, 1965.

Loewe, Michael. *Faith, Myth and Reason in Han China.* Indianapolis: Hackett Publishing Company, 1994.

Lu Xun. *Selected Works.* Yang Xianyi and Gladys Yang trans. Four volumes. Beijing: Foreign Languages Press, 1980.

Lu You 陸游. *Lu Fangweng quanji* 陸放翁全集. Taibei: Heluo tushu chubanshe, 1975.

MacCannell, Dean. *The Tourist: A New Theory of the Leisure Class.* New York: Schocken Books, 1976.

MacFarlane, Robert. *Mountains of the Mind: A History of a Fascination.* London: Granta Books, 2003.

March, Andrew L. "Self and Landscape in Su Shih," *Journal of the American Oriental Society* 86 (4) (1966): 377–96.

McDermott, Joseph P. "The Making of a Chinese Mountain, Huangshan: Politics and Wealth in Chinese Art," *Asian Cultural Studies* 17 (1989): 145–76.

McDowall, Stephen. "In Lieu of Flowers: The Transformation of Space and Self in Yuan Mei's (1716–1798) Garden Records," *New Zealand Journal of Asian Studies* 3 (2) (2001): 136–49.

———. "Qian Qianyi's (1582–1664) Reflections on Yellow Mountain," *New Zealand Journal of Asian Studies* 7 (2) (2005): 134–52.

McKenzie, D. F. "The Sociology of a Text: Orality, Literacy and Print in Early New Zealand," *The Library*, Sixth Series 6 (4) (1984): 333–65.

McMahon, Keith. *Misers, Shrews, and Polygamists: Sexuality and Male-Female Relations in Eighteenth-Century Chinese Fiction.* London: Duke University Press, 1995.

Mei Qing 梅清. *Mei Qing Huangshan tuce* 梅清黃山圖冊. Rpt.; Shanghai: Shanghai renmin meishu chubanshe, 1980.

Meinig, D. W. ed. *The Interpretation of Ordinary Landscapes: Geographical Essays.* Oxford: Oxford University Press, 1979.

Meyer-Fong, Tobie. "Making a Place for Meaning in Early Qing Yangzhou," *Late Imperial China* 20 (1) (1999): 49–84.

———. "Packaging the Men of Our Times: Literary Anthologies, Friendship Networks, and Political Accommodation in the Early Qing," *Harvard Journal of Asiatic Studies* 64 (1) (2004): 5–56.

Milton, John. *Paradise Lost.* Rpt.; Alastair Fowler ed., second edition [revised]. Harlow: Pearson, 2007.

Minford, John. "Pieces of Eight: Reflections on Translating *The Story of the Stone*," in Eugene Eoyang and Lin Yao-fu ed., *Translating Chinese Literature*, pp. 178–203. Bloomington: Indiana University Press, 1995.

Mitchell, W. J. T. "Editor's Note: The Language of Images," *Critical Inquiry* 6 (3) (1980): 359–62.

———. ed. *Landscape and Power.* Chicago: University of Chicago Press, 1994.

Morinis, Alan ed. *Sacred Journeys: The Anthropology of Pilgrimage.* Westport: Greenwood Press, 1992.

Naitō Torajirō 內藤虎次郎. *Shina kaiga shi* 支那繪畫史. Rpt.; Kanda Kiichirō 神田喜一郎 and Naitō Kenkichi 內藤乾吉 ed., *Naitō Konan zenshū* 內藤湖南全集. Volume 13. Tōkyō: Chikuma shobō, 1969–1976.

Naquin, Susan and Chün-fang Yü ed. *Pilgrims and Sacred Sites in China*. Berkeley: University of California Press, 1992.

Nelson, Susan E. "The Piping of Man," in Wu Hung and Katherine R. Tsiang ed., *Body and Face in Chinese Visual Culture*, pp. 283–310. Cambridge, MA: Harvard University Press, 2005.

Ni Qixin 倪其心 ed. *Zhongguo gudai youji xuan* 中國古代遊記選. Two volumes. Beijing: Zhongguo youji chubanshe, 1985.

Nienhauser, William H. Jr. ed. *The Indiana Companion to Traditional Chinese Literature*. Two volumes. Bloomington: Indiana University Press, 1986 and 1998.

Olwig, Kenneth Robert. *Landscape, Nature, and the Body Politic: From Britain's Renaissance to America's New World*. Madison: University of Wisconsin Press, 2002.

Ouyang Xun 歐陽詢 comp. *Yiwen leiju* 藝文類聚. Rpt.; Wang Shaoying 汪紹楹 ed. Four volumes. Shanghai: Guji chubanshe, 1982.

Owen, Stephen trans. *An Anthology of Chinese Literature: Beginnings to 1911*. New York: W. W. Norton and Co., 1996.

Oxford English Dictionary [online edition: http://www.oed.com/].

Pei Shijun 裴世俊. *Qian Qianyi shige yanjiu* 錢謙益詩歌研究. Ningxia: Ningxia renmin chubanshe, 1991.

———. *Qian Qianyi guwen shoutan* 錢謙益古文首探. Ji'nan: Qilu shushe, 1996.

———. *Sihai zongmeng wushi nian: Qian Qianyi zhuan* 四海宗盟五十年：錢謙益傳. Beijing: Dongfang chubanshe, 2001.

Pengcheng tuishi 彭城退士. *Qian Muweng xiansheng nianpu* 錢牧翁先生年譜. Rpt.; *Beijing tushuguan cang zhenben nianpu congkan* 北京圖書館藏珍本年譜叢刊, 64: 587–600. Beijing: Beijing tushuguan chubanshe, 1999.

Plaks, Andrew trans. *Ta Hsüeh and Chung Yung (The Highest Order of Cultivation and On the Practice of the Mean)*. London: Penguin Books, 2003.

Porter, Denis. *Haunted Journeys: Desire and Transgression in European Travel Writing*. Princeton: Princeton University Press, 1991.

Powers, Martin. "When is a Landscape like a Body?" in Wen-hsin Yeh ed., *Landscape, Culture, and Power in Chinese Society*, pp. 1–22. Berkeley: University of California Press, 1998.

Pugh, Simon ed. *Reading Landscape: Country – City – Capital*. Manchester: Manchester University Press, 1990.

Qian Hang 錢杭 and Cheng Zai 承載. *Shiqi shiji Jiangnan shehui shenghuo* 十七世紀江南社會生活. Hangzhou: Zhejiang renmin chubanshe, 1996.

Qian Qianyi 錢謙益. *Muzhai quanji* 牧齋全集. Xue Fengchang 薛鳳昌 ed. 40 volumes. Shanghai: Wenming shuju, 1910.

———. *Muzhai chuxueji* 牧齋初學集. Rpt.; six volumes. Shanghai: *SBCK* edition.

———. *Qian Muzhai chidu* 錢牧齋尺牘. Rpt.; *Ming Qing shidajia chidu* 明清十大家尺牘. Xianggang: Zhonghua shuju, 1938.

———. *Liechao shiji xiaozhuan* 列朝詩集小傳. Rpt.; two volumes. Shanghai: Guji chubanshe, 1959.

———. *Qian zhu Du shi* 錢注杜詩. Rpt.; two volumes. Shanghai: Guji chubanshe, 1979.

———. *Muzhai chuxueji* 牧齋初學集. Rpt.; Qian Zhonglian 錢仲聯 ed. Three volumes. Shanghai: Guji chubanshe, 1985.

———. *Muzhai chuxueji* 牧齋初學集. Rpt.; *Siku jinhui shu congkan* 四庫禁燬書叢刊. Beijing: Beijing chubanshe, 2000.

———. *Jiangyunlou shumu* 絳雲樓書目. Rpt.; *Xuxiu siku quanshu* 續修四庫全書. Volume 920. Shanghai: Guji chubanshe, 2002.

———. *Qian Muzhai quanji* 錢牧齋全集. Qian Zhonglian 錢仲聯 ed. Eight volumes. Shanghai: Guji chubanshe, 2003.

Qian Qianyi 錢謙益, Wu Weiye 吳偉業 and Gong Dingzi 龔鼎孳. *Jiangzuo sandajia shichao* 江左三大家詩鈔. Taibei: Guangwen shuju, 1973.

Qu Shisi 瞿式耜. *Qu Shisi ji* 瞿式耜集. Rpt.; Shanghai: Guji chubanshe, 1981.

Qu Shouyuan 屈守元 ed. *Hanshi waizhuan jianshu* 韓詩外傳箋疏. Chengdu: Bashu shushe, 1996.

Rée, Jonathan. *Philosophical Tales: An Essay on Philosophy and Literature*. London: Methuen, 1987.

Ren Fangqiu 任訪秋. *Yuan Zhonglang yanjiu* 袁中郎研究. Shanghai: Guji chubanshe, 1983.

Rickett, Adele Austin trans. *Wang Kuo-wei's Jen-chien Tz'u-hua: A Study in Chinese Literary Criticism*. Hong Kong: Hong Kong University Press, 1977.

Riemenschnitter, Andrea. "Traveler's Vocation: Xu Xiake and His Excursion to the Southwestern Frontier," in Nicola Di Cosmo and Don J. Wyatt ed., *Political Frontiers, Ethnic Boundaries, and Human Geographies in Chinese History*, pp. 286–323. London: RoutledgeCurzon, 2003.

Robson, James. "The Polymorphous Space of the Southern Marchmount [Nanyue 南 嶽]: An Introduction to Nanyue's Religious History and Preliminary Notes on Buddhist-Daoist Interaction," *Cahiers d'Extrême-Asie* 8 (1995): 221–64.

Rousseau, Jean-Jacques. *Les rêveries du promeneur solitaire*. Rpt.; Raymond Bernex ed. Paris: Bordas, 1977.

Schafer, Edward H. "The Idea of Created Nature in T'ang Literature," *Philosophy East and West* 15 (1965): 153–60.

———. *Pacing the Void: T'ang Approaches to the Stars*. Berkeley: University of California Press, 1977.

Schama, Simon. *Landscape and Memory*. London: HarperCollins, 1995.

Shanchuan xiuli de Zhongguo 山川秀麗的中國 [*di si jie "Hanyu qiao" shijie daxuesheng Zhongwen bisai wenda tiji* 第四屆 "漢語橋" 世界大學生中文比賽問答題集]. Shanghai: Huadong shifan daxue chubanshe, 2005.

Shao Luoyang 邵洛羊 ed. *Zhongguo meishu da cidian* 中國美術大辭典. Shanghai: Cishu chubanshe, 2002.

Shelley, Percy Bysshe. *The Complete Poetical Works of Percy Bysshe Shelley: Volume 2*. Neville Rogers ed. Oxford: Clarendon Press, 1975.

Shen Fu. *Six Records of a Floating Life*. Leonard Pratt and Chiang Su-hui trans. Harmondsworth: Penguin Books, 1983.

———. 沈復. *Fusheng liuji* 浮生六記. Rpt.; Jin Xingyao 金性堯 and Jin Wennan 金文男
　　ed. Shanghai: Guji chubanshe, 2000.

Shen Yue 沈約. *Song shu* 宋書. Rpt.; eight volumes. Beijing: Zhonghua shuju, 1974.

Shi Zhicun 施蟄存 ed. *Wan Ming ershijia xiaopin* 晚明二十家小品. Shanghai: Shanghai
　　shudian, 1984.

Shih-t'ao. *Enlightening Remarks on Painting*. Richard E. Strassberg trans. Pasadena:
　　Pacific Asia Museum, 1989.

Shinohara Koichi. "Literary Construction of Buddhist Sacred Places: *The Record of Mt.
　　Lu* by Chen Shunyu," *Asiatische Studien* 53 (4) (1999): 937–64.

Sima Qian 司馬遷. *Shiji* 史記. Rpt.; ten volumes. Beijing: Zhonghua shuju, 1959.

Soka Gakkai Dictionary of Buddhism. Tokyo: Soka Gakkai, 2002.

Sontag, Susan. *On Photography*. New York: Farrar, Strauss and Giroux, 1977.

———. *Where the Stress Falls: Essays*. London: Vintage, 2003.

Soothill, William Edward and Lewis Hodous. *A Dictionary of Chinese Buddhist Terms*.
　　Delhi: Motilal Banarsidass, 1977.

Spence, Jonathan D. and John E. Wills, Jr. ed. *From Ming to Ch'ing: Conquest, Region
　　and Continuity in Seventeenth-Century China*. New Haven: Yale University
　　Press, 1979.

Strassberg, Richard E trans. *Inscribed Landscapes: Travel Writing from Imperial China*.
　　Berkeley: University of California Press, 1994.

———. *A Chinese Bestiary: Strange Creatures from the Guideways Through Mountains
　　and Seas*. Berkeley: University of California Press, 2002.

Struve, Lynn A. "Huang Zongxi in Context: A Reappraisal of His Major Writings,"
　　Journal of Asian Studies 47 (3) (1988): 474–502.

———. *The Ming-Qing Conflict, 1619–1683: A Historiography and Source Guide*. Ann
　　Arbor: Association for Asian Studies, 1998.

Su Shi 蘇軾. *Su Dongpo quanji* 蘇東坡全集. Two volumes. Beijing: Zhongguo shudian,
　　1986.

Sullivan, Michael. *Chinese Landscape Painting – Volume II: The Sui and Tang Dynasties*.
　　Berkeley: University of California Press, 1980.

Sun Jianai 孫家鼐 ed. *Qinding Shujing tushuo* 欽定書經圖説. Beijing: [Jingshi]
　　daxuetang, 1905.

Sun Zhimei 孫之梅. *Qian Qianyi yu Ming mo Qing chu wenxue* 錢謙益與明末清初文學.
　　Ji'nan: Qilu shushe, 1996.

Sung Ying-hsing. *T'ien-kung K'ai-wu: Chinese Technology in the Seventeenth Century*.
　　E-tu Zen Sun and Shiou-chuan Sun trans. London: Pennsylvania State
　　University Press, 1966.

Tao Qian 陶潛. *Tao Yuanming ji* 陶淵明集. Lu Qinli 逯欽立 ed. Beijing: Zhonghua shuju,
　　1979.

Tian, Xiaofei. *Tao Yuanming and Manuscript Culture: The Record of a Dusty Table*.
　　Seattle: University of Washington Press, 2005.

Tuan, Yi-fu. *China*. Chicago: Aldine-Atherton, 1969.

———. *Topophilia: A Study of Environmental Perception, Attitudes and Values*.
　　Englewood Cliffs, NJ: Prentice-Hall, 1974.

———. *Passing, Strange and Wonderful: Aesthetics, Nature, and Culture*. New York: Kodansha, 1993.

Vallette-Hémery, Martine. *Yuan Hongdao (1568–1610): théorie et pratique littéraires*. Paris: Mémoires de l'Institut des Hautes Études Chinoises, 1982.

Vervoorn, Aat. "Cultural Strata of Hua Shan, the Holy Peak of the West," *Monumenta Serica* 39 (1990–91): 1–30.

Vinograd, Richard. "Family Properties: Personal Context and Cultural Pattern in Wang Meng's *Pien* Mountains of 1366," *Ars Orientalis* 13 (1982): 1–29.

———. *Boundaries of the Self: Chinese Portraits, 1600–1900*. Cambridge: Cambridge University Press, 1992.

———. "Origins and Presences: Notes on the Psychology and Sociality of Shitao's Dreams," *Ars Orientalis* 25 (1995): 61–72.

Wakeman, Frederic Jr. "Romantics, Stoics, and Martyrs in Seventeenth-Century China," *Journal of Asian Studies* 43 (4) (1984): 631–65.

———. *The Great Enterprise: The Manchu Reconstruction of Imperial Order in Seventeenth-Century China*. Two volumes. Berkeley: University of California Press, 1985.

Waley, Arthur trans. *The Book of Songs*. New York: Grove Press, 1960.

Wang Anshi 王安石. *Wang Anshi quanji* 王安石全集. Ning Bo 寧波, Liu Lihua 劉麗華 and Zhang Zhongliang 張中良 ed. Two volumes. Changchun: Jilin renmin chubanshe, 1996.

Wang Keqian 王克謙 ed. *Lidai Huangshan youji xuan* 歷代黃山遊記選. Hefei: Huangshan shushe, 1988.

Wang Shiqing 汪世清 and Wang Cong 汪聰 ed. *Jianjiang ziliao ji* 漸江資料集. Hefei: Anhui renmin chubanshe, 1984.

Wang Siren 王思任. *Wang Jizhong xiaopin* 王季重小品. Li Wu 李嗚 ed. Beijing: Wenhua yishu chubanshe, 1996.

Wang Wei 王維. *Wang Youcheng ji jianzhu* 王右丞集箋注. Zhao Diancheng 趙殿成 ed. Rpt.; two volumes. Xianggang: Zhonghua shuju, 1972.

———. *Poems of Wang Wei*. G. W. Robinson trans. Harmondsworth: Penguin Books, 1973.

Wang Yunxi 王運熙 and Gu Yisheng 顧易生 ed. *Zhongguo wenxue piping shi* 中國文學批評史. Three volumes. Shanghai: Guji chubanshe, 1981.

Wang Zhongmin 王重民, Sun Wang 孫望 and Tong Yangnian 童養年 ed. *Quan Tang shi waibian* 全唐詩外編. Two volumes. Beijing: Zhonghua shuju, 1982.

Ward, Julian. *Xu Xiake (1587–1641): The Art of Travel Writing*. Richmond: Curzon, 2001.

Watson, Burton trans. *The Complete Works of Chuang Tzu*. New York: Columbia University Press, 1968.

Watson, Philip. "Famous Gardens of Luoyang, by Li Gefei: Translation with Introduction," *Studies in the History of Gardens and Designed Landscapes* 24 (1) (2004): 38–54.

———. trans. "Prose Writings of Lu You," *Renditions* 62 (2004): 7–23.

Watt, James C. Y. "The Literati Environment," in Chu-tsing Li and James C. Y. Watt ed., *The Chinese Scholar's Studio: Artistic Life in the Late Ming Period*, pp. 1–13. New York: Thames and Hudson, 1987.

Welter, Albert. "The Contextual Study of Chinese Buddhist Biographies: The Example of Yung-ming Yen-shou (904–975)," in Phyllis Granoff and Koichi Shinohara ed., *Monks and Magicians: Religious Biographies in Asia*, pp. 247–76. Delhi: Motilal Banarsidass, 1994.

West, Stephen H., Stephen Owen, Martin Powers and Willard Peterson. "*Bi fa ji*: Jing Hao, 'Notes on the Method for the Brush'," in Pauline Yu, Peter Bol, Stephen Owen and Willard Peterson ed., *Ways with Words: Writing about Reading Texts from Early China*, pp. 202–44. Berkeley: University of California Press, 2000.

Whitfield, Sarah. *Magritte*. London: South Bank Centre, 1992.

Widmer, Ellen. "The Huanduzhai of Hangzhou and Suzhou: A Study in Seventeenth-Century Publishing," *Harvard Journal of Asiatic Studies* 56 (1) (1996): 77–122.

Wile, Douglas trans. *Art of the Bedchamber: The Chinese Sexual Yoga Classics Including Women's Solo Meditation Texts*. Albany: State University of New York Press, 1992.

Wilhelm, Hellmut. "Bibliographical Notes on Ch'ien Ch'ien-i," *Monumenta Serica* 7 (1942): 196–207.

Wilkinson, Endymion. *Chinese History: A Manual [Revised and Enlarged]*. Cambridge, MA: Harvard University Press, 2000.

Wimsatt, W. K. and Monroe C. Beardsley. "The Intentional Fallacy," in W. K. Wimsatt, *The Verbal Icon: Studies in the Meaning of Poetry*, pp. 3–18. Kentucky: Kentucky University Press, 1954.

Wollstonecraft, Mary. *The Works of Mary Wollstonecraft: Volume 7*. Janet Todd and Marilyn Butler ed. London: William Pickering, 1989.

Wong, Kin-yuen. "Negative-Positive Dialectic in the Chinese Sublime," in Ying-hsiung Chou ed., *The Chinese Text: Studies in Comparative Literature*, pp. 119–58. Hong Kong: Chinese University Press, 1986.

Wu, K. T. "Colour Printing in the Ming Dynasty," *T'ien Hsia Monthly* 11 (1) (1940): 30–44.

———. "Ming Printing and Printers," *Harvard Journal of Asiatic Studies* 7 (1942–43): 203–60.

Wu, Nelson I. "Tung Ch'i-ch'ang (1555–1636): Apathy in Government and Fervor in Art," in Arthur F. Wright and Denis Twitchett ed., *Confucian Personalities*, pp. 260–93. Stanford: Stanford University Press, 1962.

Wu, Pei-yi. *The Confucian's Progress: Autobiographical Writings in Traditional China*. Princeton: Princeton University Press, 1990.

———. "An Ambivalent Pilgrim to T'ai Shan in the Seventeenth Century," in Susan Naquin and Chün-fang Yü ed., *Pilgrims and Sacred Sites in China*, pp. 65–88. Berkeley: University of California Press, 1992.

Wu Qiushi 吳秋士 ed. *Tianxia mingshan youji* 天下名山遊記. Three volumes. Shanghai: Zhongying shudian, 1936.

Xiao Chi. *The Chinese Garden as Lyric Enclave: A Generic Study of the Story of the Stone*. Ann Arbor: Center for Chinese Studies, Michigan University, 2001.

Xie Guozhen 謝國楨. *Ming mo Qing chu de xuefeng* 明末清初的學風. Shanghai: Shanghai shudian, 2004.

Xie Zhengguang 謝正光 [Andrew Hsieh]. *Qing chu shiwen yu shiren jiaoyou kao* 清初詩文與士人交遊考. Nanjing: Nanjing daxue chubanshe, 2001.

———. "Qian Qianyi fengfo zhi qianhou yinyuan ji qi yiyi" 錢謙益奉佛之前後因緣及其意義, *Qinghua daxue xuebao* 清華大學學報 [*zhexue shehui kexue ban* 哲學社會科學版] 3 (21) (2006): 13–30.

Xu Bangda 徐邦達. "*Huangshan tuce* zuozhe kaobian" 《黃山圖冊》作者考辨, *Duoyun* 朵雲 9 (1985): 125–9.

Xu Chaohua 徐朝華 ed. *Erya jinzhu* 爾雅今注. Tianjin: Nankai daxue chubanshe, 1987.

Xu Hongquan 許宏泉. *Dai Benxiao* 戴本孝. Shijiazhuang: Hebei jiaoyu chubanshe, 2002.

Xu Hongzu. *The Travel Diaries of Hsü Hsia-k'o*. Li Chi trans. Hong Kong: Chinese University Press, 1974.

———. 徐弘祖. *Xu Xiake youji jiaozhu* 徐霞客遊記校注. Zhu Huirong 朱惠榮 ed. Two volumes. Kunming: Yunnan renmin chubanshe, 1985.

Yang Bojun 楊伯峻 ed. *Liezi jishi* 列子集釋. Beijing: Zhonghua shuju, 1979.

Yang Tingfu 楊廷福 and Yang Tongfu 楊同甫 ed. *Ming ren shiming biecheng zihao suoyin* 明人室名別稱字號索引. Two volumes. Shanghai: Guji chubanshe, 2002.

———. *Qing ren shiming biecheng zihao suoyin* 清人室名別稱字號索引 [*zengbuben* 增補本]. Two volumes. Shanghai: Guji chubanshe, 2001.

Yang, Xiaoshan. "Naming and Meaning in the Landscape Essays of Yuan Jie and Liu Zongyuan," *Journal of the American Oriental Society* 120 (1) (2000): 82–96.

Yang Xuanzhi. *A Record of Buddhist Monasteries in Lo-yang*. Yi-t'ung Wang trans. Princeton: Princeton University Press, 1984.

Yanshou 延壽 comp. *Zongjinglu* 宗鏡錄. Rpt.; *Taishō shinshū daizōkyō* 大正新修大藏經. Volume 48. Takakusu Junjirō 高楠順次郎 and Watanabe Kaigyoku 渡邊海旭 ed. Tōkyō: Taishō issaikyō kankōkai, 1924–1932.

Yao Xuan 姚鉉 ed. *Tang wen cui* 唐文粹. Rpt.; three volumes. Shanghai: *SBCK* edition.

Ye Mengzhu 葉夢珠. *Yueshi bian* 閱世編. Rpt.; Lai Xinxia 來新夏 ed. Shanghai: Guji chubanshe, 1981.

Ye, Yang trans. *Vignettes from the Late Ming: A Hsiao-p'in Anthology*. Seattle: University of Washington Press, 1999.

———. *Making it Strange: The Travel Writings of Wang Siren*. Berkeley: UCLA Center for Chinese Studies Occasional Paper #1, 2003.

Ye Yanlan 葉衍蘭 and Ye Gongchao 葉恭綽 ed. *Qingdai xuezhe xiangzhuan* 清代學者象傳. Two volumes. Shanghai: Shanghai shudian chubanshe, 2001.

Yeh, Michelle. *Modern Chinese Poetry: Theory and Practice Since 1917*. New Haven: Yale University Press, 1991.

Yeh, Wen-hsin. "Historian and Courtesan: Chen Yinke 陳寅恪 and the Writing of *Liu Rushi biezhuan* 柳如是別傳," *East Asian History* 27 (2004): 57–70.

Yi Ding 一丁, Yu Lu 雨露 and Hong Yong 洪涌. *Zhongguo gudai fengshui yu jianzhu xuanzhi* 中國古代風水與建築選址. Shijiazhuang: Hebei kexue jishu chubanshe, 1996.

Yim, Chi-hung. *The Poetics of Historical Memory in the Ming-Qing Transition: A Study of Qian Qianyi's (1582–1664) Later Poetry*. Unpublished PhD thesis: Yale University, 1998.

Yin Gonghong 尹恭弘. *Xiaopin gaochao yu wan Ming wenhua* 小品高潮與晚明文化. Beijing: Huawen chubanshe, 2001.

Yoon, Hong-key. *Geomantic Relationships Between Culture and Nature in Korea*. Taipei: Orient Cultural Service, 1976.

Yü, Chün-fang. *The Renewal of Buddhism in China: Chu-hung and the Late Ming Synthesis*. New York: Columbia University Press, 1981.

———. "Ming Buddhism," in Denis Twitchett and Frederick W. Mote ed., *The Cambridge History of China Volume 8: The Ming Dynasty, 1368–1644, Part 2*, pp. 893–952. Cambridge: Cambridge University Press, 1998.

———. *Kuan-yin: The Chinese Transformation of Avalokiteśvara*. New York: Columbia University Press, 2001.

Yu Kwang-chung. "The Sensuous Art of the Chinese Landscape Journal," Yang Qinghua trans., in Stephen C. Soong and John Minford ed., *Trees on the Mountain: An Anthology of New Chinese Writing*, pp. 23–40. Hong Kong: Chinese University Press, 1986.

Yuan Hongdao 袁宏道. *Yuan Hongdao ji jianjiao* 袁宏道集箋校. Qian Bocheng 錢伯城 ed. Three volumes. Shanghai: Guji chubanshe, 1981.

———. *Four Months of Idle Roaming: The West Lake Records of Yuan Hongdao (1568–1610)*. Stephen McDowall trans. Wellington: Asian Studies Institute Translation Paper #4, 2002.

Yuan Ke 袁珂. *Zhongguo gudai shenhua* 中國古代神話. Beijing: Zhonghua shuju, 1960.

———. ed. *Shanhaijing jiaozhu* 山海經校注. Shanghai: Guji chubanshe, 1980.

Yuan Mei 袁枚. *Yuan Mei quanji* 袁枚全集. Wang Yingzhi 王英志 ed. Eight volumes. Nanjing: Jiangsu guji chubanshe, 1993.

Yuan Zhongdao. *Notes Made Whilst Travelling and at Repose (Book One)*. Duncan Campbell trans. Wellington: Asian Studies Institute Translation Paper #2, 1999.

Yuanji 原濟 [Shitao 石濤]. *Dadizi tihua bashi* 大滌子題畫跋詩. Wang Yichen 汪繹辰 ed. Shanghai: Renmin meishu chubanshe, 1987.

———. *Shitao huaji* 石濤畫集. Two volumes. Beijing: Rongbaozhai chubanshe, 2003.

———. *See also* Shih-t'ao.

Zeitlin, Judith T. "The Petrified Heart: Obsession in Chinese Literature, Art, and Medicine," *Late Imperial China* 12 (1) (1991): 1–26.

———. *Historian of the Strange: Pu Songling and the Chinese Classical Tale*. Stanford: Stanford University Press, 1993.

———. "Disappearing Verses: Writing on Walls and Anxieties of Loss," in *idem* and Lydia H. Liu ed., *Writing and Materiality in China: Essays in Honor of Patrick Hanan*, pp. 73–132. Cambridge, MA: Harvard University Press, 2003.

Zhang Dai 張岱. *Taoan mengyi / Xihu mengxun* 陶庵夢憶 / 西湖夢尋. Rpt.; Xia Xianchun 夏咸淳 and Cheng Weirong 程維榮 ed. Shanghai: Guji chubanshe, 2001.

Zhang Guoguang 張國光 and Huang Qingquan 黃清泉 ed. *Wan Ming wenxue gexinpai Gongan san Yuan yanjiu* 晚明文學革新派公安三袁研究. Wuhan: Huazhong shifan daxue chubanshe, 1987.

Zhang Hongsheng 張宏生 ed. *Ming Qing wenxue yu xingbie yanjiu* 明清文學與性別研究. Nanjing: Jiangsu guji chubanshe, 2002.

Zhang Jipei 張繼沛. "Qian Qianyi jian Du zhi yaozhi ji qi jituo" 錢謙益箋杜之要旨及其寄託, in *Lianhe shuyuan sanshi zhounian jinian lunwenji* 聯合書院三十周年紀念論文集, pp. 215–34. Xianggang: Zhongwen daxue chubanshe, 1986.

Zhang Juzheng 張居正. *Zhang Juzheng ji* 張居正集. Zhang Shunhui 張舜徽 ed. Four volumes. Wuhan: Hubei renmin chubanshe, 1987.

Zhang Lianjun 張聯駿. *Qing Qian Muzhai xiansheng nianpu* 清錢牧齋先生年譜. Rpt.; *Beijing tushuguan cang zhenben nianpu congkan* 北京圖書館藏珍本年譜叢刊 64, pp. 671–720. Beijing: Beijing tushuguan chubanshe, 1999.

Zhao Erxun 趙爾巽 ed. *Qing shi gao* 清史稿. Rpt.; four volumes. Beijing: Zhonghua shuju, 1998.

Zhao Nong 趙農 ed. *Yuan ye tushuo* 園冶圖説. Ji'nan: Shandong huabao chubanshe, 2003.

Zheng Chunying 鄭春穎 ed. *Wenzhongzi Zhong shuo yizhu* 文中子中説譯注. Haerbin: Heilongjiang renmin chubanshe, 2002.

Zheng Yuanxun. *A Personal Record of My Garden of Reflection*. Duncan Campbell trans. Wellington: Asian Studies Institute Translation Paper #5, 2004.

Zhou Fagao 周法高 ed. *Qian Muzhai Liu Rushi yishi ji Liu Rushi youguan ziliao* 錢牧齋柳如是佚詩及柳如是有關資料. Taibei: self-published, 1978.

Zhou Qi 周齊. *Mingdai fojiao yu zhengzhi wenhua* 明代佛教與政治文化. Beijing: Renmin chubanshe, 2005.

Zhou Wu 周蕪 ed. *Huipai banhuashi lunji* 徽派版畫史論集. Hefei: Anhui renmin chubanshe, 1983.

Zhu Dongrun 朱東潤. "Shu Qian Qianyi zhi wenxue piping" 述錢謙益之文學批評, in *idem, Zhongguo wenxue lunji* 中國文學論集. Beijing: Zhonghua shuju, 1983: 71–89.

Zhu Honglin 朱鴻林. *Ming ren zhuzuo yu shengping fawei* 明人著作與生平發微. Guilin: Guangxi shifan daxue chubanshe, 2005.

Zhu Yizun 朱彝尊. *Jingzhiju shihua* 靜志居詩話. Rpt.; Beijing: Renmin wenxue chubanshe, 1998.

Zhu Zejie 朱則杰. "Qian Qianyi Liu Rushi congkao" 錢謙益柳如是叢考, *Zhejiang daxue xuebao* 浙江大學學報 [*renwen shehui kexue ban* 人文社會科學版] 32 (5) (2002): 13–8.

Zou, Hui. "Jesuit Perspective in China," *Architectura* 31 (2) (2001): 145–68.

———. "The *Jing* of a Perspective Garden," *Studies in the History of Gardens and Designed Landscapes* 22 (4) (2002): 293–326.

Zurndorfer, Harriet T. *Change and Continuity in Chinese Local History: The Development of Hui-chou Prefecture, 800 to 1800*. Leiden: E. J. Brill, 1989.

Index